SHAPING INTERIOR SPACE

SECOND EDITION

SHAPING INTERIOR SPACE

SECOND EDITION

Roberto J. Rengel

University of Wisconsin—Madison

Fairchild Publications, Inc.   New York

Director of Sales and Acquisitions: Dana Meltzer-Berkowitz

Executive Editor: Olga T. Kontzias

Senior Development Editor: Jennifer Crane

Art Director: Adam B. Bohannon

Production Manager: Ginger Hillman

Senior Production Editor: Elizabeth Marotta

Project Manager: Chris Reeves

Cover and Text Design: Ron Reeves

Layout: Mary Neal Meador

Library of Congress Catalog Card Number: 2007933128

ISBN: 978-1-56367-518-8

GST R 133004424

Printed in the United States

TP09

CONTENTS

EXTENDED CONTENTS

PREFACE

PREFACE TO THE SECOND EDITION

Over the last four years it has been immensely gratifying to hear from enthusiastic users of *Shaping Interior Space*. Many have shared with me creative ways in which they are using the text, and many others have offered insightful comments and suggestions, the most common being, "Could we get larger illustrations next time?"

Users of the text will be pleased with the design of the second edition. Steps have been taken to increase the visual appeal of the page layout. Also apparent will be the new look of most of the images. The majority of the drawings have been redrawn digitally, resulting in clearer images that have a stronger impact. Additionally, many figures have been replaced and many others added to better illustrate the concepts in the book. Other general goals have been to increase clarity, simplify the language, and reduce superfluous material and to make the text more accessible to beginning design students. New material has been added to several chapters, and the appendices have been integrated into the main text: "Walls, Ceilings, and Columns" was moved to Chapter 4; the sections on carpet borders, checkerboard patterns, and eye-level decorative bands were moved as a unit to Chapter 8; "Considerations for Office Design" and "The Art of Table Layout in Restaurants" were moved to chapter 5; and "Twenty Retail Store Partis" was moved to Chapter 6.

The structure of the book remains intact, based on the ten principles introduced in the first chapter. The order in which the principles are presented roughly follows the design process sequence, but the book's organization continues to be driven by the sequential presentation of the book's themes and not by the strict sequence of steps in the design process. The goal remains that instructors can use the chapters in the text as needed, in the order that suits them best.

Other changes include a new section, "A Project's Driving Forces," in Chapter 5 that explains the use of clients' mission statements as well as the identification and use of project design goals and strategies during the programming phase of a project, and a new capsule, "Corporate Culture." Chapter 6 remains one of the most useful chapters in the text. It has been expanded and reorganized. A new section on design concept statements covers the use and verbal articulation of character concepts in greater detail. Additional examples of concept diagrams are included.

The section on identity in Chapter 9 has been expanded to introduce the topics of personality and self-image, corporate identity, and branding. The delicate nature of this chapter, with its treatment of self-image, sophistication, and taste, continues to be challenging. The new material has helped to ground many of the concepts related to identity in relevant research from the disciplines of consumer behavior and marketing.

The production of this edition, like the production of its predecessor, has involved the efforts of many. Once again my gratitude goes to the entire staff at Fairchild Books for their continued support and their help in making this second edition a reality. Very special thanks go to Olga Kontzias for her leadership, Chris Reeves for her painstaking editing, and Ron Reeves and Mary Neal Meador for the significant graphic enhancements of this edition. Finally, I would like to acknowledge the valuable feedback received from students, educators, and other users of the text. Improvements in this edition owe much to them.

PREFACE TO THE FIRST EDITION

Few professions can claim the kind of impact on the quality of our lives that the design professions have. We cannot escape the built environment. It is everywhere and affects us daily in profound ways. Particularly important are interior spaces. It is in them that we spend most of our time, whether working, shopping, dining, or sleeping. Interior space has become the focus of much attention among design professionals. On the one hand, interior designers, once preoccupied almost exclusively with the decorative aspects of design, have become active shapers of interior space. On the other hand, architects, normally more preoccupied with the complex requirements of designing a total building, are becoming more interested in interior projects and the particular sensibilities they entail.

Designing the built environment is difficult, certainly much more difficult than it is to just talk about design. Design students learn to "do" design while in school. The heart of the designer's education is the design studio, where design is done, not just talked about. Students tackle hypothetical projects that simulate real-life conditions with the assistance of the design instructor and, frequently, others who volunteer their time to provide valuable criticism. That way, they learn to do design. After a few of these design studios they are launched into the real world to do real design.

Despite the overwhelming importance of the doing, learning design also requires some degree of talking and reading about it. It is through these less direct ways that students gain valuable insights they can try out in the studio. This book is intended as a studio companion. It discusses design, but it does so while wearing a designer's hat.

Consequently, the discussion is not historical, nor cultural, nor scientific, nor philosophical, but the talk of design. It is concerned with design's higher qualities and the ways to produce them, while not forgetting about the important and multiple contexts in which design takes place.

The book is intended for designers of interiors, with a primary focus on the particular realities of the interior design profession. The book is also intended to be helpful to students and instructors of architecture who have a special interest in the design of interior space. It has been conceived to complement the teaching of design studios and contribute in the design-teaching effort together with such other important paths to design insight and wisdom as learning by doing, learning from other students, and learning from the guidance of a conscientious design instructor. This book seeks to become part of the design instruction team and to make a strong contribution.

Specifically, this book is geared for students who are at least at an intermediate level of design. While it is written so that any design student can understand and benefit from its contents, it makes no attempt to cover many of the design basics necessary for the beginning design student. It is assumed, for instance, that the design student using this book knows about design fundamentals; can draft; and knows about materials, adjacencies, basic space planning, furniture, and other similar design elements and considerations. What this book attempts to do is take the novice designer to the next level. Inherent in this next level is an attitude that transcends the view of design as a vehicle for function and beauty alone and adopts an expanded view concerned with other significant contributions of design. Among these contributions are design's role in helping people make sense of their physical world, its role in enriching people's experiences inside buildings, and its role in affirming and expressing people's particular personalities and identities.

The designer is seen as a movie director. In this role, the designer is full of intentions beyond providing function and good looks and manipulates the qualities of both individual spaces and sequences of spaces to achieve specific results that enhance the sense of order, enrichment, and expression experienced by users. Successful implementation of this role is not easy. It requires familiarity with potential design approaches and strategies, the ability to diagnose the requirements of a project correctly, the ability to select appropriate design strategies, and the skills to execute the chosen strategies effectively.

The book is also concerned with the creative aspects of the design process, from the analysis stage through to the resolution of all the physical issues about a project. The primary focus is on spatial issues. Because of this focus, it has been necessary to draw from existing architectural literature as opposed to interior design literature, where the topic of space has not been addressed extensively. In fact, because of the nature of the topic and its location at the point where architecture and interior design meet, much of the terminology used in the book goes back and forth between the two disciplines. It is not the intent to confuse or to show preference for one discipline over the other. It just happens that the topic addressed is equally part of both disciplines.

Other than the text, the book relies heavily on illustrations, most of them simple drawings and diagrams. Although many photographs are used as examples of the ideas presented, whenever possible, drawings have been used as the primary means to illustrate points. Drawings are the language of design, and the flow from idea to sketch or drawing is more akin to design thinking than is the flow between idea and photograph. Specifically, the drawings used are loose and design-oriented, not the rigid drawings used to represent the finished product. The goal is to emphasize a process that is creative, open-ended, and evolutionary, not one that is finished and immutable.

Writing a text for use in the design studio is a difficult proposition. It is hard to go beyond broad generalities and the often-repeated, elementary design elements and principles without going out on a limb and taking chances. Going beyond the usual generalities involves showing specific ideas and ways to implement them. It requires going beyond the usual neutral stance and stating do's and don'ts with belief and conviction. It involves the risk of encountering disagreement along the way. However, a strong position is never unproductive. It establishes a definite point of departure. One can fully agree, partially agree, or disagree, but surely, it always elicits a reaction and makes one think. That's precisely what is being attempted here, to present ideas and promote critical thinking.

The book is organized around ten core principles introduced in Chapter 1. Chapters are divided into four general sections: General Principles (Chapters 2–4), Establishing the Design (Chapters 5 and 6), Developing the Design (Chapters 7–9), and Completing the Design (Chapters 10 and 11). Chapter 2 addresses what users do in buildings. The important role of place and its elements are explained in Chapter 3. Chapter 4 is a review of the many aspects of architectural space: how it is defined, enclosed, shaped, manipulated, combined, and composed into entire projects. The early tasks of the design process are covered in Chapters 5 and 6. Chapter 5 explains the importance of proper understanding in design and covers the different variables for which understanding is necessary. The process of early ideation and concept development is covered in Chapter 6. Chapters 7 through 10 get to the core of the design virtues advocated in this book: order, enrichment, expression, and resolution. Chapter 11 rounds out the book by discussing the important role of the design elements that modify how space is experienced.

Chapters in the book contain several important pedagogical features. Each chapter opens with a list of instructional objectives. Most include a short capsule that highlights commentary about a relevant topic from important sources in the existing design literature. The capsules aim not only to supplement the chapter but to encourage students to become aware of and seek these other valuable sources of design information. At the end of Chapters 6 through 11, short case studies discuss built projects designed by prominent designers, focusing on aspects of the design relevant to the chapter topics. Finally, an end-of-chapter review includes a summary, chapter questions, and, in some cases, exercises to promote understanding and discussion.

The text concludes with two appendices. Appendix 1 includes various segments covering miscellaneous supplementary topics about interior architectural elements and decorative patterns. Appendix 2 includes supplementary information relevant to the design of offices, stores, and restaurants, three common interior project types assigned in design studios.

ACKNOWLEDGMENTS TO THE FIRST EDITION

My gratitude goes to the entire staff at Fairchild Books for their help in making this book a reality. Special thanks go to Mary McGarry, who was enthusiastic about the book from the beginning, and Sylvia Weber for her editorial help and for keeping me on track. Finally, I would like to acknowledge the valuable feedback received from the following reviewers selected by the publisher, who provided much useful advice about both style and content:

Sharon Anderson, Moorpark College; Mary Anne Beecher, University of Oregon; Glen Currie, Art Institute of Pittsburgh; Anita Henson, St. Mary's University; Jerry Neilson, University of Florida; LuAnn Nissen, University of Nevada-Reno; Rachel Pike, Wentworth Institute of Technology; and JoEllen Weingart, Illinois Institute of Art-Schaumburg.

The final product owes much to their valuable input.

PART ONE
GENERAL PRINCIPLES

CHAPTER 1
Mastering Interior Design

INSTRUCTIONAL OBJECTIVES

- Explain the crucial role of the design studio in design education.

- Present several important sources of design knowledge.

- Explain the role of intentions and strategies in design.

- Introduce the concept of total design.

- Describe the evolving role of interior designers as shapers of space.

- Explain the close interrelationship between architecture and interior design in interiors.

- Introduce the ten design principles that guide this book.

You employ stone, wood, and concrete, and with those materials you build houses and palaces. That is construction. Ingenuity is at work. . . .

But suppose that walls rise towards heaven in such a way that I am moved. I perceive your intentions. Your mood has been gentle, brutal, charming, or noble. The stones you have erected tell me so. You fix me to the place and my eyes regard it. They behold something that expresses a thought. A thought that reveals itself without word or sound, but solely by means of shapes which stand in a certain relationship to one another. These shapes are such that they are clearly revealed in light. The relationships between them have not necessarily any reference to what is practical or descriptive. They are a mathematical creation of your mind. They are the language of Architecture. By the use of raw materials and starting from conditions more or less utilitarian, you have established certain relationships which have aroused my emotions.

—*Le Corbusier,* Towards a New Architecture

DESIGN STUDENTS KNOW there is more to design than mere utility. In fact, many choose to become designers because they enjoy being creative and because of the prospect that their creations will arouse the emotions of those who come in contact with them. While engineers use their knowledge and training to provide practical and efficient solutions based on the physical laws of nature and builders use their knowledge to construct projects that are structurally sound and well crafted, interior designers use their knowledge and ability to create designs that touch the human heart in ways that neither the engineer's design nor the builder's construction usually do. A good interior design reflects a design solution conceived by and for human beings. It holds in high regard not only their physical well-being but their emotional and spiritual well-being as well.

When clients hire interior designers, they know they are getting more than just a practical design solution; they are also buying style and substance. While practically all interior designers are sincerely interested in creating special interiors, some do a better job at it than others. This may be due to differences in levels of skill, levels of motivation, and, most important, levels of awareness. Many skilled and motivated designers fall short of being great designers not because they lack competence but because they are not fully aware of the range of possibilities available to create designs that arouse human emotions. The view that interior design consists of providing a func-

tional and good-looking environment is certainly incomplete. Design has much more to offer than function and good looks. It is when design intentions reach beyond these two basic necessities that designers are engaged in total design.

THE DIFFICULTY OF DESIGN

Designing good interior spaces is difficult. The number of design problems and their complexity can be staggering. Designers are required to make sense of the realities and needs of a given client; translate them into collections of spaces subdivided in special ways in response to their optimal relationships; shape and finish the enclosing surfaces of those spaces; select and design furnishings, accessories, and fixtures that match and reinforce the particular style used; and make it all work together and look good. Ultimately, full **synthesis** is the goal of every project. All the parts and pieces need to work together, but still be flexible to accommodate change over time.

One of the aspects of design that makes it so challenging is the fact that all the parts of a project have precise and delicate interrelationships. Designing interiors is like solving a giant table puzzle. What makes the interior design puzzle harder to solve than table puzzles is that the pieces can fit in not just one but many locations, some better than others. To make matters even more challenging, you may find that resolving one section of the design

$$\text{DESIGN} = \text{PROPER RESPONSE} + \text{PROPER EXECUTION}$$

Figure 1.1: Design requires proper response and proper execution. Proper response translates into accurate and insightful understanding of the design problem and a corresponding responsive design solution. Proper execution involves the tasks of design development and final resolution.

puzzle with a certain configuration may cause it to weaken or clash with another section of the project.

Total design requires the resolution of a multitude of problems at many different levels and scales. The solutions to these design problems (adjacencies, privacy, connections, enclosure, views, details, furnishings, lighting, and so on) are layered next to and over one another in intricate ways that create specific effects. On any given job, the designer needs to manipulate, control, and, ultimately, resolve these combinations, pushing, pulling, and twisting to achieve engaging and evocative designs.

While many of the practical tasks of design involve rational decision making, much about design relies on intuition and good design sense. Stanley Abercrombie has referred to the discipline of interiors as being "so subjective and so intimate, so immune to the calculations of science, so special to a singular circumstance and therefore so often ephemeral."[1] The elusive qualities of design make the application of exact rules and formulas unrealistic. Nevertheless, the use of guidelines, principles, and strategies are helpful for design students. This book offers several.

Becoming a Designer

At its most general level, design requires two things to be successful: a fitting response to the design problem and its skillful execution (Figure 1.1). Proper response requires that the design problem (and subproblems) are understood correctly and that an appropriate design strategy is formulated to solve them. Choices have to be made about how to distribute space, assemble spatial sequences, determine levels of enclosure and articulation, and so on. The choices made by the designer need to be responsive to not only the particular utilitarian requirements of the project but also the client's particular character.

Once a design direction is established, designers need to be able to execute the design with skill. This means devel-

oping the design ideas in detail and, ultimately, resolving and completing all aspects of the design. Particular shapes and articulations are given to all the design elements, and compatible furnishings and miscellaneous nonpermanent pieces are specified. The result, if responsive and well executed, will contribute much to the day-to-day experience of the users.

The Importance of the Design Studio

The inherent complexities of design make its mastery a lifelong process. So intricate and inexact is the discipline of design that many years of conscientious design practice are needed to fully understand the levels of intricacy and nuance involved. Learning design starts in school, specifically in the design studio. In the studio, students learn to design hypothetical projects, similar to the ones encountered later in real practice.

The best way to learn design is by doing. Design is not learned by memorization or the application of formulas. Students learn design by solving design problems. The tangible outputs required to communicate designs leave little room for "faking it." The drawings used in design force designers to show, explicitly, both the design intent and the specifics of the solution, thus revealing the virtues and shortcomings of the solution.

The design studio is the most important component of a design education. It is in the studio that you first learn to assess design situations that simulate real life and to make judgments that lead to a limited number of viable solutions. You have to commit to certain choices from the many possibilities available and make them work, resolving each part to the best of your abilities and within tight time constraints.

Not only the doing is critical. Equally important is the process of review and critique. It is imperative to get beyond the fear of criticism and seek design feedback from peers, design instructors, and, most important, from oneself.

Students need to constantly question their design choices. What is right or wrong about this design approach? Is the overall approach appropriate? Is anything not working? Are there any good ideas not resolved properly? Are there any bad ideas resolved brilliantly? What needs further development? These are the important questions you need to ask constantly.

Only through this kind of ongoing questioning are students able to develop the reasoning skills necessary to isolate the basic issues of a design problem, understand their implications, and develop fitting design approaches for testing and development. These are skills that need reinforcement beyond the school years, as design problems become most intricate, involving all of the complexities and problems inherent in reality. After school, you are faced with real projects that require probing and detective work instead of the fully digested and convenient summary of needs and requirements given on most school projects. Developing a habit of critical questioning will develop your mental agility to solve problems. The more you do this in school and then later, in practice, the sharper you'll become.

In addition to good reasoning skills, proper response in design requires proper perspective. Early on, it is hard to make certain decisions because it seems you have no basis on which to anchor and evaluate them. Proper perspective is developed over time. It is, therefore, important to start acquiring a personal sense of what is correct and appropriate. A good way to start is by learning from other designers and design professors. By asking questions and studying how other designers have responded to real design problems, you start to acquire a sense of what can be done. Developing an alert set of eyes and a good design memory that recalls characteristics of environments is invaluable. Once you gain some experience, you'll start developing and trusting your own personal sense of propriety.

Sources of Design Knowledge

There are many sources of knowledge and information available to designers. These include design history, current design trends, design theory, and observations made while traveling to new environments. Studying past and present design solutions helps you develop your sense of appropriateness and fit. Design history is an excellent way to gain design perspective. When studying design history,

one of your principal aims should be to understand the conditions that were present during specific times and to evaluate the kinds of design solutions conceived within the context of those conditions. By seeking to understand what made certain design approaches fit a specific set of circumstances in the past, you develop a sense of judgment, refining your sense of fit and nuance even further.

In addition to studying past design solutions, students need to become avid followers of current design trends. There are a number of excellent trade journals, including specialized ones for specific sectors of the industry. There are good design books available too. By following the work being done by today's designers, you can get a sense of the breadth of recent trends and start developing your own opinions about what is good and most appropriate.

Another important source of information for designers is the rapidly growing body of interior design research. You should become familiar with ways of accessing this important information. It can give you valuable insights about the effects of certain types of environments or their environmental attributes on users. While many areas of design have not been researched, others enjoy a good amount of published material. At present, there are countless educators worldwide engaged in research that continues to expand the available knowledge base of the field. Although it is normally not possible to utilize research findings directly in the form of rules and formulas, research findings establish a sound point of departure, especially in areas that have established conclusive findings about specific aspects of design.

Research findings can provide useful information, but you must remember that in design every case is new and needs to be looked at with fresh eyes. You can think of and use research findings in the same way you think of and use advice from people possessing expertise and wisdom; what they have to say may be perceptive and truthful. How you decide to use the information is up to you. The information will merely establish an approach, a direction. Giving it specific form for the application at hand will be your responsibility.

One last source of design knowledge is travel. Whether abroad, to a neighboring town or city, or to a local tavern, travel can provide invaluable insights to designers. Keeping a notebook of observations or taking pictures is also helpful. When you travel, things are fresh and you notice them more. There are design lessons everywhere. Whether you visit places known for their design quality or just ordinary places, you will notice many examples of elements or combinations that offer design insights. You will also notice examples of things you had never thought about or things you didn't think possible, and yet, there they are, and they seem to work!

Intentions and Strategies

There are important design considerations beyond basic function and aesthetics. These occur at different hierarchical levels, from broad overall design goals to narrow considerations about how to treat a niche on a wall. It is important to expand your own personal scope of design possibilities. The more possibilities and variations you have in your personal repertoire, the more intentionality you can bring to your projects. Intentionality is crucial to making projects come alive. Every design move should be justifiable. Nothing in a project should happen by chance. The greater your awareness of the possibilities, the broader and deeper your intentions will be—and the resulting designs will acquire new layers of meaning.

Distinguishing between design problems, design intentions, and design strategies can be confusing. They are part of one common string of thought that progresses sequentially from the identification of a problem to the implementation of a solution. **Design problems** usually involve specific needs and issues requiring a design solution. An example is the need for, say, a friendly and inviting reception area. This design problem already comes with the requirement that the space be friendly and inviting. Two general intentions have been declared from the outset. **Design intentions** are precise goals related to a design problem. They can be concerned with practical or experiential aspects of design. Design intentions for the design problem above (more specific than just "friendly and inviting") could include a bright, cheerful room with a clear, prominent reception desk and a cozy, comfortable waiting area off to one side with a focal wall and perhaps an exterior view. These more specific ideas start to introduce potential design strategies.

Design strategies are specific means of implementing design intentions by using particular physical materials, compositions, finishes, and so forth. For our example,

determining design strategies would require devising specific means to achieve a bright and cheerful room, a clear and emphasized reception desk, and so on. These might include using contrasting levels of light, varying the height of ceilings, using a reception desk with an unusual shape, creating a focal wall, or incorporating a view of the exterior into the design of the waiting area. The thing to remember is that problems, intentions, and strategies progress in their level of specificity, getting more and more detailed as you move from problems to strategies.

Every intention in design needs to be followed by a corresponding strategy. It would be frustrating to pursue even general intentions such as, say, modern formality, or evocative simplicity, or an engaging sequence without first explicitly articulating what is meant by them and, second, being equipped with a repertoire of specific strategies to achieve them. You don't need to have an exact mental picture of the way it is going to look when it's done, but having a general strategy to begin with helps. You can draw mental pictures from something you saw while traveling, or from a magazine, or even from an idea you doodled on a napkin one day. The more of these you have stored in your internal design library, the faster your own ideas will pop up when thinking about design strategies.

Ideas in your collection of personal strategies can also come from your own designs and those of your peers. Look around and become aware of what is possible and how specific strategies can be made to work. There may be cases where you see a brilliant design that happens to be the wrong solution to the problem to which it was applied. Yet some of the particulars may be especially well executed. Go ahead and make a mental or written note of the particulars and perhaps a note about what kind of application they would be more appropriate for.

Eventually, you will assemble a collection of design strategies that work in response to specific design problems, similar to a chess player having a collection of strategic moves ready to respond to any situation during a match. It is important, though, to always stay fresh and to avoid having those moves become automatic formulas. For that reason, it is useful to have some awareness of your current preferences and convictions. These tend to evolve over time as you gain experience and insight, as you mature, and as the times, conditions, and styles change.

Achieving excellence in design requires conscious effort, resolve, and hard work. Competence comes with exposure and experience, but excellence requires more. It is quite common for designers to become adequate and coast through their careers producing acceptable, ordinary design. If you truly want to become good, you need to develop a commitment to design. If it is not ingrained in you during the early years, it is easily lost. The real practice of design is full of mundane requirements that will consume much of your effort, making it very tempting to aim for ordinary, acceptable design and never progress from there. If you choose to aim for excellence, you need to start now. The first thing you need to do is develop a desire to go beyond the basics. Function and aesthetics are important, but they are just the beginning. Good design requires total design.

AIMS OF THIS BOOK

The goal of this book is to help make you a better designer. It is assumed that you have some design studio experience under your belt, have been exposed to the basics, and are ready to move into the advanced levels of design nuance and sophistication necessary for total design.

We present important aspects of both the design process and design content. Related to the design process, we particularly stress the important tasks of analysis, ideation, and resolution. Related to content, we touch on many aspects and elements of interior design. However, the focus of this book is on **spatial design**. This is an aspect of increasing importance in the field and one with which many interior design students and practitioners seem to struggle.

As interior design has become a more prominent and recognized profession, the role of the interior designer has expanded considerably. Once relegated to the selection of finishes, furnishings, and other additive aspects of design, today's designer is not merely a completer of interior designs but a shaper of interior space. Today's interior designer frequently has total control over the design. Yet many interior design students—and even practitioners—experience difficulties with spatial design and seldom go beyond simplistic and unimaginative plans with minimal three-dimensional exploration.

The view we hold of interiors is an inclusive one. Interior designs work as a unity among spaces, surfaces, boundaries, openings, sequences, furnishings, finishes, accessories, artwork, and other elements. The skillful manipulation of interior space is crucial to establishing a good place. The level of interior space manipulation can range widely. It is possible to have a gigantic undifferentiated shell and to determine the subspaces, functions, and tone by the furnishings and other nonpermanent elements alone. Other projects have the benefit of more differentiated space, with changes in volumes and all kinds of twists and turns that give them their drama and excitement. Space and its related elements are too crucial to leave to others or treat blandly; interior designers need to become adept at working with, manipulating, and controlling the spatial aspects of design.

There is a fine line between architecture and interior design in this book. Both these disciplines come together in the creation of interior environments. The lessons of this book can be equally helpful to architecture students interested in interiors and to interior design students interested in spatial design. There are still a few basic and important differences between the realities encountered by architects and designers when they face the design of interior space. The most crucial one is that architects, for the most part, shape interior space in the process of designing an overall new building, and interior designers almost always design projects in existing interior spaces, usually starting from either empty building shells without internal construction or existing spaces to be altered or completely redesigned and rebuilt. The examples in the book are aimed at the interior designers who encounter existing shells as their points of departure.

Above all, this book aims to encourage a way of thinking about design that fosters the pursuit of high ideals and to illustrate specific design strategies and concepts that you may want to experiment with. We hope this will make a contribution to your personal library of design intentions and strategies. When, where, and how you apply the ideas presented is up to you. Judging whether the way you apply a certain strategy is appropriate for the circumstances or whether the execution is successful is beyond what the book can offer. That's where the design studio, peers, and instructors come in. The appropriateness of design is a subjective matter governed by the individual peculiarities of each situation, and constant evaluation and critique pertaining to the specific application at hand is necessary to ascertain the merits of any design attempt.

This book, then, is like a bridge between you and the design studio. It presents you with new information to consider and use, but you will have to try it within the context of the studio and learn by doing. Whether the design problem interpretation is sound, whether the strategies are appropriate and fitting, and whether the execution of the design ideas is carried out skillfully will need to be evaluated by you and your peers on a case-by-case basis.

TEN DESIGN PRINCIPLES

The contents of this book are based on ten principles about interior design. These are:

General Principles
1. Buildings are for people.
2. Place is the basic unit of interior design.
3. To master place, one must master space.

Principles to Establish the Design
4. A good design solution requires a good understanding of the problem.
5. A good design starts with a simple and powerful organizational idea.

Principles to Develop the Design
6. A good design produces order.
7. To satisfy, projects need to have enriching qualities.
8. In order to have deeper meaning, projects need to incorporate a fitting expression.

Completing the Design
9. The obligation to balance and unify all the physical components used in a project is an inherent aspect of the design task.
10. Spatial design is not complete with space alone. It requires the effects of key modifying elements that contribute to the way it is perceived.

General Principles

The first three principles lay the basic ground for the view of interior design advocated throughout. They reflect a basic attitude about the interior environment and its purpose.

Figure 1.2: Even when burdened by the many physical details and problems of a project, designers need to remember that buildings are for people. Every design effort should have as its goal the utility, convenience, comfort, safety, or delight it produces for people.

1. Buildings are for people.

The fundamental purpose of all interior environments is to support people and their activities (Figure 1.2). Some buildings and individual projects may command considerable attention due to their grandness or beauty, but their most basic functions are to support the functions and dreams of those who use them.

Designers need to cultivate an appreciation and understanding of the types of rituals and events associated with different project types. By listening, observing, and, most of all, experiencing directly the realities of those who use specific project types, designers can acquire the insights and sensibilities necessary to inform their designs.

The many activities associated with the use of buildings need to be analyzed and understood. These are the subplots of the total building experience. The experiences of people approaching, arriving, moving, interacting, performing tasks, and leaving a project are all important events with important design implications. The rituals performed routinely in given types of projects, the specific occasions that vary from time to time, the people involved, and the effect of the surroundings all affect the total experience people have in buildings. Although the physical setting is only one of the components, it is an important component of the total mix and needs to be considered in relation to the other factors present at the scene.

An important consideration to remember is that different users of a project have different perceptions of a given situation depending on their role in it, their level of affinity with the situation, their familiarity with the place and the occasion, how challenging their involvement is, and how much control they have over what is going on. Designers have to be sensitive to all these considerations, for they affect the experience of the different users of a given facility.

2. Place is the basic unit of interior design.

Interior design is a unique and complicated discipline. Comparing it to other art forms is very difficult. The basic units of interior design are not points, lines, shapes, planes, or even space. Of course, these all are factors in the process of assembling interior environments, but none of

Figure 1.3: The basic unit of interiors is place. Interior environments need to be looked at holistically as assemblies of places for people. These range in size, character, and function but are always distinguishable as discrete locations where specific activities take place.

them is the basic unit of lived-in environments. The basic unit of interior design is place (Figure 1.3). Designers need to learn to think about environment in terms of place, each place having a unique character of its own depending on the choices made in putting it together. The concept of place implies that the environments we create are complex totalities that function as real and coherent locations where life takes place. This is a different way of looking at it compared to the abstractions we tend to use when we think of environments created by the addition of walls and other building components, or worse, when we think of environments as drawings on a piece of paper.

The unit of place needs to be the yardstick with which projects are measured. In the process of conceiving places of particular qualities, certain elements may automatically suggest themselves as belonging together to achieve the desired effect. Design aspects such as colors, textures, and shapes have to be fine-tuned and given individual consideration. But the overall picture has to return to the basic unit of place, as a unified totality, to really be evaluated properly.

There are not too many different generic types of interior places. In most interior projects there are identifiable locations such as rooms and circulation paths to get around. Some places, because of their function or location, are more important. Some of these are arrival spaces or the strategic locations where main paths converge. Based on these differences, each place is assigned its appropriate location and configuration. Important considerations about places are the way they are enclosed, connected to each other, and arranged so that people can sit, stand, and move in ways appropriate to the project.

Eventually, designers have to spend considerable time dealing with the individual components of place. Their judgment of all these components, however, has to be made in relation to the overall place of which they are a part and its unique characteristics.

3. To master place, one must master space.

The mastery of space and its many components is essential in the design of interior places (Figure 1.4). Most of us have spent considerable time during our formative years in enclosed rooms, either at home or school. Consequently, there is a natural tendency to equate architectural space with

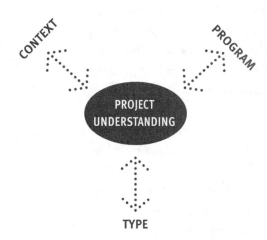

Figure 1.4: The manipulation of interior space, including its distribution, composition, and sculpting, is one of the most basic and important requirements of design.

physical elements in space can be arranged to reveal or conceal views ahead, to control movement or to free it.

Equally as important as creating good individual spaces is composing the sequences of spaces that shape the entire project. There are many possible arrangements of spaces in relation to the paths that feed them and in relation to adjacent or nearby spaces. Eventually, decisions have to be made about how all the spaces work as a system, with choices ranging from simple utilitarian compositions to elaborate classical ones.

Principles to Establish the Design

The next two principles are related to the task of establishing a basic design direction early in the design process.

4. A good design solution requires a good understanding of the problem.

Good design is responsive to particular needs, is appropriate to the circumstances in substance and style, and fits within its context. In order to achieve this kind of congruence between needs and solutions it is imperative for designers to understand the requirements of a project. Aspects to be understood include, but go beyond, the basic programmatic requirements of the project (Figure 1.5).

rooms. While in many cases space is defined as a room, in other cases it is not. Designers need to make special efforts to understand the many variations and subtleties of space.

Space can be explicit (like a room with four walls, a floor, and a ceiling) or it can be implied. In between there are many possible combinations. The level of enclosure is a crucial variable, as space can be defined with different degrees of enclosure. Defined space can be totally encapsulated or totally free. Variations in the treatment of the edges as well as the size, number, and placement of openings will create very different effects.

Space, although most often composed of regular, simple volumes, can be irregular. Sometimes the solid masses inside space can be the ones having the regularity of form, and space can be the leftover shape. Space comes in all sizes and shapes. Depending on its proportions, it acquires forces of its own and starts either to suggest stability or to induce movement. Many different manipulations can be performed when designing spaces. Individual basic forms can be added to, divided, and distorted. Additionally, the

Figure 1.5: To respond appropriately to the particular realities of a project, the designer needs to understand its context, program, and type.

There are often historical, cultural, and regional realities that become important contexts to be considered and addressed. The local neighborhood, with its physical and environmental features and movement patterns, represents an immediate and important context. The building in which the project is housed also constitutes an important context. It comes with a set of suggestive attributes and patterns of use that need to be understood and responded to.

Usually, the most direct needs of a project are associated with the requirements outlined in the design program. Most projects come with a program outlining the specific requirements to be addressed. Functions, as well as their space requirements and relationships, are included. Although most of the project requirements are likely to be included in the program, some important considerations are sometimes omitted. It can take some detective work and perceptive questioning by the designer to get to the heart of some issues not articulated in the program.

It is important to know that most projects are examples of a particular setting type having specific characteristics and needs based on its function. Whether it is a restaurant, store, or office, most projects have unique requirements characteristic of their type. Designers need to fully understand the inherent requirements associated with specific types of projects. Some of these will not be reflected in the program and will surface only if the designer is familiar with the specific nuances of the project type through study or experience.

Potential levels of understanding vary widely. A doctor may say she knows how you must be feeling, but if she has never had your disease, she really doesn't know how you feel. Only through proper questioning and a good dose of empathy can she begin to get a sense of what you are feeling. The same is true in design. You may feel you understand how a place functions, but if you have not spent time in a similar place before, your understanding will be superficial. The people who really know how a place functions, at least in their corner of the world, are its users. For complex projects, designers need to make every effort possible to get to the users if they sincerely hope to understand how the facility is supposed to work.

Proper understanding takes effort. Designers need to develop the habits of proper questioning and listening, as well as develop effective ways of recording the information collected in ways that are useful for the design. These efforts should not be limited to the beginning of a project. Although most information is collected at the beginning of a project, this information evolves, is expanded, and even changes during the life of a project. Having processes to solicit and record this information throughout the life of a project will ensure proper understanding of the project at any point during its duration.

5. A good design starts with a simple and powerful organizational idea.

The most basic design response to a given project is the organizational structure it is given (Figure 1.6). Of all the many needs and realities that must be understood about a project, the most fundamental one is a good grasp of the basic essence of the project, with as little detail as possible. This may take some effort, but once you understand a project's basic organizational essence, and whether it suggests a large central space or many small sequential units, you are prepared to make your first design move,

Figure 1.6: A project requires a proper response to its most fundamental design problem. It is embodied in a clear and powerful organizational idea, such as the one shown for a library building.

like the painter's first stroke on a blank canvas. Keep in mind, however, that having a good grasp of the essence of the design problem will facilitate, but not guarantee, an appropriate response.

A simple organizational idea (also known as organizational concept) is the start of a good project. Its success depends on its appropriateness—how well it responds to the basic design problem. The idea may be bold or jazzy, but does not need to be. Its main goal is to establish an overall organizational system that gives coherence and clarity to the project.

The generation of fitting concepts requires a good understanding of the basic behaviors that take place in the facility, the relationships of different units, the hierarchy of parts, and the flow of people, goods, or information. The process of concept generation requires the identification of dominant issues, the generation and evaluation of workable alternatives, and the selection of one to develop. This sometimes requires the painful discarding of other workable alternatives.

Principles to Develop the Design

The next three principles are concerned with specific goals initiated early and pursued in full during the development stages of the design process. During development, the basic design idea established earlier is given precise form and refined.

6. A good design produces order.

The need for order is one of the most basic human needs, especially in unfamiliar environments. A sense of correctness and confidence comes with order. Proper order provides points of reference to help people feel oriented and have a sense of where they are. It operates at many levels. Order is produced by strong and clear organization. A sense of order is also perceived when things appear to be where they belong, producing a tidy environment, where everything is in its proper place. Visual harmony produces a sense of order too. Order is also sometimes associated with situations that have good correspondence between needs and responses.

At the project level, a sense of order is perceived when the project's organization and structure are understood.

Projects with clear organizational structures, readable links between parts, and memorable spaces or elements become rich in order and are easier to understand. People seem to have a sense of where they are in relationship to the whole. Logical, well-structured sequences, clear intersections and groupings, distinctive parts, and the use of a hierarchical design approach are the kinds of attributes that contribute to a project's sense of order.

Providing healthy levels of order is sometimes not as straightforward as it appears. Every increase in order will not necessarily translate into a corresponding increase in preference. In fact, sometimes too much order can be undesirable. Designers need to learn to provide the optimal level of order for the nature of the project and for the different kinds of users of a project. The optimal level of environmental order for a clinic and a discotheque is going to be different. The same is true if you compare the desirable level of order for a first-time visitor to a large hospital to the desirable level for a staff member. In this case, the problem of providing a clear, straightforward environment for the visitor and an interesting environment for the regular user presents a unique design challenge.

7. To satisfy, projects need to have enriching qualities.

While the main function of a project is to support and enhance the activities that take place in it, projects have

Figure 1.7: Rich physical qualities bring projects to life. The shapes, patterns, textures, rhythms, and details of this bar contribute to its playfulness and richness.

a significant physical presence that strongly impacts their users. Other than providing spaces for functions with the desired levels of connection and separation between them, the physical parts of a project have the capacity to delight humans by providing enriching physical qualities and experiences (Figure 1.7). Enriching qualities and experiences can be bold or subtle, depending on the circumstances and the desired effect.

Not all enriching experiences need to provide stimulus with the intent to excite and motivate. Enriching experiences can also be the kind that helps users relax and restores their emotional equilibrium. Variety and complexity can be used to stimulate and create interest. Novelty and picturesqueness can provide momentary vacations and relax the busy mind. To determine the appropriate type of enrichment for any given space, designers need to understand and respond to their specific circumstances.

Circulation areas present special opportunities for enrichment. They can be dramatic and full of pleasant surprises. Sequences can be made interesting; events can take place along the way; surfaces can incorporate engaging details, colors, and textures; and views can provide pleasant distractions and interesting information. Areas for tasks involving mental concentration benefit from the type of environmental qualities that promote a sense of stability. Establishing meaningful visual connections with the surroundings and providing views for relief and distraction also enrich the busy mind.

8. In order to have deeper meaning, projects need to incorporate a fitting expression.

The qualities provided to enrich a project also carry with them inherent expressions of particular attitudes. Designers need to give projects the right expression. The way of allocating and dividing space, the shapes of the architectural and decorative documents used, and the colors, furnishings, and accessories incorporated in a project all carry connotations of particular attitudes and stylistic tendencies (Figure 1.8). Care has to be exercised by the designer so that the chosen expressions are the appropriate ones.

The way design elements are arranged and shaped and the characteristics of the products selected for a project can be expressive of universal human manifestations,

Figure 1.8: A project needs to express qualities that its users will relate to and support. These become the project's personality. Many businesses, like this coffee store, make conscious efforts to portray very specific personalities targeted to their audiences.

such as constraint or freedom. They can also express significant historical or cultural associations, or important programmatic requirements, such as connection or segregation. Furthermore, and quite important, design can express dominant traits about the personality of the client. Manifestations of qualities related to status, control, hierarchy, sophistication, and extroversion are all possible through design.

The expressions manifested in a project can also speak to the designer's own stylistic inclinations and personal preferences, as well as reflect the particular design tendencies of a specific location at a particular time in history.

Completing the Design

The final two principles are related to the important tasks of completing the design. In the end, all the design issues and problems need to be fully resolved and finalized.

9. The obligation to balance and unify all the physical components used in a project is an inherent aspect of the design task.

So many are the physical parts and pieces of typical interior projects that solving the functional puzzle alone is quite a challenging task. Additionally, designers are asked to make projects look good, balanced, and unified. The process of total resolution of the many components into a single unified entity is one of the greatest responsibilities of design. It starts with the resolution and refinement of the floor plan in order to make it work right and eliminate all awkward or wasteful spots.

Beyond that, parts need to be sized and balanced to look right. The relative size of things in relation to humans and to other parts needs to be addressed and resolved. The proportions of parts and sections in relation to other parts and to the compositions they are a part of also must be resolved (Figure 1.9). Parts seen together or experienced sequentially have to be balanced for proper equilibrium. Additionally, despite the inherent or intentional variety of a project, ultimately it has to read as a unified totality, conceived and produced by a single hand, while avoiding the dullness that comes with excessive regularity and repetition.

10. Spatial design is not complete with space alone. It requires the effects of key modifying elements that contribute to the way it is perceived.

While space and its enclosing surfaces establish the basis for spatial design and experience, the complete space experience includes other important environmental elements such as lighting, color, details, and sounds. The blending of all these elements becomes one of the biggest challenges and opportunities for the designer. When the many elements that comprise the spatial experience work together in coherent, synergetic fashion, the result is much more powerful than the result of merely adding their individual effects. It is when this happens that space is experienced in full, resulting in rich, evocative environments that strike a chord in those who use them (Figure 1.10 a and b).

Figure 1.9: The design task requires resolving all physical aspects of the project. The display shelves, graphics, lighting, accents, and products in this store have been carefully orchestrated and harmoniously resolved.

Figure 1.10 a and b: The spaces we create require the important modifying effects produced by lighting, colors and their values, materials, details, furnishings, and so on. It is as a totality that we perceive them through our senses and with our minds.

BEGINNING THE JOURNEY

The following chapters of this book are organized in the same order as the ten principles just introduced. Chapter 2 addresses what users do in buildings. The important role of place and its elements is explained in Chapter 3. Chapter 4 is a review of the many aspects of architectural space: how it is defined, enclosed, shaped, manipulated, combined, and composed into entire projects. The early tasks of the design process are covered in Chapters 5 and 6. Chapter 5 explains the importance of understanding the requirements of a project properly. The crucial process of early ideation and concept development is covered in Chapter 6.

Chapters 7 through 10 get to the core of the design virtues advocated in this book: order, enrichment, expression, and resolution. Chapter 11 finishes with a brief look at the important role of the interior elements that help give interior spaces many of their special characteristics.

We are ready to begin our journey. Open your mind and get ready to experiment and travel beyond function and good looks. Enjoy!

REVIEW

Summary

Good interior design projects offer more than just utility. The designs of interior environments have the capacity to delight and inspire. Design requires, at the most fundamental level, proper response to the specific problems of the project and skillful execution of the response.

The design studio is the most important component of a design education, for it is there that students perform the act of designing. Also important is the practice of reviewing and critiquing design solutions. It is through proper questioning that students develop the reasoning skills necessary to become good design thinkers. It is also important for the young designer to expand his or her range of design ideas and strategies over time, expanding the designer's collection of potential design solutions.

Today's designers are responsible for the distribution and shaping of the interior environments they design. It is therefore crucial that they become adept at working with interior space and be able to conceive, establish, develop, and complete space and its many components.

This book is organized around ten design principles. These address concepts students need to know regarding the realities of interior space and its design, and specific design issues concerned with the tasks of establishing, developing, and completing design solutions.

---

1. Stanley Abercrombie, *A Philosophy of Interior Design* (New York: Harper and Row, 1990), 165.

CHAPTER 2
People in Buildings

INSTRUCTIONAL OBJECTIVES

- Describe typical events during building visits.
- Highlight the importance of events preceding the main activity in buildings.
- Highlight the importance of secondary events in buildings.
- Highlight the distinction between stationary and transitory activities.
- Explain how situational factors affect users' experiences in buildings.
- Explain how certain variables affect how users react to situational factors.
- Explain how the various events people go through when visiting buildings add up to the total experience of the visit.

Architecture is more to do with making frames than painting pictures; more a matter of providing an accompaniment to life than the dance itself.

—Simon Unwin, Analysing Architecture

Our experience is made up largely of the activities we do to satisfy our human needs and the societal rituals we perform daily. These include learning, working, playing, and connecting with others. Although some of these take place outside, it seems like most of what we do, we do inside. We seem to spend most of our time either inside a building or in transit between buildings.

As the quote above suggests, architecture is an accompaniment to the dance of life. Our conscious awareness, however, is usually more preoccupied with the dance of life itself than the surroundings in which the dance takes place. As we move from activity to activity and from goal to goal, our mind is focused on the meeting, the purchase, the meal, or the dance. People, goods, food, and dancing partners are our primary objectives. Despite its seemingly secondary status in our lives, architecture is a crucial ingredient in the mix. Buildings provide the settings in which the various dances of life take place, and, as such, they play a vital supporting role. Buildings supply not only shelter, warmth, and safety but also favorable conditions for an effective meeting, a smooth sale, an unforgettable meal, or a flowing dance. Surely, the other meeting members, the merchandiser, the salesperson, the cook, the waiter, and the dance partner all have to do their share for our daily rituals to be successful and meaningful, but buildings and, specifically, their interior spaces carry their share of responsibilities. Human experience is a seamless phenomenon, involving not only people and their rituals but also the settings in which they occur.

Designing beyond function and good looks requires knowing the rituals people perform inside buildings and the distinct activities that go with them. These activities act as forces that push and pull in many directions, sometimes in complementary and other times in conflicting ways. Understanding this mix and the role the spaces we design plays in the whole picture will allow you to respond with fitting solutions that facilitate and enhance the building experience.

Our first task is to learn about people and their rituals in buildings. We may start by asking: What exactly do people do in buildings? There are countless activities that people perform in buildings; however, despite that fact, there are several sequential and predictable events that occur most of the time. The purpose of this chapter is to present these events so that you can learn to design with them in mind. Additionally, this chapter will cover some of the main components involved in the mix of human activity and suggest how people's experiences in buildings vary depending on these components.

BASIC EVENTS OF THE BUILDING EXPERIENCE

The basic events that take place during building visits seem to be consistent and repetitive. Many of these events take place before or after the main activity associated with the visit. By gaining awareness of these events, you can provide design features to enrich the experience of users in buildings. Let's start with a scenario of a person's trip to the theater to see a live play, taken from Martin Bloom's book *Accommodating the Lively Arts*. In one of the chapters Bloom describes, in detail, the requirements of the spaces and places of a theater. Below is a description of one patron's experiences and observations as he visits the kind of theater described by Bloom. We take it from the exterior approach toward the building to the moment preceding the start of the show.

A patron approaches the theater on foot. The approach sets the tone for the experience. The ambience surrounding the theater is festive, creating a mood of anticipation of the event to come. The marquee projects, protects, and announces the current show. It welcomes, lures, and dazzles with light. The entranceways beneath the marquee welcome him to the attraction and feature promotional signs, posters, and photos on either side. Just beyond the entranceways, the box office allows sufficient space so that the long lines of ticket buyers do not impede the flow of patrons already ticketed and entering the theater. A staff member goes back to the administration area through a door accessible from the outer lobby , but located inconspicuously. The ample space in the outer lobby allows for discrete circulation, avoiding congestion from the crowd. Patrons not yet ready to enter the theater wait in allotted spaces away from the main paths of circulation.

Although businesslike and efficient, the lobby space serves as a prelude to the performance, enhancing the anticipation for the event to come. As the patron approaches the entrance to the inner lobby and passes through the control point, he surrenders his tickets and receives a stub indicating his seat assignment. At this point he begins to sense his relationship to the theater as a whole. The locations of checking facilities, restrooms, and public telephones become quickly apparent, and the pathway to the particular portion of the theater where he will eventually be seated is clearly disclosed.

Having unburdened himself of coats and parcels, he moves freely into the highly structured environment that begins to prepare him for the coming event. Having some time to wander, he contemplates images of past events in the theater, as well as historic artifacts related to the building. The main lobby is spacious, enabling the large audience to circulate freely and facilitating social interaction. The main lobby also provides glimpses of the immediate surroundings through window openings and through doors leading onto terraces, contributing a dynamic quality and aesthetic amenity. The grand stairway to the mezzanine contributes to the overall character of the lobby, providing viewing positions from the upper level that overlook the lobby below. The overall height and breadth of the space is monumental.

The lobby has established the patron's mindset for the ensuing event, transforming him into a participant in the event about to take place in the theater. Meanwhile, the patron becomes an actor in a secondary act, the drama created by the spectators in the lobby. As the patron approaches the entrance of the auditorium, he proceeds through a transitional zone

in which the lighting and sound levels of the lobby are gradually diminished. Once inside, he takes measure of the totality of the space, gaining a sense of his relationship to it.

Understanding his position in relationship to the whole gives him a sense of security within the environment. After being conducted to his assigned row, he negotiates the space between the rows and gets to his seat. The seat, clearly identified by letter and number, is comfortable, with enough height, width, and elbow room to accommodate a wide range of physical types.

There is enough ambient light to allow him to grasp the size, shape, and appearance of the room. The colors and textures of the walls and ceilings relate harmoniously to the seating areas and tie the whole composition of the room into a cohesive whole. Narrowly focused downlights complement the ambient lighting, facilitate the reading of the programs, and provide adequate lighting levels for aisles and exits.

The focus of the auditorium lies within the performance space and the seating arrangement reinforces that focus. It provides good sight lines and acoustics so that the audience is able to see and hear the performance with ease. As the time for the event nears, individual members of the audience settle in their separate locations, begin to focus their attention on the performance space and, as they do, become a coherent and attentive body, ready to react to the stimuli of the production. As the house lights dim, the environment of the audience space gradually loses its identity and begins to yield to the reality of the stage. In it, shortly, the audience will witness a presentation of a heightened reality, one more focused and more persuasive than anything that can be experienced outside the theater.[1]

The description above provides a rich account of the many events that take place even before the start of the big event, the theatrical production itself. In the case of a theater show, the production is the main activity. Actors act on stage and the audience looks on attentively from their seats. Behind the scenes, countless workers perform their roles with scenery, costumes, lights, and other crucial backstage activities to make the production smooth and flawless. During intermission, our sample patron may take a trip to the restroom and then proceed to the lobby for a beverage and, perhaps, conversation with friends about the first half of the show and what may be in store for the second. At the end of the production, the entrance sequence is reversed. The patron proceeds from the auditorium to the cloakroom to the various lobbies and, finally, exits the building. This may be done in ceremonious fashion, as when arriving, although exiting often tends to be a bit more chaotic because of the large number of people leaving simultaneously. Figures 2.1, 2.2, 2.3, and 2.4 show four views likely to be experienced by a theater patron while approaching and entering the theater but before getting to the main hall for the show. These are only a few of the many the visitor will experience while attending a function at the theater.

A trip to the theater is representative of all the generic events a person is likely to go through in a building: approaching, arriving, waiting, moving toward the

Figure 2.2: The extensive glass facade on the other side of the arts center also marks the location assertively while fully disclosing the events in the main lobby.

Figure 2.1: The corner of an arts center strongly announces its presence. Its transparency and sculptural qualities make the building stand out as an important destination.

Figure 2.3: The main lobby of a theater is a theater in its own right. There the patrons become actors before an event, during intermission, and at the event's conclusion.

Figure 2.4: The mezzanine above the main entrance features some of the best spots for congregating before a show and during intermission.

Figure 2.6: A common arrival space in buildings housing more than one entity is a public lobby. The image above shows a rich lobby for a downtown office building.

Figure 2.5: These two exterior views show the approach to a restaurant (a) and to a medical clinic (b).

destination place, arriving at the destination, performing the intended activity, taking side trips, engaging in peripheral activities, departing from the destination, moving toward the exit, and exiting. Although the specific nature of these experiences will vary from occasion to occasion, and from building type to building type, they are, essentially, the rituals people do in buildings. Below, we examine them more closely.

Approach

Our journey to a place begins the moment we decide to go there. In most cases, we simply make a decision to engage in a certain activity, be it eating out, shopping, going to work, or meeting with friends. Although in some cases people visit a building to see the building, such as in a building tour, the majority of times the building is a secondary (although crucial) component of the activity.

Even before we can see the building, we may start thinking about it: where we will park the car, which entrance we'll use, and so on. Eventually, we see the building. It ceases to be a memory and becomes real. We start approaching it and recognize it as our destination (Figure 2.5 a and b). Depending on our familiarity with the building, the eventual entrance sequence will have different degrees of challenge. Entering the building may be challenging to the

first-timer if the building's design is complicated. For habitual users it will be business as usual.

The building surroundings and general conditions will have an effect on how we react to the act of entering. If it is a beautiful day, we may delay the arrival; if it is cold and windy, we will welcome the building's warmth; if the scenery is flat, open, and undifferentiated outside, we may welcome the building's sense of structure and enclosure. The building may be handsome, ordinary, or ugly. Depending on how apparent these qualities are and our state of mind, we may or may not pay attention to them.

The approach to the building is full of anticipation. The first sight of the building leaves an important first impression on the visitor. Depending on the type of facility, the appropriate outward appearance may need to be bold or subtle, plain or adorned, formal or informal. Many commercial businesses, such as office facilities and retail stores, make decisions about where to lease space depending on, among other things, the quality and image of the building exterior.

Overall Arrival 1

At some point we reach the building's front door, open it, and step inside, a significant event. The act of entering itself is usually straightforward and performed automatically. Few people stop and think: Wow, what an entrance!

However, it is possible for building users to notice particularly well-composed and inviting entrances, such as the one shown in Figure 2.6 for an office building.

At this point, if users are familiar with the building, they may proceed automatically toward their goal. Otherwise, it may take a few minutes, depending on the building's complexity and internal arrangement, to get oriented and figure out where to go next. It is also at this point that they get their first impression of the building's interior. Depending on what the space has to offer and their state of mind, they may notice this first space and its qualities to a greater or lesser degree.

The ultimate destination may be a short distance away, far in the back, or on a different floor altogether. Accordingly, users proceed the short distance, to the back, or toward the stairs or elevators to reach their next destination. If they take the stairs or elevators to go to a different floor, they go through a similar sequence to the one on the ground floor at the new level once they arrive.

Arrival represents a partial objective of the overall goal of arriving at the final destination. For the designer, there are opportunities to make the arrival memorable, to reveal the whole cohesively, and to make the path clear for visitors, among others.

Overall Arrival 2

As we get closer to the entrance of the destination space, the level of excitement (or apprehension) we feel is likely to increase. As we enter we go through an entrance experience similar to the one of entering the building, except here the transition is between two interior spaces, and we are actually arriving at the destination space. Again, we will have first impressions of the new space, perhaps more noticeable this time since the burden of finding our way around is behind us, allowing the mind to attend to other things.

Depending on the type of space, there may or may not be someone to greet us. An office, a clinic, and a restaurant are likely to have a person greeting us; a store may not. Here, similar to the arrival at the destination floor, we may take a moment to glance around and get oriented. If we are familiar with the space, we just proceed ahead.

This arrival, more than the others, is likely to give us a sense of accomplishment and relief, even if at a subconscious level. There are opportunities for designers to make

Figure 2.7: In buildings containing more than one facility, a second arrival takes place when one transitions into the specific place being visited. Here, we present the first views seen upon entering a dental clinic (a) and an office suite (b).

a strong first impression in the arrival space itself, as well as in the spaces seen beyond. Figure 2.7 a and b shows the arrival spaces of a dental clinic and an office suite.

Waiting

In many facilities, such as offices, clinics, and restaurants, visitors have to wait their turn. A waiting room or area is provided for that purpose. Waiting is one of those rare instances when we are neither engaged in the target activity nor traveling to it. We are at the general destination but must now wait before engaging in the main activity. Any potential anxiety related to finding the right place or getting there on time has likely subsided considerably. We now have some time on our hands.

Depending on the length of the wait and our disposable time, waiting may or may not be a relaxed experience. There may be other people waiting too, strangers in close proximity. This could be pleasurable for the person who likes to make new friends but stressful for the person who feels uncomfortable among strangers. Looking at magazines or menus may provide relief and comfort to those who would rather avoid strangers. If you bring company, this could become a welcome opportunity to talk. Eventually, the person you are there to meet with, or the waiter, or the nurse, arrives and calls your name. You are getting closer to your real goal.

A couple of exceptions to the experience described above occur in some restaurants and most stores. Some restaurants have a bar and encourage patrons to wait there. The resulting waiting experience is different since you begin to actively use the facility while waiting; in this case, you may start to consume a beverage, something

Figure 2.8: Waiting is an unavoidable reality for visitors of many facility types. Here, we present the waiting area in a doctor's office (a) and an academic building (b).

different from waiting passively. Stores are still different. Stores, except by-appointment specialty stores, require no waiting; you proceed right in and start looking around. Many stores, however, notably grocery stores and convenience stores, have some waiting at the end, this time at the checkout counter. Retailers make attempts to make this idle time productive by placing small merchandise close to the registers for last-minute impulse purchases. Some include magazines and miscellaneous tabloids for our browsing pleasure and potential purchase. This kind of waiting occurs at the end of the sequence and represents the consummation of the shopping activity, rather than the waiting-at-the-gate kind of experience at the restaurant, office, or clinic.

A different kind of waiting occurs at the theater. There, you can wait outside in the lobby where you are free to move about at will, a much more active waiting experience. Part of what makes the typical waiting room experience uncomfortable for many is the lack of control and freedom of movement. There is usually nowhere to go, plus the close proximity to strangers is uncomfortable for many.

Waiting experiences are full of anticipation and expectation. They are instances of suspended attention, sort of a limbo between one place and another. People are not burdened with the logistics and challenges of finding the place and are not yet engaged with, maybe not even thinking about, the upcoming activity. This is an excellent opportunity for the designer to make an impression, perhaps by incorporating meaningful details. Figure 2.8 a and b shows waiting areas for a doctor's office and an academic building.

Moving to the Destination

The route taken and the experience of moving toward a principal destination tend to be different for first-timers, frequent visitors, and day-to-day users of a given facility. Insiders will proceed ahead and often use the back way in. Visitors, whether alone or escorted, will be limited to the public corridors intended for them.

The walk to the destination can be straightforward and utilitarian, or it can be involved and eventful. While in transit, users get a chance to look around and get a better sense of the overall environment, even if they don't get to see it all. They form impressions based on what is revealed in the corridor and the views from it to the spaces beyond. Insiders know the environment well and are not as likely to focus consciously on it.

Moving to the destination is often the most revealing experience of visitors to a facility. The opportunities to make an impression and provide enriching experiences are plentiful. The circulation system can be experientially stimulating at different levels. At the most basic level, it can orient and provide rich experiences to the visitor. At another level, it may provide a more subtle interest, the kind you notice after repeated exposures, such as intricate details about the carpet or fabric pattern or a distant view seen through a window on the way to the final destination. This second level of stimuli could be geared to the regular visitor. At yet another level, corridors can contain elements that change over time, to provide an additional level of engagement to the daily visitor. Figure 2.9 a and b shows routes to the destinations of clinic and restaurant projects.

Figure 2.9: The road to our destination can be an eventful and expressive journey in itself. The main paths to a dental clinic's main examination area (a) and a restaurant's dining room (b) start to reveal features of the spaces beyond.

Arrival at the Activity Destination

The experience of arriving at the final activity destination varies depending on the role of the person getting there. In a restaurant, the cook will arrive in the kitchen, the food server will move around her area, the cashier will arrive at the front cashier station, and the customer will arrive at the table. Depending on the facility type and the target activity, the destination place may be a desk, a conference room, a doctor's examination room, a dentist's chair, or a dining table, among others.

The common denominator of all these cases is a sense of arrival at the heart of the activity. It will be here that users, in their specific roles, will engage in the activities they came to perform. These activities may range in duration from a couple of minutes to longer periods of time.

The experience of customers in stores, however, is usually different. The experience there is one of constant movement from one place to the next with no specific place of arrival as described above. Museums and galleries offer a similar kind of experience, featuring a progression from space to space rather than an experience involving one principal activity place. Of course, there can be a sense of arrival in stores or museums when the purpose of the visit is related to one specific item. The moment we get to that item, we arrive. Figure 2.10 a–d shows views of the final destination places for an office worker, a visitor attending a meeting at the office facility, a customer in a restaurant, and a patient at a dental office.

Engaging in the Target Activity

Once we arrive at the target destination we engage in the target activity. The nature of the activity will vary widely depending on facility type and our role in the activity. The activity may be dining at a table, working at a desk, meeting in a conference room, shopping somewhere in a store, being examined in an examination room, or watching a show in a theater. The activity may also be serving the customer at the above dining table, selling merchandise at the store, examining the patient in the examination room, or being the lead actor of the theatrical production in the theater.

Many activities are done while stationary, either standing or sitting, although some, like shopping, involve locomotion and exploration. Some activities require both. A library experience may involve considerable amounts of

Figure 2.10: The heart of any facility is the place where the principal activity is conducted. Examples of these are the workstation in the office (a), the conference table in the meeting room (b), the dining table in the restaurant (c), and the dental chair in the dentist's office (d).

both stationary and locomotive activity. We may spend as much time searching for books in the stacks as reading them at the table or carrel.

Target activities represent the functions of the facility. They require functional provisions as well as ambient ones. Spatial qualities should take all aspects of the function into consideration and respond in ways that facilitate desirable experiences and avoid undesirable ones. Figure 2.11 a–c shows people performing their target activities in various settings.

Side Trips

Side trips are usually short-term visits to other spaces in the facility for personal or other reasons. These trips are not necessarily an essential component of the target activity per se. The best known is the trip to the restroom. Whether at work, at a restaurant, or at the theater, there comes a time when users pay a visit to the restroom. This, in itself, becomes a mini-experience requiring them to leave the target destination, travel to the restroom, use the facilities, and return. In too many facilities, unfortunately, the spaces leading to and from the restrooms are not given proper design attention and do not make a favorable impression. Figure 2.12 shows the unexpected and eclectic approach used for the vanity mirrors to enliven the restroom experience in a restaurant.

Another well-known side-trip destination is the concession stand in theaters and stadiums. As a designer, you should think of the circulation leading to side-trip destinations and the destinations themselves as worthwhile secondary experiences deserving proper design attention.

Secondary Activities

Some building experiences are limited to the activity performed at the main destination and, perhaps, one side trip to the restroom. Other experiences, however, involve additional meaningful events as part of the total experience. A day at the office may involve a principal meet-

Figure 2.11: Once stationed in the right place, facility users can engage in whatever their target activity is. Shoppers are an exception. They seldom settle down or linger much since shopping at a store involves exploration and movement (a). Others, like restaurant kitchen personnel (b) and bar visitors (c), usually conduct their business within the specific settings designated for their activities.

ing in the boardroom, another meeting with staff, and a training session. In addition, there will usually be a time for lunch, whether taken in the lunchroom or outside the office. These are all examples of secondary activities, instances when functions related to the main activity take one temporarily away from the main destination place and into another space for a related activity.

For many, the typical workday at the office is loaded with these types of events. For others in the office, the entire day may be spent at the desk with side trips to the restroom and the copy room, but without any special occasion other than lunch. A visit to a clinic may involve important stops at the lab and the X-ray room. A trip to a museum may involve a talk before the exhibit opens and the usual stop at the gift shop on the way out.

One example brought up earlier is the case of the bar in a restaurant. Waiting at the bar for a table to be ready doubles as a waiting experience and a secondary activity too. The activity no longer involves the typical waiting room experience, but becomes a meaningful experience in its own right. Once your name is called, however, you leave the bar and proceed to your main destination and activity: dining in the dining room.

Secondary activities, obviously, deserve as much design attention as the main target destinations in a facility. Figure

Figure 2.12: The places we go during side trips can be designed to entertain and provoke curiosity.

Figure 2.13: Secondary activities require us to leave the principal setting to visit a related setting. An example of this is an individual examination and X-ray room in a dental facility.

2.13 shows an examination room in a clinic, an example of the kind of secondary activity places people go to.

Departing the Destination

At some point it is time to leave. This is an important transition. The reason for leaving may be because the activity has been completed (dinner is finished) or because it is simply time to leave (the store or office is closing at the end of the day). We stop doing the activity we were doing and start gathering our belongings to head out. At this point we may be preoccupied with things such as the last details of the activity (such as paying the bill after dinner) and gathering our possessions, and we may begin to anticipate and prepare for the next activities (getting to the car, making it to the movies on time, and so on).

The experience may be rushed or relaxed, depending on what the next destination is and how much time we have to get there. The departure from the target destination starts the overall departure process. It is followed by movement toward the exit and the eventual exit.

Moving toward the Exit

After getting up and gathering our possessions we proceed toward the exit. We may go alone or be escorted. If not escorted, we may need to concentrate to find the way out, depending on the complexity of the building and our familiarity with it. The walk toward the exit may be hurried or relaxed, and we may have different degrees of awareness of the surroundings depending on the level of rush, mental preoccupation, or engagement with others. Nevertheless, it is a time of movement through the premises and has the potential, once again, for meaningful engagement with the surroundings. Therefore, serious consideration should be given to the experience offered as one travels back from the destination space. It has the opportunity to be as engaging as the experience we had when traveling to the destination place at the beginning of the journey. It may be the same route taken to the target destination or, perhaps, a different one. Figure 2.14 a–c shows views of the exiting sequence from the dental clinic seen in some of the earlier figures.

Figure 2.14: Leaving a facility usually involves a sequence similar to the arriving sequence, except in reverse. The three views seen here show the experience of leaving a dental clinic: the corridor leaving the examination area (a), the path through the waiting area leading to the exit door (b), and the exit doors from the building's public lobby (c).

Final Departure

Eventually we go through the last space and finally exit the facility. In some cases, the last space and the last wall may attempt to make one final impression on us. At this point the building experience is complete and starts to become a memory. The collection of impressions has been made and is recorded in our minds. We can then start planning our next building experience, perhaps minutes away and substantially different.

These generic rituals we perform in buildings occur time and time again in different settings and in slightly different ways. They provide the designer an event-based framework useful for design. This is not to say that design should consist of a series of fragmented responses to these events. That would hardly work, resulting in choppy projects lacking flow and unity. Nevertheless, designers should become more mindful of these events, consider inherent design opportunities, and act on them whenever possible and appropriate.

USERS' RESPONSE TO INTERIOR SPACES

In addition to becoming familiar with the above rituals, designers must become aware of the situational factors that affect users' experiences in buildings and some important variables that influence how people react to their settings. We start with the situational factors.

Situational Factors Affecting Users' Experiences in Buildings

Many have tried to study the relationship between human beings and their environment, often reducing the experience of life to people, functions, and environments. The experience of life is much more complicated than that, consisting of many variables that interact in complex and changing ways. The goal of this section is to increase your awareness about the situational factors that affect experiences in buildings and the role physical settings play in the overall experience. As stated in the opening quotation to this chapter, architecture is "more a matter of providing an accompaniment to life than the dance itself." Here we take a look at some of the important aspects of "the dance itself."

The things people do in life ("the dance") can be ana-lyzed in terms of specific occasions that take place in specific places, where people play specific roles, utilize given resources, and are surrounded by specific people, objects, and building parts. All these combine in complex and intricate combinations to become unique contexts for our activities. In order to think of ways design can contribute to the enrichment of our experiences in them, we need to have an understanding of how these factors typically interact. These situational factors consist of occasions, players, resources, and surroundings, the latter consisting of architectural features, people, and objects.

Occasion

An occasion is a very particular kind of activity, such as, say, a formal dinner for the members of upper management of a given corporation. Here, the generic activity is dinner. However, it is a specific kind of dinner with specific connotations and requiring particular behaviors.

Players

The people involved in the occasion are the players. These can be locals or visitors. Both the mix of players and the characteristics of individual ones will have an effect on the occasion. Are they lively or subdued? Formal or casual? Important or ordinary? Some of the key players in our example are the members of upper management attending the dinner, but also the waitstaff servicing the group.

Resources

Resources include physical ones, such as space, equipment, and the like, plus other important intangible ones, such as time and money. Our dinner example, for instance, may be taking place in a comfortable banquet room with ample space and tables. Let's suppose that this particular corporation is going through difficult economic times and its members are holding a retreat the following day starting early in the morning. As a result, the budget for the dinner this year may be low, and the participants will not be able to stay as late as they did in past years because of the activity the next morning. Let's also pretend that this year's dinner is somewhat rushed because the room was not ready on time and they had to start late. This year's dinner, in all likelihood, will not be as pleasant as those of other years, although none of it will be the fault of the interior physical environment.

Have you ever wondered how a person will react to a particular environment? Or what type of environment is most suitable for a particular person? In order to be able to make these predictions, we need a workable model that links specific emotional reactions to the load (complexity, intensity) of a given environment. Fortunately, Albert Mehrabian and James Russell have devised a practical framework we can use to make reasonable predictions to these challenging questions. Their research has led them to conclude that people's reactions to environments are based on just a few emotional dimensions, which in turn can produce many different behaviors. The basic chain of events consists of a given environment experienced by a person, the person's processing of the conditions presented by the place and situation, and the person's behavioral reaction, be it jumping with excitement or running in disgust.

The second emotional dimensions determine how a person reacts to a situation in the environment. They are the level of arousal, the level of pleasure, and the level of dominance experienced by the person in relation to the conditions presented. Keep in mind that although our focus here is man's reaction to the built environment, there are, as we have seen, other factors at play, such as the influence of other people, the specific occasion, and so on. Arousal refers to the overall level of stimulation experienced. The qualities of an environment may excite you and increase your blood pressure and heart rate. A different environment may have the opposite effect and may cause you to feel relaxed, or even sluggish and sleepy.

The second emotional dimension is pleasure. It refers, as the word suggests, to the amount of pleasure derived from a particular environment. Some environments may cause contentment and an overall good feeling, while others annoy or depress. The third dimension, dominance, refers to the degree of control or influence one feels in relation to a specific situation. This depends on both the setting and the event. For example, working at home may be more relaxing than working at the office. The familiarity of home and the fact that you don't need to be on your best behavior give you greater control over the situation. You could be wearing your cutoff jeans and singing loudly and no one will complain. Even within the office, though, different events will produce different levels of dominance. If you are, say, a midlevel manager, you will feel more in control in a meeting with the people you supervise than in a meeting with the top executives from upper management.

According to Mehrabian and Russell, just these three dimensions of emotional reaction, in different combinations, produce all possible feelings. For example, high displeasure, high arousal, and high dominance equate to anger. Anxiety, on the other hand, involves high displeasure and high arousal but low dominance. Every feeling known, from joy to anguish, may be described as some combination of the three basic emotional dimensions.

Our emotional reaction to any given environment, then, can be measured as a certain combination of arousal, pleasure, and dominance. Depending on our particular reaction we will be more or less inclined to approach, or avoid, the environment. The graph in Figure C2.1 shows the approach/avoidance behaviors produced by different combinations of arousal and pleasure. In general, conditions of neutral pleasantness will be avoided at low and high levels of arousal and approached at some level of moderate arousal. Pleasant situations and environments will generally be approached increasingly as arousal increases up to some level of very high arousal, which will begin a downward trend in the degree of approach. Unpleasant situations and environments will be increasingly avoided as arousal levels increase. It is no surprise that an ugly but mild room is less offensive than an ugly and intense one.

The third dimension, dominance, also plays an important role in the overall effect produced by an environment. For example, an environment that produces low arousal, mild pleasure, and some dominance will be cozy and enjoyable and produce a relaxed and comfortable overall effect. Conversely, an environment that produces low arousal, mild displeasure, and low dominance (submissiveness) will cause boredom and avoidance.

Having established the basics, we can now address the important consideration of differences among people. The authors propose that the same three basic emotional dimensions be used to describe the particular emotional traits and temperaments of people. Thus, we have people of generally pleasant or unpleasant dispositions, people whose personality and/or role make them more or less dominant or submissive, and people who innately tolerate more or less arousal. This last one is the trickiest of the three dimensions.

It works like this: People, according to personality and temperament, screen out more or less of the stimuli presented by the environment in order to reduce the actual environmental load perceived. Some people screen a lot of the stimuli (screeners) and others don't (nonscreeners). Nonscreeners tend to pay attention to most of what the environment offers without attempting to discard nonessentials. As a result, they experience environments as being higher in arousal levels. Screeners, on the other hand, are selective in what they pay attention to. By subconsciously prioritizing the components of a complex situation and attending only to the relevant ones, they effectively reduce the total environmental load perceived. Therefore, the same amount of environmental stimulus will cause greater amounts of and longer-lasting arousal for nonscreeners than for screeners. That is why some people feel right at home in the loud, colorful, and blinking discotheque and others feel more at home sipping decaf tea at the muffled café in the bookstore.

If arousal serves as a magnet in neutral and pleasant environments and situations, at least up to a certain point, then the nonscreener, who is more susceptible to environmental stimulus, will feel attracted to a scene with progressively ascending arousal sooner than the screener. We have said, however, that all people tend to avoid situations when the load level gets too high. Predictably, the nonscreener will reach the point of avoidance earlier than the screener. As Mehrabian explains, the higher susceptibility of the nonscreener to become "more aroused in high-load settings causes them to exhibit more polarized approach-avoidance behaviors to pleasant and unpleasant situations: compared to screeners they have a stronger approach to high-load and pleasant places, and a stronger avoidance of high-load and unpleasant ones."[1]

While designers may be able to create a good match between the personality of a single client and the qualities produced for, say, an apartment designed for that specific person, most projects are designed for multiple, in some

Figure C2.1: Approach/avoidance behaviors for different combinations of pleasantness and arousal.

Source: From *Public Places and Private Spaces: The Psychology of Work, Play, and Living Environment, by Albert Mehrabian.* Copyright © 1976 by Basic Books, Inc. Reprinted by permission of Basic Books, a member of Perseus Books, L.L.C.

cases hundreds of, people. In those cases, obviously, it is impossible to please everyone. Nevertheless, what is possible, and makes this type of information highly useful, is to determine the collective ideal levels of the three variables that a certain environment should stimulate or offer. A good office setting would likely stimulate a low to moderate level of arousal (at least in areas requiring high concentration) and offer a pleasant environment that allows a moderate amount of control. An ideal store may strive to stimulate a moderate to high level of arousal (depending on the store) and offer high pleasantness and at least moderate levels of control and freedom (except for the full-service store). A fancy, intimate restaurant may want to stimulate a low to moderate level of arousal and offer high pleasantness (all restaurants want to be pleasant) and low to moderate control. A tavern, by contrast, wants to stimulate high arousal and offer a high level of freedom and control.

We know you like pleasant environments. How about the other two variables? Are you either dominant or submissive by nature? Are you a screener or a nonscreener? How does your personality match the types of places and situations you typically approach and avoid?

---

1. Albert Mehrabian, *Public Spaces and Private Places: The Psychology of Work, Play, and Living Environment* (New York: Basic Books, 1976), 27.

Surroundings

The interior physical environment, of course, is more than just a resource. It also has a presence of its own as an entity, as do the other people and objects in the room. We refer to these here as the surroundings. In this group we can distinguish between surroundings directly related to the occasion and those peripheral ones in close enough proximity to be perceived, even though they play no direct role in the immediate occasion. Examples of the first group would be the activity room and its features, plus all the other furnishings, objects, utensils, and the like. Examples of the second group would be the people having a dinner next door and all the sights, sounds, and smells emanating from them and their activities.

The evening's experience will be a combination of complex dynamics involving all these factors and is likely to be different for the various attendees. Some factors will be experienced in approximately the same way by all, such as consistent, prompt, and courteous service and a fantastic view. The experience of other factors may vary from person to person, such as seating assignments and the quality of the dish ordered. In some cases, the same factor will be experienced differently by different people, such as one person liking and another disliking the same dish, or someone being more annoyed than others about the rushed nature of this year's dinner.

Variables Affecting Users' Reactions to Situational Factors

Human beings, despite their similarities, are different because of their personalities and backgrounds. Some people like quiet environments and others, loud ones. Some like public over private places. Some people like old styles over contemporary ones. Some people like involvement; others are more restrained. Additionally, everyone brings with them the context of the recent past. A modest-sized room may seem splendid to someone moving in from tiny quarters, while it may seem insufficient for someone accustomed to large spaces. At an entirely different level, someone may have heard some good news and be in a happy mood, but the person next door may have just been laid off and be experiencing tremendous emotional pain.

In addition to personal traits and the recent past, a few other factors affect the way people react to events. These include their role in the occasion and their degrees of affinity, familiarity, demand, and control with the situational factors described above.

If you are part of the occasion, you have a role in it. You may be one of the people attending the dinner or you may be one of the people servicing those having dinner. Among members of upper management you may be an old member or a new member; you may be the CEO or a treasurer. Furthermore, you may be the member who helped coordinate the event and might be attending to all kinds of details during the evening.

Another factor is related to people's preferences. Individuals have unique personal affinities. Not everyone likes the same settings, people, and so on. Certain occasions, players, resources, and surroundings may be enjoyable to some and not to others. A member of the dinner example above may not like going to formal dinners; another may like them but dislike her role as the event coordinator. Another person may like both the formal dinners and her role, but have a real problem with rushed dinners. Still another person may find everything else agreeable except the style of the furniture and paintings in the room and the person he has to sit next to, whom everyone else likes.

Familiarity is another factor. People may be more or less familiar with the particular event and the players, resources, and surroundings associated with it. In our management dinner example, some members may be familiar with the ritual of the yearly dinner, their role in it, the usual setting for the event, and even the occasional shortage of money and time. Newcomers may be unfamiliar with some or all of these factors. They may have a harder time making sense of the evening. On the other hand, the event may seem fresher to them than to the bored-with-it old-timers. The level of familiarity, then, is one of the variables that influences factors like the stress level and the sense of novelty associated with a particular occasion.

Different situations demand more or less from their participants. The demand of a situation is the degree of difficulty associated with it. A casual family dinner is likely to be considerably less demanding than the formal business-type dinner in our example. Some roles will be more demanding and require more concentration than others. The management member in charge of coordinating the event will have a more demanding evening than the others. This, in turn, may be nothing compared to the demands of the cook in the kitchen. Inadequate resources will usually increase the level of demand of any task. People and environments can also be more or less demanding to relate to.

Related to the roles people play in a given event is their degree of control over aspects of the event. The degree of control people have over a given activity affects their reactions to it. This also is related to the four factors of occasion, players, resources, and surroundings. Issues of freedom and power come into play. In our example, most of the participants had no control over the occurrence of the event. It was going to happen and they had to attend. Once there, they had to play their roles. For some it was playing the corporate persona many executives play in order to be like the rest of the crowd. They had no control over the time and budget limitations. Some may have had some creative ideas on how to deal with these problems but may be reluctant to bring them up since it may be inappropriate. Additionally, they certainly had no control over the setting, the group next door, and maybe even the choice of dish (these may have been predetermined). Compare this with the control you have over a casual, relaxed lunch with your best friend on a Saturday.

PEOPLE IN BUILDINGS AND DESIGN

The context in which our lives take place is, indeed, complex. Although the physical setting is an important component of any experience, much of our satisfaction or dissatisfaction at home, work, or play is the result of factors unrelated to setting. The dance of life is intricate. Still, designers need to learn about the particular situational factors related to their projects in order to design responsive environments.

As a designer, you have no control over most of the factors that influence experience, nor should you try to take responsibility for them. It would be impossible to predict the infinite number of possible combinations of personalities, preferences, and chance occurrences that take place in particular settings; however, it is possible to get an understanding of the general factors present in a particular application of a project through familiarity with the building type, the typical roles associated with it, and some of the idiosyncrasies the current user group may share with you. Then you are equipped to use the environment as a balancing and enhancing act to do its share in the complex mix of activity components. Depending on the project and the particular setting within it, you may decide to reinforce some physical characteristics and downplay others in order to enhance the experience of as many users as possible.

Providing enhancing conditions goes beyond the production of merely functional and pleasant solutions. It takes more work too, but it is richly rewarding for users and designers alike. Although designers may have little control over who is and isn't familiar with the interior environment of a facility, they can, having awareness that there will be people with different degrees of familiarity, make adequate provisions for the satisfaction of the greatest number. Similarly, knowing the various roles involved in a particular type of building, you may make special efforts to create enriching and satisfying environments for all, regardless of role. For instance, you may attempt to provide meaningful events not only for the customer in the restaurant dining room but also for the food preparation staff in the kitchen. Of course, the magnitude of these will be different, but so will the expectations. In other words, a small gesture that may go unnoticed in the main room may elicit cheers from the kitchen staff.

If the customary activities of a given environment are intense and demanding you may want to compensate and seek a balance by providing a soothing environment. On the other hand, if it is a nightclub, you may want to actually magnify the experience by providing a charged physical environment. If the tasks performed are routine and monotonous you may want to compensate by providing a lively environment that balances the experience.

In terms of control, if the atmosphere at a particular enterprise, such as an office, is very hierarchical and employees feel powerless, you could compensate by providing environments that offer choices and some control, thus empowering them to some extent. If, on the contrary, the atmosphere is excessively loose and unstructured, a healthy supply of formal structure may be desirable.

One of the most significant ways in which the mood of a physical environment can be altered is by controlling its sensory load. Environments can be considered high or low load depending on their degree of complexity, novelty, and intensity. A dense, busy, unpredictable environment with multiple bright colors would be considered a high-load environment. A simple, ordered, predictable one, with white paint everywhere, would be a low-load one. In addition to the physical qualities of the space itself and their relative degree of intensity, it is possible to affect the load by controlling the degree of activity in the space. Very active, high-density environments, for instance, will generate high levels of motion and sound coming from various sources and directions. This, even in an otherwise plain environment, will result in a high-load environment. For more about the effect of the environment's load level see the capsule (People and the Environment) in this chapter.

These are just some examples to illustrate the kind of thinking involved in using the environment as a balancing force in interior environments. Obviously, the correct response will depend on the exact circumstances of the project and the goals of both the people controlling the project and the eventual users, as well as the insights of the designer after considering the possibilities.

It is up to individual designers to decide the level to which they will take their designs. Many designers stop after function and good looks, because they have never been encouraged to think beyond them. We challenge you to become aware of the full possibilities and seek meaningful, deliberate design interventions aimed at enriching people's experiences in buildings. There are no hard rules, just the willingness to become familiar with strategies and possibilities and to exercise good, insightful judgment during the design process.

If we compare the game of life to a dance or a series of dances, then it is your responsibility as an individual designer to know the stages of the dances, the people involved in them, and the particularities of each dance. Only then will you be able to design appropriate accompaniments.

REVIEW

Summary

Knowing the basic rituals people perform in buildings gives the designer valuable information that can be used to provide engaging experiences at every step of the process. These activities can be categorized into generic activities people perform in buildings. These start with their approach to and arrival at a building. Next comes the process of moving toward and arriving at the target destination, including any necessary waiting periods. Target destinations include primary and secondary ones. Additionally, users may need to make side trips to the restroom or other similar destinations. Once finished, they begin a departure sequence that eventually leads to the exit from the building.

In addition to these rituals, this chapter explained that the spaces we design are one of many factors affecting people's experiences in buildings. These spaces are part of the surroundings and provide the setting for life's activities. Also affecting the experience will be the type of occasion, the other players associated with it, and the resources at their disposal. How people react to a particular experience depends on their relationship to the mix above. Most notable are the role one plays in the occasion, the degrees of affinity and familiarity toward the other factors, the level of demand imposed by the circumstances, and the degree of control one has over them.

While designers have little or no control over many of the nondesign factors that make up experience, they do control one of the most important ones, the setting in which the dance of life unfolds. The environments we design can often act as a balancing force, providing the right kinds and amounts of order, enrichment, and expression to optimize the conditions around the rituals of life enacted in them.

1. Martin Bloom, *Accommodating the Lively Arts: An Architect's View* (Lyme, NH: Smith and Kraus, 1997), 12–20.

Chapter Questions

1. Name and describe the basic building events that involve arrival.
2. Name and describe the basic building events that involve movement from one place to another.
3. Name and describe the basic building events performed while stationary.
4. As a visitor to an office on the tenth floor, how many total transitions would you go through if you went there for a meeting and also made one trip to the restroom and one trip to the break room? Count from the moment you would approach the building on foot to the moment you would leave the building.
5. What makes a visit to the grocery store or to a museum different from visits to other building types in terms of the 12 basic events described in this chapter?
6. What four factors that affect our experiences in buildings were discussed in this chapter? Explain your understanding of them.
7. What five variables affect the way you react to the four factors of Question 6? Explain how they affect your reactions.

Exercises

1. Increasing your awareness of the way the basic events occur in different building types requires consciously thinking about them and analyzing how the built environment contributes to the various events. In order to get some practice, try dissecting the visits to the following settings in terms of the 12 events discussed in this chapter. You may respond to Exercises 1–3 in either outline or essay format. Check with your instructor.

   > A nightclub
   > The movies
   > The design studio
   > The library
   > A coffee shop
   > The bookstore

2. For the settings above, analyze potential scenarios related to the occasion, the players, the resources, and the surroundings.
3. For each of the scenarios proposed, analyze possible reactions by you and some of the other players depending on role, affinity, familiarity, demand, and control.

CHAPTER 3
Interior Place and Its Components

INSTRUCTIONAL OBJECTIVES

- Describe the differences between function, space, and place.

- Present and describe the basic components of place.

- Explain the different prominence levels of domains.

- Describe the components of circulation systems: arrival spaces, paths, and nodes.

- Explain the hierarchical nature of paths.

- Explain the role and importance of nodes in interior circulation systems.

- Show and describe various levels of openness of barriers.

- Explain the various levels of invitation provided by different types of connectors.

- Explain the role of project ends in providing a connection to the rest of the world outside the project.

- Explain the role of furnishings as spatial modifiers in interior environments.

- Explain the role of interior landmarks in interior environments.

In the immensity and confusion of the environment, certain portions of space assume the value of place. They are identifiable, can be pointed out by others, and suggest ways of behavior. Some places are intended for our movements and exchanges, others encourage withdrawal and isolation. The place always suggests an action or a pause, even if only mental. Its forms are associated with events which it accommodates or which it has once accommodated, and with other similar places and events.

—Pierre von Meiss, Elements of Architecture: From Form to Place

IN CHAPTER 2 we reviewed the basic events of people's experiences inside buildings and other considerations that affect the building experience. In this chapter we begin to focus on place as the basic unit of interior design. More specifically, we explain the basic components of projects in terms of place. You will see that there are not too many types of places in buildings when we generalize them into our basic categories.

We first explain the concept of place, a central one in this book. Buildings are collections of places, not of functions. The basic components of place are explained as a system we can use to conceptualize projects.

FUNCTION, SPACE, AND PLACE

In design we commonly use the terms function, space, and place. It is important to understand the differences between these three concepts and how they are related. You are most likely familiar with the idea of **function** as used in the environmental design disciplines. It simply refers to the things people (or animals, plants, or machines) do in a specific environment. These translate to specific arrangements of spaces, furnishings, and equipment and particular placements of the people within the required spaces. To use an analogy from theater, function involves the actors (users) using props (furnishings and equipment) to perform certain roles.

Space is all around us, on the exterior as well as the interior of the buildings we occupy. When we design and build projects, we claim space and subdivide it in particular ways to suit the needs of the project. The spaces so defined have specific boundaries, shapes, and dimensions. This act of definition and shaping transforms generic space into the kind of space designers

work with: **architectural space**. But designers do more than just define space. These defined spaces usually correspond to specific functions that occur in them. Their design is also developed further and given particular characteristics to suit those specific functions and to reflect the general character of the project. Openings are placed strategically, surfaces are articulated, and subareas defined during this process of customization in order to reflect the particular requirements of the people who will occupy the space and the rituals that will take place in it. The resulting environment ceases being merely architectural space (although it can still be described in terms of boundaries, shapes, dimensions, and so on) and now becomes a habitable place.

Of all the space in the theater, the space occupied by the stage has been claimed for the functions performed by the actors. It has some recognizable limits, and the actions of the actors occur on this stage. During a play, the stage scenery portrays distinct places that often change from scene to scene, each having unique physical qualities and related activities. In the interior projects we design, the settings within a particular space generally don't change that much, and defined places tend to have consistent qualities and related functions. Thus, the bar in a restaurant or the waiting room in a dental clinic remains distinguishable as a specific and unique place from day to day and from week to week.

Places are clearly recognizable as discrete entities having an identifiable purpose and a particular character. They become recognizable as having limits within which specific events or functions take place. While the terms "space" and "place" can sometimes be used interchangeably, "place" tends to describe habitable space more completely and holistically. A place can be composed of several spaces as long as it hangs together as a whole (Figure 3.1).

Figure 3.1: A place, like the one shown, is a complete setting that includes the particular space, qualities, actors, and rituals that make it a unique phenomenological entity.

A project having dozens of functions performed by different people will acquire a particular form based on the number and relationship of places created by the designer for the project. As a designer, you always have a choice of how to break the functions into discrete compartments and how to assemble these compartments. Delimitation and differentiation become powerful tools with which to achieve place. How many places you create and what size, proportion, and shape you give them becomes crucial. When they are well conceived, clear, and well placed, they give environments a strong sense of identity and make a strong impact.

In this chapter we are not concerned with properties of space such as size, proportion, and geometry. Our intent here is to discuss the generic types of places that occur in interior projects. Specific properties of space will be discussed in the next chapter.

BASIC COMPONENTS OF THE ENVIRONMENT (PLACE ELEMENTS)

At the most basic level, interior environments can be reduced to places we visit to do something (destination places) and places that help us get there (circulation systems). The spatial characteristics of these two types of places are defined by the boundaries around and the objects within these places. With these four categories (destination places, circulation systems, boundaries, and objects) and some elaboration we can establish a group of ten elements useful for conceptualizing interior space.

The group is a combination of Kevin Lynch's five elements of urban imageability,[1] Christian Norberg-Schulz's elements of existential space,[2] and some minor additions that address aspects specific to interiors. Lynch's studies revealed that people make sense of urban surroundings by making mental maps that consistently feature five kinds of elements: districts, paths, nodes, edges, and landmarks. They are defined below, where they occur. Norberg-Schulz's model of existential space features three core elements: centers, paths, and domains. For an explanation of these, see the capsule in this chapter. A description of the ten place elements follows.

Destination Places

Destination places can be categorized as domains or centers, depending on their degree of prominence.

Domains

Domains are recognizable regions or areas. They are analogous to what Lynch called *districts*. Lynch defines districts as "medium to large sections of the city, conceived of as having two-dimensional extent, which the observer mentally enters inside of, and which are recognizable as having some common identifiable character."[3] Norberg-Schulz's concept of domain is better suited for interior spaces since domains don't carry the large area connotations of Lynch's districts. Despite the difference in scale, however, the concepts are nearly interchangeable. A district is usually some neighborhood (residential or otherwise) with recognizable boundaries and a particular character based on the kind of people who inhabit it and the things they do. You may not be familiar with the neighborhood, but you are likely to have at least some idea about its general extent. In some cases there may be multiple adjacent neighborhoods, and, even if you are not familiar with these neighborhoods, you may have a general idea of the area they occupy, and maybe even a sense of where one ends and the next one begins.

The concept is the same for interior projects, although the scale is smaller. The departments in an office or retail store, the units in a health-care clinic, and the different dining rooms in a large restaurant are all examples of domains in interiors. Domains are the basic destinations in a facility. They are the places people go to perform whatever activities they came to do, be it work, shop, or eat.

Projects usually consist of a collection of domains accommodated based on the requirements of the program. They are important because they constitute the greatest area of a project. They are the spaces where users spend the most time.

Centers

Centers are special destination places. You can think of them as very special domains. The term comes from Norberg-Schulz. Centers are well-known places where particularly meaningful activities and social interactions take place. They are both the goals toward which we move and the points of departure from which we orient ourselves in relation to the rest of the environment.

Of all the places people visit inside buildings, these are the most special. In public projects, they are usually the places where important group activities happen. Examples of centers include the principal conference room in an office, the main dining hall in a restaurant, and the main lounge of a hotel. These important locations require clear and direct access; in some cases, they even require a ceremonial approach.

Centers are important during planning because they require strategic placement. You should consider their locations before those of other, less important, places. In many projects, users will orient themselves in relation to these centers. Whether they become the great big space at the entrance, the sacred space in the middle, or the prestigious (or mysterious) destination at the end of an

Figure 3.2: Centers refer to important domains rather than spaces located at the geometric center of a project. Because of their status as special destinations, their placement always requires special consideration.

Figure 3.3: This open office area in an office suite is a domain, or neighborhood, one of many similar ones in the facility.

important path, centers always demand prominent placement. Figure 3.2 shows the main auditorium in a training facility, truly one of the centers of that project.

It is important to note that not all projects need centers. It is quite common to find restaurants where all dining areas are of similar importance and retail stores with no dominant departments. Another important aspect of centers to note is that it is their relative importance that makes them a center. Figure 3.3 shows a photograph of one of many open areas in an office, one of many similar domains in the facility. Figure 3.4, on the other hand, shows a large and prestigious public meeting room of a building, leaving little doubt that it is, indeed, one of the special destinations—a true center.

Figure 3.4: This room is a center. It is one of the most prestigious spaces of this particular building and is used exclusively for very special events.

Figure 3.5: This reception area is the arrival space of an office facility. It serves as a transition between the outside and what lies beyond within the facility.

Circulation Systems

Circulation systems determine the way you move around a building or facility. To a great extent, your impressions of a particular interior environment will depend on your experience while moving from place to place through the circulation system. Here we distinguish among three basic components of these systems: arrival space, the paths themselves, and nodes.

Arrival Space

The place you arrive when visiting any facility is of such importance that it deserves its own category as an element. At the city scale there are usually many access points, but in buildings and their interiors, there is usually only one main entrance. Therefore, in interiors, much more than in cities, it is possible to control the first impression of visitors.

The **arrival space** serves to make an initial overall impression on the visitor and also serves as a departure point to the rest of the facility. It is often the place where we are greeted and where we check in and get directions on how to reach our destination within the building or project. Its importance and potential are enormous. Figure 3.5 shows the reception area of an office facility, very often the arrival space to such office suites. Figure 3.6 shows the arrival space to an academic building displaying some special articulation and lighting fixtures at the ceiling to highlight its importance.

The design of arrival spaces can contribute greatly to the sense of order, enrichment, and expression in a facil-

Figure 3.6: Some arrival spaces, such as this one, are relatively informal, without checkpoints. Notice, however, how the special decorative treatments at the ceiling help to define this as a location of above-average importance.

ity. Arrivals are occasions of transition between the inside and outside of the project. The impact of these transitions and the need to make route decisions produce greater-than-average levels of stress and, therefore, a state of heightened awareness.

Paths

Paths are the channels of movement that we use to get around. Lynch defines them as the "channels along which the observer customarily, occasionally, or potentially moves."[4] Paths connect spaces, allowing users to get from one to another. All architectural spaces need paths for movement, whether they are separated from, or integrated with, the places they serve. They can be autonomous paths occurring outside the areas they serve or integrated paths

Figure 3.7: The degree of explicitness of a path can vary. It can be very explicit (a), clear but unaccented (b), or rather loose and ambiguous (c).

occurring within the spaces they serve. Figure 3.7 a–c shows examples of different paths.

Not only do paths serve the function of transporting us to our destination but they are also the vantage points from which we perceive the totality of a project, its spaces, and their sequences. So important was this secondary function for the great Swiss architect Le Corbusier that he developed the notion of **promenade architecturale**,[5] a carefully orchestrated route that revealed a building's spaces and their overall organization.

Paths are the heart of the circulation system. Note, however, that while the circulation system refers to the total system of movement within a building or project, a path refers to a specific segment having specific characteristics. You could think of paths as channels of movement of distinctive character that allow movement toward particular destinations.

Paths are hierarchical. Not all paths move as many people or share the same degree of importance. A major corridor in a busy airport is analogous to a freeway. A highly articulated corridor in a modern office with one or more places to stop, sit, and talk is analogous to a pedestrian street. Designers should understand the conceptual and functional differences between main and secondary paths.

Main Paths

Main paths are equivalent to avenues in cities. They define the main overall circulation system and get us to prominent destinations. They, like avenues, tend to be the most public thoroughfares for movement, the channels through which visitors move. As such, they not only get people to their destinations but also provide visual and other types of sensory experiences that make important impressions

Figure 3.8: This segment of a main path in an academic building is given prominence by its generous volume, articulated forms, crafted details, and elegant materials.

on visitors and new users. Additionally, they help provide a sense of sequence and are, therefore, partially responsible for the sense of unity and cohesiveness (or the opposite, chaos) of a project. Figure 3.8 shows an example of a main path in a prominent public area of an academic building.

Main paths are important contributors to the perceptions people form of built environments. It is while moving through and looking from them that visitors collect impressions of facilities and their people. A main path's shape, proportion, degree of openness, level of detail, and number of events will communicate in important ways with users and visitors alike. This will be discussed in Chapter 4. Figure 3.9 shows a main path in a conferencing facility.

Figure 3.9: This is a main path in an institutional building. Carefully detailed, although not fancy, what really sets it apart from other paths in the building is its generous and inviting width.

Figure 3.10: Maintaining a clear hierarchy between main and secondary paths helps users feel oriented and understand the building better. Three diagrammatic schemes of circulation systems show various main and secondary path arrangements.

Figure 3.11: Nodes often occur at important junctions, along a path, or at the end of a path.

Secondary Paths

Secondary paths are equivalent to the streets and alleys of our cities. In interiors, they are often narrower and less formal than the main paths. Large facilities like office complexes and large department stores usually have a network of main and secondary paths. The secondary paths tend to be more utilitarian, although there is no reason why some of them should not delight the user. There are instances when it might be appropriate to convert a particular minor path into an experientially rewarding one.

It is not only the functional importance of a path segment that accounts for its level in the hierarchy. In a project of fairly even functional hierarchy, the designer often decides to put higher perceptual importance on a particular path or segment of a path, distinguishing that segment as principal and more important than the rest. Perceptual hierarchy, then, becomes at least as important as functional hierarchy.

Distinguishing between main and secondary paths and designing spaces that physically show the difference between the two will produce clearer, easier-to-navigate projects. Figure 3.10 shows diagrams of three circulation systems combining main and secondary paths.

In terms of configuration, there are not many path varieties. A single path can go from one point to another, it can start at one point and branch out into multiple ones, and it can also start from and return to the same point. While performing these functions, paths can have a variety of shapes. They can be straight, curved, segmented, undulating, or any combination of these. Paths can also be combined in

Figure 3.12: A centrally located break area provides employees of this facility a place to step off the main path to take a break and chat with coworkers.

many ways. They can join as well as intersect. Additionally, paths are not always level: They can also ascend or descend to higher and lower levels via ramps and stairs.

Many of people's perceptions of interior environments are experienced while navigating their paths. Later chapters will elaborate on ways paths contribute order, enrichment, and expression in interiors.

A special component of a path is the occasional nook or larger zone off to the side or at the end of the corridor where users are encouraged to step aside to converse with others informally or get away temporarily (Figures 3.11 and 3.12).

Nodes

Nodes are areas of heightened activity. Nodes are not paths themselves but, rather, places at given points along the paths. Lynch explains that they can be junctions, like a convergence of paths, or concentrations, like an enclosed square. Nodes can occur at significant intersections, off to one side along the route, or at end points. Space usually expands at these locations, and one or several magnet areas are placed in close proximity. In an urban neighborhood it may be a corner with a coffee shop, a bakery,

Figure 3.13: Paths converging in a powerful and expanded center create a major node in this educational building. Although this space may seem like a center, in our definition it is a node because it is not a destination place but a prominent juncture within the circulation system.

Figure 3.14: Nodes often serve to bring people together, as in this waiting area outside a series of meeting rooms.

a convenience store, and a post office. In an office it may be a junction where conference rooms, a break room, and the mailroom converge, thus attracting people and fostering vitality.

The distinction between nodes and centers is helpful for design purposes. Centers are the principal domains. Nodes are in-between places where paths and strategic magnet destinations converge. They become a temporary place to stop where people run into one another and sometimes stay for a while if seating is provided. An example would be a node that includes a well-placed break room or a lounge area with seating in an office setting. A node may also be created by a combination of an intersection that expands and well-integrated places to sit surrounding the intersection, such as the one shown in Figure 3.13, where horizontal and vertical circulation converge and expand to create a powerful node.

Nodes are important architectural enhancers. They provide relief, encourage social contact, accentuate transitions and entrances, and create memorable spaces along the way. Like paths, they are important components that contribute to order, enrichment, and expression. The architectural program given during the early stages of a project is not likely to ask for any nodes. Nodes happen because designers make them happen. They are strategically conceived and placed to create vital spaces of human interaction (Figure 3.14).

A clear hierarchy of domains and paths, nooks and pockets along the paths, and well-placed nodes enhances the clarity and experiential appeal of interior projects. An interior space system consisting of just domains and undifferentiated paths lacks those qualities. Figure 3.15a shows a diagram of a hypothetical project expressed in terms of undifferentiated domains and paths. Figure 3.15b shows the same space, but this time centers, main circulation segments, and nodes are included. Notice how the clarity and general appeal of the project, even as seen as a plan diagram, are enhanced by the addition of hierarchy.

Boundaries

Now that you are familiar with destination places and paths we can look at the kind of architectural elements

A   B

Figure 3.15: Projects without differentiation (a) are confusing and seldom memorable. The differentiation between domains and centers and between main and secondary paths, together with the addition of alcoves and nodes along the circulation route (b) greatly enhance the clarity and memorability of a project.

that help determine how places are connected or segregated from one another. We present three elements related to boundaries: edges, connectors, and ends. While edges are the only one of these addressed by either Lynch or Norberg-Schulz, connectors and ends are important basic elements and deserve special attention.

Edges

We look first at how paths relate to places, and how places relate to other places in terms of the levels of separation and connection their boundaries allow. **Edges**, according to Lynch, are often boundaries between two places. They can be more or less penetrable barriers, closing off one region from another, or seams, relating and joining two regions.[6]

Once a decision has been made to have two places adjacent to each other, one has to think about the desired degree of separation between them. The same is true between routes and places. We rely on barriers to separate adjacent spaces. Between the extremes of a full barrier or no barrier are other levels of potential separation. We could conveniently categorize the possibilities into four levels of barriers: solid, mostly solid, mostly open, and open. Totally solid and totally open boundaries are straightforward and easy to visualize. The in-between categories are less straightforward and require illustration.

Mostly solid refers to a barrier having some openings that provide visual, auditory, haptic, and physical connection between one space and the next. The solid portion is greater than the open one. Examples include a full-length partial-height wall 7 feet high; a partial-length full-height wall; and a full-length full-height wall with a few punched openings. Figure 3.16 shows elevation views of these examples.

With mostly open barriers the ratios are inverted and the open portions constitute a greater area of the plane than the solid ones. Examples include anything from a colonnade to examples similar to the ones in Figure 3.16, but with larger open areas. Figure 3.17 shows some examples.

Glass is a unique material that is hard to classify but falls somewhere between mostly solid to mostly open. It is a solid material. You cannot walk through it. Nevertheless, glass allows light to penetrate from one space to the next, and clear glass allows one to see through from one space

Figure 3.16: Mostly solid barriers come in many configurations. In these three examples, note that the solid area (shaded) is greater than the open area.

Figure 3.17: Mostly open barriers also come in many configurations. In these four examples, the amount of openness and connection to adjacent spaces is more than half of the barrier's area.

to separate areas will enable you to be more responsive to the optimal level of separation and more creative about the means you utilize to achieve it.

Depending on their number, size, and configuration, barriers can have immense effects on how much of the visual field is disclosed at one time, thus influencing our sense of order and orientation. They influence the sense of drama as one moves about the project. Their shapes, placement, and arrangement serve to communicate a portion of a project's expression.

Connectors

Contrary to the idea of barrier is that of access. The points of connection between adjacent spaces are important determinants of the character and flow of those spaces. Options range from the well-known (and often over-used) doorway to full-width openings between spaces. Here, we distinguish between two broad categories—gateways and passages—each with a multitude of variations. Gateways read as formal access points and invite movement between spaces, while passageways allow movement between spaces in looser, less formal ways.

Gateways

A **gateway**, as the name implies, is a clearly defined point of entry. The most common one is the doorway. So strongly do we associate the symbol of a cased opening having a swinging door with the ideas of entrance and exit that the doorway has become the quintessential example of a gateway. For our purposes, we'll distinguish between grand entryways and ordinary entryways.

Ordinary entryways have single or double doors or cased openings of comparable size that invite us to enter. We are all familiar with these. Grand entryways are more formal and monumental. They are unmistakable gateways that draw you in and are usually reserved for prominent entrances. The size of the door and frame as well as the size of the surrounding casing and the depth of the passage all contribute to their grandiosity. In interiors, grand entryways often consist of a specially detailed door or opening, usually oversized, and often placed in an extra-deep cavity. Figure 3.18 shows two examples of grand entryways in interiors.

to the next. Given the sophistication of manufacturing techniques today, it is possible to manufacture glass of various degrees of opacity. While clear glass allows us to see through it, etched glass does not. Consequently, using glass, a designer can create the desired level of transparency to fit the occasion.

Even as early as the concept generation stage of the design you should begin thinking about the desired nature and degree of separation between places and between paths and places. Being aware of the many ways

Figure 3.19: Passageways informally allow users to go through to the space beyond, without formal doors or framed gateways.

Figure 3.18: The generous arched entryway (a) is an example of an inviting grand gateway. Retail stores usually feature inviting grand gateways (b) to lure outsiders in.

Passageways

Passageways are not framed openings like the more formal gateways discussed above. They can be either tunnel-like adjoining passages between spaces or merely openings in the wall that allow movement between spaces. In the first case, they invite movement; in the second, they allow it. Many modern interiors rely on wide passageways as a way to move between spaces. Openings allow movement between spaces, but the user relies on other directional cues from the furnishings or other objects to know which way to go. Figure 3.19 shows an example: Notice how it connects and invites in a casual way without doors or cased openings.

Connectors contribute much to a project's sense of order, enrichment, and expression. Their placement controls patterns of movement and the exact points of entry to the different parts of a project, affecting both our senses of orientation and stimulation. Their placement and detail also communicate certain types of expression.

Ends

Ends are special kinds of edges. We make the distinction to differentiate between internal separations within the same project (edges) and those edges where a project ends. Ends occur at the limits of a project's allotted space.

Scholars in the design disciplines have pursued diverse avenues in search of a better understanding of the built environment. One notable scholar who has contributed much to our understanding of the significance of the man-made environment is Christian Norberg-Schulz. His primary aim, he explains, has been "to investigate the psychic implications of architecture rather than its practical side."[1] Norberg-Schulz has pursued architectural insights from every angle possible. After initial attempts to analyze art and architecture scientifically, he turned to other methods. Although a believer in the contributions of scientific methods, he found them limiting, noting that "when we treat architecture analytically, we miss the concrete environmental character, that is, the very quality that is the object of man's identification."[2] His diverse explorations into the minds of artists, philosophers, historians, and psychologists led him to phenomenology as a vehicle for architectural inquiry. It provided a mode of inquiry compatible with his desire to study architecture as a concrete phenomenon.

Phenomenology is an approach within the field of philosophy initiated by Edmund Husserl as a reaction to what he perceived as modern science's incapacity to help us understand the concrete "life-world." As Norberg-Schulz puts it, "the life-world does not consist of sensations, but is immediately given as a world of characteristic, meaningful things, which do not have to be 'constructed' through individual experience."[3] He further explains: "Phenomenology was conceived as a 'return to things,' as opposed to abstractions and mental constructions."[4] Encouraged by the potential contributions of phenomenology to architectural thinking, he embarked on the mission of developing a phenomenology of architecture.

Much of Norberg-Schulz's efforts have focused on the topics of place and dwelling. Below, we summarize some of his thinking on these topics to give you a sample of his views.

Place

The place is the concrete manifestation of man's dwelling, and his identity depends on his belonging to places . . . [by place] we mean something more than abstract location. We mean a totality made up of concrete things having material substance, shape, texture and colour. Together these things determine an "environmental character," which is the essence of place. . . . A place is therefore a qualitative, "total" phenomenon, which we cannot reduce to any of its properties, such as spatial relationships, without losing its concrete nature out of sight.[5]

Because of their qualitative nature and levels of complexity, Norberg-Schulz believes places cannot be properly described by methods that rely on abstractions of concrete phenomena to arrive at neutral, objective knowledge. Lost by such approaches "is the everyday life-world, which ought to be the real concern of man in general, and planners and architects in particular."[6]

Places have a specific concrete presence. They can be either natural or man-made and are experienced as environments having a particular set of qualities, that is, particular characters. Concentration and enclosure are the properties of man-made places, be they cities, towns, or individual buildings. At any of their scales, man-made places are collections of things grouped together and somehow bound. Norberg-Schulz analyzes them in terms of "space" and "character." Space refers to the three-dimensional organization of the elements that make up place. He looks at space not as a mathematical concept but as an existential dimension. Character refers to the general atmosphere of a place. While spatial organizations may have different characters, space and character operate as a unit, and specific spatial organizations limit the possible characterizations within them.

The elements of existential place are center, path, and domain. At the heart of the notion of place is the center. The ultimate environmental center is the home, the center of each individual's personal world. Centers are known places where meaningful activities and social interactions take place. They are both the goals toward which people move and the points of departure from which they orient themselves in relation to the rest of the environment.

Beyond the home, other places become centers in our lives. Friends' houses and the meaningful public buildings of our lives, such as school, community center, and church, become centers. At different scales, certain specific rooms and spots within those buildings also become centers. Regardless of scale, a center, because it is a place, has recognizable limits. There is a definite sense of inside and outside defined by a physical or symbolic boundary between here and there.

The next basic property of human existence is the path. Any center, or place, exists within a context, never in isolation. As such, a place is physically related to the rest of the world around it. Thus, starting from the very center of a place, we can identify directions such as up and down, and left and right. As Norberg-Schulz explains, "the simplest model of man's existential space is, therefore, a horizontal plane pierced by a vertical axis. But on the plane man chooses and creates paths which give his existential space a more particular structure."[7] The path connects the known with the unknown and its presence sets in motion a cycle of departure and return. Contrary to the center, which is static and contained, the path is continuous and dynamic. Paths represent a direction to follow toward a goal, but, as Norberg-Schulz explains, "during the journey events happen and the path is also experienced as having a character of its own. What happens along the way, thus, is added to the tension created by the goal to be reached and the point of departure left behind."[8]

The last basic property of existential space is the domain. As we travel regularly along the same path toward a meaningful destination, the areas we pass on either side become somewhat well known, even if we don't enter them directly. Norberg-Schulz calls these areas domains and distinguishes them from the areas beyond them, the real unknown. Domains are not just the "everything else," but are distinct from one another and identifiable because of their boundaries or some other unifying characteristic, such as grouping of parts or common visual characteristics. The difference between domains and centers is that each person belongs in certain centers, and, therefore, these become his or her particular, personal goals. Despite the cohesiveness they may enjoy, domains are not destinations or goals, although they might very well be for some-one else. For us domains are "relatively unstructured 'ground' on which places and paths appear as more pronounced 'figures.'"[9]

Places, paths, and domains form the basic schemata for man's orientation and, thus, according to Norberg-Schulz's view, constitute the elements of existential space. Depending on where we find ourselves, a certain environment may be dominated by one or another of these three properties. The experience of driving toward a familiar destination may be dominated by paths and domains. Then, all of a sudden, one enters familiar and meaningful territory and the experience gets transformed into a progression of centers at different scales, starting with the entrance into the familiar neighborhood and culminating with the final arrival at the dinner table.

The elements of existential space exist at different levels. The first and smallest level is determined by the hand and what it can grasp. It is the level of small things and objects. The next level is determined by the body. It is the level of the furniture on which we can sit, recline, or lie down. The third level is the house, or individual building, which allows movement and comprises defined territories. Beyond these, and less useful for the purposes of people concerned with interiors, are the urban, landscape, and regional levels.

The levels of house (meaning also familiar individual buildings) and things are the most relevant to the designer of interiors. The house represents the very center of human existence. It gives man a place to be, a place in which to stay and spend time in safety and comfort. Within it, of course, there are also rooms, each a place having a unique character. As we get into the smaller objects of life, the furnishings and other items of our lives, we get into objects of very precise forms that we come to know intimately. These are the objects with which our hands and bodies come into the most intimate contact. The fireplace, the dinner table, the bed, and even the chest of drawers become true foci in our lives and are known in the most direct ways. In fact, it is the progressively smaller levels of the hierarchy that give the larger ones their character. Thus, the character of the neighborhood is determined largely by its buildings, the character of the buildings by their details and objects, and so on.

Dwelling

By tracing its linguistic evolution, Heidegger uncovered the meanings associated with the word *dwell*. Combining these meanings, he defined dwelling as "to be at peace in a protected place."[10] To this, Norberg-Schulz adds some linguistic derivations of his own, and adds that through dwelling the life-world becomes habitual and "known." He goes on to distinguish among four modes of dwelling related to their scale, level of development, and how collective or individual the interactions occurring within are. The four modes are natural dwelling, collective dwelling, public dwelling, and private dwelling. For our purposes, the last two are the most significant. Public dwelling occurs within a community with shared common values and beliefs, such as the employees of a given company. In fact, it usually takes place in a public building. Private dwelling refers to the private and personal kind of dwelling required to develop one's individual identity. It finds its most pure expression in the home.

True dwelling requires a meaningful relationship between a person and a given environment. In other words, one has to establish a meaningful relationship with both the space and the character aspects of the given place. Where a person is and how he or she is in a given place have to be understood. Norberg-Schulz labels these two required psychological functions orientation and identification. "To gain an existential foothold," he explains, "man needs to orientate himself . . . he also has to identify himself with the environment."[11] Orientation is concerned with the spatial relationship of things, while identification is concerned with the qualities of places. The two are always present, although they don't necessarily have to correspond. In other words, it is possible to feel oriented in a place and not identify with it, and vice versa.

Orientation ties directly to our previous discussion of the three properties or elements of existential space: centers, paths, and domains. The designer's task becomes to translate these into physical form in a way that produces a good environmental image likely to facilitate the process of feeling oriented. For this, Norberg-Schulz uses Kevin Lynch's influential ideas on environmental imaging and his concepts of districts, paths, nodes, edges, and landmarks, which work nicely with the existential space concepts of center, path, and domain. The place elements introduced in this chapter, in fact, are a combination of the concepts from both Lynch and Norberg-Schulz.

Perhaps more important than orientation is the function of identification with a given environment. Identification means to relate meaningfully, to truly belong. It requires proper correspondence between the interior and exterior worlds of the individual, where the environment embodies aspects of existence meaningful to the person. This is the aspect that Norberg-Schulz feels has not been given proper attention in modern society, where "attention has almost exclusively been concentrated on the 'practical' function of orientation, whereas identification has been left to chance."[12] Proper dwelling requires the proper alignment of interior self, body, and exterior world. The interaction between internal and external things can be tricky to decipher. Norberg-Schulz believes that the identities of man and environment feed off each other. He explains: "Identity . . . consists in an interiorization of understood things, and . . . growing up therefore depends on being open to what surrounds us. Although the world is immediately given, it has to be interpreted and understood, and although man is part of the world, he has to concretize his belonging to feel at home."[13]

1. Christian Norberg-Schulz, *Genius Loci: Towards a Phenomenology of Architecture* (New York: Rizzoli, 1980), 5.
2. Ibid., 5.
3. Christian Norberg-Schulz, *The Concept of Dwelling* (New York: Rizzoli, 1985), 16.
4. Norberg-Schulz, *Genius Loci*, 8.
5. Ibid., 6.
6. Ibid., 8.
7. Christian Norberg-Schulz, *Existence, Space and Architecture* (New York: Praeger, 1971), 21.
8. Ibid., 22.
9. Ibid., 23.
10. Norberg-Schulz, *Genius Loci*, 22.
11. Ibid., 19.
12. Ibid., 21.
13. Ibid., 20.

These are the boundaries within which you design a given office, store, or restaurant. They may or may not be important, depending on the circumstances. In a high-rise building, the outside walls are ends that relate to the exterior context and are thus important. Exposure to views, the sun path, or important visual or symbolic elements outside rely on the proper placement of spaces in relation to these ends. Figure 3.20 shows an end made usable with seating and pleasant views to the exterior. Similarly, while the exterior edge of an intimate—and therefore introverted—restaurant may not be that important, the opposite is true at a sidewalk cafe, where an important goal is to connect with street activity. Ends are significant because they dictate the limits of your space and the type of relationship with adjacent spaces. For a retail store, for instance, it is important to use the main front end, such as the storefront, to entice potential buyers. In Figure 3.21 the focus is inward, toward the store.

Ends at a project's perimeter often feature some level of transparency, allowing us to see beyond. They are important in providing a sense of orientation. They also provide daylight and views, important stimulators and enhancers.

Objects

Finally, we will now inspect the role of objects in the orchestration of place. Objects in space are a very important aspect of interior environments and, as such, their characteristics have a significant impact on movement and access. By objects we refer to major objects in space, such as furnishings and significant fixtures or decorative objects.

Furnishings

Under the general term **furnishings** we refer to fixtures, furniture pieces, and equipment of sufficient size to influence the experience of space. Designers of interiors often rely heavily on these to choreograph the interior experience, and, therefore, they represent an important category among our place element groups.

Examples of influential furnishings are freestanding fixtures or display cases in stores, tables in restaurants, and systems furniture in open office spaces. These types of furnishings tend to work more as space modifiers than space creators except in cases where they are tall enough to provide a real sense of enclosure. In these cases they have an effect on the visual lines of a space and become important screening devices; their placement becomes critical, and a tug-of-war between placement for function and placement for effect is common.

Perhaps the main attribute of furnishings in interior environments is how their placement affects the use of space

Figure 3.20: Ends can become special, as shown in this example of an informal and bright sitting area with views to the exterior.

Figure 3.21: An important end boundary of a retail store is its front. A generous and inviting gateway and a mostly transparent front dissolve the barrier, revealing the merchandise to lure shoppers inside.

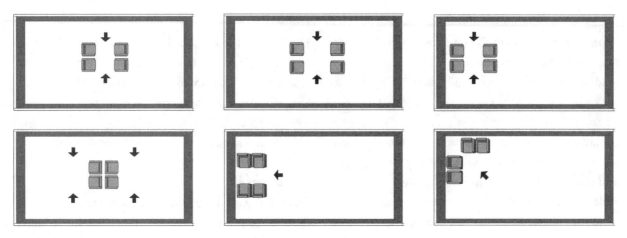

Figure 3.22: The number, placement, and arrangement of furnishings have important effects on the resulting use patterns of a space, as illustrated by these six simple scenarios.

Figure 3.23: This furniture arrangement complements the overall effect of the waiting area, defining two very distinct seating areas that become focal points in the space.

Figure 3.24: The high density of the workstations and medium-height panels are two of the principal factors that give this space its spatial character.

and controls movement. The placement of furnishings dictates which areas of the floor remain open for human occupation as well as become circulation patterns in space. Figure 3.22 shows six different furniture arrangements in a simple waiting space and the resulting use patterns.

The way furnishings are grouped can also contribute to the definition of place. A group of furnishings can help define regions and, when used repetitively, can contribute a sense of continuity and rhythm (Figure 3.23). Furnishings can also have a strong effect on the general density of a space. Depending on their size, number, and spacing they can produce various effects, from spare to crowded. In Figure 3.24 the furnishings, although low, have a major impact on the use and overall density of the respective spaces. The tall office cubicle panels in Figure 3.25 act as walls, defining the

Figure 3.25: The high furniture panels act like walls in this tall space, hiding the work areas behind them.

corridor strongly and reducing the sense of clutter, since the desks on the other side are hidden.

Furnishings contribute to order, enhanced experience, and expression. The paths dictated by their arrangement affect our experiences as we move around them. The degrees of balance and harmony in their layout greatly influence the project's sense of order.

Landmarks

Lynch defines **landmarks** as "simply defined physical object[s]. Their use involves the singling out of one element from a host of possibilities."[7] Their key physical characteristic is singularity, some aspect that is unique or memorable. Landmarks are more clearly identifiable if they have a clear form, if they stand out against their background, and if there is some prominence of location and/ or scale. At the scale of interior space we rarely encounter the plazas with memorable monuments or the distinctive high-rise buildings that frequently become the landmarks at the city scale. The designer of interiors relies on other, less grandiose, types of landmarks. Possibilities include special features such as accent walls, art pieces, and special displays. Although typically more modest than their urban counterparts, interior landmarks stand out and are remembered. Like landmarks in cities, they are the kind of prominent and recognizable features you are likely to use when you tell a friend to meet you by the sculpture, or by the pink wall, or by the information kiosk. Figure 3.26 a–c shows three conceptual examples of landmarks.

Landmarks give people points of reference around which to get oriented and contribute to both the experience and sense of expression of a space. Landmarks can be especially effective if they can be seen from multiple locations, even from a distance, and if they occur at key intersections of a project. Figure 3.27 a and b shows two examples of interior landmarks: a prominent statue in a lobby area and a magnificent stained-glass window in a library.

Landmarks, like nodes, mark important locations of projects. As such, they contribute much to order and orientation. Whether seen from a distance as goals to move toward, or discovered unexpectedly as surprises, they can serve to enhance users' experiences. Furthermore, their specific character, form, and occasional to the expressive qualities of a project.

Figure 3.26: Special walls (a), sculptures (b), and two-dimensional artwork (c) are examples of potential landmarks in an interiors project.

Figure 3.27: Statues and prominent sculptures, so effective as outdoor landmarks, are also highly effective inside (a). Two-dimensional artwork, in this case an oversized stained-glass window that takes the entire wall, can also be memorable and, thus, effective as a landmark (b).

REVIEW

Summary

More than a collection of spaces, the interior environments you design are collections of places. Although the parts and elements of a project are always numerous, there are only a few basic components of place. Being aware of these will help you conceptualize settings more effectively.

The main activity of interior environments usually occurs in their destination places. Most of these are what we call domains. Centers are domains of special importance by virtue of their functional or symbolic prominence. Circulation systems provide networks of movement to get to the destination places. These include the project's arrival space, the network of paths to move around the facility (main paths and secondary paths), and nodes. Nodes are special locations along paths or at their intersections that incorporate magnets to attract people and increase vitality.

Projects, their places and paths, are confined and defined by boundaries. These include edges, barriers, connectors between spaces, and ends. Barriers provide separation, connectors yield passage between areas. These can be formal and strongly defined gateways or informal and less defined passageways. Ends are the outermost boundaries of a project, where a project meets the rest of the world, be it the suite next door, a public corridor of the building, or the exterior.

Interior places contain objects of different kinds. Furnishings are important spatially. The number, size, and placement of large pieces of furniture, fixtures, and equipment have a major impact on interior space and how it is perceived. Landmarks are prominent objects that usually occur in special locations of a project. These can be pieces of artwork or prominent building elements or fixtures. Their main attribute is singularity. They stand out and are remembered.

1. Kevin Lynch, *The Image of the City* (Cambridge, MA: MIT Press, 1960).
2. Christian Norberg-Schulz, *Existence, Space and Architecture* (New York: Praeger, 1971).
3. Lynch, 47.
4. Ibid.
5. B. Leupen, C. Grafe, N. Köinig, M. Lampe, and P. de Zeeuw, *Design and Analysis* (New York: Van Nostrand Reinhold, 1997).
6. Lynch, 47.
7. Ibid., 48.

Chapter Questions

1. Think of important buildings in your life, past and present. What special domains, that is, centers, can you recall? Can you recall special nodes along the circulation system? Describe them.

2. How would you introduce nodes in an office project? How about in an educational setting or clinic?

3. Try to recall some prominent, main interior paths. Were they appropriate for the occasion? Describe them.

4. What memorable arrival spaces have you experienced? What made them good or memorable?

5. How would you make a secondary path experientially rich? Could you do it without spending too much money?

6. Can you recall successful partially solid or partially open barriers? Describe them.

7. Where would you use a partially solid barrier?

8. Where would you use a partially open barrier?

9. Recall and describe grand gateways you have experienced.

10. Can you describe effective passageways that invited passage without demanding it?

11. Can you describe effective passageways that didn't necessarily invite passage but allowed it?

12. Recall and describe successful transparent project ends you have seen.

13. Can you recall projects with tall furnishings that created a corridorlike effect as you moved between them? Describe them.

14. Can you recall instances where the furnishings enhanced or disturbed order due to their level of density or the level of order or disorder of the smaller objects placed on them? Describe them.

15. Describe interior landmarks you have seen. How are they effective? How are they memorable?

16. In what ways, which have not already been mentioned, would you create interior landmarks?

17. Diagram your current academic building in terms of the ten place components covered in this chapter.

CHAPTER 4
The Basics of Space

INSTRUCTIONAL OBJECTIVES

- Explain different ways to define space.
- Present the hierarchy of spaces.
- Introduce the concepts of containment and encapsulation.
- Explain the effect of openings and edges on enclosure.
- Explain the role of edges on the definition of positive and negative space.
- Present four room-size scales useful for interior design.
- Describe five basic geometric forms used in interior spaces.
- Present different approaches to manipulate spatial form.
- Explain the concept of disclosure in design.
- Describe basic approaches to the design of circulation systems.
- Present basic types of path-to-space and space-to-space relationships.
- Present basic organization systems for interior projects.
- Present four basic spatial approaches commonly used in interior projects.

Everyone who has thought even casually about the subject knows that the specific property of architecture—the feature distinguishing it from all other forms of art— consists in its working with a three-dimensional vocabulary which includes man. Painting functions in two dimensions, even if it can suggest three or four. Sculpture works in three dimensions, but man remains apart, looking on from the outside. Architecture, however, is like a great hollowed-out sculpture which man enters and apprehends by moving about within it.

—*Bruno Zevi,* Architecture as Space: How to Look at Architecture

CHAPTER 3 WAS DEVOTED to the idea of environments as collections of places. We addressed the differences and relationships among the concepts of function, space, and place and introduced the elements of place. These elements were discussed in terms of their role and significance, without elaborating on specifics concerning the treatment and manipulation of spaces. This chapter focuses on fundamental aspects of space. The aim is to learn to define and manipulate both individual spaces and systems of spaces.

A key to the success of a project is the proper arrangement of its parts according to function and hierarchy. It is also necessary to properly manipulate individual spaces to make them come alive and have engaging effects. The manipulation of a space involves the control of its shape, size, degree of enclosure, and relationship to other spaces. Possibilities increase with the designer's level of knowledge and skill. The more you know about the properties of spaces and ways to manipulate these properties to create specific effects, the better equipped you'll be to enrich the experience of users in your projects.

The spatial response to interior design projects varies widely. Decisions about the subdivision, placement, and composition of spaces respond primarily to the basic functional requirements of the project. A customer service office facility intended for the handling of telephone inquiries will require different spaces than, say, an accounting firm. The customer service facility will require large open spaces furnished with clusters of small cubicles where workers can receive calls from customers. The accounting firm, in turn, will need many private offices where accountants can work privately with a high degree of concentration.

In the two examples above, the ratio of enclosed space to open space will be very different, the accounting office having a far greater area of enclosed space. Suppose the accounting firm has a floor devoted to training consisting of several large training rooms. This would also result in a high enclosed-to-open-space ratio. Yet, even if the total ratio of enclosed to open space was similar, the nature of their arrangement would be different. The training floor would consist of a few large rooms with easy public access, while the typical office floor would consist of many small private rooms.

Whether a project is more or less open, more or less rigid, or more or less innovative will depend greatly on its own set of circumstances. It is up to the designer to understand these and determine what type of arrangement is most responsive to the particular set of requirements at hand. In all these cases, it is the project that suggests the appropriate organization and treatment of spaces. A designer must be able to interpret the needs of the project and know how to shape and manipulate space.

In this chapter, we look at individual spaces and their spatial properties first. Then we look at some basic relationships between adjacent spaces and, finally, spatial organizations for entire projects. For much of the information contained here we are indebted to the contributions of previous authors who have tackled the subject of architectural space, particularly Francis Ching,[1] whose work has clarified its many manifestations.

PROPERTIES OF INDIVIDUAL SPACES

It will be helpful to first acquire an awareness of spatial design for single spaces before dealing with the orchestration

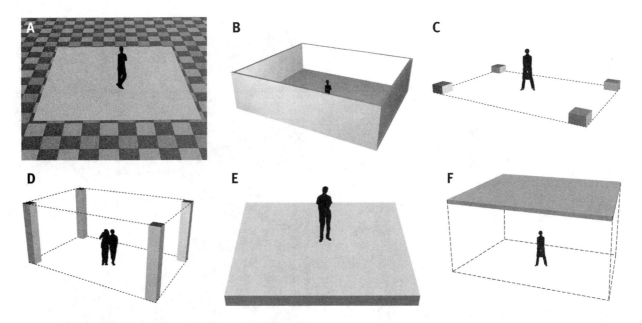

Figure 4.1: Space can be defined by marking the boundary on the floor (a), erecting walls at the edges (b), marking strategic points along the edges with objects or columns (c and d), raising the floor area inside the boundary (e), and dropping the ceiling plane over the space (f).

of complex spatial organizations and sequences. We will devote the first parts of this chapter to the examination of the issues of spatial definition, enclosure, size, form, permeability, and mobility in individual spaces.

Spatial Definition

Space, whether claimed (as a spot claimed with a blanket for a picnic in the park) or allocated (as the kind of space distribution designers perform), is usually marked or defined in some way. In the picnic example, you lay a large blanket over the desired spot, add the picnic basket and perhaps a few other personal items, and the space in the park becomes yours for the afternoon. In interiors, spaces are also demarcated in order to differentiate them from neighboring spaces and create different territories. A variety of architectural and interior design elements are used to define space. Depending on the choice of elements and their composition, space can be explicitly defined or simply suggested. Also, it is possible for various layers of a spatial hierarchy to operate simultaneously, creating multilayered arrangements. We look at space-defining elements first.

Space-Defining Elements

Space is defined by the marking of its boundaries. This is done by establishing and marking the lines that repre-

sent the limits between inside and outside. Designers use various devices to accomplish *space definition*, the most recognizable being a vertical plane (usually a wall) placed along the boundary. This can be a solid wall or some sort of permeable screen. It can be full in height or a partial wall. Another way to define space is to just mark its corners with an object such as a column (or any other device), and, thus, define four (or more) corners that establish a particular space. Furthermore, one can define a space by differentiating its floor and/or ceiling plane from its surroundings through changes of level and/or material between adjacent areas. Figure 4.1 a–f shows examples of these basic space-defining methods.

Space can be defined two- or three-dimensionally. *Two-dimensional definition* is achieved by claiming an area through the marking of its limits on a two-dimensional plane, usually the floor or the overhead plane. The extent of space demarcated is mentally completed by projecting upward or downward (depending on the case), and the implied volume of space is understood. In the picnic example above, the blanket demarcates an area using the floor plane. Note that you can demarcate territory two-dimensionally by marking the limits of the boundary only (fully or partially), or by changing the entire surface treatment of the floor or ceiling plane inside the territory through variations of material, color, texture, or pattern.

Figure 4.2: The suspended spheres at the corners help to complete the volume suggested here by defining its height.

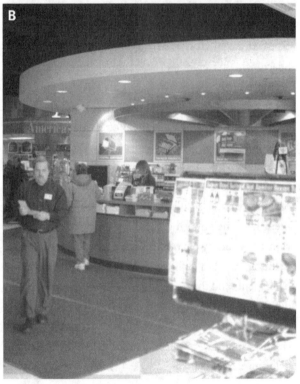

Three-dimensional definition is more explicit about the vertical extent of the defined volume. It not only defines the territory claimed but also indicates its vertical dimension. A minimal way to achieve this in a square space would be to place four objects (such as suspended spheres) on the four corners at the desired height (Figure 4.2). This would complete the "box," suggesting the full extent of the space defined.

The issues of height and mass are important in establishing the precise character of a boundary. Points at corners and markers along a boundary line on the floor merely establish the boundary. If the line is solid and has some height, it becomes a partial wall and partial separation is created. If the line extends to the ceiling above, complete separation is accomplished.

We have mentioned four common ways of demarcating space: marking points, marking lines, and articulating the ceiling or floor plane. In interior projects, three types of space-defining elements can be placed strategically on these locations: objects (furnishings, columns, accessories), permeable barriers (colonnade, glass, partial walls), and full barriers (solid walls). In practice, these can be combined to create different configurations having strong spatial definition. Figure 4.3 shows two examples.

Literal and Implied Space

Space definition can be literal or suggested. The explicitness of definition varies, depending on the defining elements used and their placement. Solid, full-height walls at the boundaries define the edge assertively with

Figure 4.3: A simple system of posts and beams, as the one shown from Steelcase, can create a strong sense of space without walls (a). Similarly, ceiling elements, such as the floating curved ceiling (b), can define space strongly.

Figure 4.4: In a, even though all the walls continue beyond the limits of the defined rectangular space, their placement on the boundary lines, together with the strong corner demarcation achieved by the two foreground elements, help to define the rectangular area shown. The space in b is defined by a combination of full and partial walls, a row of columns, a partial ceiling plane, and two types of contrasting floor patterns.

a physical barrier that provides separation from one space to the next. When space is implied by objects at the corners or overhead planes, the resulting definition is not as strong, although it is still effective and even preferable when openness is desired. A wide range of possibilities exists between the extremes of fully explicit and fully implicit space. Figure 4.4 shows two examples of implied space: In Figure 4.4a, a rectangular area is defined by partial planes and a corner column. In Figure 4.4b, several spaces are defined within a larger rectangular area.

Hierarchy of Space Definition

Space definition can occur at different levels simultaneously. Inside a building, say, a restaurant, you may be sitting at a table (space 1), which is part of a well-defined group of tables (space 2). The group of tables may be part of several groups of tables under a section defined by a lowered ceiling (space 3). This lower area, in turn, may be open to and part of a larger overall dining area in the restaurant (space 4), which may represent one-half of the total dining area (space 5). See Figure 4.5.

Knowing the various ways of differentiating space can help you create separations in bold or subtle ways. In the example above, differentiation is achieved as follows:

Space 1: Object – A single recognizable object, the table
Space 2: Group – A group of closely spaced tables reading as a discrete region
Space 3: Section – A collection of several groups of tables under a space defined by a lowered ceiling

Figure 4.5: Spaces such as this hypothetical restaurant often have many levels of spatial definition defined by grouping or common enclosure.

Space 4: Volume – Two sections within the same overall volumetric space
Space 5: Overall project – Two sides of a restaurant, each with its own volume but linked as one overall project

An advantage of multilevel space definition is that it gives a sense of being part of various "spatial groups" simultaneously and, thus, helps to maintain a sense of place at the various levels of the hierarchy.

Enclosure

Closely related to levels of spatial definition are levels of enclosure. As we saw above, a space can be defined strongly without having to be enclosed. Some spaces, of course, need to be fully enclosed for functional or practical reasons. Those spaces require not only definition but also a sense of separation and containment. Private offices, conference rooms, changing rooms, and restrooms all demand enclosure, some more than others. Other spaces, like open retail or office areas, do not require enclosure and can remain open within themselves and in relation to adjacent spaces.

There are many levels of definition between the two extremes of full enclosure and full openness. The choices made by designers regarding the openness or enclosure of spaces greatly determine the spatial character of a project. In this section we will examine various levels of enclosure, the characteristics of their space-defining edges, and the effect of different kinds of wall openings. We will begin with containment and encapsulation, two important concepts related to enclosure.

Containment

Some spaces are not only recognizable as well-defined areas but actually provide a strong sense of **containment**. Containment is a concept that refers to a space's ability to gather people and/or objects. You can test the containment capabilities of any given space by thinking of it as a container with more or less ability to hold its contents without spilling them. The three spaces shown in Figure 4.6 a–c provide some degree of containment. The example with the L-shaped corner walls provides the strongest containment because of the sealed corner it offers. If you were to pour "contents" into these three shapes, the L-shaped configuration would best be able to contain them without spilling.

Figure 4.6: Containment is related to the perceived sense of shelter. You can think of containment as gathering without spilling. In examples a–c, example c shows the best ability to "contain without spilling."

This concept is important in living environments because it translates into a sense of grounding and protection. The potential of the L-shaped configuration in Figure 4.6 to give us both a sense of protection and visibility appeals to our innate need for security. The configuration provides protection from two sides. Only the front sides are open, but they are visible straight ahead when looking diagonally from the sheltering corner. There are also configurations that provide stronger containment than the L-shape. Examples include U-shaped configurations and completely "boxed" rooms.

Encapsulation

Encapsulation is another term related to enclosure. It refers to the degree to which the enclosure of a space creates a seal from adjacent spaces. A fully encapsulated space is a fully sealed room with full walls on all sides, a floor, a ceiling, and no openings. Until the early twentieth century, the norm in spatial design was to subdivide an overall space into many smaller encapsulated rooms. You always knew when you were entering a new room. In some cases, you walked through the actual rooms to go from one to another. The location of the doors established the path. Later on, corridors were added and one could move between spaces without passing through them. Still, the actual habitable spaces remained encapsulated, autonomous rooms separated from one another.

With the modern movement came more open configurations. Space was not to be encapsulated as in the past. Instead, space was thought of as a continuum of infinite space that could be defined minimally in order to distinguish one area from the next while maintaining flow and continuity. Edges were ambiguous and loosely defined by the strategic placement of a few nonaligning walls.

A   **B**   **C**

Encapsulation was avoided except when absolutely necessary for privacy. Some of the work by Mies van der Rohe and Frank Lloyd Wright represent the best examples of this approach to space planning. See Figure 4.7 and the capsule "Destruction of the Box."

Today, architects and designers employ many different levels of spatial definition. These range from the fully encapsulated to the barely differentiated. Although no strict categorization of the levels of enclosure exists, we may distinguish among four general levels to get an idea of the range.

Loosely defined space is implied or suggested space. No visual, acoustic, or haptic separation is required between it and the adjacent spaces. It relies on providing enough spatial clues to make the space readable. Strategies may include definition of corners, that is, marking enough spots along the periphery of the space or providing planar definition from above or below through floor or ceiling changes to demarcate limits.

In *moderately defined space* edges are explicit in at least two, sometimes three, sides. Space starts having a moderate degree of containment. Some visual separation may be desirable depending on the application, although it is possible to achieve strong definition with partial-height elements that allow strong visual connection between spaces.

Contained space has maximum containment capacity by having walls on all sides. It provides visual separation when the walls are above eye level but no acoustic or haptic separation is necessary. Therefore, it can have some

Figure 4.7: These two houses by Mies van der Rohe represent the opposite of encapsulation. Spaces are free and flowing and not sealed in boxes.

openings that achieve containment with partial height elements that do not provide a complete seal at the corners or overhead.

Encapsulated space not only has walls on all sides but the overhead and floor planes are connected to create a sealed space, a totally enclosed room. Visual, acoustical, and haptic separations are required. Figure 4.8 shows examples of a contained space and an encapsulated space with the front walls removed.

Figure 4.8: Contained space has surrounding walls but is not sealed (a). Encapsulated space is sealed on all sides (b).

A **B** **C**

Figure 4.9: Closed corners facilitate the readability and increase the sense of containment of a room (a). Partially open corners (b) and fully open corners (c) can define and contain a space but with some degree of ambiguity.

Openings

The size and location of openings have a strong impact on the sense of containment of a space. Figure 4.9 shows the impact different opening configurations have on the perceived level of enclosure in a simple square room. The room with the strongest integrity at the corners (Figure 4.9a) has the strongest sense of containment. The room in Figure 4.9c, despite defining the space successfully, doesn't contain the room as strongly because of its open corners.

The location of openings in relation to one's approach also affects the first impression of a room's degree of enclosure. In general, spaces with an opening straight ahead will not have as strong a sense of enclosure as spaces with a solid barrier straight ahead as you enter (Figure 4.10).

Spatial Edges

We have seen how important spatial edges are in determining the degree of enclosure. We have also seen how edges can be, but don't need to be, defined by physical barriers. Alternatively, they can be defined by changes in the materials or levels of ceilings or floors, by the strategic placement of freestanding objects, and by strategic alignment with adjacent elements. In considering spatial edges, next we explore the physical barriers that define and shape space. They tend to be of three kinds: vertical walls or screens around the sides, the horizontal base plane on which we stand (the floor), and a horizontal (although sometimes sloped) plane overhead (the ceiling).

Vertical Edges

Walls or screens of various heights and thicknesses, whether freestanding or part of an adjoining room, are the most common vertical edges. Important design con-

Figure 4.10: A wall straight ahead as you enter a room will contain the space. An opening straight ahead, on the other hand, produces a sense of openness.

siderations include the relative degree of openness or closedness achieved by them, as well as their figural and textural character. The degree of openness is affected by the horizontal continuity of the barrier (it may be continuous or have gaps), the number and size of openings, and the barrier's height. We focus here on the issue of heights. Continuity and openings will be discussed later.

A vertical solid barrier can range from a low, bench-height partition to a full-height partition reaching the ceiling plane above. It is useful to distinguish among three different heights: below eye level; above eye level, but partial; and full. Each produces a distinct effect.

Edges that are below eye level include low partitions, furnishings, and fixtures. These provide physical separation, but visual, auditory, and haptic connections are maintained. They are useful in instances where both definition and a strong sense of connection are desired.

Edges that are above eye level but of partial height also include partitions, furnishings, and fixtures. They provide not only physical but visual separation while maintaining auditory and haptic connections. You can still hear sounds from the adjacent space and feel the same air and temperature. These edges are useful when both visual privacy and a sense of connection are desirable.

Edges that are full height are most often walls and other partitions. They provide physical, visual (in most cases), auditory, and haptic separation between spaces and are commonly used where a full separation is desired. Figure 4.11 shows examples of these three types of vertical edges.

Horizontal Edges

Base planes (floors) and overhead planes (ceilings) are the two types of horizontal edges that help to complete the spatial definition of enclosed space. Ceilings are not always horizontal but are included under horizontal edges for convenience, since they are commonly horizontal in interior spaces.

Floors are limited in their capacity to enclose and define space. They are always level (except at ramps) and for commercial applications require minimal changes in height because of issues of accessibility. Material, color, texture, and pattern variations are the most common ways of treating floors for space definition and differentiation.

Although floors are limited in their ability to differentiate space, ceilings offer many opportunities to do so. They offer two advantages. First, there is no issue of accessibility with ceilings since we don't walk on them. Second, being overhead, they are highly visible. Variations are commonly achieved by level changes or shape changes (Figure 4.12 a–c).

Although elevation changes at the ceiling are most effective, changes of ceiling material, color, texture, and pattern can also be used to distinguish between adjacent areas. The

Figure 4.11: Below eye level, above eye level, and full height enclosing planes produce dramatically different perceptual effects when seen in space.

Figure 4.12: Ceilings are very effective in differentiating adjacent areas. Ceiling height changes (a), ceiling shape variations (b), and material changes (c) can all be effective to define edges.

range of surface manipulations is not as wide as it is with floors, given the fairly neutral treatment normally provided for ceilings. Nevertheless, transitioning from a monolithic, smooth ceiling system to a grid and tile system at the same

Scientific developments in the early twentieth century revolutionized the way people thought about the universe. It was seen as having four dimensions, time being the fourth dimension. Space and time became part of a relational continuum, with space changing as one moved in time. Artists, writers, and filmmakers started to adopt this new way of thinking about space, a radical departure from the perspectivism of the Renaissance, which perceived space from a single fixed point. This new idea soon influenced architects and designers. After all, of all the arts, it had the potential to affect architecture and interior design the most.

In addition to the new thinking, the development of new construction techniques utilizing steel and concrete made it possible to use slender skeletal support structures, thus providing the freedom necessary to revolutionize interior layouts. Perhaps the most significant design-related outcome resulting from these changes was the destruction of the box. Until then, interior environments consisted of collections of contained spaces arranged in various configurations. All of a sudden, corners opened up, walls disappeared, dividers and partial walls were introduced, and a freer way to design came about. While the use of open flowing space has been prominent for many years, many design students still tend to design in boxes.

Frank Lloyd Wright was one of the most important catalysts for the destruction of the box, something that consciously preoccupied him as early as 1904, while designing the Larkin Building; however, it wasn't until later that this idea started to flourish. "Unity Temple is where I thought I had it, this idea that the reality of a building no longer consisted in the walls and roof," Wright explained. "In Unity Temple you will find the walls actually disappearing; you will find the interior space opening to the outside and see the outside coming in. You will see assembled about this interior space, screening it, various free, related features instead of enclosing walls. See, you now can make features of many types for enclosure and group the features about interior space with no sense of boxing it."[1]

Wright's destruction of the box entailed the opening of the corners, the use of walls as independent screens, and the detachment of the wall-to-roof connection. He explained: "I knew enough engineering to know that the outer angles of a box were not where its most economical support would be, if you made a building of it. No, a certain distance in each way from the corner is where the economic support of a box-building is invariably to be found. . . . Now, when you put support at these points you have created a short cantileverage to the corners that lessens actual spans and sets the corner free or open for whatever distance you choose. The corners disappear altogether if you choose to let space come in there, or let it go out."[2] In this way the corner was opened up: lesson number one.

The next task was to manipulate walls to open up space. "These unattached side walls," Wright said, "become something independent, no longer enclosing walls. They're separate supporting screens, any one of which may be shortened, or extended, or perforated, or occasionally eliminated."[3] So, walls started to acquire a new meaning. They were no longer continuous, uninterrupted enclosures placed exactly at the boundary of each room and sealed hermetically at the corners. They were now screens full of possibilities. Not only was it possible to free up the corner but now, by moving and shortening walls, it was possible to really open up a space and make the inside and outside continuous: lesson number two.

Next, Wright continued the liberation by transforming the connection between the horizontal plane and the vertical plane: "No one has looked through the box at the sky up there at the upper angle, have they? Why not? Because the box always had a cornice at the top. It was added to the sides in order that the box might not look so much like a box, but more classic."[4] According to Wright, it was possible to do more than just free up the four, or however many, corners of a room and move the walls within the room. By shortening the top of a wall along its length and using a transparent material such as glass to join the wall and roof so it appeared to float, it was possible to fully liberate space and do away with the

Figure C4.2: Floor plan of Mies's German Pavilion.

Figure C4.3: Floor plan of Mies's Tugendhat House.

Figure C4.1: Evolution of the destruction of the box: enclosure at boundary, supports at four corners (a), partial enclosure at boundaries, supports "in" from corners (b), minimal enclosure, strategically located "free" walls act as supports (c).

box: lesson number three. Figure C4.1 shows representative sketches of the evolution from box to free plan.

Not only did it become important to break the box between interior and exterior but also the boxes within buildings in order to create more flowing arrangements symbolic of the times. Wright was not the only one concerned with the destruction of the box and the general opening up of interior space. Other well-known architects followed suit and experimented with various approaches to the same problem. The de Stijl movement in The Netherlands offered its own antibox theories involving dismembering via the disjointment of planes and their strategic positioning. Some of the best examples of such an approach can be found in the work of the German-born architect Mies van der Rohe. Some of his early designs employed a minimal number of strategically placed wall planes to achieve openness, flow, and connection to the exterior. A great example of this approach is his German Pavilion for the 1929 International Exposition in Barcelona, Spain (Figure C4.2). Mies, whose slogan was "less is more," succeeded

in giving us one of the purer examples of free-flowing space unimpeded by structural walls and also provided one of the earliest examples of unadorned richness. His design relied on the purity, beauty, and texture of the chosen materials. Another notable example from Mies was the Tugendhat House in Czechoslovakia (1930) shown in Figure C4.3. This house employs an approach similar to that of the German Pavilion (light-weight skeletal structure and independent screens) to maintain a similar sense of openness and sparseness, despite the more demanding programmatic requirements of a real house.

In a similar vein as these two designs by Mies is Philip Johnson's well-known Glass House in New Canaan, Connecticut (1949) shown in Figure C4.4. It features an all-glass envelope and three masses, two linear masses providing storage, and one cylindrical mass containing the bathroom and a fireplace. These serve to subdivide the open space into three areas: a large living and dining area and two smaller areas, the bedroom and the kitchen. In this example, it is not thin screens but functional masses that serve as screens and perform the dividing task.

Figure C4.4: Floor plan of Johnson's Glass House.

A

B

C

Figure C4.5: Floor plans of Mies's Farnsworth House (a), Wright's Robie House (b), and Wright's Zimmerman House (c).

Other good examples of functional masses serving as screens can be found in Mies's Farnsworth House in Plano, Illinois (1950), and Wright's Robie (1909) and Zimmerman (1950) houses (Figure C4.5 a–c). These offer illuminating examples to the designer of interior space about how a single interior mass, strategically placed and carefully articulated, can screen, house, and divide while helping to keep the rest of the space free and open.

By using these simple approaches, designers can produce simple and flowing designs. Most interior design projects occur in empty open shells where the structural systems are already in place. The designer is given a clean space on which to plan the new project. Partitions and masses don't have to support any loads. They are free. They can be thin, curved, or movable. Spaces can overlap with and flow into one another. Imagine the possibilities!

Suggested Exercises

1. Pretend you are Wright. Start with a boxlike floor plan and destroy the box. Concern yourself only with the relation of the room to its exterior. Open up the room to achieve inside-outside continuity, by moving or shortening walls, freeing up corners, and any other devices you can think of.

2. Put on Mies van der Rohe's cap for a while. Using grid paper, take a rectangular area and subdivide it into subareas using thin planes, as Mies did with the German Pavilion. Try at least two versions.

3. Similar to the examples shown in Figure C4.5, in an otherwise open rectangular room, design a single mass that incorporates some function and, because of its strategic location and shape, helps to divide the room into various zones.

4. Pretend you are given a hypothetical store space to design. Without getting into design specifics, use one or more masses and one or more screens to define and subdivide several spaces in the store. Pretend the footprint of the space is approximately 40 by 120 feet.

1. Edgar Kaufmann and Ben Raeburn, eds., *Frank Lloyd Wright: Writings and Buildings* (New York: Meridian, 1960), 284.
2. Ibid., 285.
3. Ibid., 286.
4. Ibid.

Figure 4.13: Articulation of walls and ceilings helps to produce spatial texture at a much different scale than the smaller surface texture, like that of a rough wall.

Figure 4.14: The enclosing planes here go back and forth between being a mold that shapes space and being a shape itself. Where the wall recedes in, it acts as the mold that gives shape to cylindrical space in front of it. Where it projects out, it becomes the cylindrical shape itself. This example illustrates another important and related lesson: a wall does not always have to be limited to a thin, straight membrane between two areas.

elevation, for instance, is often enough to achieve a subtle separation between areas. See Figure 4.12c.

Textural and Figural Aspects of Edges

In addition to their role of separating and containing spaces, edges contribute to the textural qualities of the space. We normally think of texture in relation to surfaces. Yet space can also be thought of as having texture. It is called **spatial texture**. *Random House College Dictionary* defines *texture* as "the characteristic physical structure given to a material (or space) by the size, shape, density, arrangement, and proportions of its elementary parts."[2] While spatial texture is often determined by the objects (furnishings, suspended lights, and so on) in the space, the defining surfaces can also play an important part in supplying texture.

Enclosing walls can be smooth and plain, but they can also be highly articulated, thus adding textural qualities to the space. Ceilings and floors also offer opportunities to add spatial texture. For instance, ceilings can be subdivided into modules, rhythmic bands can be used, and so forth. Figure 4.13 shows a space with a textured side wall and ceiling. Spatial texture also occurs when spaces are left open to the structure above, such as in a room without a dropped ceiling. The structural members and other elements normally hidden by a ceiling establish a texture of their own. Mechanical ducts, sprinkler lines, and electrical conduits, boxes, and fixtures become visible and can add texture, although sometimes a chaotic texture.

Positive/Negative Spaces and Masses

An important contribution of defining edges is their role in defining the shape of space, both positive and negative. In **positive space**, space is the figure (recognized shape) and the surface is the background (leftover space). In **negative space**, space is the background and the surface is the figure. You cannot give geometric figural shape to a space without the contribution of the surrounding edges. A round room needs concave walls, an octagonal room needs eight wall segments, a domed space needs a domed ceiling plane. We rely on the shapes we give these edges to give the space its shape. We will discuss the basic shapes of rooms later in this chapter.

It is the enclosing surfaces of rooms that define their shape. In general, at any one time, either the enclosing plane or the shape of the space it defines has a more recognizable regular shape. Sometimes an enclosing wall takes on a figural recognizable shape and the leftover space in front of it ends up with an irregular, sometimes unrecognizable shape. In these cases the wall, and not the shape of the room, is seen and recognized as a shape and becomes dominant. In some cases, a certain wall may fluctuate back and forth, alternating between being the recognizable shape and being the background, thus letting the space have the recognizable shape. Figure 4.14 shows a hypothetical example of this phenomenon. A portion of the wall shown defines a circular space in front of it, and, further ahead, the wall takes on the shape of a cylindrical mass.

Size

It may seem as if designers have relatively little influence on the size of spaces. Most project programs prescribe the floor areas required by the different project functions, leaving little flexibility in the matter. Yet, while designers are often given specific size requirements for the spaces needed, they do have opportunities to influence the perceptual size of spaces.

Designers can sometimes influence the size of the spaces they design to accentuate or downplay the perceptual size of the space. This is done by manipulating a room's plan and height dimensions. Such manipulations can enhance qualities related to size, such as grandeur or intimacy.

When we say room scale we mean the overall relative size of the space or room. For our purposes, it may be useful to think of spatial size in terms of four broad categories: monumental scale, generous scale, functional scale, and intimate scale. Designers should be familiar with the connotations of each and become adept at applying them.

There are no specific guidelines that prescribe specific dimensions for these various room scales since they depend on the specifics of the situation and are therefore relative. More important than thinking in terms of specific dimensions is understanding the traits of these different scales, the appropriate time to use them, and the experience they produce. A brief explanation of each follows.

Monumental scale is the scale of grand cathedrals and palaces. It is usually conceived of as part of the architecture, used on very special buildings and very infrequently. Its key traits are verticality and spaciousness on a grand scale. It is always easily recognized.

Achieving monumental scale in interior projects is sometimes impossible due to the limited size of most existing interior building sites. Yet multifloor lobbies in some new office buildings and spaces in older buildings with large volumes sometimes present opportunities to achieve monumental space. This grand scale often presents design compositional challenges related to the large amounts of empty space overhead and the usually expansive surrounding surfaces high up. Decisions about the modulation and general treatment of these surfaces and spaces must be considered carefully to achieve satisfying and balanced results (Figure 4.15a).

Figure 4.15: Space comes in many sizes. Depicted here are representations of four basic scales: monumental (a), generous (b), functional (c), and intimate (d).

Generous scale is the scale of very comfortable office and hotel lobbies, spacious dining areas in restaurants, and generous shopping areas in stores. It is more easily achievable than monumental scale, as it doesn't require as much volume. It is often up to the designer to push the limits of space and make otherwise ordinary spaces more generous. As with monumental scale, the feeling of spatial generosity relies heavily on the extension of the vertical dimension. Change an 8-foot-high, 5-foot-wide corridor to 10 feet high, and you will create a generously scaled corridor. Give a low lobby space a 14-foot-high ceiling, and you will have a generous lobby. Generous scale is important in design and is often achievable. All that's required is the awareness to recognize potential opportunities for it, the willingness to make it happen, and the ability to justify it. Figure 4.15b shows an example of a generously scaled room.

Functional scale provides an adequate amount of space to fulfill the basic requirements of a room or space. All of us see it every day and know it well. It ranges from sizes that are minimally acceptable to sizes that are slightly more comfortable but not generous. An example of the minimal approach is a project designed to meet the minimum requirements stated in the building codes. This is often the direction followed for projects requiring maximum efficiency and economy. In these cases, room sizes and corridor widths are minimal. In multilevel buildings, the floor-to-ceiling heights are kept as low as possible to permit the stacking of as many floors as possible. The functional scale need not be dictated by the minimum dimensions in reference and code books. It can certainly be more comfortable.

The functional scale will often do the job but will rarely motivate or inspire. However, this is the scale of everyday normal design and cannot be totally avoided. A good strategy to follow is to learn to use functional scale selectively and to balance it when possible with strategically placed generous scale spaces that provide relief and comfort (Figure 4.15c).

Intimate scale is the scale of small spaces for one or a few occupants. Tighter spaces and lower ceilings are not only allowed but desirable. This is the scale of niches, alcoves, and inglenooks. It is also the scale of small but

Figure 4.16: Shown here are three examples of actual environments of different scales, ranging from intimate (a), comfortable, yet cozy (b), and grand (c).

comfortable conference rooms and cozy theaters. The difference between spaces of intimate scale and spaces on the minimal end of the functional scale is that intimately scaled spaces are used when intimacy is appropriate. When designing intimately scaled spaces, care is taken to avoid an oppressive feeling.

You should not limit your idea of good spaces to comfortable, generous, and grand spaces. Learn how to create purposely cozy spaces and to use them where appropriate. The library study carrel, the small break room in an office, and the dining table in an intimate restaurant become better spaces when endowed with the coziness of intimate scale (Figure 4.15d). Figure 4.16 a–c shows three actual environments ranging in scale from intimate to grand.

Form

Another important property of space is its **form**. For our purposes, in this section the definition of form is limited to the basic configuration of space, such as rectangular, circular, and so on. In other words, its shape.

The form of space has important implications concerning the dynamics of the space and its centers of energy. In general, spaces either have shapes that are narrow or linear, inducing movement, or have shapes with boundaries that are approximately equidistant from the center, such as squares and circles, which tend to be more static and promote habitation. Our discussion below focuses on

Figure 4.17: The extent and shape of the vertical dimension can produce dramatically different spaces given the same floor area. Here we see how they affect three square rooms of equal size.

A

B

C

Figure 4.18: Long rectangular rooms are often more comfortable when subdivided. These illustrations show divisions created by articulations on the side walls (a), actual dividing screens (b), and the grouping of furnishings and/or fixtures in the space (c).

rooms and spaces belonging to the second category. We also focus on rooms having regular geometric shapes.

Square Space

Square spaces are pure, formal, and static. They are spaces to be occupied and normally do house a function. Square spaces have a strong sense of definition because of their strongly defined and uniform corners. They also provide a strong sense of enclosure because of their four prominent walls. Furthermore, a square space possesses a strong sense of centrality. Although the only plan variation possible for square spaces is their size, square spaces can acquire different characteristics depending on the treatment of the third dimension. Different heights and ceiling shapes will give similarly sized rooms a substantially different feel (Figure 4.17).

Circular Space

The circle, like the square, is pure, formal, and static. The circle, however, more than the square, is a highly memorable shape. Circles can be places for habitation as well as circulation spaces. Unlike the square, the circle has no corners. However, it does possess a strong center and a very readable surrounding envelope that, like the square, provides a strong sense of containment and enclosure.

Rectangular Space

Rectangular spaces have different properties depending on their size and proportions. For that reason it is useful to divide them into two categories: short and long rectangles. The short rectangle is any rectangle whose length to width ratio does not exceed two to one. The proportions of the short rectangle produce spaces with a strong sense of place. Depending on their intended use and their size, these spaces can be left as one space with one center or subdivided into two or more zones, each having its own center.

In a long rectangular space, the length exceeds its width by a ratio greater than two to one. The long rectangle is very dynamic. It suggests movement along the long axis. Very long rectangular spaces sometimes become perceptually uncomfortable unless they are subdivided into smaller units. When they get very long and narrow, they start to acquire the qualities of a corridor. Subdivision can be accomplished by the articulation of the enclosing surfaces to suggest subcompartments, by the addition of physical edges between sections, or by the arrangement of the contents into subgroups (Figure 4.18 a–c).

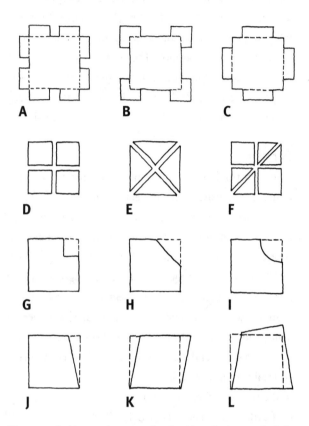

Figure 4.19: The right triangle is the most functional triangle for design. Notice the two basic variations possible for the placement of furniture. In this example, the problem of acute angles at the ends is avoided because the angled wall stops and the ends are left open.

Triangular Space

The triangle, such as the equilateral triangle, is generally considered a problematic shape for interior spaces because of its functionally problematic acute angles. Nevertheless, it can sometimes be used successfully. In fact, one type of triangular shape can be used successfully in interiors to create dynamic areas while maintaining adequate functionality: the right triangle.

The right triangle is a dynamic shape because of its long diagonal side and the tension created between the right-angle sides and the diagonal side. All objects within the space can be placed either parallel or perpendicular to the two sides forming the right angle (Figure 4.19a), or placed diagonally in relation to the diagonal side (Figure 4.19b). Circulation can follow either the diagonal or the two sides of the right angle. In most cases, however, it will be more efficient to have circulation moving along the diagonal.

The triangle, even the equilateral triangle, can be used selectively for impact. Like the circle, the triangle is very memorable when kept pure. It is possible to truncate the sharp corners for increased functionality or to avoid configurations with acute angles, as shown in the two examples in Figure 4.19.

Manipulation of Form

All the basic shapes described above can be used in pure form or manipulated a number of ways for effect. Below is a brief description of four common manipulation techniques: aggregation, fragmentation, segmentation, and distortion. These are derived from Rob Krier's studies of form manipulation.[3]

Aggregation consists of the addition of smaller, ancillary spaces to larger spaces, such as the pure shapes described above. The art of creating the side niche or alcove is something every designer should learn and practice. In the case of aggregation, the main form remains

Figure 4.20: In this example a square form is subjected to form manipulation techniques including aggregation (a–c), fragmentation (d–f), segmentation (g–i), and distortion (j–l).

dominant and recognizable and the ancillary spaces read clearly as additions (Figure 4.20a–c).

Fragmentation occurs when a pure shape is broken up into smaller fragments in such a way that, by virtue of their proximity and configuration, the overall shape remains recognizable (Figure 4.20d–f). It is also possible to achieve fragmentation by modulating a given spatial envelope into smaller compartments, as long as the overall shape is maintained. This is similar to aggregation, but in the case of fragmentation the total shape defined by the subspaces is the basic form without any protrusions.

Segmentation occurs when incomplete shapes (segments of a known shape) are complete enough that the shape is recognizable. The level of definition of the segment needs to have enough resolution to make the form readable. If this is done appropriately, the mind will complete closure of the shape suggested (Figure 4.20g–i).

Distortion is achieved by inflecting the edges of a known form in order to alter it while keeping it somewhat recognizable. This is normally done for effect, based on specific design intentions such as the addition of texture or the creation of a more dynamic composition. The level of distortion is up to the designer and the circumstances. The key is for the basic shape to remain readable; otherwise, the shape gets transformed into an entirely different shape (Figure 4.20j–l).

Permeability

One of the principal aspects of interior architectural space is its degree of **permeability**. Projects require important decisions concerning the extent to which air, smells, views, and paths are open from one space to the next. Designers have control over these variables, and, in most cases, are able to fulfill the functional requirements of the program with any number of scenarios of different degrees of permeability.

In this section we concentrate on two aspects of permeability: disclosure and mobility. **Disclosure** refers to how much of a space, and the other spaces beyond, is revealed as you walk around. **Mobility** refers to the relative degree of restraint or freedom a particular spatial arrangement affords those who move in it. As a designer, you can play the role of movie director controlling movement and the kinds of things seen along the way to create specific experiences.

Disclosure

Imagine that on a given day you visit two offices for business meetings. You arrive at the first one, open the door, and find yourself in the reception area. From it, you can see a good portion of the facility. To the right are clusters of systems furniture with low dividing panels that let you see all the way to the end of the space. To the left are more low workstations. If you move to the side, you can see all the way to the back of the room where a group of private offices is located against the end wall of the space. Straight ahead is the reception desk with a partial-height dividing wall behind it. Behind the wall is the route leading to a particular room with a central formal entrance: the conference room, your destination.

The second office space is quite different. Upon entering, you arrive at an enclosed reception area with high walls on all sides except for an opening to the left. From that room you get a glimpse beyond but can't really see what's going on. Once your contact person arrives, she takes you to the conference room. To get there, you go through the opening on the left and enter an enclosed corridor. You cannot see much except for what's straight ahead. At one point, the corridor opens up into a large square area, an intersection. From there, you get a quick glimpse to either side, barely making out what lies beyond. You continue straight and arrive at a small anteroom, walk through it, and arrive, finally, at the conference room.

Figures 4.21 and 4.22 show schematic views of these two spaces. It is evident that the level of visual disclosure is remarkably different between them. The first space is very open; the second is enclosed and quite controlled.

Figure 4.21: There is full visual disclosure in this example of a trip to a conference room in an office. The visitor sees most of the office upon entering as well as on the way to the conference room.

Figure 4.22: There is very little visual disclosure in this version of a trip to a conference room. The high degree of compartmentalization prevents the visitor from seeing beyond the high walls.

These two scenarios illustrate one of the basic distinctions of interior space: the distinction between open plans and compartmentalized plans. The first category features large open spaces, which can be apprehended as a whole, with their parts and subdivisions acting as freestanding objects. The amount of visual disclosure in these projects is substantial. The second category describes projects that are subdivided into compartments that are experienced sequentially, one at a time. Visual disclosure in these projects is very restrained.

Levels of visual disclosure are determined by the number, type, and placement of view-obstructing elements, whether they are permanent architectural elements or less permanent elements, such as furnishings, pieces of equipment, or even plants. Their heights dictate whether uninterrupted views of the space or just an occasional glimpse are permitted. Low height elements will allow views. Elements higher than eye level will provide substantial blockage. Views will therefore range from panoramic views to glimpses and vary depending on whether what's seen is a wide general view or a carefully planned and focused vista.

We discussed how edges of different heights provide different levels of enclosure. We were dealing with simple, regular shapes. In reality, many spaces will have combinations of architectural elements, furnishings, and other objects of various heights positioned at various depths in space and producing numerous combinations of disclosure, depending on their height and placement (Figure 4.23). Additionally, these barriers can have different degrees of transparency, depending on whether they are solid, have openings, are translucent or transparent, and so on.

Disclosure within the Space

Disclosure within the space refers to the level of disclosure inside the immediate space occupied. It is determined by the objects, furnishings, masses, and architectural elements within the space. Disclosure, whether within the space or beyond it, should serve three important functions: provide orientation, focus attention, and provide relief.

Orientation

The level of disclosure provided within a single space can help or hinder the users' ability to feel oriented. You may choose to make the understanding of both the project as a whole and its component parts crystal clear by providing full disclosure. This is desirable in a large space of a project serving many first-time visitors. Conversely, in other instances, you may choose to make this understanding more of a gradual process as one moves through the space. Small rooms are easy to grasp all at once. Larger spaces, especially those with tall elements within, have the potential of being either interesting and engaging or confusing and discouraging. This depends on the composition of view-obstructing elements within them.

The extent to which and the rate at which spatial information is revealed creates unique and specific experiences regarding orientation. If you allow visibility, you will make the process of understanding a particular space easy. Large or complex spaces will demand more clarity while smaller, simpler spaces may welcome some intentional complexity, as long as an acceptable degree of clarity is maintained.

Focus

Most spaces have a functional focus. Depending on their nature, they may sometimes even have more than one. In most teaching classrooms, for instance, there is one main focus: the front of the room, where the lecturer stands. A restaurant, in contrast, may not

Figure 4.23: Planes, objects, and screens layered in space control what you see within a space as well as beyond the immediate space.

have a single communal focal point, and instead may be designed to highlight each seating section so that each becomes an individual focus. An office space may have both individual foci at the workstations and a central team-oriented area. It is part of the designer's responsibilities to emphasize some views and deemphasize others in order to focus attention where it's needed. Guiding the eye toward focal areas can be done in subtle ways with elements such as lines, or more boldly, through room shapes and other techniques.

Relief

In contrast to the idea of focus is that of relief. While a functional focus tends to be task oriented, relief is usually distraction oriented. You can think of relief as intentional distraction for the purpose of restoring tired or bored minds. Few designers may think consciously about providing relief to space users; however, many interior places can benefit from foci created for the purpose of relief. Try to remember, for instance, those times you have been inside a crowded elevator, surrounded by strangers. There are two basic ways you can find some relief. One is to look straight ahead at the back of the person in front of you or at the floor (boring and awkward). The other is to look at the changing floor numbers displayed on the dial above the door (better). The number display provides not only helpful information (letting you know how close you are to your destination floor) but also an acceptable area you can direct your attention to for distraction and relief.

Similarly, you may find opportunities to provide relief in settings like waiting rooms, office work areas, restaurants, and clinics. This type of internal relief usually translates into some sort of focal area, focal surface, or focal object. These, when supplied, are the areas where we direct our attention to get a momentary mental vacation. A focal area may be as simple as an open space amid an otherwise enclosed area. A focal surface can either provide information or something pleasant or stimulating to look at. A focal object can be an enclosed room strategically located amid an otherwise open area or a memorable freestanding object like a nice kiosk, a display, or a piece of sculpture.

Not all spaces require internal relief, but many benefit from it. Becoming sensitive to this need will make you seek ways to provide visual relief and encourage those momentary mental vacations people often need.

Disclosure beyond the Space

Disclosure beyond the space is concerned with what is revealed beyond the immediate occupied space. It can be what is seen when looking toward an adjacent space or while looking outside. Like its internal counterpart, disclosure beyond can provide orientation, focus, and relief.

Orientation

There are different ways in which you can gain orientation while seeing what lies beyond, whether looking inside or toward the exterior. Even though what lies outside or in the next room is there for you to see sooner or later, you, as the designer, can control the experience by manipulating the rate and nature of the disclosure. You can reveal everything at once, gradually, or piece by piece, to elicit some specific desired response, be it suspense or surprise.

The exterior provides important informational clues that help our general sense of orientation. Seeing outside gives us a sense of the approximate time of the day, the weather conditions, and what side of the building we are on.

The degree of control you have over disclosure of the exterior varies depending on the circumstances. You often have no control over the kind of windows you inherit with your project's building or the degree to which you can modify them. Most office buildings have windows all around the perimeter, and in an effort to maximize natural lighting and views, we leave them untouched. How we arrange the masses of enclosed spaces inside can, however, produce different experiences in relation to external disclosure. It is usually how we treat the foreground that will determine how much of the outside we can see at any given point in a place.

Internal disclosure beyond the immediate space provides important internal orientation that helps users get a clear mental picture of where they are in relation to the overall footprint of the facility. In general, the orientation provided by a clear view of what lies beyond is helpful in promoting a sense of order, although a totally given disclosure provides no suspense and can become boring. However a designer chooses to do it, manipulating the rate of disclosure to adjacent spaces is sure to have an impact on the users, as they become more or less clear about what lies beyond. The appropriate rate of disclosure depends on the circumstances and can only be judged on a case-by-case basis.

Focus

Focus between spaces calls attention to important features or destinations on the other side. You can highlight a nice feature of the next space to provide a pleasurable experience or you can reveal a key destination ahead to give people the proper direction in which to move. A proper orchestration of spaces and a helpful level of disclosure from one space to the next can provide the rewarding experience of moving from one goal to the next.

Relief

As with disclosure within the space, you can also provide relief, and brief mental breaks, with views to other interior spaces or to the outside. Techniques for providing relief through other adjacent interior spaces are similar to those for providing them within the same space. They include using contrast (open versus closed) or focusing on special objects or surfaces that provide relief. Relief is also achieved by exposure to and disclosure of the exterior. Here, relief is associated with the feeling of spatial expansion one has when looking at the open space beyond as well as the picturesque qualities of certain views.

As important as the decision to reveal the exterior of a space is the decision on how to achieve it. How do you reveal, for instance, a particular side of a building that has a magnificent view? Can the view be seen as you approach that side of the building, thus generating a sense of anticipation? Do you reveal a glimpse, arouse the user's curiosity, then hide it momentarily before finally revealing it in full? Do you reveal it in chunks? Or, do you keep it hidden until the last possible moment and then, all of a sudden, surprise the user with the magnificent view? These are all viable options. The solution depends on the particular circumstances and your sense of what is appropriate and desirable.

Mobility

One of the ways building interiors affect our experience is by controlling the freedom we have to move about. When we start to think about circulation as more than a utilitarian commodity and consider its role in creating experience, we quickly become aware of the kind of control designers have over the experiential qualities related to movement. A project may have strongly prescribed paths or a somewhat freer circulation system. The goal of the thoughtful designer is to reach a compromise between the need for economy and clarity, on the one hand, and manipulations for particular experiential effects, on the other.

As a designer, you control whether or not people will have access to move in certain directions, and when they do have access, the level of relative constraint and freedom inherent in the route to get there. A place may only have one route that leads to it, and it may be a direct and clear route. Another place may have three alternate routes leading to it, and they may be indirect and meandering. Below we discuss three common ways of designing a path for movement: a controlled route with only one choice of travel direction, a controlled route with more than one travel direction, and a free route with many travel directions and loose boundaries.

Controlled Mobility: Only One Way to Go

Controlled mobility occurs when there is a well-defined route (usually some sort of corridor) that everyone must follow to move around a given space. You move only within this corridor and there is little or no chance to improvise. In the case of a controlled mobility/single direction route you have only one way to move back and forth between any two points. See Figure 4.24a. The center aisle in an airport terminal is a perfect example of this scenario. This linear aisle represents the only way of moving back and forth between the spaces in the terminal.

Controlled Mobility: Multiple Direction

This type of route features controlled movement, but, in this case, offers a network with more than one single way to move around and get to a destination. The paths may be tight and controlled, but at least you have more than one to take (Figure 4.24b). Having choices is not necessarily better. In some instances, you will want to provide multiple routes; other cases will be better served by having only one.

Figure 4.24: Movement in space can be controlled and unidirectional (a), controlled and multidirectional (b), or free (c).

Free Mobility

Free mobility occurs when routes are not explicitly differentiated by hard elements and simply become (or at least they seem to be) the leftover "space between things" (Figure 4.24c). There is usually some sort of implied route preconceived by the designer, but its definition is left loose and often somewhat ambiguous. Usually, you want enough differentiation so the user feels that it's okay to go down a suggested path. In areas that serve locals only, you can have a higher degree of intentional ambiguity. The users will be familiar with the space and will know it is okay to move in the suggested circulation spaces.

COMPOSING MULTIPLE SPACES

So far we have focused on characteristics of single spaces, such as ways to define space, different levels of enclosure, levels of visual disclosure, and patterns of movement within single spaces. Now we turn our attention to multiple spaces, starting with basic relationships between spaces and paths, and concluding with ways of organizing entire projects.

Space/Path Relationship and Level of Autonomy

Depending on the relationship between a space and the path providing access to it, different levels of spatial autonomy can be attained. Figure 4.25 shows a range of possibilities. Figure 4.25a represents high autonomy. Despite the space's adjacency to the path, one enters it on the side

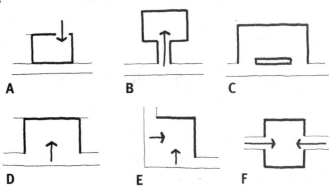

Figure 4.25: Space/path relationships involve issues of proximity and access. A path may be adjacent to a space but access may not be direct (a). Conversely, a space may be somewhat offset from the path but may enjoy direct access through a secondary space (b). The designed relationship may also combine both proximity and convenient direct access (c, d, and e), and, in some cases, the path may go right through the space (f).

opposite the path, therefore providing no easy linkage. Figure 4.25b shows another autonomous space. In this case access is straight from the main path, but it is through a transitional route, thus affording separation between the path and the space. Figure 4.25c and 4.25d show spaces right off the path, the only difference being the added wall in 4.25c, which provides increased separation and some autonomy. Figure 4.25e is similar to 4.25d, but entry occurs at a corner intersection with paths occurring on two sides of the space. Finally, Figure 4.25f shows an integrated configuration in which the paths go right through the space and provide no separation between path and place.

In cases where paths are kept physically detached from and outside the spaces they serve, the spaces remain autonomous and experience no intrusion from users going to other destinations. This type of arrangement is useful for major thoroughfares serving spaces requiring at least a moderate level of privacy.

Figure 4.26: Space to space relationships involve issues of both proximity and access. Two adjoining rooms do not necessarily need direct access between them (a and b), but they may have an opening between them for better accessibility (c).

These paths are usually adjacent and parallel to the spaces they serve. Depending on the circumstances, they can either stand out physically or blend in. Differentiation can be achieved through subtle strategies, such as minor ceiling height variations, or through bold ones, such as the use of totally different decorative approaches with strong physical barriers between them.

In the case of paths that pass through the served spaces, there is a planned, intentional intrusion. In these cases you, as the designer, have determined that the resulting integration between the path and the served space or spaces is desirable or, at least, acceptable. This is sometimes the case with secondary thoroughfares that tend to have local traffic, thereby not causing objectionable levels of intrusion. In most of these instances the path blends spatially and decoratively with the served space or spaces.

The Art of Joining Spaces

There are only a few ways to join adjacent spaces. We will point out six types of relationships between adjacent spaces. These vary in their relative degree of connection and integration.

Adjoining Spaces with No Physical Connection

In these cases, two spaces are attached as shown in **Figure 4.26a** but have no direct connection between them. In fact, the points of access are on opposite ends. Although they are close in proximity, the spaces are far apart in mutual accessibility.

Adjoining Spaces with an Off-Side Connection

Here spaces are attached and, as above, lack a direct connection. In this case, however, both spaces are open to the same circulation spine, making it relatively easy to move from one to the other (Figure 4.26b).

Adjoining Spaces with a Direct Connection

In these cases, spaces are attached and also have a direct connection through the common wall providing direct passage between them. This connection may range from a standard door to a wide and generous opening (**Figure 4.26c**).

Proximate Spaces with an In-Between Space as Connection

Here spaces are adjacent, although not quite attached. They are connected by a third, smaller space providing direct linkage between them. This arrangement is useful when a strong and somewhat formal sense of transition is desired (Figure 4.27a).

Interpenetrated Spaces

With **interpenetrated spaces**, both spaces overlap partially, sharing a common area of ambiguous ownership. With this type of arrangement access is direct and flows from one space to the next, especially as one approaches the territory in the ambiguous common area (Figure 4.27b).

Superimposed Spaces

In the case of **superimposed spaces**, two (or more) spaces are literally superimposed over one another, creating

Figure 4.27: Adjacent spaces may be joined by an intermediate, in-between space that provides access between them (a) or, in the case of interpenetrated spaces, by the common space they share, in which case one can be in both simultaneously (b).

Figure 4.28: Superimposed spaces go beyond interpenetration. They actually coexist and share a major portion of their space. The above examples show superimposition of two linear spaces (a), one linear and one circular space (b), and one square and one circular space (c). Notice that in all these cases the shared space is in the center.

a new spatial definition and geometry. Depending on the treatment of the surfaces and ceiling planes, both spaces can have equal dominance or one can dominate the other. Figure 4.28 a–c shows some examples of superimposed spaces. The relationships between the spaces can be orthogonal, symmetrical, rotated, and so on. Also, it is possible to superimpose multiple shapes on top of each other, creating increasing degrees of complexity.

Composing Systems of Spaces

Most projects consist of not two but many spaces, organized within some kind of cohesive structure. The connection of adjacent spaces remains a common theme throughout all the design phases. Questions about the relationships between project parts have to be resolved and be part of an overall organization scheme.

The ways of combining these elements for a specific project may seem endless. Yet, the realities of the project and the specifics of context help to narrow down the possibilities. Also influential are the preferences of the user as well as the designer. The synthesis of all these factors gives shape to a project. Ultimately, the final project includes some kind of organization as well as a particular spatial approach.

Here, we will look at some of the basic choices you have as a designer to address the overall organization of the project. We will discuss several ways to arrange a project based on the circulation system and suggest four distinct spatial approaches you can adopt as the compositional rules for a given project. We will start with arrangement alternatives based on circulation, an approach suggested by Stanley Abercrombie, who analyzed plan types based on their circulation.[4]

To devise organization systems for entire projects it is possible, theoretically, to begin with the circulation system as an organizing force and then plug in the spaces where appropriate. In reality, both the spaces and the routes feeding them are part of an inseparable system and need to be considered together. Once you have a feel for the required spaces in a project you will have to think of arrangements that will work for the project within the given site configuration. This inevitably will force you to make some decisions about how you will move people around. For that reason, thinking of project organization in terms of its circulation system makes a lot of sense.

Below we present six movement-based models you can use to organize projects. Each is illustrated with examples of different geometries that work within that particular system.

Linear Systems

You may choose to use a **linear system** consisting of linear circulation with spaces on one or both sides. If there are spaces on both sides, you can balance them equally or make one of the two sides wider than the other. The circulation spine of linear systems can also go through the spaces it feeds, becoming part of those spaces (Figure 4.29a–c). There may be special goals (destinations) at the two ends of linear systems. Additionally, special spaces can occur near the center or even at more than one point along the route if the path is long enough.

Linear organizations may undulate and the linear paths may twist and turn. As long as the general character remains linear, we can still call them linear. Whether L-shaped, U-shaped, or linear segments at random angles, the system is still linear if its character remains linear. Where you have corners in L- and U-shaped configurations, these become potentially important junctions

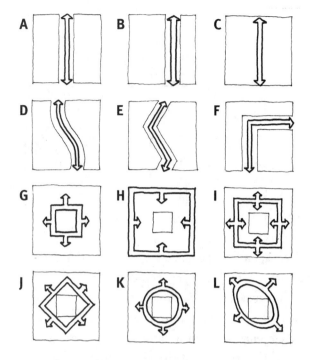

Figure 4.29: Linear and loop organizations have many possible variations, as these diagrams illustrate.

reserved for special destinations. Figure 4.29d–f shows additional variations of linear organizations.

Loop Systems

When a linear system closes itself up, forming a loop, it takes on a different character both geometrically and functionally and becomes a **loop system**. A loop can also be circular, segmented, or free-form. Its distinguishing attribute is that it is a closed system with no loose ends. A loop can be single- or double-loaded. An inner loop feeding outward and an outer loop feeding inward are both examples of single-loaded loop systems (Figure 4.29g–h). Double-loaded loop systems feed both an interior zone (inward) and an exterior zone (outward), as shown in Figure 4.29i. A double-loaded loop system requires many decisions regarding the placement of spaces. The central inner zone, for instance, can be either a space of great importance, or a utilitarian space. As with linear systems, the corners in loop systems have the potential of being special strategic destinations, and thus, loop systems can have diverse geometries. Figure 4.29j–l shows some examples of alternative geometries.

Axial Systems

Axial systems consist of routes arranged around an axis; typically, these routes intersect at right angles. They often feature a main linear axis intersected by a secondary one. These configurations tend to be formal because of the linearity of the routes and their often perfect intersection at or near the center of the space. Oftentimes this center coincides with an important central space. The ends in both directions are all potential strategic locations, as are the four corners defined by the right-angle intersections.

While the traditional use of axial circulation systems tends to be formal and symmetrical, it is entirely possible to use this approach with asymmetrical compositions or even nonorthogonal configurations. These, of course, would instantly transform the formality usually associated with axial arrangements. Figure 4.30a–c shows some examples.

Radial Systems

Radial systems are characterized by linear routes that emanate radially from a common center. The common center can be a major place or an important node. It does not need to be at the geometric center of the project, although it often is. Other potential locations for the central space are edges and corners, whether inside or outside (Figure 4.30 d–f). One drawback of this type of arrangement is the difficulty of using the wedge-shaped areas between the circulation spines efficiently.

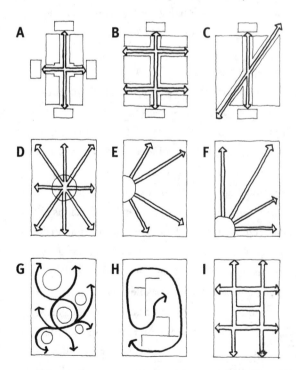

Figure 4.30: Variations of axial (a–c) and radial organizations (d–f) are shown, as well as two examples of free organizations (g and h) and one example of a network (i).

Free Movement Systems

Free movement systems are characterized by a free flow and at times an apparent lack of coherent geometry. Their success relies on the compositional balance achieved by the placement of project elements around which one circulates. These can be linear elements, like the walls of Mies van der Rohe's houses, or free-floating masses acting as islands. Given the many free-form configurations possible, it is difficult to generalize about specific attributes of these configurations. Free movement systems are viable and appropriate organizations used in many interior settings that do not require the strict geometry or formality of the other systems described here (Figure 4.30g–h).

Network Systems

Network systems are characterized by fairly complex circulation systems that are interconnected and form a network. They usually occur in large complex projects or smaller ones with intentionally intricate circulation systems, as is common with some retail projects. For large projects with many circulation segments, maintaining a sense of hierarchy among the parts will help to ensure a sense of legibility and order. In contrast, in many retail settings, the segments are undifferentiated to achieve intentional disorientation. Figure 4.30i shows an example of a fairly straightforward network system.

Spatial Approaches

Project particularities such as size, complexity, client type, and site configuration will suggest some of the above organizations more than others. We just described six basic types of spatial organization based on patterns of movement. You also need a clear direction about the general compositional approach to be used for the project. This requires not only route configuration but decisions about the character of spaces and the type of spatial model dominating the approach. Earlier we talked about different approaches to space definition, enclosure, and disclosure. When you consider all the variables, the number of possible compositional combinations can seem staggering.

Although the many ways of combining circulation systems and spatial approaches yield a great number of different solutions, we suggest four basic approaches to the orchestration of space: the functional approach, the

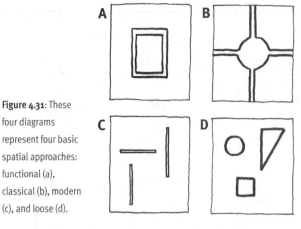

Figure 4.31: These four diagrams represent four basic spatial approaches: functional (a), classical (b), modern (c), and loose (d).

classical approach, the modern approach, and the loose approach. Using these four approaches as a point of departure may facilitate your efforts to arrive at a model suitable for your project; however, do remember that these are only points of departure, and variations and combinations are often desirable. Descriptions of each follow. Figure 4.31 a–d shows representative simple diagrams for each approach.

Functional Approach

The **functional approach** is, perhaps, the most common. The time and budget pressures experienced by both clients and designers tend to produce, by default, projects that follow the functional approach. This model uses an efficient, engineered approach that frequently features a highly efficient loop or network type of circulation system with spaces efficiently organized on both sides of the circulation.

You will have to adopt the functional approach for many projects during your career. They may seem boring, although there is no reason why they have to be so. As long as you are aware that the functional approach is what a particular project requires you can avoid wasting time with other unrealistic approaches and focus on making the best of the project despite the limitations of the approach. You may be able to compensate for the strict circulation system by developing other aspects of the project. You may also find clever ways to articulate the important centers and nodes.

Classical Approach

The **classical approach** is formal and features a high degree of compartmentalization. It is likely to be symmetrical and ceremonial. Possible circulation organizations are linear, axial, and radial. Formal offices, restaurants, hotels, and retail stores can use this approach. With the proper accompanying finishes it can convey class and sophistication.

Modern Approach

The **modern approach** is based on the clean modern compositional principles of certain modern designers such as Frank Lloyd Wright and Mies van der Rohe. It features simplicity and clean lines. General spaces are often loosely defined, not encapsulated. Movement tends to flow from space to space. Open spaces, even if not enclosed, are well defined and shaped geometrically so that they become positive spaces. Arrangements tend to be asymmetrical but balanced.

Loose Approach

In the **loose approach**, solids float in space in well-balanced arrangements. These solids tend to stand out as figures. The leftover space around them is often irregularly shaped and includes circulation and other adjoining open spaces. These spaces tend to be casual and are often playful as well.

REVIEW

Summary

The definition and manipulation of space is essential to the production of designs that go beyond function and provide order, enrichment, and expression. This chapter reviewed some basic considerations necessary for the composition of single spaces and systems of spaces.

Important spatial properties of individual spaces include their level of definition, the type of enclosure they provide, their size, shape, and form, and the degree of disclosure and movement they afford. Space can be articulated in many different ways, some literal and others implied. It can be highly contained and even totally encapsulated. The perceived degree of enclosure varies with the position of openings such as doorways and windows in the space. Walls sometimes act as backgrounds to the shape of space and at other times become the shapes themselves.

Spaces come in different sizes and shapes. Designers have considerable control over these variables. Spaces also have specific enclosure characteristics, and their form can be manipulated by techniques such as aggregation, fragmentation, segmentation, and distortion.

Levels and patterns of disclosure can be manipulated to create specific effects. Disclosure, whether within a space or beyond the space, affects a user's sense of orientation; it also contributes a sense of focus and relief.

When designing adjoining spaces, whether a space-to-path or a space-to-space relationship, issues of proximity and connection come into play. Spaces can be proximate without being directly accessible. They can have moderate or high levels of accessibility between them, depending on the location of openings and the geometry of the spaces. Some spaces are literally superimposed onto one another.

As one moves from designing a couple of spaces to the design of the entire project, certain organizational systems appear more appropriate than others. Based on movement patterns, potential systems include linear, loop, axial, radial, free, and network organizations. You may stick to one approach for a project or use a combination of two or more.

Finally, to help you think of approaches to the organization and spatial character of interior spaces it is useful to think in terms of four basic models that represent four different stylistic directions. These are the functional approach, the classical approach, the modern approach, and the loose approach.

---

1. Francis D.K. Ching, *Form, Space and Order* (New York: Van Nostrand Reinhold, 1979).
2. *Random House College Dictionary* (1987), s.v. "Texture."
3. Rob Krier, *Elements of Architecture* (London: Academy Editions, 1992), 26–33.
4. Stanley Abercrombie, *A Philosophy of Interior Design* (New York: Harper and Row, 1990), 17–25.

In the course of designing interior space, designers always have to deal with walls, ceilings, and columns. Floors are another enclosing surface, although floors have limited opportunities for articulation. They simply need to be flat and, even so, everyone, regardless of physical ability, can move unimpeded from place to place. Walls, ceilings, and columns, on the other hand, present opportunities for articulation.

It is common for the novice designer to think of walls as something that happen when you need a room, of ceilings as something you need in order to hide ugly mechanical ductwork and suspend lights, and of columns as things that are just there and about which you can do nothing. There is much more to these important spatial elements.

Walls do more than just enclose rooms. They contain, define, separate, decorate, and can actually do work for you (Figure C4.6). Most individual walls are experienced as at least two, frequently more, realities. The darkened

wall in Figure C4.7 is experienced as four different realities, three individual ones from inside the three rooms, and one from the other side of the offices. In other words, that particular wall could have four totally different expressions! Since walls have not one but two sides, proper consideration must be given to the appearance and effect of each side. Although walls normally conform to the thickness produced by the particular combination of the materials used and their widths and thicknesses, not all walls need to be of uniform depth. Either one or both sides of the wall can take off and expand to meet your design intentions (Figure C4.8).

THE MANY FACES OF WALLS

Figure C4.7: Walls have many sides. The dark wall shown is seen independently from three offices and from the open area outside the offices.

THE 2 SIDES OF WALLS

Figure C4.8: Walls have two sides. They may be straight, angled, curved, wide, or narrow.

WALLS

1. CONTAIN/DEFINE

2. ENCLOSE

3. SEPARATE

4. AS OBJECT

5. AS FUNCTION

Figure C4.6: The many functions of walls: contain (1), enclose (2), separate (3), as object (4), as function (5).

Walls embody different personalities according to the roles they assume (Figure C4.9) and the treatment given them by the designer (Figure C4.10). They certainly do not have an obligation to extend to the ceiling (at least the nonstructural walls normally used in interiors). So, they can be of any height and shape you want. Different heights create different conditions (Figure C4.11), as do different shapes (Figure C4.12). You can even put a wall to work for you. Figure C4.13 suggests just a few of the many possibilities.

WALLS

1. GRAND WALL

2. STATIC WALL

3. MOVING WALL

Figure C4.9: Some of the many types of walls: the grand wall (1), the static wall (2), the moving wall (3).

EXPRESSIVE WALLS

A.

B.

Figure C4.10: Walls can be expressive through surface treatment (a), or articulation and content (b).

PARTIAL HT. WALLS

Figure C4.11: Walls are not always full height. Partial-height walls, however, come in many heights.

WALLS - SHAPES/FORMS

Figure C4.12: Some of the many shapes walls can assume: undulating (a), gable (b), diagonal end (c), semicircular (d), tilted (e).

UTILITARIAN WALLS

Figure C4.13: Walls can be utilitarian and incorporate files (b), work counters (c), or both (a).

Some walls do have to extend all the way to the ceiling (or beyond) to meet particular enclosure and privacy requirements. Even in many of those cases, however, it is possible to maintain some visual continuity and light penetration through the use of glass. Even when privacy is required, a modest amount of glass can be used to achieve continuity between sides (Figure C4.14). Glass can also cover large areas to produce major connections between sides. The detailing of how this happens, by the way, presents opportunities for many different design expressions. The way glass panels are subdivided creates different looks with their own personalities (Figure C4.15), as do the weight and material of the trim used (Figure C4.16).

Ceilings can also perform expressive functions. In addition to the many effects that can be produced by ceiling height variations (Figure C4.17), the shape of ceilings can also be expressive. As Figure C4.18 shows, undulating ceilings, shallow gables, and vaults (half and full) are some of the possibilities.

Figure C4.14: Walls can let light from the perimeter in through clerestory glass bands (a), sidelights (b), or both (c).

Figure C4.15: Large areas of glass can be subdivided minimally (1), moderately (2), or extensively (3).

Figure C4.16: The weight of the trim framing window walls can be minimal (1), light (2), or heavy (3).

Figure C4.17: Ceiling height variations can produce many different effects.

Figure C4.18: The articulation of the ceiling is one of the designer's main tools. Ceilings can be subdivided to define areas (a), undulated (b), gabled (c), or vaulted (d and e). Shapes don't always have to be completed symmetrically. It is possible to have, for instance, partial vaults (f and g).

Finally, structural columns, while impractical to remove, offer opportunities for expression. Depending on how you cover them (shapes and materials used), different effects can be produced. Figure C4.19 shows different approaches in plan, while Figure C4.20 displays different shapes in section. The fact that other effects are possible through detailing and articulation is

Figure C4.20: The shape of covered columns can assume many shapes: fully covered and full height (a), partial height (b), leaning (c and d), or spreading and partial height (e).

Figure C4.19: Columns can be given different shapes depending on how you cover them. They can be left rough (a), covered with a rectangular shape (b), a round shape (c), a triangular shape (d), or made to disappear on one side (e).

COLUMN

Figure C4.21: Columns can be articulated by varying the widths of their different sections. There are, of course, many other ways of articulating columns.

Chapter Questions

1. Explain the related concepts of space definition, containment, and encapsulation. When does a space go from definition to containment or encapsulation?

2. Recall monumental spaces you have visited. What was your reaction to them?

3. Can you recall a corridor, room, or open space you have experienced that had a very generous scale?

4. Recall intimate-scale spaces you have seen. How did they feel?

5. As a designer, you will often be faced with decisions about whether to make a certain space a little more generous or more intimate. Depending on the space, its setting and use, you may favor one approach over the other. What kinds of spaces would you make more generous? Which ones would you make more intimate?

6. Think of at least two instances where you would use each of the following:
   a) An off-the-path room with a short direct path to it
   b) A corner space completely open to both side paths. Would you differentiate the path from the space or have it blend with the space?
   c) A path running through the heart of a space

7. Sketch and briefly describe at least two instances where you would use each of the following:
   a) Two adjoining spaces with a prominent opening on the common side
   b) Two adjacent spaces with an intervening connecting space
   c) Two interpenetrated spaces
   d) Two superimposed spaces

8. In what types of applications would you consider the following systems?
   a) A linear system
   b) An axial system
   c) A radial system
   d) A free system

9. Describe two ideal types of projects for each of the following approaches:
   a) The functional approach
   b) The classical approach
   c) The modern approach
   d) The loose approach

Exercises

The recommended type of drawing for these exercises is a three-dimensional drawing, such as an axonometric or a perspective. In some cases, however, a floor plan will work. Check with your instructor to determine the type of drawings you should use.

1. Draw two minimally defined rectangular spaces, one straightforward and literal, the other implied.

2. Draw three rectangular rooms enclosed by walls. Add openings (number, size, and placement are up to you) to achieve the following:
   a) A very open space with minimal enclosure
   b) A space with an open feel but a moderate sense of containment
   c) A strongly contained space with as much openness as possible

3. Draw at least two similarly sized spaces with enclosing edges of different heights and different levels of transparency (using screens) to produce two very different effects.

4. Draw one space in which you use the ceiling to define:
   a) A subspace in the center
   b) A path along one side

5. Draw a large space using the floor plane to define a subarea near the center.

6. Draw two square, two circular, and two short rectangular spaces in which you use the placement of doors to achieve different circulation patterns. These will be rooms that users must go through, so the rooms will all need at least two doors—an inlet and an outlet.

7. Draw two long rectangular spaces and subdivide each into three compartments by using a combination of different techniques, such as wall articulations, dividing planes, furniture arrangements, or placement of doors.

8. Draw three rooms using one of the basic forms we studied and manipulate their form by using:
   a) aggregation
   b) segmentation
   c) distortion

9. Using the concept of disclosure, draw a large space where the view within the space provides a general sense of orientation. This can be achieved by providing a constant (or periodic) view of a central prominent element, by providing a view of a set of regular elements that indicate a route, by providing an extensive disclosure that allows you to see the whole, and by other techniques as well.

10. Draw a portion of a retail space where the disclosure provided helps to focus attention on one particular display area.

11. Draw either an office or restaurant space where disclosure is planned in such a way that users get at least one instance of internal relief from their work station or dining table.

PART TWO
ESTABLISHING THE DESIGN

CHAPTER 5
Understanding

INSTRUCTIONAL OBJECTIVES

- Explain how a project occurs within a given historic, cultural, and geographic context.

- Explain the contextual impact of the surroundings on interior projects.

- Explain the contextual impact of the building in which the project occurs.

- Present the concept of types and show its relevance to interior projects.

- Present the roles played by a project's internal players.

- Present examples of external context analysis.

- Present examples of internal context analysis.

- Present an approach that seeks to understand a project's most basic realities.

- Present approaches that seek to distinguish among projects of the same type.

- Present a format to acquire specific detailed information about important project spaces.

- Present a format to collect detailed information about relationships between project spaces' aspects.

- Present ways of expressing the driving forces of projects.

My own approach is to try to first understand the characteristics of the project. Before I try to conceive a formal answer I, with my partners and members of the team, become familiar with the site and its physical and cultural environment, the specific functions and purpose of the building, and relevant historical precedents. We have long meetings with users and clients to try to learn as clearly as possible the particulars of their hopes and needs.

—Cesar Pelli, Observations for Young Architects

BEFORE A DESIGNER can begin to design a project, it is necessary to collect pertinent information about the project and its needs. This information is collected during the programming (data collection) phase through conversations, surveys, group sessions, and observations. Successful design solutions rely on decisions based on accurate and complete information. Otherwise, no matter how thoughtful and skillful the design efforts, the project could easily provide good solutions to the wrong set of problems.

At some point toward the end of programming, or immediately after it, the information collected is sorted out and analyzed to get an overall understanding of the project and its particular requirements. The process of shaping interior space starts with the understanding gained during this important stage. Only when a project is based on accurate and well-understood information can we know for certain that the stages that follow (ideation, development, and resolution) will be addressing the right design problems. The diagram in Figure 5.1 a–d shows the progression through the basic stages. Each stage is based on information gained or arrived at during the previous one, allowing design ideas to become more detailed and refined as we move forward.

Understanding requires a considerable amount of analysis. During this stage all the project's evident realities, both inherent and contextual, are considered. The following aspects of the project need to be understood properly in order to produce a responsive design.

Context
1. general context
2. surroundings
3. building in which the project will take place

Internal Players
4. client
5. users

The Project Itself
6. type of project being designed
7. project's parts and their functions
8. relationship among the various parts
9. relationship of the parts to the whole

The better the above considerations are understood, the better your position to supply a solution that responds well to them. It all starts, however, by making sure you are responding to the appropriate needs of the project.

The analysis stage, particularly for large or complex projects, can be overwhelming. While collecting data and starting to think about project needs and strategies, it is important to remember that design needs to fulfill, first and foremost, the project's functional purpose. This is the most basic requirement of design. While some of the higher aims of design advocated in this book are important, their pursuit would be empty if they were not carried out in the process of responding to functional purpose.

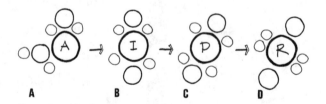

Figure 5.1: Design involves a series of stages that progressively solve the problem with greater accuracy and detail. This diagram represents the four basic stages: *analysis* of data to achieve understanding (a), *ideation* to generate potential approaches that solve the design problem (b), *development* to articulate the concept chosen in more detail (c), and *resolution* to refine and resolve all aspects of the project (d).

Order, enrichment, and expression complement and enhance function but they are never a substitute for it. Even a designer's own artistic purposes need to be carried out in the process of providing function. Cesar Pelli makes this point eloquently when he states: "The artistic purposes of the architect need to somehow combine with the many purposes and functions of clients and users. Skillful architects manage to achieve their personal artistic goals while respecting the goals and needs of those for whom the building is being designed. This balance is simple to propose and difficult to achieve."[1]

While purpose and its specific functions shape a project from the inside out, physical context shapes a project from the outside in. Responses to this collection of internal and external forces determine the arrangement of project parts and are, therefore, a critical aspect of the process of shaping interior space. This chapter will focus on the task of gaining proper understanding about both the project's functional purpose and its contextual circumstances. We will look at context first.

CONTEXT

A project is part of many contexts. It takes place at a certain time in history (historical context), within a certain culture (cultural context), and in a specific location (regional and local contexts). Each context comes with its own set of rules within which designers need to operate.

General Context

Designers are usually familiar with the contextual rules within their geographic area of operation, such as stylistic tendencies related to particular cultures and time periods. The situation is different, however, any time the designer steps into a different culture, region, or neighborhood. In these cases the rules change, thus requiring different design responses.

Designing in a historic district, a foreign culture, or within a neighborhood having a particularly strong stylistic character are all instances requiring proper understanding by the designer. When confronted with these unfamiliar circumstances we need to carefully study and understand what their contexts suggest and then respond accordingly.

Surroundings

A project's immediate physical context, its surroundings, is the most tangible context and requires proper understanding by the designer. For convenience, we can divide surroundings into two categories of different scales: the neighborhood and the specific site. Neighborhood characteristics usually have a greater impact on the designs of new buildings than on interior spaces. They can, however, be relevant to interiors when they have dominant tendencies, as in the case of an old historic neighborhood. It is, however, the project's immediate site that provides the most significant information requiring a design response.

The immediate site can significantly influence the placement of a project's parts. Contextual realities from the site often play a major role in determining a project's plan. Unfortunately, the realities outside the project's bounding walls are frequently ignored in interior projects and many opportunities to take advantage of or avoid problems associated with the context are missed. Designers must realize that exterior realities present both amenities and problems that need to be taken seriously if a project is to have a harmonious and complementary coexistence with its setting.

Response to context in interior projects is somewhat different from such response in architectural projects. In architectural projects, architects consider the site's location, orientation, and configuration in order to make proper decisions about where the building should be placed on the site, as well as how it is to be oriented, two of the most important decisions in building design. Based on the particular realities of the site for a given project, the building is located on a given spot, oriented a certain way, and configured to fit the location.

In contrast, most interior design projects occur in buildings that either already exist or, if new, are designed by others. The designer is therefore confined by the given boundaries and geometry of a predetermined building and must work within its constraints, taking advantage of its strengths and downplaying its weaknesses. This presents a unique architectural condition. On the one hand, the designer cannot change the building in response to the site since the building has already been shaped. On the other hand, the building itself now becomes another layer of the context since it is the container within which the interior design will take place.

Even when the building already exists, the exterior context needs to be acknowledged and responded to by the interior designer. It will become one of your tasks to locate interior rooms and spaces according to what the exterior has to offer. Significant immediate contextual considerations are the neighborhood, existing natural features, circulation around the site and access points to the building, and environmental issues.

Immediate Neighborhood

The immediate neighborhood consists of those surroundings close enough to the project building to have an effect on it. Depending on the project, this may be anywhere in extent from a segment of a street to an area of several blocks. The main things to look for are the surrounding buildings (size, character, proximity) and patterns of use. Figure 5.2 shows a diagram of an office building with observations about significant aspects of the immediate neighborhood that will need to be considered during design.

Figure 5.2: External features, mainly the characteristics of neighboring buildings and their users, can inform design decisions. In this example, a prominent civic building across from the building site becomes a significant presence that demands a design response. The selection of which areas will have access to views of this building becomes an important design consideration.

Natural Features

Three natural features require analysis: single natural elements, such as significant trees and other plants; regions of particular character, such as woods, lakes, and clearings; and topographic characteristics of the site, such as slopes, peaks and valleys. Some natural site features, like a lake, may provide visual relief. Others, like a group of trees, may provide shade to cool the building.

Charles Moore wrote about the importance of outlook, a concept related to the relationship of interior spaces and the exterior "in which something outside the room attracts the attention of the inhabitant without requiring him to give up those advantages enclosure brings. Outlook occurs through openings, generally windows, and is, in effect, another kind of focus."[2] Put simply, it refers to pleasant features outside that can serve as focal points for the people inside. Such instances of favorable outlook usually demand a design response; thus, a room or space should be located on the side that faces the desirable feature. "The distinguishing characteristic of rooms enfronting the outside," adds Moore, "is that they are arranged in relation to something beyond themselves, and the chief advantage of this arrangement is that it allows the rooms to have an outlook over whatever they face and share its qualities. By the same token, it is only useful if there is something worth facing: either something already there; or something made and shared."[3]

Figure 5.3 shows a diagram identifying significant natural elements around an academic building.

Circulation and Access

The analysis of circulation patterns and building access (both vehicular and pedestrian) provides useful information about patterns of movement adjacent to the building. It provides information about how people get to the subject building (by car, bus, bike, or on foot), and which side they approach it from. Additionally, information about general patterns of movement outside helps determine what parts of the building people walk by the most, providing insights about where to place internal functions that need more or less visibility and exposure. Figure 5.4 shows the circulation and access diagram for the school building previously introduced. It identifies, among other patterns, two important parallel arteries, one intended primarily for pedestrian circulation (adjacent to and parallel to the building's long dimension), and one farther down dedicated to vehicular traffic.

Environmental Features

Environmental features include factors such as general climate characteristics and the sun path, as well as prevailing winds and sources of external sounds (including noise) and smells (including offensive ones). These factors are often influential in the zoning of interior functions. Exposure in relation to the sun path determines which spaces will get the morning sun (and the resulting light, heat, or glare it provides) and which will get sun in the afternoon.

Concerns for the proper placement of interior functions in relation to the outside are not anything new. As early as the first century B.C., the Roman architect Vitruvius wrote about the virtues of giving proper exposure to the different rooms in buildings according to climatic considerations:

Winter dining rooms and bathrooms should have a southwestern exposure, for the reason that they need the evening light, and also because the setting sun, facing them in all its splendor but with abated heat, lends a gentler warmth to that quarter in the evening. Bedrooms and libraries ought to have an eastern exposure, because their purposes require the morning light, and also because books in such libraries will not decay. In libraries with southern exposures the books are ruined by worms and dampness, because damp winds come up, which breed and nourish worms, and destroy the books with mould, by spreading their damp breath over them.[4]

Figure 5.3: This diagram shows a survey of natural features outside the project site for an academic building. The most significant natural feature in this example is the trees on the north, behind the building, which provide pleasant, filtered views from the rooms located on that side of the building. The lawn in front of the building slopes away from the building, resulting in expansive views, even from the lower floors.

Figure 5.4: This kind of diagram shows the analysis of circulation and access points to the building, showing both vehicular and pedestrian circulation and giving the designer useful information for design.

While much has changed since Vitruvius's days, such as the advent of sophisticated heating and air conditioning systems, designers have a responsibility to consider a room's placement in relation to the outside. Issues ranging from functional needs to energy conservation will influence decisions of room placement.

Figure 5.5: Conducting an analysis of environmental factors, such as this one for a restaurant site, helps to identify sources of light, glare, noises, winds, and smells.

Awareness of the source of winds, sounds, and smells is also important, and rooms should be placed in appropriate proximity to them. Figure 5.5 shows an environmental feature diagram for a restaurant contending with sights, sounds, and smells.

Building

Beyond its surroundings, the building that houses an interior project presents a context of its own. It has its own geometry, circulation, modularity, column placement, core-to-perimeter distance, and, in some cases, unique configurations or characteristics. Depending on the project to be accommodated and the building's features, these may be seen as assets or liabilities. Significant aspects of a building's context include the interior context, the circulation patterns, and the features of the actual project space, the site.

Interior Context

The analysis of **interior context** considers the space to be occupied in relation to the rest of the building. The pertinent factors include the location of the space within the overall building, the neighbors within the building,

the location of building systems and features, the adjacent building's activities, and the surrounding sounds and smells. Is the space in a corner, in the middle, on the perimeter, by the entrance? Is it on the sunny or the shaded side? Who are the neighbors in adjacent suites? What do they do? Do they generate noise or offensive odors? Performing this kind of analysis will provide useful insights to help you make appropriate design decisions. Figure 5.6 shows a diagram analyzing the interior context of a site in a regional shopping center. This tenant is located near the food court, meaning employees and customers will have to contend with distracting noise and tempting smells throughout the day. It also means the store will be seen by a great number of people.

Circulation

Analyzing circulation patterns provides insights about movement systems within the building, points of access to and egress from the space or suite, and egress from the floor or building. Circulation patterns are crucial for any business that relies on proper exposure, such as restaurants and retail stores. Locating such businesses in strategic areas of high exposure is paramount to their success.

Figure 5.6: The interiors of large, multiuse buildings act as homogeneous neighborhoods. These, like exterior neighborhoods, feature miscellaneous functions and neighbors that can have an impact on your project. In this example of a store site inside a shopping center, the analysis reveals two nearby stores with similar merchandise (competition) and the location of a food court near the site (good exposure).

Points of access are important both for the ease of the visitor and the convenience of the locals. Appropriate egress patterns are necessary to ensure safe exiting during emergencies. All these factors will affect the choice of location within a building and design strategies once a location has been chosen. Figure 5.7 shows a circulation analysis diagram for the store near the food court introduced above.

Features of the Space

Here the concern is with the project space itself. Whether the client is occupying the entire building, an entire floor, or a portion of a floor, the aspects needing attention are the same. Among them are the size of the floor area to be occupied; the space's shape and overall geometry; significant features, such as the size, location, and spacing of columns; the characteristics of the perimeter wall; window spacing; light penetration and exposure to outside views; and the location of miscellaneous building components, such as mechanical equipment, ducts, and sprinkler systems.

Figure 5.8 shows a space feature diagram for a floor of an office building. It shows some of the internal aspects of the site that will impact the design of the space, such as column locations and sizes, perimeter window characteristics, and clearance heights to existing mechanical ductwork overhead.

We turn our attention now to some basic differences among floor plates to understand the significant variations one encounters from building to building. Figure 5.9 shows three of the many configurations possible in office buildings with central service cores. We will concentrate on the geometry of the buildings and the use of space they allow. Figure 5.9a features a rectangular floor plate with a two-part building core. The configuration provides usable space in the very center of the building as well as space around the two core masses. Articulations on either end of the building, behind the cores, provide special spaces for potentially special functions. The designer will have to work around rows of interior columns on either side of the core when rooms or furniture workstations are laid out in those areas. Figure 5.9b also consists of a rectangular floor plate. The linear core occupies most of the center spine and is pushed toward one side of the building,

Figure 5.7: Similar to an external circulation analysis, this internal version identifies patterns of movement inside. In our example, the proximity to the food court and a major anchor tenant is likely to ensure substantial pedestrian traffic nearby.

Figure 5.8: This diagram focuses on the internal space features of a floor in an office building. Existing conditions are surveyed and notes made of key dimensions and locations of significant elements such as overhead ductwork.

Figure 5.9: Building configurations vary significantly. A task during the understanding stage is to analyze the configuration of the floor plate and determine what it presents as opportunities and challenges. The unique configurations and geometric features of these three office buildings may or may not be suited to house a particular prospective tenant, depending on the particular needs of that tenant.

Figure 5.10: In addition to geometry, factors such as which side is front and which one has the entrance will have an effect on design. Notice the different configurations these hypothetical stores assume as the location and number of exposed sides and the entrance location change.

opening up space on the opposite end. The zigzagging at the four corners produces eight corner locations instead of four, a welcome feature for any organization requiring many corner offices for its executives. Figure 5.9c is another predominantly rectangular plan with a central core. Like the previous example, its core is also off-center resulting in one tight, and one generous, end. Its most distinctive feature is the curving wall on one end. This feature can present planning challenges. It may be a blessing or a curse depending on the requirements of the project to be accommodated, although most competent designers would be able to put it to good use in any case, even if some efficiency is lost.

We will now examine some basic configurations of simple spatial geometries and see the effects of shape, exposure, and point of entry on the resulting space layout. These are the kinds of spaces you may encounter as sites for a small office, a retail store, or a restaurant. Figure 5.10 shows four basic shapes for a retail store: the narrow rectangle, the normal rectangle, the square, and the L-shape. A basic diagram is shown for each of the shapes for two scenarios: one with access on the narrow side (Figure 5.10a$_1$–d$_1$) and one with access on the wide side (Figure 5.10a$_2$–d$_2$). Additional diagrams show the effect of visual exposure (glass) on a second side plus corner entrances (Figure 5.10a$_3$–d$_3$). Notice the way the schemes change depending on configuration, orientation, point of access, and the number of sides visually exposed to the outside.

Let's return to office buildings and examine two floor plates and their interior contexts (Figure 5.11). The service cores of these two buildings occur along one end and not at the center of the building as is more customary. Figure 5.11a occurs in a large multistory office building. It offers a large usable central area. The service core elements occur along one of the long sides, thus providing freedom in the center but also potential challenges when planning for multiple tenants on one floor. Additionally, one side features six bay windows and overlooks a magnificent civic building and related grounds across the street. The opposite side has a panoramic view of the downtown in the foreground and of a lake in the background. Finally, there are eight large freestanding interior columns in the space that will require careful planning around them.

Figure 5.11b shows the floor plate of another office building. It features a narrow rectangular floor area with elevators on one of its short ends and minimal core elements elsewhere. Distinctive features of this building include a high perimeter-to-area ratio and a short distance from the perimeter to the center. Additionally, it features two areas of special architectural articulation: one bay window on the wall near the entry side and an outward-expanding, curved area on the far end. Looking over a vacant lot, there are some good views of the civic building, although there are plans for an adjacent building that will likely block some of these views.

Understanding what the building and its surroundings have to offer is an essential part of the analysis task. Good analysis and understanding will increase the likelihood that project parts are placed in the most appropriate loca-

tions and that the configurations used are complementary to the building's geometry.

The following are design considerations to keep in mind:

- Orient spaces in response to what's outside, seeking or avoiding outside features as appropriate.
- Take advantage of the building's geometry.
- Plan your modules carefully if the building has many interior columns. Use a module that works with the column spacing.
- Carefully plan modules along the exterior perimeter to work with the existing module of window mullions and solid elements.
- When planning tall spaces, consider limitations posed by existing elements overhead.
- Decide which characteristics of the building you want to adopt, feature, ignore, downplay, or hide.

INTERNAL PLAYERS

The internal players who most affect decisions of a project are the client and the users. By client, we refer to the owner or the designated representative in charge of the project. By users, we mean the actual people who will spend time in it, either locals or visitors. Often, the client is also one of the users, such as when the president of a company is the project's client in addition to being one of its users.

Clients

The client is the person controlling the project on the owner's side. This is often the owner, although sometimes a designated representative is in charge of managing the

A　　　　　**B**

Figure 5.11: These two floor plates of office buildings reveal some information about their size and geometry. It is not until we have the details of the surrounding context, as described in the text, that some of the real opportunities can be understood.

project. In any case, the client is the person or group of persons who makes important decisions about the project. Clients decide, first of all, that there is a need for the project. They tend to be practical people and are responsible for the feasibility of the project. As such, they are always deeply concerned about issues of function, cost, and schedule. Clients have a tremendous influence on the projects they control. They decide how money will be spent and approve or reject design proposals from the designer as they see fit.

The client's influence can be either beneficial or detrimental to the project, depending on the client. "A good client," says Cesar Pelli, "used to mean the supportive patron, one who would approve all proposals and agreed on whatever direction the architect wanted to give the design. Such patrons are now very rare. Good clients are needed more than ever, but today that means people who care about the building and the art; are involved through the whole design process; are explicit in their needs and goals, likes and dislikes; and make clear and timely decisions. We can learn much from our clients and depend on them to keep us on track as we move toward the most appropriate, functional, and exciting buildings for their needs."[5]

Users

If clients set the tone for projects, users shape their content. Buildings and their interiors are for users. The client may or may not be one of the active users of the building. As we saw in Chapter 2, the outlook of users varies depending on their role within the building or project. In a restaurant, for instance, the roles of the maître d', the chef, the bartender, the food servers, and the cashier are different, and this influences their individual opinions about the needs of the project. The view of a patron who comes in to dine is, likewise, quite different from those of the group above. The patron's opinion will be colored by impressions gained while entering, waiting for a table, proceeding

to the table, ordering, consuming the food, visiting the restrooms, and paying the bill. The staff members' opinions of their experience will be influenced by how much the facilities, as well as other factors, ease the execution of their roles. For the cook this will mean a functional kitchen, an adequate supply of ingredients, and a competent help staff. For the food servers it will mean a manageable workload, comfortable traffic paths between tables and kitchen, and functional waitstations.

In Chapter 2 we mentioned the difference between locals (those people who work in a facility) and visitors (those people who visit the facility but don't spend much time there). Clovis Heimsath makes a similar and useful distinction by dividing user roles into served and service roles.[6] The restaurant example above serves to illustrate this point. All the players in the first group above, such as cooks, food servers, and busboys, perform the role of service. The patrons are the ones served. Another useful distinction is the one between "front-of-the-house" and "back-of-the-house" functions. Front-of-the-house functions are public ones, such as those performed in the dining area of a restaurant or in the main hall of a theater. These functions tend to be performed in the more image-conscious areas of a facility, areas where a facility's purpose is consummated, be it eating, shopping, or watching a movie. Back-of-the-house functions are sup-

Figure 5.12: The people shown here are performing service roles in restaurant settings. Figure 5.12a shows the hostess in a front-of-the-house service role. Figure 5.12b shows cooks performing back-of-the-house functions.

port functions, usually highly utilitarian in nature. Some workers never leave the back of the house while others operate strictly up front. Still others, like food servers in a restaurant, go back and forth between these two worlds. Hotels, restaurants, hospitals, and theaters are service-oriented institutions involving massive behind-the-scenes activities that support the experiences of those being served in the front of the house. Figure 5.12 a and b shows individuals performing service roles in an eating establishment.

Understanding users and their roles is crucial for a project. Users perform the usual functions associated with their roles, but they often perform them in distinct ways. In some cases, workers of a company may have a specific style because of their collective personality, a certain tone set by the owner, particular company traditions, or some other reason. This accounts for differences among groups performing similar roles in different establishments. This sense of unique tone and attitude becomes a consideration that influences the expression given to the project. The food servers at a formal, exclusive restaurant are likely to have a different collective personality than a group of servers at, for instance, a school cafeteria, although both groups perform a similar role.

THE PROJECT ITSELF

The project itself is the central concern of all predesign and design activities. In this section we examine five key aspects of projects: the project type, the project's essential purpose, the parts of a project, their relationships to each other, and their relationship to the whole.

Project Type

Most projects are a specific application of a **project type** that has been done before. Whether a retail store, a restaurant, a theater, a clinic, or an office, projects share commonalities with similar projects of the same type done previously. Therefore, it is usually unnecessary to invent ways of solving old design problems, as long as the existing solutions work. Studying these old solutions can teach invaluable lessons and provide insights. The practice of analyzing prototypical solutions to common project types, with all their variations, is a good habit for designers to adopt.

Whenever you find yourself working on a type of project new to you it is helpful to spend some time studying past projects of the same type (called precedent studies). This can be done by reading the literature available on this type of project. Information is widely available in reference books as well as in specialized books and magazines. Better still are the insights gained by actually visiting similar projects and spending time observing and using them.

Projects of a common type share a basic purpose, a number of core elements essential to their function, and some recurring issues that always have to be addressed. Following is a cursory analysis of a few common project types. The intent is to give you a basic idea of the kind of information useful in understanding a certain type of project. The information given is, therefore, representative and does not attempt to present a full analysis of all the types. Detailed information about different project types is readily available in reference books for architectural and interior standards. When carrying out a project it will often be necessary for you to consult these guides to get more detailed information.

A Retail Store

Essential Purpose

A retail store brings consumers and merchandise together.

Means of Achieving Purpose

The goal is to bring the consumer in and entice him or her to buy. Presenting merchandise at every turn will increase the chances of the customer buying.

Dominant Features

The most important physical presence in a store is the merchandise. Everything else is secondary. Merchandise rules.

Basic Components

Storefront display, merchandise, fixtures, cashier, provisions for trying on merchandise, such as shoes or clothing. Also, merchandise stock in the back.

Common Issues

Stores require proper merchandise display with appropriate customer service and surveillance. The staff, sometimes limited, needs one or more strategic central locations from which to oversee all the public areas of the store to monitor customers.

Crucial Aspects

The way merchandise is displayed (the fixtures, lighting, and so on), how the design moves the consumer around the store and presents the merchandise, and how the staff can monitor customers, both to assist them and to prevent theft.

Particularities of the Experience

Retail stores can offer simplicity and clarity in applications where the customer wants predictability and efficiency (such as in a grocery store). At the other extreme, they can offer complexity and ambiguity to disorient and entice. In most cases, the shopping experience is performed in transit. Whether in a grocery store or a fashion boutique, the customer is on foot moving from aisle to aisle or from rack to rack. Sales staffs spend their day attending to customers, arranging merchandise, and conducting transactions at the cashier desk. They are usually on their feet all day long.

Opportunities

Retail stores offer opportunities to use design strategies related to order, enrichment, and expression. Depending on the type of store, greater or lesser levels of order may be appropriate. The experience of customers can be enhanced by providing creative circulation patterns as well as creative merchandise placement and display. Strategies can be explored to help bring merchandise and customer together. There are also opportunities to enhance the experience of those who work in stores by increasing the comfort of their stations and providing visual relief in overly busy environments.

Prototype

Retail stores come in all shapes, sizes, and styles. There are many variations on the theme, depending on the industry, the intended audience, and the level of service offered. Figure 5.13 shows a prototypical diagram for a simple generic store.

Figure 5.13: The following basic elements are included in this prototypical diagram of a store: window display, entry, checkout/cashier, perimeter displays, freestanding displays, employee areas, and merchandise storage.

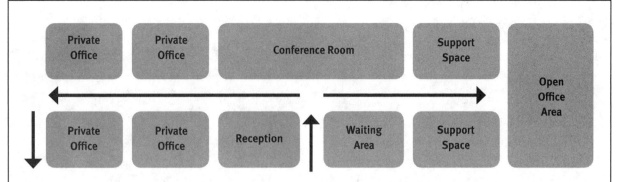

Figure 5.14: The following elements are included in this prototypical diagram of a small office: reception, waiting area, conference room, support spaces, private offices, and an open office area.

An Office

Essential Purpose

People come together in offices to perform work related to their line of business; the work is part of the process of performing some service (medical, legal, design, and so on). The nature of the work is typically administrative and involves the production and communication of information through documents transmitted by manual and electronic means.

Means of Achieving Purpose

Typical tasks include talking on the phone, reading and producing letters or documents, and staging meetings and presentations.

Dominant Features

People, furnishings, and equipment dominate the visual field in office settings.

Basic Components

The workplace consists of private offices, large open areas shared by many workers, conference rooms, and miscellaneous support areas for arriving, waiting, copying, storage, and so on.

Common Issues

The amount of floor area occupied, the ratio of open to enclosed areas, and the amount of flexibility desired are some of the common issues encountered.

Critical Aspects

Space efficiency, the interface with technology, and the accommodation of changing needs are some of the critical aspects.

Particularities of the Experience

Most activities are performed at a workstation, a desk, or a conference table. There is a marked increase in the use of computers. Workers do most of their work while sitting, except when in transit between areas or when standing and presenting. Work is performed individually as well as in teams. Depending on the type of office, a number of visitors (clients or customers) will stop by every day.

Opportunities

Office environments can easily be boring because of the constant repetition of elements and tasks and the need for economy. There are many opportunities for designers to manipulate the sense of order to achieve an appropriate level for the office's size and level of complexity. Design interventions provide enrichment and can be explored for both circulation and stationary areas to add interest and variety for workers. Given the wide variety of corporate personalities, it is also possible to manipulate expressive components to seek a proper fit between the company and its environment.

Prototype

It is somewhat difficult to describe a generic office without discussing subtypes since offices vary significantly from subtype to subtype. Even among generic offices there are major differences between the open office plan and the closed plan. For the purposes of generating a workable prototypical plan we will use a combination of open and closed areas (Figure 5.14).

Resolving an office design project requires a good understanding of the many units in the office, their roles, and their relationships with one another. The first step of any office design solution is to carefully place all elements for optimal function. The second step is to organize these into a coherent system of open and enclosed areas. Below, we present some useful considerations for the organization of open and enclosed areas and a conceptual model for space planning based on the kind of work people do.

Office design projects normally take place within the shell of an office building in a business district (usually downtown) or an office park. Typical floors consist of a core (usually somewhere near the center of the floor) containing elevators, exit stairs, mechanical and electrical rooms, and restrooms, with open space around it that is leased to businesses.

SOLIDS AND VOIDS

One of the most important design tasks for office projects is the previously mentioned disposition of solids (enclosed spaces) and voids (open spaces). Private offices, conference rooms, storage rooms, coffee rooms, and copy/supplies rooms are enclosed spaces. We will consider the first two "people rooms" and the others "service rooms." Additionally, there are open spaces. These include corridors and common open areas with systems furniture.

Offices vary widely. Some offices (e.g., law firms) are very hierarchical and consist mostly of enclosed private offices. Other offices (e.g., a customer service center) consist of mainly open space with systems furniture. Below, we consider various generic office design scenarios within a hypothetical office building shell and point out some important planning considerations.

Figure C5.1 shows four different schemes within the same building shell. Figure C5.1a and C5.1b are for offices requiring many private offices along the perimeter, such as in the case of a law firm. There are three main things we want to point out. First, if at all

Figure C5.1: Depending on the project type enclosed rooms may occur along the perimeter or floating inside. Other elements such as walls are used to separate adjacent spaces.

possible, leave certain areas open to the exterior to allow natural light into and views out from the space. You don't need a lot of them, just a few well-placed ones will do the trick. Second, don't use window space for service rooms. Put those inside and try to integrate them with the core. The core is a solid mass that is already there. In cases like these, it often makes sense to grow the core by continuing its shape outward (as shown at the ends) or by creating a carefully conceived protrusion (as shown along one side in Figure C5.1b). Third, articulate long walls. Where you have long stretches of walls, as in these examples, they will appear flat and monotonous unless you articulate the plane to provide variety. The guidelines given in these two examples are not exact prescriptions for how to do it, just reminders to do something to articulate these long planes.

Figure C5.1c and C5.1d show two schemes for a very different kind of project: the mostly open project. This type of project may require a few enclosed offices but usually has some requirements for the usual service rooms (or spaces). The problem with the mostly open plan is its tendency to have too much openness, making it perceptually uncomfortable, disorienting, and potentially monotonous. A useful strategy is to use the few required rooms or service areas to subdivide the floor into more manageable neighborhoods. Figure C5.1c shows free-floating elements. It features a floating room and a few narrow service walls. These don't need to be full height, but should be tall enough to achieve separation between the areas. They may incorporate files, work counters, coffee areas, copy areas, and so on. Figure C5.1d shows a similar approach, but, in this case, many of the elements are attached to the core at strategic locations. Notice how in these two schemes, the floor is divided into four or five areas of more comfortable sizes and proportions than if the entire floor was left open.

Now we will consider cases that feature a balanced mix of open and enclosed areas. We start with two cases requiring a few people rooms along the perimeter. In other words, there are just a few of those rooms, but they have to be on the perimeter, by the windows. In these cases, a useful strategy is to group the offices and put them all on one or more sides, so that the other sides can remain fully open (Figure C5.2). The idea is to let the open areas have significant uninterrupted exposure to natural light and views. Notice that service areas are still incorporated as attachments to the core. As seen in Figure C5.2a and C5.2b, their size, proportion, and location produce different leftover open spaces.

Figure C5.2c and C5.2d show two schemes with balanced open and enclosed areas where the enclosed spaces don't have to be on the perimeter. The scheme in Figure C5.2c incorporates all the rooms (people and service) into the core. It is possible, as shown, to extend fin walls beyond the main shape if one desires to give an open area a better spatial definition. Finally, Figure C5.2d shows a scheme featuring two floating blocks consisting of back-to-back (although they could just as well be single) rows of offices. Their strategic placement in this case also utilizes these masses as space dividers.

Figure C5.2: Many projects feature rooms attached to the building cores. Examples of these in combination with floating and perimeter rooms are shown.

The service areas in this scheme are attached to the ends of the core, and there is a floating dividing wall that may incorporate some utilitarian function.

WORK PROCESSES AND SPACE PLANNING

Most office projects have some open areas that utilize systems furniture. In fact, many projects almost exclusively consist of open planning. Open space planning does not consist of generic rows of equal cubicles stretching over vast open areas in buildings, although we have seen examples like that. Open space planning has become quite sophisticated, with strategies and customizations to cater to every conceivable working process. Steelcase, the giant systems furniture manufacturer, provides us with a useful model for thinking about work processes and devising appropriate corresponding design solutions.

WORK PROCESS EXAMPLES

| Individual Processing | Group Communicating | Individual Analyzing and Creating | Collaborating |

Figure C5.3: Four basic work styles can be identified based on levels of interaction and autonomy. Used with permission of Steelcase.

Figure C5.4: Hypothetical layout for individual processing work process. Used with permission of Steelcase.

The model considers the work a person or group performs in terms of two variables: interaction and autonomy. Somebody's work may require much interaction with others or it may be solitary, individual work. It may also range from the autonomy the worker has over such things as to how, when, and where the work is done. Putting the two variables together along vertical and horizontal axes we can see the four possible combinations (Figure C5.3). These define four different types of work approaches requiring different design responses. A designation has been given to each of the four work processes. They are described below.

Individual Processing (Low Interaction, Low Autonomy)

This type of work involves pragmatic, repetitive tasks like inputting data, preparing reports, filing, and doing repetitive telephone tasks. It's individual, steady, and repetitive work. Required individual work spaces are usually compact, with some but not much privacy. The overall space density is usually high. Telemarketing and customer service centers are good examples of this work process. Figure C5.4 shows a generic example of an office area planned using this type of approach.

Group Communicating (High Interaction, Low Autonomy)

This type of work process, unlike the one above, requires the sharing, transferring, and/or exchange of information. Although the key word is sharing, workers and groups still require a certain amount of privacy. Also, workers are not sharing the entire time. Their work could be described as individual work with frequent exchanges. In these cases, it is crucial

Enclave offers a private retreat from the active group environment.

Figure C5.5: Hypothetical layout for group communicating work process. Used with permission of Steelcase.

Shared stand-up space for the printer and fax.

Figure C5.6: Hypothetical layout for collaborating work process. Used with permission of Steelcase.

to understand the extent of the physical sharing in order to optimize the balance between openness and enclosure. Figure C5.5 shows an open area planned to facilitate interactions among groups of four and between one group and adjacent ones.

Individual Analyzing and Creating (Low Interaction, High Autonomy)

This type of work is individual and intense. It's strategic, cerebral, and focused and requires an environment that facilitates concentration (i.e., privacy). It normally implies a private office, although it is possible to create conditions favorable for this kind of work with systems furniture by using tall privacy panels and locations away from the main flow.

Collaborating (High Interaction, High Autonomy)

This type of work also requires cerebral analysis and creative thinking, except a good amount of it is done with others. You could think of it as group problem solving. Not all the work is done in groups, though. Consequently, this type of work requires both individual privacy and one or more spaces to come together. Figure C5.6 shows a team area that features both individual workstations and a prominent central space where one or more groups can come together.

These distinctions between different work processes give us important insights into what we can use to better design individual open areas. These open areas often accommodate varied and complex work requirements and become small microcosms in themselves. Using the proper type of individual workstation, team clusters, and relationship between teams or clusters are all imperative to enhance the productivity of the office.

A Restaurant

Essential Purpose

The basic purpose of a restaurant is to provide the patron with a meal. The experience of dining out, however, can satisfy more than the need for food. Other potential benefits include the convenience of not having to prepare the meal, the quality of the meal (sensual gratification), the quality of the service (pampering), and the quality of the overall experience (entertainment, shared activity, and so on).

Means of Achieving Purpose

A meal selected by the patron is prepared on the premises and served at a table or counter.

Dominant Features

Tables and chairs dominate a restaurant. There is often a bar as well. Amount and type of decorations vary from case to case.

Basic Components

Despite the differences, there are common factors in restaurants. They feature front- and back-of-the-house activities. The most important components are the kitchen and dining areas. Other components include bars, an entry foyer with a waiting area, a cashier station, and restrooms.

Common Issues

Issues include decisions about the kind of restaurant, and thus, the kind of experience to provide. What's the menu? What's the atmosphere like? Important decisions need to be made about the levels of privacy, sound, and light to be offered. Other issues involve the subdivision of space and traffic patterns.

Critical Aspects

Restaurants are tricky businesses and often fail. Many of the critical aspects for success (such as location, target population, number of tables, menu choice, and quality of food and service) are outside the control of the designer. Providing an appealing, comfortable, and efficient backdrop to the show performed by the cast of employees is the contribution of the designer.

Particularities of the Experience

For the patron, the majority of the experience takes place while sitting at a table. The patron's focus can be directed at the table and its contents, toward accompanying guests, or toward views away from the table,

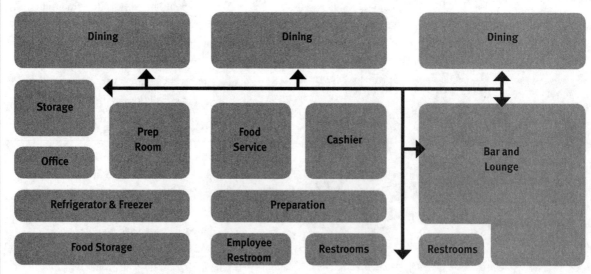

Figure 5.15: Prototypical diagram of a restaurant. Notice how the functions are divided by the circulation into front-of-the-house functions (top and right) and back-of-the-house functions (bottom left quadrant).

either within the restaurant or outside it. For the staff, the experience varies widely depending on their role as kitchen staff, waitstaff, bar staff, or management staff.

Opportunities

Spatially, the biggest opportunities in restaurant design are those involving the subdivision of space and the placement of tables to create desired levels of privacy as well as connection. Additionally, there are above-average decorative opportunities given the thematic character of many restaurants.

Prototype

The experience in a restaurant can vary depending on whether one is there to get a quick, inexpensive, practical meal or to experience an unforgettable meal in a luxurious setting while being pampered by the waitstaff. As with retail stores, there are many variations depending on the type of food served, the location, the clientele, and so on. Figure 5.15 shows a prototypical diagram for a generic restaurant. Refer also to the capsule titled "The Art of Table Layout in Restaurants."

CAPSULE | The Art of Table Layout in Restaurants

Two realities operate simultaneously in restaurants: the back-of-the-house reality and the front-of-the-house reality. On the one hand, restaurants are like factories, requiring the assembly of products from raw materials that come in periodically. The creations are made on demand and on the spot, requiring great organization and efficiency. On the other hand, there is the front-of-the-house experience. Above all, this experience should be pleasant. Although it is clear that the highlight of the experience is the meal itself, all the surrounding factors help to shape the total experience. Sights, sounds, and smells are some of the important environmental contributors. Themes and styles transport patrons to a temporary reality with a very special mood and character.

Designers have little control over such aspects as the quality of the food or how courteous and expedient the service is in a restaurant. They do, however, enjoy great influence over the ambiance of the place. Thoughtful composition, sensitive and well-conceived lighting, and appropriate detailing are some of the ingredients for success. As we have stated before, success requires both good ideas and good execution. You should plan to devote much time to these matters. It is not these that we want to highlight here.

Instead, we address a more mundane but very important aspect of restaurant design: seating. The goal is to help you with this often time-consuming task so that you can produce a layout quickly and move on to more intricate tasks of the design, such as developing the theme and mood through detailing, color, lighting, and so on.

We begin by considering the two types of possible spaces in which you have to do your layout: the narrow space and the wide space. The first one implies a linear type of arrangement and has several possible layouts, depending on the actual width of the space. The second one presents more options and requires some preliminary decision making. With narrow spaces you can pretty much go at it and start your layout; however, with wide spaces having a central zone you have to decide what you are going to do with the center. Figure C5.7 shows your three basic choices. You may put

Figure C5.7: The center of deep plans presents the designer with different options. The designer may choose to emphasize or deemphasize the sense of center. The area may be compact or elongated, centered (as shown) or off-axis.

something other than seating in the middle, such as a mass with waiter stations and/or decorative or focal elements (e.g., planters, fountains, and so on), as shown in Figure C5.7a. Your second choice is to have a central seating area, in turn surrounded by narrower, perimeter areas (Figure C5.7b). Your third choice is to eliminate the center through the addition of one or more dividing elements (e.g., linear partial-height walls, planters, and so on). The solution shown in Figure C5.7c, an example of this approach, divides the room into four zones, one per side.

Before we begin looking at layout ideas, let's take a moment to reflect on the limited number of seating zones and table types. There are only two types of seating zones: perimeter and open. Perimeter seating is against a wall or some other boundary. Open seating, as the name implies, is in the open. Table types for perimeter seating include the booth, the two- or four-person against-the-wall table, and the two- or four-person against-the-wall table/banquette combination. You can also, of course, use one of the open-seating table arrangements along the perimeter. Open-seating table arrangements include the round table for four or more, the angled (usually 45 degrees) square table for four, the nonangled square table for two or four, and the nonangled rectangular table for four (seating on long sides). Those are pretty much the possibilities. There are, however, many possible ways of combining perimeter and open seating. The layout you choose depends on the proportions given by the space (or created intentionally by you through subdivision), the

Figure C5.8: Linear layouts with parallel walls

Figure C5.9: Linear layouts with central seating rows

mix of tables desired for the restaurant, and your own preferences.

We give our layout ideas below, starting with narrow arrangements. Figure C5.8 shows six layouts consisting of two parallel perimeter walls (no central zone). The layouts in Figure C5.9 feature a center row between two parallel perimeters. Figure C5.10 shows layouts with a central zone of two rows. In Figure C5.11, a partial-height, dividing island is used along the center, thus subdividing the overall space into two narrow spaces. The environment still reads as one room, because the center divider is low. The island reads as an object in the middle.

Figure C5.12a features a perimeter on the left and a zone on the right. Notice that it is no longer one or two rows of tables in the open but a larger area that reads as a zone. The layout in Figure C5.12b is slightly different. From left to right, it reads as a perimeter/single row/zone arrangement. Finally, Figure C5.13 shows how a large central zone can be subdivided into smaller regions. Whenever possible, avoid very large, undivided zones with a sea of tables. Sitting at one of the center tables is not a very pleasant experience. One feels lost in the middle. In a restaurant it is reassuring to feel anchored against, or at least close to, a wall column or some other element with anchoring properties.

Figure C5.10: Linear layouts with wider central zones.

Figure C5.11 Rectangular room with seating island as space divider.

Figure C5.12: Layout with perimeter rows and central zones.

Figure C5.13: Rooms subdivided into two linear zones through central linear seating

A Library

Essential Purpose

A library is a building where recorded knowledge is stored and made available to the public. The public sometimes looks at the materials in the library; however, materials are often borrowed and taken home for limited periods of time at the end of which they must be returned. A strict control of materials leaving the facility is necessary in order to avoid theft.

Means of Achieving Purpose

Knowledge finds its way to users through various media. Information is stored in books and other media such as audio, video, and CD-ROMs. Computer usage is becoming widely prevalent and is already transforming the way we store and distribute knowledge.

Dominant Features

Dominant elements in public areas are book stacks to store books, carrels and tables for people to use, and computers to perform searches.

Basic Components

These include a prominently situated control desk, staff areas, search areas with computers, and public areas with stacks and tables. In public community libraries, there is often a division between the adult and children's sections. Specialized areas include a section for periodicals and one for audiovisual materials.

Common Issues

A challenging issue with libraries is distributing zones in order to achieve a good balance between stacks and reading areas as well as between quiet and loud areas.

Critical Aspects

The back-of-the-house activities in libraries are essential for their proper functioning. Adequate facilities to receive, catalog, and distribute books are imperative. Environmental and sunlight controls to protect books and a proper control point near the exit to monitor people leaving the facility are also important.

Particularities of the Experience

For the library user, activities include searching for materials (first at a computer and then physically searching for the material in the aisles), reading or

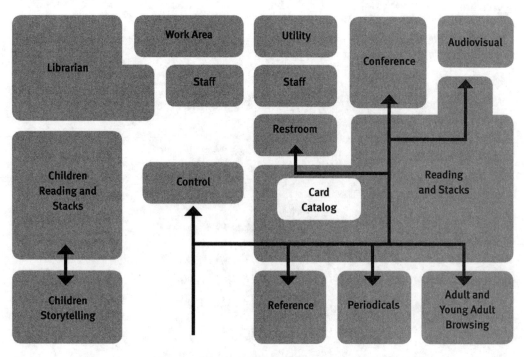

Figure 5.16: Prototypical diagram for a small community library.

studying the materials within the library, and checking out materials. A library scene involves a combination of transitory patrons looking for materials, settled ones enjoying the materials found, and others returning books or checking out new ones.

Opportunities

Libraries require orientation and clarity. For that reason, order is paramount in libraries. Subtle design gestures to enhance experience are adequate as long as they don't dominate and distract the user. The same is true of attempts to provide expression.

Prototype

Figure 5.16 shows a prototypical diagram for a community library.

A Theater

Essential Purpose

The theater brings audience and actors together. The actors dramatize aspects of reality and present them in focused, heightened ways that help the audience experience them much more intensely than in real life.

Means of Achieving Purpose

The theater achieves its purpose via live performances of theatrical productions.

Dominant Features

Theaters are examples of functions dominated by a central principal space. Although there are a series of spaces (often prominent) leading to them, and many crucial spaces behind them, there is little doubt that the combination of stage and auditorium represent the heart of any theater facility.

Basic Components

Like restaurants, theaters have front-of-the-house and back-of-the-house functions. The back-of-the-house functions can be quite extensive, housing dressing rooms, rehearsal rooms, costume storage rooms, workshops, and the stage itself. Front-of-the-house functions are public and include entry foyers, lobbies, and the auditorium itself.

Common Issues

The proper design of back-of-the-house spaces is always a challenge in theater design. Although not public and prominent, these need to facilitate smooth back-of-the-house operations if productions are going to be successful. Also important are all aspects of crowd management and control, including means of egress in case of emergency.

Critical Aspects

Because of the nature of live performances, all aspects of production (back-of-the-house activities) need to be coordinated and executed flawlessly. There are no second chances. Although the execution of the production relies heavily on the skill and preparation of the actors and the production staff, a well-functioning back-of-the-house facility is essential to make them work as smoothly as possible.

Particularities of the Experience

Preshow and intermission are times when the activities of the crowds become a show in itself. Theaters are prominent public places in which to see and be seen. Once in the hall, the spatial volume of the auditorium is often impressive, but when the lights are dimmed, everything vanishes except the production itself. Theater audiences experience the production while seated. There may be several thousand pairs of eyes focusing on exactly the same thing on stage at once.

Opportunities

Theater design, because of its complexity, is often done by specialists. There are opportunities to make the public spaces outside the auditorium a stage of sorts, where the drama and excitement of the patrons become the event, enhancing the theatricality of the whole experience. There are also opportunities to build anticipation

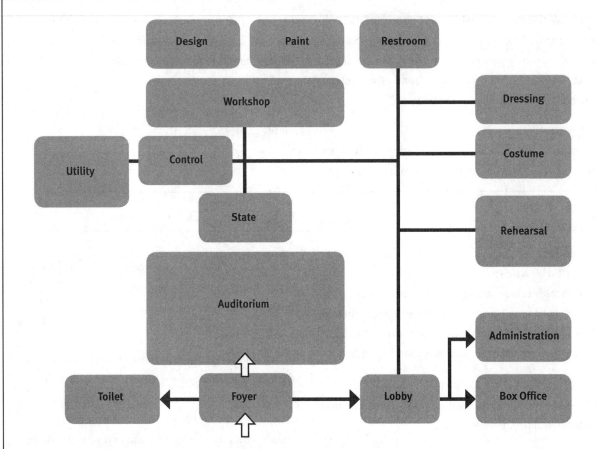

Figure 5.17: Prototypical diagram for a community theater.

through the progression of spaces leading to the main hall. In the main hall, there is always the challenge of making the immense space rich and dignified when the lights are on and giving patrons something worthwhile to look at while they wait for the show to start.

Prototype

Figure 5.17 shows a prototypical diagram for a community theater.

As these simple descriptions show, there are always a few essential functions intrinsic to a particular project type. Before one embarks on the design of an unknown type of project it is necessary to study and understand its type and its basic characteristics. Having this knowledge will provide a solid foundation from which you can start to design.

Understanding the basic type is only the beginning, though. Types occur at various levels of specificity and detail. In addition to belonging to a basic type such as "store" or "office," projects are usually a **subtype** of a general type, such as "shoe store" and "interior design office." Consequently, even though the spirit of retail is similar from store to store, the requirements for, say,

a shoe store and a candy store are very different. Even within the same subspecialty there are variations. A shoe store that sells exclusive Italian footwear, for instance, is likely to be organized differently than a budget family-footwear store. It is necessary to think beyond the basic project type and consider the particularities of a project: its specific niche, approach, or philosophy. A handful of factors define the varieties within types. These include product or service offered, target customer profile, particular style or kind of product or service, level of quality, type of service or delivery, image or theme projected, and, in some instances like restaurants, type of experience promoted. Let's apply these to retail stores and restaurants as examples. Consider, first, the two stores profiled below:

STORE A	STORE B
Product: Fashion	Product: Fashion
Store format: Small Boutique	Store format: Large Warehouse
Customer: Young Females	Customer: Entire Family
Style: Chic and Trendy	Style: Traditional
Quality and Price: Moderate	Quality and Price: Low
Service: Full-Service	Service: Self-Service
Image: Irreverent, Urban	Image: Rugged, Country

Clearly, the two profiles shown for these stores suggest different design directions, the urban boutique needing to be small, articulated, and to have some flair; the country warehouse needing to be large and rustic.

Let's now consider two restaurants:

RESTAURANT A	RESTAURANT B
Product: American Food	Product: Italian Food
Store format: Stand-alone Restaurant	Store format: Leased space downtown
Customer: Families	Customer: Young Professionals
Style: Steakhouse	Style: Trattoria
Quality and Price: Moderate	Quality and Price: Moderate
Service: Table Service	Service: Table Service
Image: American Prairie	Image: Urban Casual

Here again, the different profiles of the two restaurants are likely to result in two spatially and visually different restaurants. Despite their differences, they will both have the basic components of all restaurants, such as a waiting area, perhaps a bar, one or more dining areas, and all of the back-of-the-house spaces, such as a kitchen and a storage area.

Sometimes two different subtypes imply substantially different arrangements, almost different typologies. Let's consider two different office types. A financial investment firm and an interior design firm have different requirements, even though they are both office types (Figure 5.18 a and b). The investment firm consists of perimeter offices with support staff on the inside; in the interior design office the perimeter is occupied by systems furniture clusters housing the workers in a more democratic fashion.

Let's compare three different jewelry stores now. The three small stores in Figure 5.19 all share the basic components of a jewelry store: window displays up front, display cases inside, an area to complete transactions, and several back-of-the-house rooms. Yet they are different from one another in their spatial organization. What at first may appear to be differences in the designers' interpretations of a jewelry store are actually insightful responses to three slightly different approaches to selling jewelry.

The store in Figure 5.19a has a linear arrangement leading to a transaction counter centered in the back. The arrangement is simple and straightforward. Customers stand in front of the display cases at either side and move from front to back and are assisted as needed by

Figure 5.18: Two office subtypes. The investment firm (a) is made up, primarily, of enclosed private offices, while the design firm (b) consists almost entirely of open office spaces.

A B C

Figure 5.19: Three variations of the jewelry store. The way of conducting business transactions varies from one example to another. Store (a) is the most informal. Store (b) is a bit more formal. Store (c) is the most formal and ceremonial.

someone standing behind the counter. Sales take place at the counter and the transaction is completed at the counter in the back. The jewelry store in Figure 5.19b is also housed in a long and narrow space. In this case, however, the linearity of the space is deemphasized. Instead, a somewhat static space is created in the center of the store as defined by four wall protrusions and the furniture arrangement. Here the customer is encouraged not only to stand in front of a particular display case but to sit down in one of the provided chairs, where they are assisted by a salesperson sitting opposite the display case. The center space reinforces the invitation to get comfortable and stay for a while. Unlike the first case, the sale occurs, and is also completed, at the display cases.

The approach to the customer/salesperson interaction in the store shown in Figure 5.19c is similar to the one in Figure 5.19b. They sit across from one another at one of the display cases. The difference here is that the store consists of not one main space but a progression of four spaces culminating in a formal and climactic closing area at the end. The sales transaction takes place and is completed ceremonially in a raised circular space that features two small desks; there are no transaction counters. This approach is much more formal than those of the first two stores.

Projects, then, despite forming part of a type, are specific applications of that type. Their particularities need to be known and understood. It is these particularities that give projects the nuances that make them different and, in some cases, special. They have important implications for the use, subdivision, and expression of space.

The Project's Parts and Their Functions

Few tasks are as important during the understanding stage than accounting for all the required functions, understanding how they work, and determining what kind of space and layout they require. Some functions occur only once, others repeat themselves; some are large and some small; some are really important and others not so important. Yet, they all have to be included and worked into some kind of cohesive system.

Despite a designer's familiarity with the parts of a given project type, it is only by working with a project's client and users that a list of complete requirements can be generated. The goal is to account for all functions and to learn the particular application for the given project. The type and number of spaces need to be identified and desired qualities described. Figure 5.20 shows a typical summary of spaces for two departments in an office.

Beyond accounting for all spaces, however, it is also useful to set specific criteria for at least the principal spaces. Figure 5.21 shows a list of requirements for the entry area of a college building. It gives specific information about function, relationships, qualities, and so on. Sometimes brief descriptions of spaces are written and included in the program. Figure 5.22 shows an example for the college building. This programmatic information goes beyond the space names, quantities, and sizes usually given in the summary. Having this kind of detailed qualitative information will fuel the search for thoughtful and detailed design solutions.

Finding out how a certain client wants to treat a given part of a project is important. You may have your own ideas about how to design a certain project part; yet,

Space Summaries by Department

Management

Position	Office (S.F.)	W. S. (S.F.)	Quantity	Total (S.F.)
President	300		1	300
Executive Vice President	225		1	225
Comptroller	175		1	175
Account Assistant		64	2	128
Collections Person		64	1	64
Human Resources Director	175		1	175
Research Director	175		1	175
Secretary (for Pres., VP, HR/RD)		74	3	222
TOTAL			11	1464

Advertising / Public Relations Account Management

Position	Office (S.F.)	W. S. (S.F.)	Quantity	Total (S.F.)
Advertising Account Executive		150	4	600
PR Account Executive		150	1	150
Advertising Account Supervisor		64	4	256
PR Account Supervisor		64	2	128
Advertising Secretary		56	2	112
PR Secretary		56	1	56
TOTAL			14	1302

Figure 5:20: The quantitative data of programming documents includes space summaries showing allocations of required spaces and square footages for every part of the project.

Room	Entry

Function
  Occupancy
  Activities
  Time
	• General building entry.
	• Common lobby area connects to major public rooms.
	• Residential entry of common lobby allows the residences to be secured, but use the main building circulation.
	• Open all hours—provide security at residential entry.

Space
  Area
  Height
  Configuration
	• 180-square-foot general building entry.
	• 900-square-foot common lobby.
	• 120-square-foot residential entry.
	• Spaces should be tall and feel generous.
	• Establish clear patterns of circulation—plan for the first-time visitor.

Relationships
  To other rooms
  To outside
  To grade
	• The building entry and common lobby should be clearly visible to the campus and be open and welcoming—provide some outdoor cover at entry.
	• The residential entry should provide a convenient connection to campus but draw the residents through some of the common circulation to promote interaction.

Light and Air
  Natural light
  Electric light
  Outlook or "inlook"
  Natural ventilation
  Mechanical ventilation
	• Provide generous windows—emphasize openness and views in and out.
	• Do not overlight circulation with artificial light.

Special Elements
  Focus
  Edges
  Machines and
    service
	• Restrooms should be conveniently located relative to common lobby.
	• Provide places to sit and wait in visible spots near both entries, including some protected outdoor areas.
	• Provide niches, walls, and other elements for information and display.

Materials and Details
  Character
  Floor
  Wall
  Ceiling
	• Hard, durable floor surfaces with area carpets in areas of heavy traffic.
	• Natural wood trim.
	• Plaster walls and ceiling.

Figure 5.21: Design criteria for the entry space of a project include function, relationships, materials, and so on. Courtesy of Gary Moye.

INTERNATIONAL COLLEGE NARRATIVE DESCRIPTION OF SPACES

1. *Common Space*		
1.1 Entry Lobby		Entry place and the orientation area for the International College.
	General Building Entry	should be visible and welcoming to the university community. Connect to:
	Common Lobby	which provides orientation and public circulation to the principal program realms of the college. The character of the circulation should encourage interaction through appropriate openness and visibility to public college activities.
	Residential Entry	provides a secure entry to the residences in a convenient location off the common lobby. Residents will have a security pass to enter the residences.
1.2 Events Room		A flexible and divisible gathering space for formal catered dinners, receptions, and speakers and for college or university social occasions such as international coffee hour, potlucks, and dances.
	Catering Room	adjacent to the events room provides a staging location for serving formal dinners and receptions.
	Storage	for tables, chairs, portable stage and dance floor.
	Restrooms	in a convenient, discreet location near the event room.
	Men	
	Women	
1.3 Exhibit Display Area		Located along an articulated edge of common lobby circulation, or in a separate but visible room. Locked glass cases provide a secure place to display unsupervised exhibits.

Figure 5.22: Short verbal descriptions are used to capture and communicate the essence of each area. Courtesy of Gary Moye.

unless you understand the client's intentions and the particular realities of the project, you may be off target. Let's take two entry sequences to two office projects to illustrate this point.

Figure 5.23 shows entry sequences to two office suites. They occur in the same building. Both clients are relatively formal and conservative; in one case, a law firm, in the other, an accounting firm. The main difference between the two office suites is that one suite (Figure 5.23a) is a satellite office of a larger firm and the other suite (Figure 5.23b) is a one-of-a-kind main office. The client for

A   B

Figure 5.23: Entry sequences to two office spaces in the same building. Sequence (a) utilizes the elevator lobby space for the office's modest reception area, while sequence (b) brings the reception area inside into a grand two-story lobby space at the heart of the office.

A   **B**

Figure 5.25: Two typical modules of teaching laboratories to be used (and repeated) in the planning of a science academic facility.

Figure 5.24: This office is composed by the aggregation of repeated modules that combine enclosed offices and open areas in between them.

the one-of-a-kind suite wants a grand reception area. The elevator lobby space is not suitable to become a tall and grand space. Consequently, the lobby is used as an arrival space only. From there, a short formal corridor leads to the center of the suite where a grand two-story space serves as the reception area. It, in turn, serves as a gateway to the rest of the office, completing the entry sequence. The reception area for the satellite office, in contrast, occurs within the elevator lobby itself. The modest reception space is appropriate for the client's modest intention. From it one proceeds through a formal corridor that leads to an internal conference room straight ahead and to the rest of the office on either side.

Collecting detailed project information can be an arduous task. Few clients will have it available and ready to use. The existing facilities of the client may not be a good or complete example of what is desired for the new facility. It often takes a multitude of meetings, needs surveys,

field observations, and several checkpoints to compile an acceptable list of project parts and their requirements. The process of collecting this information occurs during programming, and you may or may not be involved in the process. In cases where you have not been involved, it is a good practice to check the validity of the program. A program may have been done several months (or years) earlier and requirements may have changed, or a program may have been hastily put together to get a general idea of the project and may not be totally accurate.

Projects may consist of a series of unique and discrete parts in some sort of arrangement. They may also consist of typical parts that repeat. In these latter cases, it is the aggregate created by the addition of many typical units that determines the overall layout of the project. An example of this would be an office project composed of the repetition of typical neighborhoods. Such is the case in the office project shown in Figure 5.24. The typical module of the office consists of a U-shaped arrangement of offices with workstations for secretarial staff inside the space created by the configuration. Here again, the module repeats itself. It is subject to some modifications at the ends and near the center, where two office spaces are combined to create a conference room. In both these cases we see how modules, or neighborhoods, are assembled from the repetition of basic units and these, once determined, are themselves repeated, giving the plan its configuration.

Determining optimal configurations for specific repetitive units is often done early in the process. These are then tested as additive configurations in order to determine their functionality. Figure 5.25 a and b shows layouts for the teaching labs in a science building. The layouts

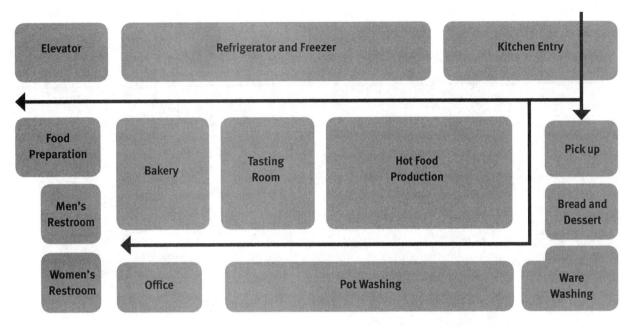

Figure 5.26: A single space worth understanding early is a restaurant kitchen; optimal relationships among its various parts facilitate a smooth and productive operation.

explore different arrangements and dimensions for the rooms. Once optimized, the arrangements become critical for the development of the section of the floor plan where they occur.

Other times, a highly specialized part, occurring just once, is important enough to merit the designer's detailed attention during the early stages of a project. Such is the case of the kitchen in a restaurant (Figure 5.26). The kitchen is the hidden heart of a restaurant operation. It needs to be conceived appropriately from the beginning, as it represents a large area of the total restaurant footprint. Its preliminary configuration will provide important information related to its size and shape.

Relationship among the Various Parts

The next thing to understand about project parts is how they relate to one another. Project parts need to be accommodated in the project site in such a way that they fit and work together, sort of like a puzzle. In order to assemble the project's puzzle, it is necessary to combine parts into groups. These groups, in turn, are assembled as a project. In this section we will focus on parts and groups.

One of the basic ways to give structure to the parts of a project is by analyzing desired adjacencies. This is done by determining which other units a particular unit needs to be in close proximity to, and which ones it should maintain some distance from. You can think in terms of three basic relationships between parts: attraction, indifference, and repulsion. You probably are familiar with this practice and have some experience using the adjacency matrices and diagrams normally used to illustrate adjacency information graphically. These graphic tools can be useful and convenient and are used widely. Figure 5.27 shows examples of matrix and bubble adjacency diagrams.

These tools, if used incorrectly, especially in large and complex projects, can also burden and confuse. The potential danger with the use of adjacency matrices, for instance, is one of unnecessary fragmentation. It is common practice, especially among young designers, to indiscriminately list every single space given in the program on both axes of an adjacency matrix and start indicating desired relationships between spaces. This is problematic for two reasons. First, it creates an unnecessary degree of complexity in projects other than the most simple. Second, it tends to promote a myopic view of the project, encouraging the analysis of fragmented parts only in terms of how any two parts relate to each other. While the mutual relationship of many spaces to each other is

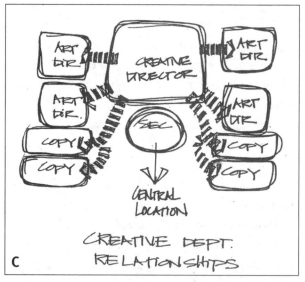

Figure 5.27: Matrix (a) and bubble (b and c) diagrams for an advertising agency project. Notice how much easier it is to intuitively grasp relationships in the bubble diagrams.

important, there are many cases of two given spaces having no relationship whatsoever.

The unit used for the analysis of adjacencies does not need to be the individual space. Although this will work well for small projects, it will be unsuitable for large ones. The advertising agency example of Figure 5.27 shows how the use of the matrix can become cumbersome. Adjacencies of large projects are best done hierarchically. Early on, your goal is to understand the project in terms of its groupings. This approach will accelerate your understanding of the project and save you valuable time. The size of the beginning unit will depend on the size and complexity of the project. The initial search for the relationship between parts should be for these groupings. The first question asked should not be about the relationship between any two parts. Instead, the questions should be what are the basic groups in this project? And then, what are their parts?

A hospital, a project of considerable complexity, should serve to illustrate the points made above. If you were to list all the components of a hospital on the two axes of an adjacency matrix and get information from hospital experts about ideal adjacencies, two things would happen. It would take a very long time to make sense of all the information and you would find out that many pairs of spaces or functions have no relationship. It would be difficult to arrange many spaces in relationship to everything else due to ambiguous data. Approaching the search hierarchically would help you make sense of the project. Several levels of hierarchy are necessary for such a complex building type.

Let's start with the basic components of a general hospital. Data at this general level would produce a diagram,

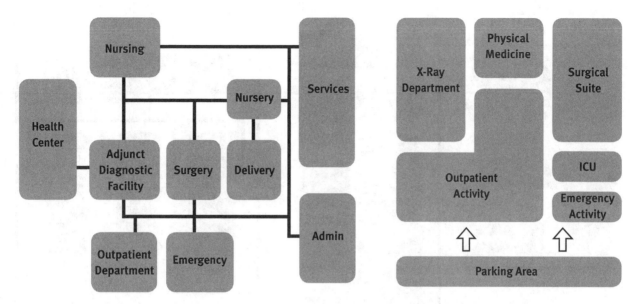

Figure 5.28: Main components of a hospital.

Figure 5.29: Outpatient Unit in relation to adjacent departments.

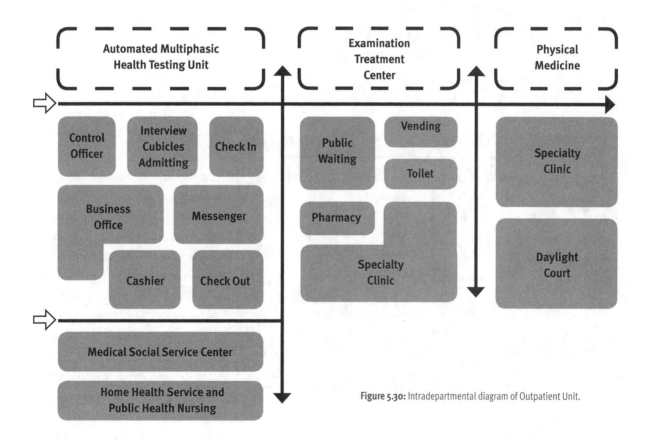

Figure 5.30: Intradepartmental diagram of Outpatient Unit.

as shown in Figure 5.28, that seems manageable. Every one of the components shown, however, has a complex internal organization of its own. Let's take the outpatient unit next to the emergency area to illustrate this. Figure 5.29

shows its relationship to the other units of the hospital. Figure 5.30 shows a diagram of the components within the outpatient unit and their relationships. If we focus on the specialty clinics, a new set of relationships at another

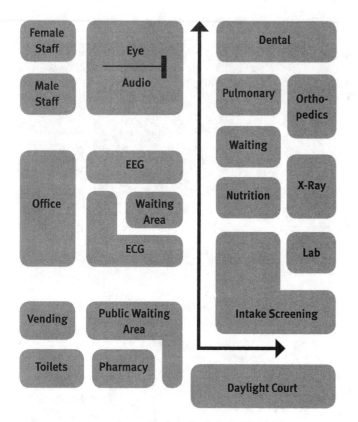

Figure 5.31: Components and relationships within Specialty Clinics area in the Outpatient Unit.

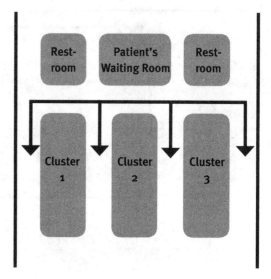

Figure 5.32: Outpatient Unit's Examination Treatment Center components and relationships.

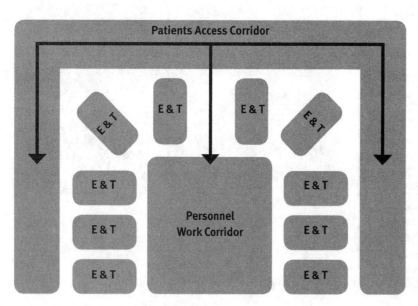

Figure 5.33: Examination Treatment Center clusters' components and relationships.

the components shown in Figure 5.33. Investigating relationships between components of this outpatient unit is necessary and relevant, but seeking relationships between the detailed components of this unit and those of, say, the administration of the hospital, would not be. Taking small parts out of context (without regard to their departments) and trying to understand their relationship would be highly unproductive and confusing.

At the appropriate level in the hierarchy, determining desired adjacencies between pairs of spaces is both necessary and useful. Here again, matrices and bubble diagrams can be both helpful and limiting. They are helpful because they give us a general idea of desired adjacency between any two spaces. They are limiting because they lack detail and nuance and, therefore, fail to tell the full story.

hierarchical level is revealed (Figure 5.31). Similarly, if we go back to Figure 5.30 and focus on the examination treatment center, we see it is subdivided into various clusters, as shown in Figure 5.32, which, in turn, are assembled of

Most adjacency matrices and diagrams distinguish the various levels of adjacency desirability among spaces, such as high priority, medium priority, and low priority. While this is helpful, it will seldom give us enough information to introduce specificity and nuance in our designs. A more complete and helpful approach would be one expressing desirable relationships between spaces utilizing three kinds of data: the level of proximity desired, the importance of achieving that level of proximity, and, for adjacent spaces, the nature of the desired connection/separation between the two spaces.

In addition to proximity, determining a desire for distance is also important. Figure 5.34 lists possible relationships between units. These relationships range from a desire for close proximity to a desire for great distance. Figure 5.34 also incorporates a way to express the degree of importance of the request as well as a means of indicating the degree of connection between adjacent spaces.

Issues other than the functional adjacency needs between project parts are also helpful to determine how to group the various parts. These issues arise because of common characteristics or needs of spaces otherwise functionally unrelated. They include grouping according to privacy needs (public vs. private), degree of acoustic quality (loud vs. quiet), degree of accessibility (accessible vs. remote), need of exposure to exterior (internal vs. external), and enclosure extent (open vs. enclosed). These criteria will frequently bring together spaces that otherwise don't need to be together, unless, of course, doing so creates other functional problems. Figure 5.35 shows a diagram of a library organized by acoustical zones.

Adjacency Options

- ❏ Interlocked
- ❏ Adjoining
- ❏ Across the hall
- ❏ A couple of rooms away
- ❏ Down the hall
- ❏ On the same side of the floor
- ❏ On the same floor
- ❏ Don't care
- ❏ Not next to
- ❏ Not close to
- ❏ Far away
- ❏ Totally open, no barrier
- ❏ Open to allow flow but some physical separation
- ❏ Barrier with door between the two spaces
- ❏ Barrier with no direct point of entry

Figure 5.34: Adjacency Options form.

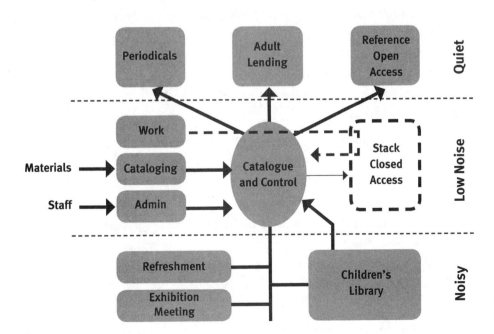

Figure 5.35: Acoustical zoning diagram for a library.

A Project's Driving Forces

Projects, we know, are much more than a series of rooms and spaces serving utilitarian functions. They embody and enable the performance of human rituals having specific nuances and meanings. In order to start making sense of the kinds of issues that may not come up in the quantitative analysis of a project, it is necessary to get a sense of the main driving aspects of the project. Most projects have a handful of main issues that stand out above the others. It is vital to understand these as early as possible in the process and to externalize them in some way. A very useful model is the one employed by the office of architect Gary Moye. His approach consists of identifying early the main guidelines or themes of a project and developing preliminary goals and strategies related to those driving themes.

The example that follows grew out of a series of workshops with user groups for a project to design an International College at a major university. The objective of the workshops was to facilitate the emergence of common themes to guide the project. As explained in the document, "the guidelines offer a synopsis of the themes which were developed by the group, within a structure which will serve the programming, site selection, and design phases of the project." The guidelines are developed as patterns, "design statements that describe and analyze project-related issues and suggest ways in which those issues might be resolved. The design guidelines articulate shared values which will guide the development of the project. As the project progresses the concepts and characteristics will test the validity of future decisions and the diagrams and strategies, which now hint at the means to fulfill the International College ideals, will become more precise and literal."[7]

Figure 5.36 explains the format used to present the guidelines. In Figure 5.37, the seven guidelines that emerged from the workshops are given a one-word title and explained very briefly. Specific characteristics and strategies originating from the discussions are then presented for each of the seven guidelines. Figures 5.38, 5.39, and 5.40 show examples of the way the guidelines were developed and presented in the program. Figure 5.38 addresses the guideline "community," Figure 5.39 addresses the guideline "oasis," and Figure 5.40 addresses the guideline "place."

Design Guidelines

The design guidelines for the University of Oregon International College grew out of a series of workshops where a group representing the users of the college discussed the nature and provisions of a residential college. Some of the concepts described below were established at the beginning of the workshops through individual interviews; others grew out of the group workshop discussions. The characteristics and strategies listed under each concept were assembled from the discussions and evolved and were reviewed by the group over time. Since the intent of the workshops was not to force the project into a predetermined framework but to allow common themes to emerge, the development of the guidelines was parallel to but not the focus of the workshops. For the full record of the workshop sessions refer to the workshop appendix.

The guidelines offer a synopsis of the themes that were developed by the group, within a structure that will serve the programming, site selection, and design phases of the project. They are intended to carry out the principle of "patterns" described in the University's Long Range Campus Development Plan. Patterns are design statements that describe and analyze project-related issues and suggest ways in which those issues might be resolved. The design guidelines articulate shared values that will guide the development of the project. As the project progresses, the concepts and characteristics will test the validity of future decisions and the diagrams and strategies, which now hint at the means to fulfill the International College ideals, will become more precise and more literal.

(continued)

Design Guideline Organization

The guidelines are organized to follow this general format:

Concept

General principle, which applies to the academic, social, and residential mission of the International College

Characteristic		Strategy
Attributes that support the general principle.	Diagram	Means identified to achieve the desired attributes.

Figure 5.36: Design guidelines format description. Courtesy of Gary Moye.

Summary of Concepts

Community

The college supports a residential learning community that integrates domestic and international students in an intensive and challenging experience at the university.

Center

The college is a focal point of "things international" on campus, is a symbol of internationalization, and contains some services and facilities unique to the International College.

Culture

The college fosters artistic and cultural expression.

Threshold

The college expresses a sense of openness to the University and is a "door" to the globe.

Oasis

The college cultivates interdisciplinary academic, cultural, and social experiences unavailable in existing departments. It is a setting where all faculty and all students can do special things.

Fit

The college serves and enhances the university, complements existing international programs, and respects the university's established development guidelines.

Place

The college is a positive physical environment that attracts residents, faculty, and visitors.

Figure 5.37: Summary of concepts for a college building project. Courtesy of Gary Moye.

Community

The college supports a residential learning community that integrates domestic and international students in an intensive and challenging experience at the university.

Identity

The residents belong to an identifiable and independent spatial unit within the college.		Residences "read" as residences Internal focus Residents have a backyard

Integration

The college fosters the integration of academic, social, and residential life.

Located near other residences

Convenient and informal relationship between living and learning spaces

Interaction

Spatial variety, physical connections, and visibility within the college promote interaction at many scales.

The structure of the living environment promotes "mentoring"

Living, dining, and bathing occur in shared spaces to promote interaction

Windows and visibility "advertise" gathering

Tangential circulation allows gatherings to coexist with passersby

Retention

The nature of the interaction at the college retains the interest of upper-level ICOL students and draws in students, faculty, and visitors from the university.

Accessibility to different things in a cluster or on a level

Study and work space for ICOL students who live elsewhere

Variety of accommodations attracts returning students

Security

A clear, securable separation exists between the residential spaces and the facilities open to the university community.

Transition or zone between living and learning spaces

Visitor access only to university-related spaces/Resident access to the whole place

Figure 5.38: The goal "community" broken down into more specific strategies. Courtesy of Gary Moye.

Oasis

The college cultivates interdisciplinary academic, cultural, and social experiences unavailable in existing departments. It is a setting where all faculty and all students can do special things.

Enrichment

Cultural and educational events and "happenings" are visible and conveniently accessible to college residents and to the university.

Public gathering areas in accessible and visible locations to the residents and university community.

Places for firesides, slide shows, films, music, and receptions

Exchange

Interaction between students and faculty is personal, frequent, and informal. The college is a good place to spend spare time together.

Department hearth for impromptu meetings

Catered dinners

Visitors stay as guests

Nearby social spaces for games and relaxation

Faculty firesides

Visibility of faculty and administrators

Innovation

Learning occurs outside the classroom and in different parts of the college. Students and faculty have individual and group access to information and communication technology.

Formal and informal places for classes to meet

Computer resource center near classrooms

Language lab

Study areas and computer access in the residences

Inventiveness

The college has "flex space," which can be programmed for different users and different activities.

"Spec office" with an anchor tenant

Exhibit space open for different uses.

Lecture hall and classrooms can be configured for a variety of uses

Figure 5.39: The goal "oasis" broken down into more specific strategies. Courtesy of Gary Moye.

Place
The college is a positive physical environment that attracts residents, faculty and visitors.

Coherence

The organization and definition of spaces promote a natural comprehensibility in the building.

Clear, positive rooms and circulation patterns

Integration of service and served

Hierarchy of spaces and activities

Variation

The spatial variety in the college supports different activities and different needs.

Different types of places to do things together

Places to be noisy, quiet, alone

Openness

Views and connections inside and outside give the college a sense of openness and informality.

Tangential circulation

Generous windows

Interior windows

Light

The atmosphere of the building is bright.

Natural light in every room

Balanced lighting systems

Reflective surfaces

Comfort

The rooms in the college are inviting and pleasant to inhabit.

South-facing orientation

Materials that are pleasant to touch

Adequate ventilation and control

Longevity

The fabric of the building is durable, maintainable, and can adapt to different uses and tastes.

Figure 5.40: The goal "place" broken down into more specific strategies. Courtesy of Gary Moye.

Another useful approach, developed by Donna Duerk, consists of the identification of issues, goals, and performance requirements.[8] Figure 5.41 shows an example of a student's adaptation of Duerk's approach for the design of a hypothetical advertising agency. Other formats may work as well. The important thing is to identify the main issues or guidelines early and to envision ways to address them.

Goal Statements and Performance Requirements	
Issue 1:	**Levels of Interaction**
Goal	the environment should provide an energizing environment that supports teamwork while also having areas where individuals can achieve their desired level of privacy
PR1:	the office should provide a diverse selection of work areas
PR2:	teamwork areas should be integrated within departments
Strategy:	use of spanner tables and pass-through areas at workstations facilitates interaction while overhead cabinets, panels, and orientation provide privacy; use of flexible small convergence room encourages reconfiguration
Issue 2:	**Image/Ambiance**
Goal	the environment should achieve a balance between bold creativity and professional conservatism
PR1:	the office should be visually stimulating in order to foster creative thinking
PR2:	important client areas and upper management spaces should portray a reserved professionalism
PR3:	the balance should be achieved through visual separation or a careful transformation
Strategy:	use of a '50s/retro/techy style to portray the nature of the agency; use of traditional full-height walls in private offices and client-centered areas blended with varying ceiling heights (from open to above to islands of suspended acoustical ceiling); use of rough, cold materials balanced by more polished, warmer finishes
Issue 3:	**Hierarchy**
Goal	the environment should express the relatively flat organizational structure of the agency, distinguishing top management from the remainder of employees
PR1:	orient employees so they can take maximum advantage of exterior views
PR2:	upper management should have private offices while most employees have workstations
Strategy:	use of clearly distinguished departments and workstation areas that can accommodate various positions; use of minimal full-height and partial-height walls

Figure 5.41: Example of a format consisting of the identification of project issues, goals, and performance requirements, followed by a responsive design strategy.

Synergy: Efficiency and Impact

Good projects achieve efficiencies that go beyond the additive result of their individual components. Three strategies that help achieve this are creating spaces that serve more than one function or can be shared; creating meaningful use of space between the programmed spaces; and creating spaces that add up to more than the sum of their parts in ways other than function.

Spaces that can be shared include conference and workrooms shared by departments in office settings and classrooms shared by different units in schools. Spaces that serve more than one function can include theater lobbies, community rooms in offices and civic facilities, and the well-known cafetorium (cafeteria/auditorium combination) in some school settings. This sharing results in economies for all the groups involved.

Meaningful in-between spaces can sometimes be added to projects to enhance the experience of their users. This is often the case in large projects where pockets along the circulation and off main public areas provide spaces for users to congregate, rest, or stop for a moment to reflect or perform a secondary activity. You may recall our discussion of nodes in Chapter 3.

The principle of spaces adding up to more than the sum of their parts was eloquently expressed by Charles Moore while talking about house design: "A good house will have resonances that extend beyond a set of discrete elements. The principle is that, in the assembly of parts, one plus one must equal more than two.... To make one plus one equal more than two you must, in doing any one thing you think important (making rooms, putting them together, or fitting them to the land), do something else that you think important as well (make spaces to live in, establish a meaningful pattern inside, or claim other realms outside)."[9] The way to give special qualities to otherwise plain and utilitarian spaces and functions requires purpose and resolve beyond the mere assembly of parts in functional ways. That's where order, enrichment, and expression come in. These start to emerge during ideation, the topic of our next chapter.

CAPSULE | Affordances

You may wonder, with good reason, to what extent the built environment can influence human behavior. This is a difficult question, but we can provide an acceptable answer with the help of James J. Gibson's concept of affordances.[1] This term is derived from "to afford" but does not exist as such in the dictionary. As conceived by Gibson, it refers to the way the particular configuration or arrangement of an object or setting makes it suitable for some overt activity. The horizontality of a concrete slab on the ground together with the natural law of gravity afford the possibility of walking on it with ease. The covered shelter at the park affords a good refuge when it rains. One does not necessarily have to run toward the shelter when it starts to pour outside, but the potential for refuge is there for those who desire it.

A good amount of what designers do is to create environmental opportunities and constraints. As seen from the examples above, the presence and arrangement of certain features encourage and facilitate certain actions and behaviors. Similarly, the absence or specific arrangement of certain features eliminate or discourage certain actions or behaviors. If the slab mentioned above was on a very steep incline instead of being flat, walking on it would be difficult for most people. Incidentally, the neighborhood's young and daring skateboarders would probably be delighted with the possibilities created by the inclined arrangement. At the park, if the shelter was not provided, one would not have the potential for refuge against the rain. Cover from the rain would be impossible, not because of imposed difficulty, but because of the omission of a sheltering structure.

Designers have great control over the provision or omission of features. They also enjoy considerable control over the specific arrangements of a project's parts and pieces. By manipulating these variables, they encourage certain behaviors and discourage others in response to the needs of the project. The environments they design, with all their inherent affordances, represent an environment full of potential; however, just because certain affordances are provided does not necessarily mean that they will be used, or even noticed. Perception of the possibilities offered by the environment varies depending on the straightforwardness of the affordance as well as the needs and motivations of the people using it. Motivations are particularly significant in determining whether and how a presented affordance is interpreted. As a result, sometimes the same condition is interpreted differently by different people. The half-open window in the house kitchen, for example, affords exposure to fresh air for the occupant, but it also affords a potential burglar an opportunity to get into the house.

Affordances occur at various levels of explicitness and sophistication. Many affordances are direct and obviously related to the requirements of the program, such as the provision of a desk, a chair, and four solid walls for someone who works in an office and needs privacy. Others are less tangible but work in subtle ways to influence behavior, such as the act of progressively widening a corridor to encourage movement in a particular direction. Still others serve secondary and even nonprogrammed desirable activities. These are often the most rewarding ones and the ones responsible for creating great environments. Just by being conscious of human nature and tendencies, the thoughtful designer can add meaningful gestures to a project. A place to rest somewhere in the middle of an excessively long path is likely to be used and appreciated by many users. It would be good to have it whether the program asked for it or not.

Other affordances can allow secondary activities in certain places, or even the transformation of those places in order to perform double duty. The introduction of comfortable lounge seating in many bookstores has transformed them from places to browse, buy, and leave to places where lingering in comfort is strongly encouraged. Likewise, providing a strategically placed pivoting or otherwise moving panel can, on demand, transform two moderately sized rooms into a large one suitable to host the periodic all-staff meeting or annual open-house party in an office setting. Windowsills of such construction, height, and depth as to permit sitting may help increase the seating capacity in the new "great room" during those special occasions.

Therefore, it is through the ability of built environments to invite certain activities and discourage others that they often exert their strongest influence on behavior. The concept of affordance is a useful one. You may start thinking of different ways of arranging or detailing parts of projects in order to add humanizing gestures, support secondary activities, and create areas that serve double duty. You may also want to look at your designs and see how they can discourage undesirable or inappropriate behaviors. You may also check for unintentional invitations or denials. The concept of affordance implies that there are many different degrees of a space's permissiveness related to any specific behavior. At one extreme, you can create conditions that not only allow but actually mandate a certain behavior, such as when entering a corridor with turnstiles that will not let you go back, thus imposing one particular type of action, forward movement. At the other extreme, you can deny access to an area from a given side by having a solid wall between the two areas. In between these extremes, affordances can exhibit different intermediate degrees of invitation or denial, such as strong invitation, subtle encouragement, possibility without encouragement, possibility with some difficulty (discouragement), or very difficult possibility (strong discouragement). As the designer, you are the permission granter. Think hard and choose wisely.

---

1. James J. Gibson, *An Ecological Approach to Visual Perception* (Boston: Houghton Mifflin, 1979).

Rob Goffee and Gareth Jones have developed an interesting model of organizational culture based on a pair of variables related to how human beings interact in organizations. The two variables are sociability and solidarity. The authors describe sociability as "a measure of friendliness among members of a community. . . . The level of sociability at a company is often the first thing a new hire notices. . . . When a coworker has a birthday, it gets celebrated. When a coworker lands in the hospital, he or she gets visited. . . . High sociability promotes high morale, creativity, and collaboration. On the negative side, close friendships among members of an organization may promote tolerance for poor performance and an environment in which "the best compromise gets applied to problems, not the best solution."[1]

Solidaristic relationships, the authors explain, "are based on common tasks, mutual interests, and clearly understood shared goals that benefit all the involved parties, whether they personally like each other or not."[2] The no-nonsense emphasis on the work to be done means that groups high in solidarity are industrious and productive. The organization is likely to have very clear goals and procedures that must be strictly followed. On the negative side, high-solidarity organizations can be heartless and even brutal at times, showing little regard for workers who don't conform to their goals and procedures.

Combinations of high or low levels of sociability and solidarity yield four possible cultures, which the authors call **networked** (high sociability, low solidarity), **mercenary** (high solidarity, low sociability), **fragmented** (low in both), and **communal** (high in both). These four tendencies, in turn, can be classified as either positive or negative, depending on how well the approach responds to the competitive environment at a particular time.

The four types of cultures have an effect on not only physical space but also patterns of communication, use of time, and sense of identity. In terms of physical space, a networked organization may have an open-door policy and more personal displays in workers' offices and cubicles; a networked organization may enjoy an above-average amount of social spaces such as break rooms and lounges. Mercenary organizations may exhibit arrangements that are highly functional and help to get the work done. Space allocations are likely to be related to achievement, and one may see more merit ribbons and awards hanging on the walls than family pictures.

In communal organizations space is shared both formally and informally, there are few barriers between departments, and the office-by-rank mentality is nonexistent. There are likely to be places for socialization, personal displays, and corporate symbols around the office, all coexisting harmoniously. The fragmented organization, by contrast, is likely to be characterized by closed doors that promote individual work and discourage socialization. There may be a conspicuous lack of both personal and corporate displays around the office.

Understanding the corporate culture of a client is critical because it may give the designer important clues as to the proper way to dispose of space, allocate square footages, and devise appropriate connections or separations between departments.[3]

MISSION STATEMENTS

Another important piece of information that often helps designers understand a company is the company's mission statement, the document used to express the essential goals and shared values of the company. Although these can be, as Wally Olins puts it, "the corporate version of the old Boy Scout oath, which demanded, as I recall, that thirteen-year-olds should be clean in body and mind," reflecting "the wish rather than the reality,"[4] most companies have a mission statement, and they are often included in the programming document prepared by the designer during this stage. Most mission statements are like a declaration of all the predictable and generic things that shareholders and the public expect to hear (quality, profit, integrity, and so on), but they can give the designer good clues about the personality of the company. A few examples should help illustrate their nature and how they can give us important clues about the company.

Autodesk, the software company, has the following vision and mission statements:

Vision: To create software tools that transform
ideas into reality.

Mission: To create quality software solutions and support services that foster innovation, creativity, and productivity for customers and partners around the world.[5]

While the vision statement is broad and vague, the mission statement gives clues about the company's commitment to innovation and its global nature. These are traits that could be used or alluded to in the actual design for the company's facilities.

Some companies extend their missions beyond quality and profits and integrate a broader societal component. For instance, Ben & Jerry's Homemade Inc., the premium ice-cream makers from Vermont, declare their social mission as follows:

To operate the company in a way that actively recognizes the central role that business plays in the structure of society by initiating innovative ways to improve the quality of life of a broad community: local, national, and international.[6]

Their statement speaks to a commitment to seek ways to enhance the lives of those around them. For Ben & Jerry's, mission goes beyond quality and profits—although they make sure to include quality and profits in other sections of their mission statement document.

The mission statement for Coca-Cola, the soft drink giant, in addition to mentioning value, quality, service, leadership, and so forth, adds some useful clues for designers when it declares: "We refresh the world."[7] One can easily start imagining ways to create an environment that conveys the idea of refreshment.

Southwest Airlines Co., the low-fare, high-customer-satisfaction airline, uses a statement that conveys a sense of the quality of the human interactions they seek to have with both customers and employees: "The mission of Southwest Airlines is dedication to the highest quality of Customer Service, delivered with a sense of warmth, friendliness, individual pride, and company spirit."[8] One can sense the warm and friendly qualities that could be expected from their facilities.

In order to service clients properly in a competitive marketplace, designers need an intimate knowledge of the companies they serve. A company's personality, culture, and mission become important aspects to be understood.

1. Rob Goffee and Gareth Jones, *The Character of a Corporation: How Your Company's Culture Can Make or Break Your Company* (New York: Harper Collins, 1998), 27.
2. Ibid., 28.
3. Ibid., 21–43.
4. Wally Olins, *Corporate Identity* (Cambridge, MA: Harvard Business School Press, 1990), 28.
5. Jeffrey Abrahams, *The Mission Statement Book* (Berkeley: Ten Speed Press, 1999), 78.
6. Ibid., 96.
7. Ibid., 132.
8. Ibid., 394.

REVIEW

Summary

Designers need to understand the specific realities of the projects they design. The basic understanding of a project is acquired during the predesign phase. In general, designers need to get a good understanding of the realities of the context, the internal players, and those of the project itself.

All projects occur within, and are influenced by, specific historic, cultural, and geographic contexts. Additionally, and varying from project to project, are the contextual realities of both the immediate surroundings of a project and the building in which it occurs.

The immediate neighborhood provides an important context with specific adjacent buildings, important long-standing patterns, and so on. The site and nearby surroundings provide specific natural features, circulation patterns, and points of access to the building. Environmental features such as the sun path, climate, sounds, sights, and smells are also crucial considerations.

The building in which the project takes place also offers an important context at an even more immediate scale. Particular aspects to be analyzed include the other tenants in the building and the public circulation inside the building. Additionally, it is necessary to analyze the physical features of the space designated for the project. A thorough understanding of the space's size, geometry, internal components, perimeter conditions, views to the outside, and so on always provides essential information.

Another important aspect requiring proper understanding is the nature of the project's internal players, usually the client and the users. The users are those people for whom the building is intended. The building must, by all accounts, work for them and their own particular circumstances.

Perhaps the most important aspect requiring understanding is the project itself. All projects are instances of project types that have been designed and built before. Therefore, there is a substantial body of knowledge about most building types, as well as built examples, often nearby. Every type also has different applications, or subtypes. Even among different subtypes there are specific variations, like those among different kinds of clothing stores.

The specific requirements of the project must also be understood. Each part and its role in the overall scheme needs to be identified and understood. Additionally, the relationships among parts, their hierarchy, and the project's driving forces need to be analyzed and understood.

1. Cesar Pelli, *Observations for Young Architects* (New York: Monacelli Press, 1999), 126.
2. C. Moore, G. Allen, and D. Lyndon, *The Place of Houses* (New York: Holt, Rinehart & Winston, 1974), 102.
3. Ibid., 173.
4. Vitruvius, *The Ten Books of Architecture*, trans. Morris Hicky Morgan (New York: Dover Publications, 1960), 180–81.
5. Pelli, 181.
6. C. Heinsath, *Behavioral Architecture: Toward an Accountable Design Process* (New York: McGraw-Hill, 1977), 52.
7. Gary Moye, Facilities Program: International College, University of Oregon (Private Document, 1994), 3.
8. Donna Duerk, *Architectural Programming: Information Management for Design* (New York: Wiley, 1993).
9. Moore et al., 147–48.

Chapter Questions

1. Name and describe the four contextual aspects discussed under surroundings.
2. Name and describe the three contextual inside-the-building aspects discussed.
3. Explain the difference between clients and users.
4. Think of as many subtypes as you can for different kinds of retail stores, restaurants, and offices.
5. Name the various adjacency categories mentioned in this chapter.
6. What factors other than adjacencies can assist in grouping project parts?

Exercises

1. Analyze the building that houses your design department. Use diagrams to illustrate significant factors for the building's interior and the building's surroundings.
2. Analyze the building that serves as context to the project you are currently working on in your design studio. Use diagrams to illustrate significant exterior and interior factors.
3. Perform a typological profile study similar to the ones shown in this chapter for a church, your school building, a movie theater, and a ski club.
4. Produce a series of detailed bubble adjacency diagrams for your current project. Proceed hierarchically. First do one diagram of the main project parts, and then proceed to do one for each major department or section.
5. Formulate a series of concepts, characteristics, and strategies for your current project using:
   a) the format shown in Figures 5.36, 5.37, 5.38, 5.39, and 5.40
   b) the format shown in Figure 5.41.

CHAPTER 6
Ideation

- Explain the meaning and function of concepts in design.
- Explain the difference between character and organizational concepts.
- Identify the stages of concept development.
- Present an approach to spatial organization using the place elements.
- Explain how to select a design idea from a project's dominant issues.
- Suggest ways of formulating concept ideas.
- Explain how to draw parti and functional concept diagrams.
- Explain how to prepare graphically strong concept diagrams.
- Explain how to write concept statements.

Just as the success of any design will be limited by the wisdom of the concept it follows, the wisdom of any concept is limited by the vision and knowledge of the designer who conceives it.

—*Stanley Abercrombie*, A Philosophy of Interior Design

IN CHAPTER 5 WE LOOKED at some of the variables that make each project unique, such as the users, context, and program. We also explained the importance of making sense of large amounts of information and reviewed some of the graphic tools designers use to account for project requirements and their relationships. At the conclusion of the analysis stage, you should have a good understanding of the client's nature, the project's parts, how these relate, and the context (physical, cultural, and historical) in which the project will take place. In some cases, you may even have a preliminary vision for a potential design solution.

Ideation is one of the most critical stages of successful design. It is also one of the most challenging. After all the project entities have been accounted for and the relationships between parts have been understood and diagrammed many times over, designers have to come up with a suitable approach for the project. For some designers this is a paralyzing moment in the design process; for others it is the most exciting moment in the design process. You can compare what happens during this stage with the first broad strokes on a painter's canvas. These thoughtful first strokes communicate the artist's intentions and commit the painting to a certain approach, one that will be refined and added to as the work progresses. This chapter is about the process of moving from an understanding of the project and its requirements to the production of insightful concepts that respond to its unique circumstances. We emphasize the importance of achieving proper fit between the realities (needs, context, and so on) of the project and the approach taken to address them. We discuss the design concept, with a presentation of both character and organizational concepts. As you will see, the decisions made during this early design stage become the foundations upon which the rest of the design is built. It is essential, then, that they are sound and fitting.

SEARCHING FOR PROPER FIT

Designers are often hired to provide solutions to projects with complex and sometimes conflicting requirements. A company may want to reduce the amount of leased space while increasing morale and productivity; a store may want to emphasize certain merchandise without a decrease in sales of the deemphasized merchandise; a restaurant may want to increase seating capacity while preserving a sense of intimacy. Good solutions to these types of problems require imagination and insight on the one hand, balance and compromise on the other.

The concept of fit in design refers to the appropriate correspondence between a set of requirements and the design solution that addresses them. It is analogous to the correspondence between clothing and bodies. Using this familiar analogy, you can easily recall instances of great fit or tight fit. You may also recall instances when a pair of jeans was comfortable but was the wrong style, or when the jeans fit comfortably and were stylistically appropriate but were inappropriate for the occasion for which you needed them (a job interview, a wedding, and so on). Similarly, the concept of fit in interior design is concerned with issues of comfort, style, and occasion. One of its unique challenges, however, is that interior design concepts start with no predetermined form. Where in fashion you always know you are designing for the human body, with its predictable form and structure (despite the infinite particularities within the human body category), in contemporary interior design you not only dress the body, you shape it.

The ideation stage, more than any other, is responsible for establishing the design's basic fit in relation to the project's needs. During this stage of design the most basic overall decisions concerning project parts and places, as well as their placement, shape, and orientation, are made. The process of assembling places and functions, as you will see, involves much more than transposing adjacency diagrams to a given floor plate, placing dividing walls between functions, and then selecting elegant finishes. This rarely produces a satisfying design. A successful design requires the organization of all required functions within a coherent conceptual and physical structure that will make users' experiences orderly and engaging. This is accomplished with an insightful and fitting overall basic strategy, also known as the **design concept**. The concept produced during this stage is eventually developed, refined, and articulated to achieve the final design.

THE CONCEPT

A successful design possesses a structure that is uniquely derived from the requirements of the project and a character that reflects the nature and personality of the users. These are the attributes that give the project a real sense of cohesion and identity. Yet the design concept remains one of the most misunderstood topics among interior design students. Part of the blame for this can be attributed to the myriad of existing definitions for "the concept" as well as the mystical connotations implied by some of them. Furthermore, no clear explanation of the process of generating concepts exists.

What Is a Design Concept?

American Heritage Dictionary defines *concept* as "a general idea or understanding, especially one derived from specific instances or occurrences."[1] Based on this definition, a concept in interior design could be said to be a general strategy or approach for the solution of a design problem having specific circumstances. A design concept aims to conceive a response to solve a design problem in a very particular way. Projects, however, are made up of not one but many problems of different scope and level of importance, and the solution to each of these problems requires the use of appropriate strategies. Each one of these ideas or strategies is a concept. There can, in fact, be dozens of concepts for a single project.

In order to work with concepts, then, you have to be able to understand their hierarchy. There are big concepts and little ones. It's the big concepts that we are most con-

cerned with here, although the smaller ones are important to resolve design issues at more detailed levels. Most important, those smaller concepts are subordinate to the big ones in such a way that, in the end, the finished product reads as one cohesive whole.

Every design project requires a main concept at the overall project scale. This **main concept** addresses the main design problems of the project and provides a dominant structure or idea that all other design ideas adhere to. While the distinction between major and minor concepts and the need for one big concept may seem plausible enough, there are still some nuances that need to be understood in order to grasp how to use concepts in design.

A major misconception about design concepts in design is the belief that they consist of one single big idea. While some main concepts may consist of a single idea, most consist of a handful of ideas that, together, constitute a single, or at least consistent, approach. Students are often paralyzed by the difficulty of having to synthesize an entire project into one idea when they are legitimately trying to respond to dozens of important issues. A concept consisting of a single idea is unrealistic in most cases. Thinking in terms of a series of ideas pointing to one dominant approach is a more realistic proposition.

Another misleading notion is the suggestion that concept ideas arise out of spontaneous flashes of inspiration. Again, this is far from the truth; neither students nor practitioners should sit and wait for such flashes to strike. The generation of concept ideas involves a great deal of systematic left-brain thinking and analysis. While it is true that ideas may arise spontaneously after a thorough analysis of the design problem and a period of incubation, there are no guarantees that this will happen. The best advice is to approach the process systematically and rely more on rational, insightful thinking than on flashes of inspiration.

To further confuse the novice, main concepts can be expressed in many different ways depending on the criteria used. Concepts can be philosophical (less is more, equal amounts of space for all, and so on), thematic (a western bar), functional (a two-wing configuration separating two distinct groups), artistic (a balanced composition of bold colors), mood related (a place that induces tranquility), or stylistic (a space that projects an outlook toward the future while remaining rooted in past tradition). Does the designer adopt one of each? Of course not. How can a designer arrive at a dominant concept then?

You may begin to realize the challenge of working with and selecting "the concept among concepts." Is there a best approach? Although there is no simple answer to this question, we can say that all projects have salient aspects that become important design drivers. These may be external, such as contextual forces, or internal, driven by function, desired image, or brand characteristics. Many projects have more than one such driving factor, and it is up to the design team to decide which factor or factors will drive the overall design response. The design response will, of course, translate into how the project's floor plan is organized (most visibly at first through diagrams and loosely drawn floor plans), what architectural forms and elements are adopted (most visibly at first through loosely drawn elevations and three-dimensional sketches), what detailing approach is used (most visibly at first through loose sketches), what materials are chosen (most visible at first through samples or rendered sketches), and what furnishings, accessories, and other appurtenances are incorporated.

In some cases, a particular way of performing the functions that occur in the project will drive the design. One example of this is the way the Swedish furniture company IKEA has chosen to display and sell their products. Their approach is quite different from the approach taken by conventional furniture retailers. At IKEA, the customer selects products from showroom areas on the upper floors, writes down the product information (name and number) on a note pad provided, and, ultimately, picks up the "boxed" products from the rows and rows of shelves on the warehouselike ground floor. One then proceeds, with oversized shopping carts full of boxes, to the checkout areas and pays and finally loads up the goods in the convenient loading areas just outside. To address this unique way of selling furniture, the entire facility is designed to facilitate the flow from one stage to the next.

Sometimes the main concept is driven by style, image, or theme. These tend to occur in highly creative environments such as restaurants, stores, clubs, and hotels. The intentionally minimalist showrooms designed by Claudio Silvestrin for Giorgio Armani are an example of these high-image kinds of projects.

At other times, a series of more pragmatic organizational concerns, such as relationships between departments and clear circulation systems, determines the main concept idea. Design concepts can only be determined on a case-by-case basis when the particularities of a project are known. They are externalized through verbal statements, concept diagrams, and concept sketches.

Design Concept Statements

Written statements are most often used to convey character (image) concepts. They come in many varieties. Upon examination of the many kinds of concept statements ordinarily written by students and practitioners alike, one notices a broad range of approaches with different degrees of clarity. Some designers repeat, sometimes in great detail, the needs and wants of the client; others write detailed play-by-play accounts of the experience, starting with the moment one enters the space; some talk about their intentions to create a productive office or a stimulating restaurant. The list goes on and on. The problem is that many written concept statements never get to the point.

The point of design concept statements is to tell the audience, as efficiently as possible, about the designer's approach to solve the design problem. Your statement may be as brief as "to create an intimate candlelit environment comprised of multiple zones" or "to place all the important public functions along the perimeter of the space to take advantage of the magnificent views." The main thing is that the design concept statement needs to address what you will do (or have already done) to solve the design problem.

As straightforward as this may appear, many young designers struggle with written concept statements. Let's examine four of the most common problems.

Problem 1: Statements that regurgitate the project goals from the program.

> For example, someone may repeat "the concept is to create a new office facility for a client that wants to consolidate units" directly from the information given in the program. This information is not a design concept but part of the design problem definition.

Problem 2: Statements that state the obvious.

For example, "the concept is to create a productive and functional office environment" or "the concept is to design a restaurant that will attract customers." It is obvious that offices need to be productive and restaurants need to attract customers. Those things go without saying. A design concept statement has to go beyond that.

Problem 3: Statements that use many adjectives without really saying much.

For example, "the concept is to design a grand and magnificent space that will be a source of delightful inspiration to all." This may be an adequate beginning but is still too vague; plus, there are many ways of producing grand and magnificent spaces and no hint is given here about the specific approach to be taken.

Problem 4: Statements that are lengthy descriptions of every single feature of the project.

There is no need to describe every feature of the project in the concept statement; the statement should include only the main aspects that are driving the design.

What then makes a good concept statement? Although there are many approaches to the verbal externalization of concept statements, the best concept statements share the following three attributes:

1. Design concept statements speak more about the design solution than the design problem.
2. Design concept statements are selective.
3. Design concept statements are economical.

Let's examine these one at a time.

Design concept statements speak about the design solution.

The first attribute requires that the concept state something about the design solution and not the design problem. These are two closely related but different elements that together help to give the project definition. The design problem, however, precedes the design strategy to be used. Consider the following statement: "The concept was to create a luxury residence for discerning, affluent empty-nesters and semiretired executives seeking a California coastal lifestyle." Is this a design concept? To test a concept to determine whether it is a design concept, simply ask yourself the following question: Does this statement tell me anything about the approach to the design solution? In the example above, the answer is no. While the statement tells us a great deal about what kind of residence the project will be, it defines the problem without stating the solution. Nevertheless, having a clear project definition is an important step that needs to take place before the design concepts are generated. Clients have to define, with some level of specificity, what type of project it will be, who is it for, whether it will be formal or casual, and so forth.

Consider now the following statement for a restaurant: The idea is to deliver "excellent food and service at a reasonable cost in a casual but intriguing environment," attracting "a wide range of customers—from formally dressed theater-goers to casually dressed diners."[2] Here again, the statement is helping to define the kind of restaurant it will be but, so far, is not saying anything about the designer's idea of how to accomplish this. The statement is part of the design problem statement, which speaks to the owner's goals and vision.

If the preceding statements are about design problem definition, the design concept has to be a response to these kinds of statements. So, the designer studies the situation, and after some consideration decides on a design approach to take. After all, many design solutions could reasonably produce the luxury residence and the casual and intriguing restaurant prescribed above. Let's examine a design concept statement written by a student to address an office project: "The concept behind my design . . . is openness and visual stimulation. All spaces are designed to pull you from one to the next smoothly. The angular rooms and shapes are intended to create an energetic feel in the workplace." Notice that the statement is talking about the designer's response to the design problem. Notice too that the statement mentions both the student's intentions (openness, stimulation, creating an energetic feel) and some specific ideas about how to achieve these (spaces that pull you, angular rooms and shapes). Now, consider another student's design concept statement for the same project: "The goal of this design is to create an innovative and dynamic environment that is attractive to Identity Consortium's image-conscious clients and employees. This is achieved through an open and flowing configuration of space and the use of modern classic pieces paired with an exposed and slightly industrial contemporary setting." Once again, notice the presence of both design intentions and more specific strategies for accomplishing them.

While the designer's initial design concept statement might be somewhat vague and broad, as the design progresses the means for achieving it become progressively more defined. Consider the following example, a Levi's Dockers Shop by Bergmeyer Associates, Inc. One can imagine how the designer (perhaps with help from the owner) may have come up with the main idea and how over time the more specific strategies (and other discarded ones) may have evolved.

What? (design idea): Design a store that "recalls soothing images of days on holiday."

How? (design strategy): Use "a nautical theme and vacation vignettes."

But how? (more specific design strategies): "Merchandise backdrops of wicker furniture and sailing, plus V-grooved panels stenciled with the Dockers logo, cherry soffits, and backlit art glass and props."[3]

Design concept statements are selective.

The second attribute of good design concept statements is selectivity. One cannot possibly hope to address every single issue of the project in the design concept. The process requires the designer to assess the design problem and exercise proper judgment in selecting the concept's driving forces. When we examine the design concept statement for an office project stated earlier ("The concept behind my design . . . is openness and visual stimulation. All spaces are designed to pull you from one to the next smoothly. The angular rooms and shapes are intended to create an energetic feel in the workplace.") we notice that the designer chose to focus on just two things: openness and visual stimulation. Surely there were many other important factors of that project but, for this designer,

openness and visual stimulation drove the main design direction. Here is another example: "The main concept behind my design is energy. By using an organic plan and strong color I hope to energize people and draw them through the entire space." A single idea—energy—was selected to lead the design approach.

Design concept statements are economical.

The third attribute of good design concept statements is economy. Consider the following succinct concept statement for a Los Angeles restaurant "featuring space-age dining for the jet set": "Use high-tech lighting and a lunar-look interior to invoke a futuristic fantasy that reflects the building's flying saucer architecture."[4] Beyond selectivity, this statement also exercises a great deal of economy by packing a lot of information into a rather brief statement. Even when one has more to say, it is possible to slim down the concept statement through selectivity and proper editing. In the concept statement for the Identity Consortium office project introduced earlier, the designer's main goal and three strategies to achieve it are packed into a 48-word statement. That's economical.

Design Concept Drivers

In the process of conceiving a design concept for a project, the designer will look at the realities of the project and decide how to express the main concept. This will depend on many factors, including the project type, inherent challenges of the site, the twist given to the project, personal intuition, and so on. Design concepts will range from the pragmatic to the symbolic and emotional. Next are some examples showing a variety of concepts driven by different aspects of the project.

The first example is driven by existing physical constraints on the project site. An Italian restaurant in Philadelphia occupied a space that was left over following the construction of a mezzanine office space. As a result, the ceiling over most of the restaurant was low, presenting a difficult design challenge. The design concept involved finding an inventive solution to this problem. The designer's response? "Create a vaulted ceiling in the high space along the window dining section to achieve volume. Use floating abstract planes in the low-ceilinged areas to provide relief and achieve an attractive sculptural effect."[5]

Design concepts for restaurants are often determined by some sort of theme related to the kind of food served and its place of origin. If the theme is Italian, designers try to make patrons feel like they are in Italy; if the theme is French, attempts are made to recreate the feel of a French bistro or sidewalk cafe. Consider the following two examples:

RESTAURANT 1:

Food Concept: American Southwest

Designer's Idea: Convey the feeling of a stage set using abstractions of plateau landscapes and buildings as architectural elements.

Design Strategies: Utilize architecturally sculptured plaster walls painted with colors and textures found in the desert Southwest. Use simple, spare furnishings and halogen spotlighting to further enhance the stage-set character. [6]

RESTAURANT 2:

Food Concept: Caribbean seafood with a large market selection of fish and seafood.

Designer's Idea: Recreate a Caribbean great house with the influence of British colonial design elements.

Design Strategies: Use gentle arches to separate dining areas and highlight the seemingly domestic scale of architectural detailing. Use lattice, cove lighting, and tropical murals to further add to the feeling of endless tropical expanse. [7]

Design concepts for highly thematic kinds of projects such as restaurants, shops, and clubs usually allow the designer a great deal of room for creative and personal inspiration. Barbara Lazaroff explains the approach she took when confronted with the task of designing an Asian-French restaurant: "I began to sketch the yin and yang logo, and the 'energy waves' I added, along with the emotional ideas of balance and flow, were the inspiration for many of the forms at Chinois. . . . I wanted to create a relaxed, yet exotic environment. I refer to my design as 'my five-year-old fantasy of what China would look like'; it doesn't look like this, but who cares—all the better."[8]

Other ways of approaching design concept statements include the use of statements that try to paint a picture of the experience you can expect in, say, a restaurant, and statements that evoke a certain spirit, be it of a past era or a certain attribute, such as elegance, austerity, or intimacy. The next three concepts are examples of these approaches.

The first one, from a student, tries to evoke the warm, energetic, and pampering characteristics of a restaurant.

Patio

"Patio blends Japanese and Spanish architecture and flavors into an exciting experience that will warm you from the inside out. Cozy up in a booth to the glow of a candle or enjoy the energy of the kitchen as chefs prepare meals before your eyes. If you need some relaxation after a hard day in the office, sit down and enjoy appetizers in a lounge bed. Take off your shoes to feel the fresh cool grass against your toes in our indoor courtyard."

This concept statement uses enticing sensory images to communicate the experience of being at the restaurant. The final examples are concept statements for two perfumeries, the first, for Lancôme in Paris, is by Jacqueline and Henri Boiffils and the second, for The Garden Perfumery in London, is by McColl Architects.

Lancôme

Design Problem Definition: Create a combined shop/institute of beauty imbued in an atmosphere of aseptic luxury and elegance.

Design Concept: Create an establishment characterized by stripped-down structural austerity through the use of symmetrical forms, the strategic disposition of products, exhibited as if they were valuable jewelry or museum pieces. [9]

The Garden Perfumery

Design Problem Definition: Create a perfumery that reflects a combination of romanticism and a certain sophistication. Attract, through the design, passersby in this central and exclusive area of London.

Design Concept: Evoke the spirit of The Garden Perfumery's products through the products themselves. Display them in a diaphanous way, converting them into the principal decorative element, to which all other design decisions are subordinate.[10]

Organizational Concepts

We have made a distinction between character concepts, those which inform the image and identity of the

A   **B**

Figure 6.1: Scheme (a) is a better response than (b) to a given programmatic requirement to arrange private offices along the exterior perimeter of the building.

project, and organizational concepts, those which inform the organization and layout of a project. Character concepts give a project its image; organizational concepts help organize the project's parts. As we saw above, character concepts are usually formulated and expressed verbally. Organizational concepts can be described verbally but are most often externalized as diagrams.

A good organizational concept does several important things. First and foremost, it establishes a responsive scheme. It is the organizational idea behind it. Additionally, it provides a strong initial foundation for order, enrichment, and expression. We will examine each of these separately.

A   **B**

PEDESTRIAN ALLEY ⟵ LIVELY STREET ⟶

Figure 6.2: Scheme (b) provides a better response to the pedestrian alley on the east and the lively street on the north and turns its back to the service alley on the west.

Establishing a Responsive and Coherent Scheme

The **scheme** you develop from your concept must represent an appropriate response to the project type, its particular programmatic requirements, and the context in which it occurs. The fundamental organizational issues of a project are resolved at this stage. The examples below show both successful and unsuccessful early schemes in response to type, program, and context.

Figure 6.1, for instance, shows two designs for a law firm. The user has clearly stated the need that partner and attorney offices be located on the perimeter, by a window. Furthermore, the stipulation has been made that partner offices be located at corners. The scheme in 6.1b, however

considerate to the support staff, is wrong for this application. The scheme in 6.1a is more responsive to the programmatic requirements given.

Figure 6.2 shows two schemes for a casual restaurant in a northern climate. The restaurant faces a pleasant pedestrian alley on the east side, a lively street with shops on the north side, and a service alley on the west. Both schemes shown are workable; however, scheme 6.2b takes better advantage of the desirable exposure to the northern street and the pedestrian alley and, thus, is a better response to the particular contextual realities of the site. These examples, however simple and obvious, help to illustrate the common-sense notion that crucial project requirements require proper design responses.

The processes of establishing an organizational concept require that you think of the project as a puzzle of reduced but essential pieces that must be arranged with insight and precision. This has to happen first, before you get bogged down with the many little problems at the micro level. Those get resolved as the design is developed. Once a basic scheme has been devised, the details can be tested within the devised structure. At that point, the basic scheme generated from the organizational concept goes through a fine-tuning process, as all the detailed parts are plugged in. After a process of give and take, the scheme and all the project parts get resolved. This process itself produces changes along the way as new understandings are acquired.

A good organizational concept also helps to produce a coherent scheme. If a project's organization is to be ultimately coherent, it needs to be based on a solid foundation. That is why organizational concepts are so important. They force the designer to make explicit decisions about an organizational structure based on the particularities of the project. One of the necessary requirements to produce a basic scheme is thinking about the project in terms of a few essential components. Reducing the parts to a minimum requires some abstraction. Thinking in terms of the place elements introduced in Chapter 3 becomes extremely helpful. For instance, you may be able to abstract a complex project into four distinct domains and two centers of equal importance connected by a circulation system. For the purposes of the scheme, the project is reduced to six main components and a circulation loop. This makes it simple and focused. The aim is not to negate all the detailed pieces of the project but to collapse them into fewer groups.

Next, it is necessary to arrange these parts in response to the realities of the project. The main concerns are placement of parts, circulation, and configuration. Issues such as public versus private; the shape, size, and proportions of the site; and the hierarchical importance of the parts play a major part. Figure 6.3 a–c shows three possible schemes for the hypothetical four domains/two centers scenario

A **B** **C**

Figure 6.3: After distilling the fundamental parts of a project, you must decide how to arrange them as a system. There are many possible schemes composed of four districts and two centers. Three are shown here.

described above. We could easily and quickly think of a few additional configurations. The reduction of parts makes the exploration of scenarios easier and faster.

In addition to the tendency to try to solve everything at once, the tendency to literally transpose adjacency bubble diagrams into a given site and make that "the scheme" sometimes becomes a problem. This is where many projects lose their sense of coherence, becoming an agglomeration of parts rather than a unified structure. In a good project, a strong structure serves as a backbone to the scheme; the literal transposition of a bubble diagram into the site rarely produces such a structure. Figure 6.4 illustrates how the adjacency diagram for a small sales office can be manipulated and given different form to fit the circumstances. Figure 6.4a shows the diagram, 6.4b shows a literal translation, and 6.4c, 6.4d, and 6.4e show three different schemes based on the diagram. These diagrams can and must be controlled by the designer. Some configurations will address the project's circumstances better than others, and it is up to the designer to select the most responsive configuration.

Establishing Order, Enrichment, and Expression

One of the virtues of a scheme based on a sound structure is the order it automatically produces. Order implies proper arrangement, something that is determined during the development of the organizational concept. As we will see later, this order also needs to be made legible, a design concern that needs to be addressed and developed throughout the entire design process.

Simple arrangements tend to work best. While one may fear that a simple scheme will be dull and uninteresting, even the simplest schemes can be given enough perceptual interest through other means, such as the enrichment and expression techniques discussed later. Even if

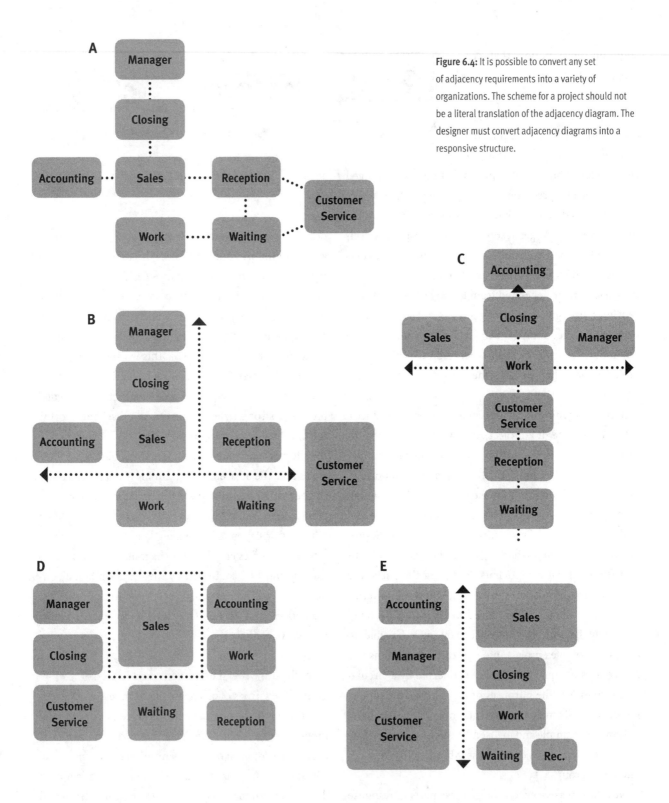

A

B

C

D

E

Figure 6.4: It is possible to convert any set of adjacency requirements into a variety of organizations. The scheme for a project should not be a literal translation of the adjacency diagram. The designer must convert adjacency diagrams into a responsive structure.

the project is inherently complex, it can be arranged in an orderly fashion and be clear and legible. You may find it useful to review the various space organizations presented in Chapter 4.

Similar to order, enrichment can be initiated during the ideation stage. An experienced designer thinks simultane-

ously about form and detail while generating organizational concepts. Young designers should also think simultaneously about order, enrichment, and expression while generating concepts. For now, refer to the simple manipulation for enrichment illustrated in Figure 6.5 a and b. Notice how the basic scheme was manipulated to produce a configura-

Figure 6.5: Drawing (a) shows the basic idea and drawing (b) the developed one. The curved forms and nodal points added in (b) provide a richer experience.

A

B

Figure 6.6: Subdividing into modules, adding parts, and projecting or recessing planes are all ways of articulating planes.

tion that provides a richer experience. While many such form manipulations occur later in the design process, they can be, and often are, introduced at this stage.

Expression normally has more to do with character as expressed in verbal design concepts like the ones introduced earlier in this chapter, yet some aspects of expression have to do with form and geometry, two aspects of design introduced at this stage of organizational concept development. Different arrangements, for instance, carry different connotations about levels of openness, formality, and progressiveness, while different sizes and geometries imply different levels of power and influence. Additionally, bold form, often introduced at this stage, can certainly be a very powerful expressive component of the design.

Not only do the size and proportions of rooms and spaces have expressive qualities, manipulations of the enclosing planes can also be rich in expression. Articulation and inflection of a scheme often start dur-

ing the concept generation stage. **Articulation** refers to the modification of planes or volumes by their skillful modulation into clearly expressed subparts to facilitate legibility, add interest, and afford order a greater degree of complexity. Some spatial articulation can occur during the ideation stage, while surface articulation usually occurs later in the process. Figure 6.6 shows three levels of surface articulation for a wall plane.

Inflection means deviation from a given course, as when a straight scheme becomes angular or curved. This type of manipulation, like articulation, often starts during the generation of the organizational concept. It is important to distinguish between articulation and inflection. Figure 6.7 shows three diagrammatic transformations of a straight wall into curved walls. In Figure 6.7b, the course of the wall stays the same and an undulating curvature is added for flair and interest. This is an example of articulation. In Figure 6.7c, the wall is no longer

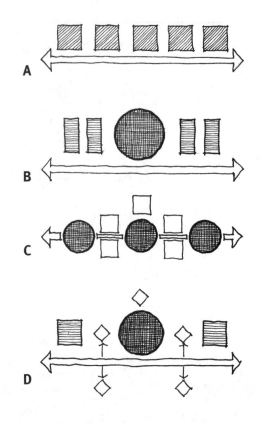

Figure 6.7: Scheme (b) articulates the straight wall, (c) inflects it, and (d) does both.

Figure 6.8: A basic plan arrangement can be transformed by using inflection and articulation. In these examples, straight paths and walls are transformed into angled and curving ones.

Figure 6.9: Spaces and functions in projects have different levels of importance or dominance. Some projects have no dominant space (a), while some have one or more centers (b–d).

a straight wall. It is now curving to the right. This is an example of inflection. Figure 6.7d combines the previous two examples to produce a wall that is both articulated and inflected from its original state. Figure 6.8 shows various straight and crossing path schemes transformed with angular and circular inflections.

Considerations in Determining a System of Organization

There are four important aspects to consider when coming up with the organizational concept for a project: placement, circulation, massing, and geometry.

Placement

One of the main challenges to be addressed with the organizational concept is determining where to place the different rooms and spaces that need to be accommodated. Factors involved include the function of each space, the relative prominence of each space, and the relationship

among the spaces. It is also helpful to think in terms of the place elements introduced in Chapter 2.

Because of their functions, various rooms require proper placement: Public areas generally want to be in the front, private areas need to be tucked away, and shared areas should be centrally located. Some spaces may be prominent due to their symbolic importance (a grand dining room) or their functional importance (the sample room in a design firm). Both rooms need special placement consideration; however, the grand dining room could be placed at one end of the building with, perhaps, a grand corridor leading up to it and the sample room needs to be centralized in relation to the design studios.

In terms of hierarchy, you may have one project in which all spaces have approximately equal importance or prominence and, at the other extreme, another project in which a single space is dominant. The hierarchical combinations are virtually limitless (e.g., a project with three

Figure 6.10: This basic concept diagram (a) and developed floor plan (b) for an academic building project feature a dense layout of enclosed rooms and one distinct area of prominent shape and location.

major and five minor spaces and a project with one dominant, two intermediate, and five minor spaces). Projects will suggest specific arrangements in most cases. The diagrams in Figure 6.9 a–d illustrate these examples. Figure 6.10 a and b includes a concept diagram for an administrative suite in an academic building where the main shared public spaces get a prominent location and unique shape and the resulting floor plan.

The way spaces relate to one another will also determine their organization as a system. Relationships determine issues of proximity. Some spaces may belong together and form a cluster. Other spaces may need to be as far apart as possible. Relationships also determine issues of centrality. Some spaces, like the sample room discussed earlier, need to be accessible to other spaces and, therefore, need to be centralized. In Figure 6.11, a scheme for the afore-

mentioned academic building is based on the designer's understanding of how the different units function in relation to one another. Because of their autonomous functions, the designer treated them as independent suites, adjacent to one another but not connected.

In terms of placement, the designer decides who gets the "sweet spots" and who gets the undesirable pockets, who gets the peace and quiet and who gets the noise, who gets the morning sunlight, who gets the afternoon sunlight, and who gets no exposure to the sun at all. Who gets the window? Who gets the nice view? Who gets the exposure up front? These and other similar questions need to be addressed in the process of placing the spaces of a project. Fortunately, these decisions are not made in a vacuum. As we saw in Chapter 5, all project types require basic configurations in order to function properly. Nevertheless, there is room for variation. Does the bar in a restaurant always need to be close the entrance? Do private offices always need to be on the perimeter? Obviously, the answer is no.

It is useful to think of a project in terms of the place elements introduced in Chapter 3 in order to arrange its parts. Arrival places, paths, nodes, districts, and centers are especially useful for the overall organization of space in interior projects. You may think of destination places as either centers or districts, or you may treat some intersections as special nodes. Figure 6.12 shows diagrams for a hypothetical retail store and a shopping center, both reduced to these five elements.

The other place elements should not be underestimated at this early stage. They too can become important elements in the organization of a project. Figure 6.13a shows a conceptual diagram for a project in which a strong separating element (edge) is a crucial part of the concept. Figure 6.13b shows the diagram for a project in which a landmark is central to the concept scheme.

Circulation

In Chapter 4 we discussed the important role of movement in the shaping of space. Quite simply, you cannot generate an organizational concept without committing to a circulation system to link your spaces. Whether movement will be free or constrained, dignified or casual, grand or minimal needs to be reflected in the organizational concept. One of the main aspects an organizational concept must clearly show is the main circulation pattern being proposed. Consider the circulation pattern shown in Figure 6.14 a and b, and compare it to the circulation patterns shown in Figures 6.10 and 6.11; the three very different circulation approaches for the same project greatly affect the resulting schemes. Once again, refer to the organization systems presented in Chapter 4.

Figure 6.11: This diagram shows a radically different idea for the same project shown in 6.10. Here the area is subdivided into more private suites to give departments the autonomy they desire and to enhance department recognition. Moving the main circulation to the perimeter makes better use of the magnificent views beyond the long, tall glass wall.

Figure 6.12: These concept diagrams are depicted in terms of our five basic place components: arrival space (A), paths, centers (C), domains (D), and nodes (N).

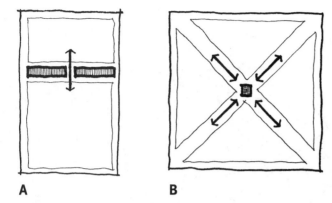

Figure 6.13: Diagram (a) shows a project with a strong edge separating two sections. Diagram (b) shows a project with a central landmark as generative force.

Figure 6.14: These two concepts feature strong diagonal circulation within different configurations.

Figure 6.15: These two concept diagrams for an office suite successfully group the enclosed areas and pull them away from the window to create comfortable open areas adjacent to the perimeter light and views.

Massing

The best organizational concept diagrams address the massing of the overall project. Specifically, they address the relationship between enclosed areas (solids) and open spaces (voids). One of the difficulties young designers have is in clearly visualizing three-dimensionally what they are creating with their schemes. Common problems are the creation of masses having awkward configurations and plans that are excessively fragmented.

The goals are to create masses with good configurations and to create well-shaped and comfortably scaled open areas. Specific strategies include grouping enclosed rooms together, attaching to existing walls or masses instead of starting new ones, and carefully watching the integrity of the shapes of both the solid masses and the open area. Figure 6.15 a and b shows a scheme in which the enclosed rooms of an office suite have been carefully grouped, resulting in masses of good shape and comfortable open areas. Generally speaking, it is a good practice to have less rather than more masses in space and simple rather than complex configurations.

Figure 6.16: Notice these two schemes for the academic building introduced in Figure 6.10. Although both schemes aim to bring users to a central node, the resulting experience is very different by virtue of their respective geometric compositions.

Geometry

Another aspect that should be visible from the organizational concept diagrams is the intended geometry for the project. Is it straight? Angular? Circular? Many projects are straight; many others have interesting geometries, some using angles, some using curved surfaces, some using combinations. Whatever the intentions, they should start being visible in the diagrams produced during the ideation phase. Figure 6.16 shows two diagrams for the same project, each with its own unique organization and geometry. Notice the impact the geometry has.

Stages of Concept Generation

The process of generating concepts varies from designer to designer; however, the process of concept generation should encompass a handful of important steps. In the next few paragraphs, we explain these steps and recommend a sequence that will help you become comfortable with this important design stage.

As we said earlier, at the heart of a concept is an idea or series of ideas that establishes the basic design approach for the project. There can be subapproaches that complement the main approach, but a strong concept has to have one identifiable main approach. The formulation of this approach (or structure, in the case of organizational concepts) is the main goal of the concept generation process. There are, however, other tasks that must occur before and after this formulation. We recommend the following stages of concept development:

1. Understand the project.
2. Identify salient issues.
3. Conceive workable approaches.
4. Externalize the approaches.
5. Evaluate the approaches.
6. Consolidate ideas and choose a direction.

A good concept relies on the proper understanding of the project and identification of its *salient issues*. Once you have identified these salient issues, you are ready to use logic and intuition to formulate potential design approaches. These approaches are then externalized through drawings and verbal statements. Once externalized, you can evaluate them, consolidate ideas if necessary, and, ultimately, choose the most appropriate direction.

Understanding the Project

In Chapter 5 we discussed the factors that make up a project's reality: the nature of a project's user population, the realities of its context, and the requirements of the program. Chapter 5 also reviewed some of the tools used by designers to consolidate and make sense of information. The understanding of this information is basic to the development of appropriate concepts and must precede the concept generation stage. Additionally, an understanding of the project as an example of a particular type as well as a unique manifestation of that type is also useful for the generation of concepts. The level of understanding achieved during the early stages of a project represents just the initial level of the project's understanding. You will never have the luxury of full understanding at the onset, but you will hopefully understand the requirements and existing realities enough to move forward. The more you get immersed in the project, the greater the level of insight and understanding become, resulting in design refinements as you go.

Identifying Salient Issues

At this stage, it is not enough to understand the project's users, context, type, and program. To truly understand the essence of a project, the designer needs to exercise his or her judgment in order to identify its *salient issues*. These vary from project to project, and sometimes they are more obvious than others. A particular program requirement, a crucial functional relationship between project parts, a gifted (or problematic) site exposure, a particular feature of the building or site, and a desire for a particular historical or symbolic gesture are all examples of salient issues.

Some projects are loaded with salient issues, while in others the designer may struggle to identify a handful. Salient issues can be self-evident (as in the case of a project within a historical district) or explicitly requested by the user (as in the case of a particular relationship between two departments or units). Some important issues are the product of reflection and insight (as when the designer realizes that a particular unit is more, or less, important than was previously thought). They can even be the product of an accidental discovery (such as the way the sun's rays penetrate one side of the building in the late afternoon). Completing statements like the ones listed below can help you identify salient issues for a project.

- This project is all about . . .
- Truly significant aspects of the site include . . .
- Unique aspects of this project include . . .
- The functional requirements obviously point to an organizational pattern that . . .
- A few adjectives that fit this project are . . .

Once you have identified some salient issues you must choose which ones to use to generate the project's design concept. When it comes down to generating ideas for concepts, designers have to rely on their ability to think not only analytically but creatively, and to make selections from among competing ideas. Once the salient issues are identified, you must scrutinize them closely and pinpoint their relative importance and their potential to influence decisions about organization, form, and aesthetics. Figure 6.17 shows the salient issues for a hypothetical project.

Figure 6.17: The four considerations listed are important issues to address; each has the potential to become the dominant aspect of the concept.

Conceiving Workable Approaches

The next task is going from a short list of salient issues to concept ideas. There is a myth that concepts have to be unique and different. This is not so. While concepts are often unique and different, they are frequently straightforward and ordinary. There are times, in fact, when the most extraordinary thinking results in ordinary, but fitting, design approaches. While insight and creativity play a role in the generation of concepts, rational, systematic thinking is just as important.

A period of reflective, critical thinking follows the generation of salient issues. This is usually done with pencil in hand, as many ideas are sketched loosely in diagram form along the way. The goal is to generate ideas for the main approach, ideas that respond to an important essence of the particular design problem. Some designers believe there is a period of incubation during which the subconscious digests information, eventually leading to inspiration and insight. This inspiration and insight, again, does not necessarily lead to innovation and far-out ideas but to a focused, appropriate response. The ideas are the result of insight, not divine inspiration. You could call it informed and fitting inspiration.

The ideas generated in response to salient issues may come up as a logical, sequential development or may pop up either while sketching or even unexpectedly, while doing something else. Ideas usually arise as thoughts, mental pictures, or diagrams or drawings while you sketch. It is important to capture ideas when they arise, even before judging them. We recommend that students initially generate and record more than one (approximately three) design concept approaches. As a rule of thumb, if it pops up in your brain, record it. This brings us to the next step, formalizing the approach through externalization.

Externalizing the Approaches

The two ways to externalize concept approaches are visual and verbal. Visual approaches include diagrams and sketches; verbal approaches can be short statements, such as the ones shown earlier in this chapter, or longer descriptive scenarios. Let's take a closer look at each of these approaches.

Short statements can be effective for recording ideas, even when dealing with organizational ideas. A good short statement should include a description of a physical arrangement or relationship and the effect it produces. For example, the following two statements serve to concisely articulate a specific design intention: "a binuclear arrangement that splits control" or "a long evocative wall that provides a strong linear and unified backdrop to activity." Statements don't need to be long, provided they express the basic approach clearly.

Scenarios are longer descriptions that describe a sequence of events and their effect. Scenarios get more specific and detailed. Although scenarios are better suited as tools to articulate experiential intentions later during the development phase, they can be used to describe complex relationships or projects whose functions have a sequential nature. They are also helpful, given their highly descriptive nature, to integrate organizational and character concepts. The following scenario integrates the organizational and character concepts for a hypothetical restaurant/bar:

The project consists of a series of aligned chambers, each transversed by a cross-axis leading to related zones at either end, except the last one, which includes an additional termination point straight ahead. One enters into a small chamber that serves as a welcoming area. To either side are waiting areas, each one having its own unique character. Moving forward, one enters the second chamber. To the right is a bar area, to the left a comfortable lounge. Next is the third chamber, which leads to two dining areas, one on either side. The one on the left is more private and formal. Still ahead are two more chambers. The next one incorporates a bar within it and leads to two different lounge areas. These are more part of the club than the restaurant. Finally, the last chamber, which also serves as a control point to the club. Straight ahead is a dancing area with a band stage at the very end. To the left is a bar and informal seating area (more for standing and hanging out). To the right is a more comfortable seating area.

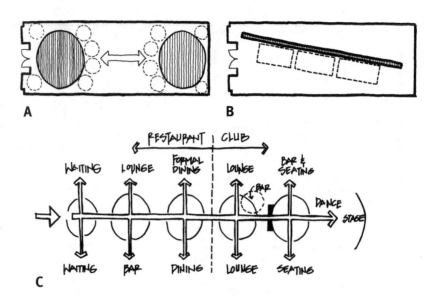

Figure 6.18: Graphic diagrams convey ideas differently than verbal descriptions. The overall organization is grasped almost instantaneously.

Scenarios are tools to describe qualitative attributes of projects. It would be easy to take the previous scenario to the next level of detail. Notice how the added qualifiers and details paint a more vivid picture of the scene:

The project consists of a series of aligned cylindrical chambers. They are each distinct in their finishes, progressing from the subtle to the bold, and are transversed by a cross-axis expressed by straight paths from side to side, which lead to related zones. . . . One enters into the first chamber, the smallest and the only one immediately adjacent to the exterior. During the day it is bathed in natural daylight that reflects off the light-colored fabric on the walls and the polished stainless steel trim. This chamber serves as a welcoming area, incorporating a free-form cherry wood and green marble maître d' station. To either side are waiting areas. The one on the right is neutral, formal, and elegant; the one on the left is casual and a bit more colorful, the wood becom-

ing reddish. As one moves forward, one enters the second chamber after passing a low, dark, and compressed transitional space.

While these scenarios are good tools for developing and externalizing, keep in mind that the eventual concept statement written for the project should be brief, as emphasized earlier.

Diagrams, as we have seen, are great devices for recording organizational concepts. Proper evaluation of organizational concept ideas cannot occur without some form of plan diagram that gives preliminary architectural form to the idea. Figure 6.18 a–c, for instance, shows diagrams of the three concepts described above by short statements and scenarios.

Also useful in addition to plan diagrams are three-dimensional sketches. When it is necessary to address qualitative issues or visualize three-dimensional form, it is useful to turn to **conceptual sketches** instead of diagrams. The three-dimensional sketches in Figure 6.19 for the long wall scheme and the first chamber of the restaurant/bar are more effective than the plan diagrams in conveying a loose idea of the spatial qualities of these spaces. Conceptual sketches make it easier to visualize ideas and make their subsequent evaluation easier.

Figure 6.19: Three-dimensional concept sketches force designers to illustrate, and others to see, a more literal translation of design ideas.

Evaluating the Various Approaches

The evaluation of concept ideas is one of many instances of evaluation during the design process. Each stage of design requires at least one formal evaluation. During the ideation stage, both the quality of the approaches generated (the soundness of the ideas) and their design interpretation (their actual interpretations on paper) should be scrutinized, however vague and abstract they are at this point. As you evaluate, you should ask yourself the following questions: Is this approach appropriate and fitting given the realities of the project? Is it likely to facilitate meeting the project goals? Below, we evaluate the three examples given earlier.

1. Binuclear Scheme
   - Does it make sense to divide the project into two nuclei, as proposed?
   - Is the proposed way of doing this (in Figure 6.18a) appropriate?
   - Could the idea of separation, if deemed appropriate, be interpreted differently?
2. Long Evocative Wall Scheme
   - Is the idea of the long wall appropriate?
   - Does it address one of the main project issues?
   - Could it be executed successfully?
   - Are there other approaches to achieve the desired simplicity and unity?

3. Multichamber Scheme
   - How much does the chamber idea contribute to the desire to subdivide the project into zones?
   - Is it really necessary to subdivide the project?
   - How would these spaces be perceived?
   - Is the resulting fragmentation detrimental?
   - Are there other ways of implementing such a scheme?

Raising these types of questions helps to discard or modify problematic ideas and retain only the best. These are not the questions you want to be asking late during design. These are fundamental form-generating issues, and once you buy into them you want to commit to them for the duration of the project.

Given the sequential nature of the design process, it is important to resolve issues appropriate to any given stage prior to moving on. The next stage will have its own group of challenges requiring attention. Ideas adopted during any given stage will provide a foundation for the next stage. It would be wasteful to start second-guessing and changing concept ideas late during the design, when layers of additional decisions have been made based on the earlier ones.

Consolidating Ideas and Choosing a Direction

Having evaluated the merits of a concept or group of concepts and identified the merits and drawbacks of each, you are in a position to choose the best idea or, possibly, combine aspects of various schemes in order to generate a new hybrid concept. The goal is to select a winning concept for further development. In some cases, time and other resources permitting, you may carry more than one concept forward for further exploration.

DIAGRAMS

While language, both spoken and written, is the vehicle to describe character concepts, graphic diagrams are the vehicles to externalize, visualize, and communicate organizational concepts. These are usually in the form of sketchy, diagrammatic floor plan views, although three-dimensional drawings are also possible. There are many styles of drawing diagrams. Two particularly useful and straightforward types are presented here: parti diagrams and functional diagrams.

Parti Diagrams

The *parti diagram* represents the scheme at its most basic. It expresses the essence of the solution without getting into any kind of detail. In order to capture only the basic essence,

it distills the approach to its most basic components, nothing less and nothing more. If the approach is rigid, formal, and symmetrical, it captures that symmetry and formalism. If the approach is curvilinear and divides the project into two nuclei, it captures that flair and division. The parti diagram is not concerned with details about specific areas; that's the realm of the functional diagram.

A good parti idea helps to establish a sound organization on which to develop the rest of the project. It helps to communicate the single most dominating idea. Figure 6.20 shows two parti diagrams for the same office project. The diagram in Figure 6.20a consists of two movement axes (the principal originating at the entry point) intersecting at 90 degrees at a central, important space. From there, the axes continue toward three special end destinations. The leftover spaces define four zones or districts within which the project's functions will be organized. The diagram in Figure 6.20b shows a simple loop around a central rectangular mass with a special destination at one of the far corners. Three leftover zones are defined, two long and narrow ones along the main sides and one at the far end of the building.

Functional Diagrams

Functional diagrams are an outgrowth of the parti diagram that include more detail. They show the massing of the project (enclosed versus open areas), the organization (linear, radial, looped, and so forth), the main circulation system, and the specific placement of prominent destinations. They are typically shown diagrammatically but close to scale. While the parti diagram establishes the basic approach to the solution, the functional diagram starts testing its workability. It starts looking more like a floor plan, although an abstract one. In the process of doing one or more of these you start realizing that some ideas work better than others. In cases where a good concept idea proves unworkable you must revise or abandon it. Figure 6.21 a and b shows the parti and functional diagram for an office project.

It is likely that you have already used block plans in your design process. Functional diagrams are similar to block plans, yet they differ in two important ways. With block plans there is the dangerous tendency to lay out a bunch of rectangular shapes on the plan to see if and

Figure 6.20: Two parti diagrams show the basic essence of the scheme: arrival point, movement system, basic arrangement, basic geometry, and special destinations.

A

B

A

B

Figure 6.21: Functional diagram (a) and parti (b) for an office project. Notice the difference in the amount of information and detail between them.

how they fit. They typically lack imagination. Functional plans, in contrast, are based on powerful (we hope) organizational structures that give projects cohesiveness and personality. They include additional information, such as massing, and they also define a specific geometry for the project. Relationships from the bubble diagrams are respected but do not dictate the scheme.

The second difference is their scope. The purpose of block diagrams is to solve the puzzle of space distribution. The design problem is seen as the need to fit and distribute spaces in the site. Functional diagrams go beyond this requirement and make conscious efforts to create meaningful places at different scales and provide a stimulating experience. A good functional diagram, for instance, not only identifies separations between parts but makes initial decisions about the character of such separations. Additionally, early ideas about the experiential character of circulation, the manipulation of daylight and views, and the location of focal points and planes are explored in the functional diagram.

Like block plans, functional diagrams are also responsible for making all the requirements fit and for respecting the desired adjacencies. In fact, the determination of locations for the different functions and their sizes, con-

figuration, subdivision, and relationships all need to be addressed and resolved in the functional diagram. The thing to remember is that all this is done within the context of creating a strong sense of place and a stimulating experience. Notice the difference between the block diagram in Figure 6.22b and the functional diagram in Figure 6.22a.

Despite the relative accuracy needed for functional diagrams, they should be loose enough to facilitate speed in generating them. Two important requirements toward this end are to draw them freehand and to use bubbles and other abstract representations of space and spatial features. Keeping the process loose and quick allows the designer to explore different alternatives during the ideation stage of design, plus it encourages spontaneity. Having multiple schemes enriches the process of exploration. If you draw the contents to scale and with acceptable precision, you will have specific reliable criteria to judge against while you make informed evaluations and selections.

A

B

Figure 6.22: The differences between a (b) block and a functional (a) diagram for a project can be considerable. The block diagram may help sort out spaces, but the functional diagram incorporates more design thinking, displaying a specific design approach and incorporating focal points, important nodes, and so on.

Figure 6.23: Personal concept sketches are usually very quick and loose.

Graphics for Diagrams

Diagrams help us communicate with ourselves and others. They help us capture ideas when they arise and record them for later use. Concept diagrams that arise while we generate ideas can be quite personal and loose. There is no need to be too careful when sketching these for your own use. In fact, looseness and spontaneity are to be encouraged during the creative process. There will be plenty of opportunity to develop them later. Figure 6.23 shows examples of some of these kinds of loose concept diagrams.

When diagrams go from private to public they require an increased level of clarity and resolution. In this section, we address the qualities that public diagrams must possess and the graphic techniques to produce them.

Requirements

A good public diagram, whether a parti or functional diagram, possesses three basic virtues: clarity of content, clarity of intention, and economy of means. *Clarity of content* means that all the pertinent pieces for that diagram need to be shown and delineated clearly. *Clarity of intention* means that the design intent, at all levels, needs to be clear enough so others can understand it. *Economy of means* ensures that information is kept simple. For both parti and functional diagrams the designer decides what will be included and excluded. For parti diagrams, the designer must show the essence of the approach with the fewest possible elements. For functional diagrams, the designer must present a more thorough and inclusive idea without including too much detail.

Of particular importance for clarity of intention is differentiation through hierarchy. Accordingly, the graphics you use in your diagrams must be hierarchical. The types of symbols you use, the weight you give them, and how you use tone and texture are crucial if you want to produce clear, readable, good-looking diagrams. Figure 6.24 shows two levels of graphic resolution. Figure 6.24a is clean but flat. Even though all the parts are there, the diagram lacks differentiation. Figure 6.24b

incorporates a hierarchy of line weights and different arrow types. It has tone, texture, and special symbols to represent areas of special importance. The second diagram contains more layers of information than the first due to the increased sense of hierarchy. The effect is impact and appeal.

Diagram Grammar

You only need to use a few symbols and a handful of simple graphic techniques to produce clear and strong diagrams. Only three types of basic symbols are necessary to produce concept diagrams: bubbles to define areas, lines with arrows to indicate circulation, and special symbols to represent special spots or events. Next, you need ways to differentiate among same type symbols to convey hierarchy. This is accomplished by varying the size of the symbol, the line weight of its outline, and/or the texture you use inside the symbol. Figure 6.25 shows some of the various symbols and their variations. That's your vocabulary. It's that simple. The secret lies in practicing and becoming competent at executing these drawing techniques. Figure 6.26 shows two very simple abstract diagrams in a basic and enhanced form.

Figure 6.24: Two levels of diagram graphic resolution.

Figure 6.25: The graphic vocabulary for diagramming includes graphic symbols to differentiate bubbles for hierarchy, different lines and arrow styles to indicate movement systems, and special symbols to convey special locations.

Figure 6.26: These simple diagrams show the enhanced readability of diagrams achieved when you use simple graphic devices, such as varied line weights and textures inside the shapes.

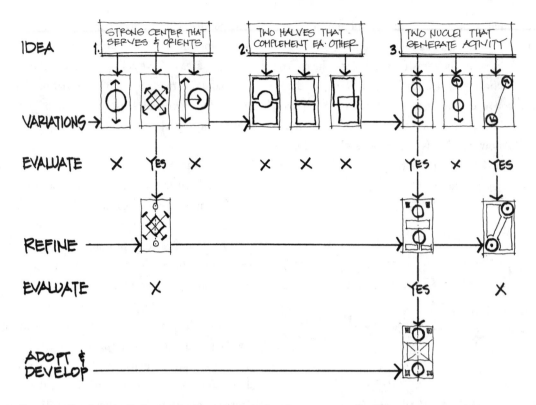

Figure 6.27: Hypothetical path of concept development and selection.

Diagram Development

Depending on your habits and personality, you might be the type who likes to work with only one idea at a time—staying with it, modifying it, and transforming it until it is resolved. Conversely, you may prefer to generate multiple ideas with variations and narrow them down through successive evaluations and selections until you have arrived at the winning solution. The second approach is the one we recommend to young designers. Seasoned designers may have success with the focused approach, but the rest of us will have a greater chance of arriving at an optimal solution by exploring multiple ideas. The only caveat here is for those who might be inclined to exaggerate and explore too many ideas, and for those who get stuck with several ideas and cannot decide on one and move forward. If you have such tendencies, be aware of it and put some limits on your horizontal thinking. Figure 6.27 shows, in diagram form, a hypothetical path to a winning solution using the multiple idea approach.

The Next Task of Design

The tangible outcome of the ideation stage is a solid design direction for the project. It will consist of two concepts, one to capture the desired image or character and the other to determine the project's physical organization.

The next task is development. There is usually some overlap between tasks, and, before the end of ideation, you may have already taken some steps toward establishing ideas related to development. During the development stage you elaborate and refine your design ideas and intentions. This leads to the necessary modifications and manipulations that help transcend mere utility and embody the project with a real sense of place, full of order, enhanced experience, and expression.

One of the remarkable aspects of design is that, despite the constraints imposed by the requirements of a project, there is ample opportunity for personal interpretation. A good way to illustrate this is to compare library designs by two late, famous architects: Louis Kahn and Alvar Aalto. Kahn's library at the Phillips Exeter Academy and Aalto's at Mount Angel Abbey are projects whose forms, although derived based on similar understandings of the needs of a library, differ substantially.

Exeter Library was conceived both as a place to celebrate knowledge (through books) and a place for community (students coming together). Kahn saw a library "as a place where the librarian can lay out books . . . and the reader should be able to take the book and go to the light." He felt that reading should occur individually by a window, in a private carrel. In response to this his design solution consisted of two concentric square doughnuts, the outer one being the place to read by the light, away from the books. The inner doughnut was the place to store books away from the harmful effect of direct sunlight. The hole in the middle was a great central space, a multistory atrium from which one can enter and see books all around through large circular openings. In this fashion the invitation to books takes place, and one can grab a book and go to the light to read (Figure C6.1). The central hall is the heart of the building as community,

Figure C6.1

Figure C6.2

both symbolically and functionally, for it is there that you run into and interact with others.

The design for Mount Angel Abbey Library, like that of Exeter, was developed in part based on the relationship between a person and a book in light. At Mount Angel Abbey we also find carrels and reading rooms around the perimeter, by the light. The book stacks are toward the center, between the readers and the central area, similar to Kahn's approach at Exeter. That is, however, where the planning similarities between these projects end. While concentric square doughnuts defined Exeter's form, Mount Angel Abbey's form is fan-shaped, as is the case with other Aalto libraries. Although his fascination with this shape is seen in many of his other buildings, the use of the fan shape is especially appropriate in his libraries. One of the basic functional requirements of library buildings is the need for a control point from which the librarian assists and monitors patrons. Aalto gave great importance to such points, placing them at the narrow end of his fan-shaped buildings, the rest of the library expanding outward from it (Figures C6.2 and C6.3). The book stacks are arranged radially from the desk such that the librarian has visual control over the entire library space.

Although there is no monumental lobby space at Mount Angel, Aalto provided a space to serve as the heart of the library and, like at Exeter, one from which the library and the books are seen and the invitation to books

Figure C6.3

Figure C6.4

occurs. This is the mezzanine between the control desk and the rest of the library. It is enhanced with dramatic lighting, making it an important focal area. This circular area features counters and chairs and is itself an interior place for reading. Although it is not at the perimeter, like Kahn's reading areas were required to be, the abun-

dance of natural light it receives makes it consistent with the idea of reading by the light (Figure C6.4).

These two libraries, designed by two of the greatest architects of the modern era, are both exceptionally good libraries. While the basic type requirements for a library were well understood by both architects, they had enough differences of emphasis and interpretation to produce two radically different designs.

CAPSULE | The Quick Concept Diagram

Presented here is a quick approach to organizational concept generation. It consists of five steps:

1. Establish basic distribution of spaces
2. Establish main circulation
3. Articulate general solids, voids, and screens
4. Articulate and/or inflect the scheme
5. Test the idea

The first step consists of laying down on paper, more or less to scale, the basic spaces of the project. By basic we mean the principal areas. To do this, you have to generalize. If there is a requirement for a cluster of offices, for example, you use only one shape for the entire group. By grouping related functions together, you should be able to reduce the entire project into just a few components. Figure C6.5a shows the requirements for a hypothetical project expressed in terms of five areas placed within the project's site. For our purposes we will keep the example generic. Let's assume that the areas have been placed after carefully considering adjacency and exposure requirements.

The next step (often developed in conjunction with the first step) is to clearly establish the main circulation. Every project has a main axis, loop, or network for moving around. Your task is to decide where this main circulation goes and to reflect it in your concept diagram (Figure C6.5b).

The next step is to consider the project three-dimensionally. Up to now, we have been thinking about our hypothetical project in terms of five general areas. Now we start defining open and closed areas. Some of the areas are likely to be open, others are likely to consist of enclosed spaces, and still others may be a combination of open and closed. Furthermore, the relationships between the circulation path and open areas and between adjoining open areas may be open, closed, or somewhere between.

Figure C6.5c shows the areas of our hypothetical project articulated into closed rooms (shaded), open areas, and screening devices between areas. This is when you start to orchestrate the project massing by making these decisions and reflecting them on your study diagrams.

Figure C6.5 The three basic steps for "quick" organizational concept generation: Disposition of major spaces (a), introduction of main circulation (b), preliminary definition of solids, voids, and screens (c).

Figure C6.6 Articulation and inflection: You can establish some preliminary articulation early on (a), and/or inflection, if appropriate (b).

Work loosely on tracing paper, and don't be afraid to change or discard ideas. Crumpling a sheet of tracing paper with a bad solution into a ball and tossing it away can be as pleasurable as keeping a good one.

Once you have the basics of a solution established (which you think will actually work when tested), you may perform some basic articulations and/or you may inflect the scheme by turning it, curving it, and so on. Keep in mind that not all projects need to be turned or curved. Figure C6.6a shows our basic scheme with some form articulation added; Figure C6.6b shows it inflected through a diagonal maneuver. Don't get too detailed. Before you do so, you want to test your idea and see whether it is going to work. Up till now you have been using approximations and working loosely, and now is the time to draw the idea up at a larger scale, to draw furniture and other contents (quickly but accurately), and to see whether it really works. If you are lucky, it will work nicely, and all the pieces will fit efficiently and harmoniously. In most cases, though, you will find that you have to manipulate the geometry to make things work. In some cases, you will find that the idea requires so much modification that it loses its integrity. In those cases it is best to abandon the idea and pursue a new scheme.

Figure C6.7 shows six schemes for a hypothetical store project illustrating different ways of inflecting the forms. The space has been conceived as two longitudinal spaces connected side-to-side at various points. One of the long sides is a little wider and incorporates the cashier's station. Figure C6.7a shows the scheme in basic form with some definition starting to emerge at the transition zone. In C6.7b the side walls and the transition zone show a more refined articulation. Figure C6.7c is similar, but in it, an uneven spacing of the center columnlike element-

Figure C6.7 The same scheme (a) can be articulated and/or inflected many different ways. Articulation can establish a regular (b) or hierarchical (c) distribution. Inflection can be diagonal (d), undulating (e), or sweeping (f). There are many other possibilities in addition to these.

sYis explored. It results in a wider cross-opening at the center. Figure C6.7d explores a diagonal arrangement of the same basic idea, and Figures C6.7e and C6.7f explore curvilinear solutions. Notice that the idea is basically the same. Despite the wide variations of geometry, the concept scheme remains two elongated spaces with multiple connections between them.

You can see that the same basic idea can be varied through articulation and inflection. Deciding which scheme is the best for the project requires testing them to see which one works best and which one best reflects the personality of the project.

CASE STUDY

Sifting through Programmatic Complexity to Provide Clarity and Convenience: The Duchossois Center for Advanced Medicine

DESIGN FIRM: HLM DESIGN

Health-care projects are among the most complex design projects. The complexity is due in part to the many functions involved and the intricate relationships between them. Solutions often result in complicated arrangements that create wayfinding and general orientation problems. The Duchossois Center for Advanced Medicine provides valuable lessons about the process of shaping a large project based on a sound understanding of its basic parts and units. It also illustrates how conceptual decisions about how an organization wants to conduct its business get translated into physical form. This project is a good example of how, even for a large utilitarian and institutional project, design must transcend function and incorporate visual and experiential qualities that portray its sponsor with pride and offer the visitor pleasant and inspiring experiences.

The center is an enormous health-care facility associated with the University of Chicago. Overall, it occupies 525,000 square feet distributed among six floors. Approximately one thousand patients visit the center daily and more than one thousand physicians and health-care professionals staff it. When a project gets to be this size, its complexity can be truly overwhelming. In this example, we briefly examine the way this project was conceptually shaped based on its particular needs and operational goals. Additionally, we show some representative examples of the kinds of design features that helped to humanize this large institutional building.

The predesign process included and was informed by a comprehensive master facilities planning exercise. Existing facilities and conditions were surveyed and trends as well as needs were analyzed and evaluated. A user group of over two hundred faculty and staff members provided programmatic data and assisted in the evaluation of working modules and similar facilities. During the conceptual stage, several stacking options were developed and evaluated. Clinic module prototypes were also

developed and scrutinized. Finally, similar facilities using comparable health-care delivery models were visited.

The basic programmatic requirement for the center was to provide a one-stop health-care system that would house the adult specialty clinics of the University of Chicago hospitals plus outpatient diagnostic and treatment facilities. The center wanted to adopt a health-care delivery system based on the principle of patient-centered care, having as its main goal the provision of maximum convenience to the patient. As part of the health-care delivery approach, group practices would not be physically grouped by medical or surgical specialty, as is the norm. This facility would have only one group practice, which would diagnose and treat diseases by organ specialty. The operational model adopted was one that brings physicians and equipment to the patient to facilitate multidisciplinary participation and patient convenience. Instead of the patient moving from department to department within the facility, the patient would remain in one place and physicians and equipment would be the ones moving. Figure CS6.1 shows a conceptual diagram of the type of physical organization implied by this model.

In order to consolidate ambulatory care practices, it was necessary to combine space and equipment for multifunctional "centers." Floor plate arrangements had to facilitate the access to and sharing of space and equipment and, at the same time, remain within acceptable limits of complexity to prevent disorientation and frustration. The concept featured two parallel linear halves on each floor,

Figure CS6.1: Diagram of prototypical patient-centered organization.

one containing the clinical programs and the other the diagnostics and treatment functions. These were offset in order to make space for a curved vehicular plaza at the street level and create a sense of entrance on one side of the building. The planning that followed was all based on this structural organization, as shown on the diagrammatic stacking plans in Figure CS6.2.

To provide visual relief and enhance orientation, two atria were incorporated. One is by the main public access point and connects levels one and two. The other atrium connects levels four through six. A large linear space with a vaulted skylight above, it divides the facility in the middle, with the clinics on one side and the diagnostic and treatment functions on the other. The large atrium serves as a major internal focus area. The waiting and circulation areas on floors four through six are located adjacent to it (Figure CS6.3).

Once the basic block of clinics for the facility was determined, module prototypes were developed and evaluated. Figure CS6.4 shows a diagrammatic plan of a prototypical medical module. Modules had to be flexible enough to meet the needs of medical and surgical specialists within the allotted square footage and structural grid. Each module contains examination rooms and support functions such as reception areas, clinical coordinator space, work areas, and toilet rooms. Also part of the module is a peripheral zone containing materials management support spaces and toilet, lounge, and conference rooms for staff use.

An important goal of the project was to increase the perception of quality of ambulatory care practice as well as to promote the convenience and dignity of patients. To this end, a number of physical and service-related amenities were incorporated, such as convenient drop-off areas, valet parking, a skybridge connecting to an existing parking structure, convenient and modern scheduling and registration systems, a sophisticated signage system for orientation, comfortable and private changing areas, electronic information systems, a food court, a sundry shop, and a commercial pharmacy.

Beyond providing basic conveniences, the success of a project relies heavily on the sensitivity of the design treatments and their ability to create a desired and appropriate image. In that respect, the design of the center has much to offer visitors, as illustrated

Sixth Floor:
A. General & G.I. Surgery / Transplant
B. Gastroenterology
C. Hematology, Oncology, Dermatology
D. Hematology, Oncology, Nephrology
E. Lab Testing / G.I. Offices
F. Gastrointestinal Procedures
G. Infusion Therapy / Cancer Resource

Fifth Floor:
A. Endocrinology
B. Cardiac, Thoracic, Vascular Surgery
C. Cardiology
D. Cardiology / Pulmonary Medicine
E. Lab Testing / Medicine Admin.
F. Donation / Apheresis
G. Heart Procedures
H. Pulmonary Procedures

Fourth Floor:
A. Orthopedic Radiology / Therapy
B. Orthopedic Surgery / Rehab.
C. Rheumatology
D. Neurosurgery / Neurology
E. Lab Testing / Surgery Admin.
F. Neurophysiology Procedures
G. Ear Nose and Throat Surgery

Second Floor:
A. Food Court / Express Registration
B. Urology
C. Pain Therapy / Pre-Surgery Testing
D. Bridge to Parking / Mitchell Hospital
E. Mammography
F. Ambulatory Surgery

First Floor:
A. Registration / Billing Inquiry
B. Eye Center
C. Radiation Oncology Clinic
D. Entrance Lobby / Security
E. Pharmacy / Building Admin.
F. Radiology

Ground Floor:
A. Mechanical Space
B. Radiation Oncology D&T
C. Future Kitchen
D. Tunnel to Mitchell Hospital
E. Instrument Processing
F. Mechanical Space

Figure CS6.2: Diagrammatic stacking plans.

Figure CS6.3: The large open atrium from levels four through six serves to provide relief and orientation.

Figure CS6.4: Diagrammatic plan of a prototypical medical module.

Figure CS6.5: Lobby of the Pediatric Specialties Clinic.

Figure CS6.8: High-end waiting and registration area.

Figure CS6.6: Rhythm, pattern, and color in corridors.

Figure CS6.7: Lobby serving the General Medicine Clinics.

here by images taken from the third floor. Figure CS6.5 shows a playful and inviting lobby serving the Pediatric Specialties Clinic. Even the corridors, so often dull and totally utilitarian in institutional projects, are given life and interest through rhythm, pattern, and color (Figure CS6.6). The lobby serving the General Medicine Clinics is, appropriately, more serious and straightforward and features visual qualities once unheard of in health-care facilities (Figure CS6.7). In this case, the connotations expressed by the design are of class and elegance. Similarly, the waiting and registration areas shown in Figure CS6.8 convey the above-average degree of design care given to these important public functions of the facility.

Store design offers some of the best opportunities for creativity and expression in the design field. The main goal of stores is to present merchandise in such a way that makes shoppers want to buy. Crucial design aspects are the effective display of merchandise, the use of interior design to reinforce a particular image or identity, and the effective movement of people through the store.

It is possible to produce, even for a small store space, a wide variety of expressions just by varying the placement and orientation of fixtures and other space elements. Below, we present twenty different parti diagrams for a small retail store. The goal is not to give you specific models to copy but to present examples of the basic typological possibilities for you to study in order to develop the kind of thinking that will help you come up with powerful organizational ideas for your store projects. Keep in mind that generating a strong scheme is only the first step in designing a store, and there are many important design features at smaller scales, such as the materials used, the way they are detailed, the fixtures used, and their exact placement. Nevertheless, a strong scheme is crucial to the design of any store. Without one, no matter how beautiful the materials, the detailing, and everything else, the design is not likely to work well as a whole.

Figure C6.8 shows the first eight diagrams. Organizations with central, linear circulation are featured in Figure C6.8a–d. The circulation in Figure C6.8a and C6.8b is determined by the available central space left by the placement of displays and fixtures. Figure C6.8a is asymmetrical, and the circulation spine is just left of center. Figure C6.8b is perfectly symmetrical and is strongly defined by the regularly placed fixtures on either side. Figure C6.8c and C6.8d are also central schemes. The central spine on

these is defined not by leftover central space but by some architectural device, such as the floor material and/or the shape of the ceiling above. The shapes of these spines are the main components of these two schemes. Everything else is organized around this dominant central organizational element. Notice that other than the linear aspect of circulation these two schemes expand to create nodes, a central circular one in Figure C6.8c and two square (rotated) ones in Figure C6.8d.

The two schemes shown in Figure C6.8e and C6.8f feature looser, less formal central spaces. In Figure C6.8e, circulation is not straight and axial like the ones before, but is offset around the center of the store and moves to the left side, from which it continues toward a focal end at the rear of the store. Movement in Figure C6.8f is diagonal from front to back with objects and displays also placed diagonally on either side of, and helping to define, the circulation spine. Figure C6.8g and C6.8h feature not circulation but displays along a central axis. Circulation occurs on either side, along the space defined between the linear central displays and the wall displays. They are very similar except that in Figure C6.8g the central fixtures are dominant, while in Figure C6.8h they complement the sides rather than imposing dominance.

Figure C6.8 a –h: Eight store partis: linear asymmetrical (a), linear symmetrical (b), linear, strongly defined, and symmetrical with dominant center (c), linear, strongly defined, and symmetrical with two nodes (e), two-segment offset (e), diagonal (f), prominently occupied central axis (g), occupied central axis (h).

Eight more schemes are shown in Figure C6.9. The schemes in Figure C6.9a–c are hybrids. Figure C6.9a proceeds from a central display with circulation to either side, to central circulation, and then back to a central display with circulation around it. Meanwhile, Figure C6.9b is a combination of linear asymmetrical movement along the left side and a diagonally oriented central area. Figure C6.9c combines symmetrical diagonal movement in the front and back with linear two-sided circulation in the central zone. The next two diagrams feature diagonal bounce schemes. These force you to move diagonally from featured area to featured area. Figure C6.9d is organized around a main central element and features many pockets strategically placed along the side walls. Figure C6.9e is organized around a series of focal points along both the center and the two side walls.

The next three schemes are examples of compartmentalized space. In these, the store is subdivided into explicit compartments, almost like rooms. Figure C6.9f is a simple two-compartment scheme with circulation along one side. The schemes in Figure C6.9g and C6.9h are both symmetrical and axial with circulation occurring down the middle. Figure C6.9g features two circular compartments with a transition passage at the center of the store. Figure C6.9h is a three-compartment arrangement featuring a small central compartment.

The geometry of schemes, of course, can be inflected. Schemes can be curved, angled, or otherwise inflected as long as the move is compatible with the identity of the store. The four diagrams shown in Figure C6.10 are examples of inflected schemes. Figure C6.10a is angled on one side and straight on the other. Figure C6.10b features both angles and free-floating shapes prominently. The schemes in Figure C6.10c and C6.10d are curvilinear. Figure C6.10c features an undulating compound curve around a central dominant circular shape. Figure C6.10d features a sweeping curve along one side and a smaller opposite curvilinear element anchored on the side wall.

Figure C6.9 a –h: Eight more store partis: straight-angle hybrid (a), straight and diagonal hybrid (b), diagonal and straight combination (c), diagonal (d), diagonal bounce scheme (e), two-compartment off-center (f), two circular compartments (g), three rectangular compartments (h).

Figure C6.10 a –d: Four inflected partis: diagonal/straight combination (a), sawtooth (b), undulating curve (c), sweeping curve (d).

The approaches presented above (central linear circulation, central linear displays, loosely organized centers, hybrids, diagonal schemes, compartmentalized schemes, and inflected schemes) are not all the possible approaches, but they cover a fair amount of them. The actual interpretation, articulation, and execution of each approach, however, is subject to infinite variation. That's part of the beauty of design. Not only do you have many approaches to choose from to solve a design problem but you can customize each of them to suit the specific needs of a project.

REVIEW

Summary

The two principal tasks during the ideation stage are to establish the project's character concept, concerned with the image of the project, and its organizational concept, concerned with the arrangement of parts. During this stage the project's many realities and needs are synthesized into specific design approaches to be developed further.

To begin exploring concepts, it is necessary to have a sound overall understanding of both the project's general requirements and its salient issues. Concepts are almost always derived in response to one or more of these salient issues and are externalized as short statements, descriptive scenarios, diagrams, and sketches. Once recorded, they can be evaluated, making it easier to select specific ideas for further development.

Character concept statements should not repeat the design problem. Instead, they should say something about the solution to the problem. Character concept statements should also be selective and brief. Organizational concepts provide the structure used to shape a project's spaces and their relationships. They establish an organization that is responsive to the project's realities and, at the same time, provide coherence and order.

For purposes of establishing the scheme of a project it is useful to think in terms of the organizational systems introduced in Chapter 4 as well as the place elements introduced in Chapter 3: arrival space, centers, districts, nodes, and paths. Thinking in these terms helps to reduce the number of project parts to the most essential and to establish a sense of hierarchy in the project.

In terms of character, the outcome of this stage is a solid verbal statement describing the designer's intentions and strategies to solve the design problem. In terms of spatial issues, the required outcome is an organizational concept that establishes a sound organizational structure. It should contain the basic design decisions on which future decisions will be based. Two important kinds of diagrams used to depict organizational concepts are the parti diagram and the functional diagram. The parti diagram conveys the structure of the project in its most minimal way. The functional diagram adds more detail and, in general, establishes locations for the project's destinations and a coherent circulation system to get to them.

1. *American Heritage Dictionary* (1985), s.v. "Concept."
2. Charles Morris Mount, *Restaurant Style* (Glen Cove, NY: Showcase Edition, 1995), 60.
3. Rosalie Grattaroti, *Great Store Design* (Rockport, MA: Rockport, 1994), 70.
4. *Interiors Magazine* (March 1997): 58.
5. Morris Mount, 140.
6. Ibid., 45.
7. Ibid., 86.
8. Martin E. Dorf, *Restaurants that Work: Case Studies of the Best in the Country* (New York: Whitney, 1992), 100.
9. Francisco A. Cerver, *Commercial Space: Shop Windows, Cosmetics* (Sussex: Rotovision, 1996), 22.
10. Ibid., 91–92.

Chapter Questions

1. You have seen that there are many kinds of concepts and that it is often confusing to know what someone is referring to when they talk about the project's concept. Explain, in your own words, what "the concept" of a project means to you.

2. Refer back to the concept for a design project you have done in school. How was it expressed (short statement, scenario, diagram, sketch)? How many ideas were involved? Was it predominantly an organizational concept or a character concept?

3. In your opinion, what kind of project understanding is most crucial to develop good concepts?

4. Think of your current design project. Name three to five salient issues, explicit or implicit.

5. Have you done concept diagrams before? Were they more like the parti diagrams or the functional diagrams described in this chapter? Explain.

6. Can you explain the main differences between a block plan and a functional diagram?

7. How do you ensure, during the ideation stage, that every required function is accounted for?

8. Explain two ways you could perform a manipulation for enrichment during the ideation stage.

9. Explain two ways you could perform a manipulation for expression during the ideation stage.

10. Think of examples of centers, nodes, landmarks, and edges for a house, a store, a restaurant, and a dance club.

11. What are the main characteristics of a good written concept statement?

Exercises

1. Identify the salient issues for the design project you are currently working on. Is there a dominant one?

2. Based on the responses above, list five potential concepts (organizational and character) for your design project.

3. Choose three other design projects you have worked on in school, and write two concept statements for each. Emphasize a different aspect of the project for each of the two concepts.

4. Select one organizational concept for your current design project and develop three variations.

5. For the design project of your choice, produce the following: a short concept statement, a concept scenario, a quick, loose concept diagram, and a sketch for a particular space or area.

6. For the three projects in Exercise 3 above, select one concept and draw both a parti diagram and a functional diagram.

PART THREE
DEVELOPING THE DESIGN

CHAPTER 7
Order

INSTRUCTIONAL OBJECTIVES

- Describe different kinds of order related to fit, visual harmony, and orientation.

- Explain three basic factors that facilitate spatial understanding.

- Explain the role of the ten place elements in facilitating project imageability.

- Describe strategies to facilitate the legibility of project parts.

- Describe grouping strategies to facilitate orientation.

- Explain ways to facilitate the understanding of relationships between parts.

- Explain strategies to promote the awareness of motion and sequence.

- Explain strategies to promote the understanding of projects as a whole.

- Describe the limits and possibilities of enclosed corridors related to orientation.

- Show the effects of varying the size, placement, and orientation of single and multiple masses in space.

- Show the effects of different levels of boundary legibility.

- Show the effect of partial-height elements related to disclosure and orientation.

> *Order must be understood as indispensable to the functioning of any organized system, whether its function be physical or mental.*
> —*Rudolf Arnheim,* The Dynamics of Architectural Form

FROM VITRUVIUS IN ANTIQUITY to modern times, writers on the subject of architecture and the environmental design disciplines have spoken about the importance of order in design. Bernard Leupen put it quite simply: "Every design is based on order . . . the need to order is prompted more than anything else by our general desire to arrange the world so as to make it easier to understand."[1]

The design of building interiors requires the disposition and placement of many parts whose proper and systematic arrangement is crucial to the success of the project. This is true whether it concerns the arrangement of furnishings within a space, the composition of an elevation, or the structuring of a series of spaces. Stanley Abercrombie has stated that "the reasoned relationship of parts to parts, of parts to wholes, of buildings to places, the power of repetition and modularity, the perception of complete units, the expression of construction realities, and the signification of inherent meaning—all are born only of order, not of chance."[2] A sense of order helps the users of a building understand their environment and their relationship to it, so they may feel oriented and at ease. It also produces a general sense of harmony in the visual environment.

In Chapter 6 we looked at how during the ideation stage designers establish the main organizational principles needed for the generation of the project's floor plan and stated that a project's sense of order originates during that stage. In this chapter we explore the idea of order and its many dimensions manifested in the design of building interiors. We will look at some of the ways order is produced in architectural interiors. Of these, we will focus on spatial order, how to establish it and how to reveal it. Specific design strategies to achieve spatial order, including the use of the place elements introduced in Chapter 3, will be discussed as well as the importance of the composition of a project's enclosed and open areas.

ORDER IN BUILDINGS

The concept of order is broad and operates at different levels. Below, we explain three basic types of order related to built environments. We discuss the way the sequential nature of interior environments relates to order and describe three important factors that facilitate the understanding of and sense of orientation in interior projects.

Kinds of Order

Order in design is manifested in many ways. Different functions have to be organized into a cohesive scheme that works effectively as a unit, architectural and decorative elements have to be balanced in harmonious arrangements, and spaces have to be arranged in a way that facilitates orientation. Below we discuss these three important manifestations of order in the design of building interiors.

Order Related to Proper Fit

When we think of order, we think of organization. Order is certainly concerned with the organization of parts. It is also more than that. A project must be organized in such a way that its parts are recognizable and their sum produces a coherent whole; it must do this in the process of addressing the needs of a particular architectural program in a particular setting. Compositional order that does not respond well to the project's function and/or context is not good order. Response to function and context involves an order of its own that must be addressed and solved properly.

When a project's functions have been arranged in such a way that relationships between parts have been addressed properly and the relationship of the project to its context has been optimized, we could say there is a good fit between the problem and its solution. This is one level of order. This type of order is simply characterized by a proper response to the project's requirements. It requires **functional fit**, the proper response to the functional programmatic requirements of the project, as well as **contextual fit**, the proper response to the opportunities and challenges of the surroundings and inherent characteristics of the project.

Functional fit is achieved when the design solution addresses the essence of the overall design problem and its subproblems at the functional level. It can be judged based on the level of fit achieved between the program and the resulting project organization. Contextual fit is concerned with establishing meaningful connections and responses between the project and its context. It can be judged by the project's level of response to its internal and external contexts.

Furthermore, the solution to the design problem should be accomplished economically, resulting in no missing or unnecessary extra parts. We could call this an **order of economy**. A project that achieves these types of order demonstrates that the essence of the design problem has been understood and responded to efficiently at every scale.

Order Related to Visual Harmony

Interior design, being concerned with the composition of parts to assemble a whole, shares many characteristics with the other visual arts. They require the proper placement of, and equilibrium between, different components to achieve an agreeable aesthetic effect. This represents yet another kind of order in interior environments, **architectonic order**. The aesthetic effect we refer to is not concerned with issues of style but, rather, with the perceptual correctness of the composition of parts in the visual field. Relevant here are such architectural issues as the proper use of scale, the correct handling of proportions, and the proper balancing of project parts to achieve a harmonious state of balance and equilibrium. These concerns have been articulated from ancient times, beginning with the first treatise on architecture by Vitruvius, and remain relevant today. The sense of resolution and correctness that derives from the proper composition of architectural components gives environments a sense of equilibrium and stability (Figure 7.1).

In addition to architectonic order, there is another, more mundane kind of order concerned with the orderliness of objects in general. Relevant here are the orderly arrangements of furnishings, equipment, or fixtures in space as well as the orderly arrangement of other smaller and harder-to-control items, such as papers on a desktop or books on a shelf. We have all witnessed, frequently in our own dwellings or work spaces, the disturbing effect of disorganized environments due to the clutter created by the stuff of daily life. While designers lack control over the tidiness of their clients once the project is occupied, they surely have the opportunity to provide proper storage spaces to facilitate the organization of all these small objects that constantly conspire to clutter our environments.

Order Related to Orientation

Christian Norberg-Schulz distills the basic act of dwelling into two basic and crucial psychological functions: identification and orientation. Orientation is relevant for our purposes here. It is concerned with "man's need to orientate himself, to know where he is."[3] Romedi Passini has defined spatial orientation as "a person's ability to understand the space around him and to situate himself."[4] We can all relate to this basic human need which, when fulfilled, gives us a sense of security and well-being. Conversely, the effects of disorientation can range from mild apprehension to actual terror, depending on the circumstances.

Within the topic of orientation we can distinguish among the order produced by the clarity of the spatial organization, order produced by the proper disclosure of the external context for orientation purposes, and order produced by the clarity of the internal circulation system.

Figure 7.1: Visual harmony is achieved when the parts of a composition achieve a sense of perceptual correctness and balance.

This chapter focuses on order related to orientation. We will examine the role of place elements in facilitating our understanding of the interior environment, strategies to organize space for strong legibility, and the effect of the disposition of open and enclosed spaces on our ability to read the produced spatial organization. First, though, we need to examine some important aspects of order and interior environments.

Levels of Order

The design of environments requires the assembly of multiple parts into a whole that possesses some level of organization. By the mere act of arranging a group of functions or spaces into some logical organization the designer brings order to potential chaos. The act of building, itself, demands a reasonable use of regularity and, thus, order. Pierre Von Meiss reminds us of this fact: "To build we must use fairly simple geometry. It is first of all a necessity for design and above all for building. . . . Regularity is thus the very essence of building"[5] (Figure 7.2).

The synthesis of programmatic requirements into an orderly arrangement of spaces and the use of regularity, uniformity, and simple geometry in construction, by themselves, have the potential to establish a basic order, the kind produced by the proper assembly of parts; however, a project's sense of order has to go beyond mere regularity and neatness. You should seek to produce meaningful wholes, paying attention not only to the neat organization of parts but also to their assembly into a system based on a clear organizing principle. The organizing principle may be simple or complex, but it has to be perceivable. Considerations about the relationship to context, internal hierarchy, relationships of spaces, and the way to move around the project have to not only work well together but also respond to the organizational principle adopted.

The ideation stage discussed in Chapter 6 gets at the root of the search for an adequate organizational system for a project. Organizational concepts, we saw, not only seek a suitable organizational system but also endow the project with a sense of hierarchy. Of all the tasks performed during design, early development of the plan is key to ensure the provision of structure based on an organizing principle. The plan sets the topological distribution of the project, locating parts and functions according to the organizational principle chosen. Morphological concerns related to its form are also important. They need to be developed insightfully to ensure that the project will be perceived and understood as intended. With this in mind, we look next at the way we perceive interior projects in order to gain some insight into the kinds of spatial arrangements and features that facilitate our perception and understanding of a project's organization.

Experiencing Interior Spaces

Interior spaces are never experienced in the same way as the floor plans we draw to represent them. Floor plans allow us to see an entire floor at once and to quickly grasp its organization. In real life, walls and distance prevent us from having that kind of instantaneous total disclosure of an entire floor. We usually experience environments one space at a time and form impressions that rely on mental maps we conceive by remembering the spaces we have left behind together with the space that we occupy and the spaces we see ahead. Figure 7.3 shows a sequence of main and secondary spaces, displaying the fragmentary and sequential ways we experience most building interiors.

Figure 7.2: The realities of the physical world demand regularity and repetition in construction. Many designs, in fact, emphasize these properties.

Figure 7.3: Most interior projects are experienced in sequences. This drawing shows a series of linked but distinct spaces arranged in a storylike sequence.

Since we don't see entire environments at once, our mental picture is fragmented and relies on memory and our individual abilities to form accurate cognitive maps based on the information seen. Environmental information and clues are perceived, understood, organized in our minds, and later remembered, helping us compose a collection of individual impressions into a coherent total image. Achieving order related to orientation can thus be more difficult than it appears. Designers have to not only produce responsive spatial arrangements and organize them based on unifying principles but make them readable and memorable as well.

In Chapter 2 we summarized the rituals we perform in buildings, starting with the sense of anticipation prior to entering and ending with our departure from the building. The sequence in which we experience a particular environment will affect the ease with which we understand it. Projects that have a predictable and consistent sequence, museums, for example, can be planned to reveal themselves in some logical progression, having a definite beginning, middle, and end.

Not all projects have predictable, rigid sequences, though. Their legibility will depend on how their spaces are revealed through design.

Factors that Facilitate Understanding and Orientation

From our discussion so far we can state a goal for designers concerning order: Projects should be designed to facilitate a sense of spatial understanding for users of varying levels of familiarity. How exactly is this done? Our next topic presents three general factors that facilitate understanding of and orientation within interior environments.

Except in the simplest of spaces, most environments are understood after repeated exposures. At some point, during one of the visits, the environment starts making sense in our minds, sometimes instinctively, sometimes from the discovery of an important part of the environmental picture, and other times after conscious efforts on our part to try to understand how things go together.

As we move around space, our mental pictures of the environment evolve. Because most environments are experienced one space at a time, it is the collection of diverse and fragmented pieces of environmental information gathered from many locations at different times that add up to our total picture of that environment.

Three factors identified by Kevin Lynch as components of environmental images at the city scale give us a useful model to understand environmental images of interior spaces. They are identity, structure, and meaning. Lynch reminds us that while it may be useful to abstract these for analysis, in reality, they are always interrelated.[6]

Identity

Identity is the quality of individuality objects possess that allows us to distinguish them from other objects and recognize them as separate entities. Related to identity is what Lynch called **imageability**, the quality of some physical objects that makes it likely that they'll evoke a strong image in the mind of the observer. Whether due to their shape, color, or arrangement, highly imageable objects are likely to produce "vividly identified, powerfully structured, highly useful mental images of the environment."[7] Projects rich in order have a strong identity both in their parts and as a whole.

Structure

Structure refers to the spatial or pattern relation of the object to the observer and to other objects. It is concerned with the relationships among the different entities and how these are assembled as a unified whole. As discussed above, the presence of an organizing principle behind the arrangement will make it easier to comprehend and appreciate. We also said that this organizing principle could vary in its complexity. Depending on the project, it may take a while to decipher this organizing principle. Once it is discovered, though, one can make intelligent assessments of the space without having to figure out all the parts. Understanding the organizing principle is like understanding a pattern. Once you discover it, the structure makes sense, even if it is complex. A strong organizing principle, together with a well-orchestrated assembly of parts, will endow the project with greater legibility, allowing users to grasp the structure more easily.

Meaning

Meaning refers to the significance the object has to the observer, whether practical or emotional. While meaning often works somewhat independently of the physical characteristics of environments, it is a crucial variable in the mix of how we perceive environments. Some places are remembered not by the singularity of their form or their placement within a structure but by the significance they have for us. Whether due to the symbolic association, practical function, or degree of familiarity, these places stand out in our mental maps even if lacking in memorable features. As we invest time in projects, they become familiar to us and acquire more significance in our lives. With meaningful places we rely less on mental pictures of spaces having particular features because we see them as places associated with certain functions, people, and events having specific degrees of significance to us.

Of the three factors discussed above, the first two, identity and structure, rely the most on design. Meaning is usually assigned to places for reasons other than their physical attributes. Nevertheless, places that are rich in meaning can be further enhanced by how legible and distinct we make them (identity) and where they are placed within the total organization (structure).

DESIGNING FOR ORDER

So far we have made a strong case for the importance of order and orientation in design. The order afforded by design can help orient us in space by facilitating our understanding of our environment, its place within the larger context, and our position within these environments at any particular time. Now we turn to ways of achieving order in our designs. We will start with the role the place elements play in facilitating order and orientation. Next, we will review ways of facilitating project understanding at various scales. Finally, we will examine the implications of spatial massing and composition.

The Role of the Place Elements in Providing Order

In Chapter 3, we introduced the place elements, a group of environmental entities useful for the creation and understanding of places. These were derived from the five elements Kevin Lynch used to classify physical forms related to urban environments and also from Christian Norberg-Schulz's elements of existential space. Other studies worldwide have corroborated Lynch's findings.[8] A study focused on wayfinding in interior environments by Romedi Passini and his collaborators revealed that Lynch's five elements were useful in classifying physical elements people use to describe aspects of building interiors.[9]

Lynch's elements are significant because his studies show that it is this group of elements people use to describe their images of environments. The ten place elements introduced in Chapter 3 are crucial in producing order and orientation in interior environments.

Domains are the departments in an office or store, or the different dining areas in a large restaurant. Figure 7.4 shows an example of a domain in an office environment.Their approximate placement and size are important in developing an accurate mental map of the whole. Understanding the boundaries between circulation spaces and these domains, and, in some cases, those between one domain and the next is also important to the formation of accurate mental maps.

Centers are domains of special importance. They become memorable because they are significant. Consequently, whether physically distinct or not, we remember these spaces and sometimes even organize our mental picture of environments around them. Knowing their inherent importance, designers can further emphasize them to evoke a powerful and lasting image by endowing them with distinct physical features. An important

Figure 7.4: Domains are legible as areas of particular characteristics, uses, and extent. This "neighborhood" in an office setting is a domain. Our mental pictures of some environments feature collections of related domains.

Figure 7.5: This conference room in an office setting is an example of a center. Sometimes centers are highlights among less meaningful domains; other times they are of such importance they become, literally, central features of the organization.

Figure 7.6: Arrival spaces are of great perceptual importance because they function as gateways to the rest of the project. Here, the arrival space of a restaurant reveals glimpses of what lies ahead.

conference room (Figure 7.5) may very well be one of the centers of an office facility.

Unlike cities, most interior environments have only one principal point of entry. The space it leads to, the arrival space, is crucial to our understanding of the environment. It is the first point of reference from which the project emanates. As such, it is the kind of reference space around which we tend to organize the other components of an interior environment. The nature of the sequences that follow from this space and how much of the space beyond is visible from the arrival space can have a significant impact on our ability to understand the total environment. Arrival spaces give us the first impression of a project and represent the first point of reference from which to construct our mental map of the environment (Figure 7.6).

Paths are crucial to our sense of order and orientation inside buildings. It is while moving through them that projects are revealed. A strong and clear circulation system may be legible enough to become the structure around which we organize our mental picture of interior environments. This is not coincidental. You may recall that in Chapter 4 we derived our organization systems for entire projects from the circulation systems. These truly have the power to be generative elements that dictate the overall organization of projects. In many projects, if you understand the circulation system, you understand the organization of the project. The corridor shown in Figure 7.7 is the main spine from which the spaces of that project will be seen and accessed.

Figure 7.7: We experience projects while walking on their paths, some revealing more than others. Here, a path allows the user to catch glimpses of what lies ahead.

Figure 7.8: Nodes are important points of reference. Whether small or large, like the one pictured here, they are strategically placed and often have distinctive features that make them memorable.

Nodes tend to be memorable for a number of reasons. First, they are places of intense activity, full of vibrancy, energy, and meaning. Second, they tend to be physically distinct due to the dynamic qualities of converging paths, expanding space, and so on. Third, due to their strategic placement and often increased size, they are visible from multiple locations and, frequently, they offer opportunities for a wide visual scope. Nodes are often a central, important space, such as the one shown in Figure 7.8. They enhance our sense of order because we tend to remember them vividly. This makes them important points of reference in our mental maps of interior environments.

Next, we group edges, connectors, and ends together because their significance to orientation is similar. These three elements help determine the extent of domains and clarify distinctions about where one area ends and another begins. Their range of legibility varies but can sometimes be strong, as in a full and massive barrier between a private domain and a public and busy path. Figure 7.9 shows a wall in an office facility creating a strong edge between the circulation and work areas. Strong edges can be memorable building elements. As such, they become a tool that can enhance our ability to remember project parts and thus improve our mental pictures of projects.

The significance of furnishings for imageability is that they are recognized as objects with distinct figural qualities. Most often we see them in groups and read them as regions of furnishings. These regions can be read as

Figure 7.9: This edge between a corridor and the work areas in an office facility provides clear spatial demarcation.

Figure 7.10: Furnishings can function as recognizable groupings that define areas or as single, distinct landmarks. Here, a seating group defines an area of its own.

domains having uniform characteristics. Distinct qualities given to a specific group of furnishings can help make that region memorable and, therefore, more legible. For instance, a person might recall a specific area of a project where the furnishings were arranged at an angle as opposed to being straight like everything else. Figure 7.10 shows an example of furnishings that can be read as distinct groupings within a larger space.

The main trait of landmarks is distinctiveness. These are, perhaps, the most noticeable of all place elements. Landmarks are clearly remembered. Their inclusion in projects and their strategic placement for maximum visibility from multiple locations make them excellent points of reference that can significantly improve our ability to understand and get oriented in interior settings. Common landmarks inside buildings include open staircases, especially if monumental in nature (Figure 7.11a), and other prominent building elements (Figure 7.11b).

Figure 7.11: Landmarks in interiors are usually prominent features, such as an internal staircase (a) and a giant circular window (b).

The insightful use and manipulation of the above place elements can help increase the legibility of interior environments. When they are orchestrated into a cohesive system they produce especially coherent environments. The organizational decisions made during the ideation stage are crucial in establishing such an appropriate orchestration. These are further refined to make order and structure clearer and easier to read, but it must be emphasized that it all originates during that all-important stage of concept formulation.

Figure 7.12: The offset and slight increase in detailing are enough to highlight this section of a wall and make it distinctive.

Promoting Project Understanding

Project understanding takes place at many levels. We distinguish five principal levels for discussion: individual parts, groupings, relationships between parts or groups, sequences, and the project as a whole. We will look at these next and suggest strategies for facilitating project understanding at each of them.[10]

Individual Parts

An individual project part may be a space or a mass. While not all parts need to be comprehended as individual entities, many do stand out as single features. We offer four design strategies to increase legibility at this level:

1. **Distinctiveness**: Parts with strong figural qualities read clearly against the background formed by adjacent elements. Ways of achieving distinctiveness usually rely on uniqueness and differentiation from nearby spaces or masses. Also necessary is a clear, uncluttered presentation of the object in question. Figure 7.12 illustrates how a simple offset or slight increase in the level of detail of a wall makes it stand out as a part.

2. **Simple Form**: Gestalt psychology established that our eyes are drawn to simple shapes first, usually focusing on the simplest one and proceeding to more complex ones only after the initial one has

Figure 7.13: Simple form, whether spatial or solid, is easier to remember. Pure shapes, such as this square room, are instantly recognizable.

Figure 7.14: Dominance requires accentuated contrast in size, shape, or level of finish. This example features contrasting size, shape, and surface treatment.

Figure 7.15: Contrasts in scale and light are used to differentiate one area from another.

been grasped. Consequently, shapes that are simple, clear, and composed of few parts will be easier to perceive. The principle of simple form applies to both the perception of mass and the perception of space itself. Simple volumes, such as the cube in Figure 7.13, help make spaces distinguishable.

3. **Dominance**: Dominance is similar to, yet different from, distinctiveness. While in both cases the part in question is differentiated from the rest, in the case of distinctiveness it is merely different, and with dominance it is clearly dominant. Oftentimes, these parts become landmarks around which other parts are organized. Dominance can be established by means of size, intensity, or interest. In Figure 7.14, the protruding part is not only different but also clearly the dominant feature of the composition.

4. **Contrast**: Contrast is a useful strategy to achieve differentiation among adjacent parts. It helps make entities more readable, especially at the point or edge where parts come together. A common use of contrast is the contrast of scale, as shown in Figure 7.15.

Groupings

Functions or spaces are often clustered together in groups and read more as a group than a collection of parts. Individual parts may or may not be discernible. We present four design strategies useful to achieve legibility of groupings:

Figure 7.16: Rooms clustered together read as a group, even if their resulting boundary is irregular.

Figure 7.17: When objects, furnishings, or even rooms occur together inside a common boundary they read as a group. This group of tables is held together by its enclosure.

Figure 7.18: Objects sharing the same orientation, such as these angled furniture clusters, reinforce their sense of group.

1. **Clustering**: Clustering consists of grouped spaces in tightly configured conglomerations (Figure 7.16). Parts may butt against one another or just come close. In any case, there has to be a high degree of proximity between them for the group to read as a cluster. The resulting shape may be simple and regular or irregular, expressing the individual volumes, protrusions, and indentations of the component parts. The key to their legibility is that the cluster read as a single entity.

2. **Common Enclosure**: In the case of parts sharing a common enclosure, the parts may be grouped tightly, as in a cluster, or loosely. What unifies them and makes them read as a single group is their common boundary, which serves as a collecting device unifying all parts within it. The tables inside the common container shown in Figure 7.17 are grouped by virtue of being inside the same boundary.

3. **Common Orientation**: In the case of parts sharing a common orientation, closely spaced parts are oriented in the same direction and, consequently, read as a group. In these cases, proximity between elements is as important as the common orientation. Figure 7.18 shows an example of similarly oriented furniture clusters.

4. **Datum**: A datum is a powerful unifying device used to group dissimilar parts through a common field or ground. It can be a vertical backdrop

Figure 7.19: A datum groups parts, even if disparate, together by acting as a common backdrop. In interiors it is usually a plane below, above, or behind the parts. In this example the raised floor platform serves as a datum for the parts sitting on it.

against which a number of parts are arranged, a floating ceiling plane grouping several parts underneath, a unique flooring plane or pattern on which a group of parts are arranged (Figure 7.19), or, as in the case of common enclosure, a full enclosure helping to group a number of parts inside it. Key to the success of a datum is correspondence of extent between the datum and the parts it groups. It has to read as if the background wall, the overhead plane, or the distinctive floor had been custom measured to house the parts they group.

Relationships between Parts or Groups

The next aspect requiring legibility is the relationship between parts. Positional relationships between parts as well as the nature of the connection between adjacent ones can be made easier to perceive and understand. Two design strategies are discussed:

1. **Clear Intersection**: Clear intersection occurs when joints or seams between parts are visible and clearly articulated. This usually involves an edge or a connector. Whether they are tall or low, full- or partial-length, separating barriers that reveal the two sides enhance the readability of the relationship between them. Other than walls, clear intersections can be achieved through intermediary spaces,

ceiling or floor treatments, furniture arrangements, and so on. Figure 7.20 shows an example of a separation between two areas clearly revealed by the characteristics of the dividing partition.

2. **Visibility**: Visibility simply refers to the increase of the visible field by means of openness, expanded views, transparencies, or overlaps, such as in the space shown in Figure 7.21. Open environments are generally much easier to figure out because the relationship between parts is clearly seen.

Sequences

Sequences are concerned with how two or more spaces link together to form a pattern and give users clues about where they are or where they are heading. We discuss three design strategies here that facilitate legibility of sequences:

1. **Gradation**: Gradation is achieved through subtle asymmetries, gradients, and any method of differentiation that successfully makes one side gradually become different from the other. The differences can be subtle, but as the observer notices them, he or she understands the progressive differentiation and can, therefore, distinguish among them, especially between the contrasting ends. The widening effect of the corridor in Figure 7.22 makes it easy to distinguish which end of the corridor you are in.

2. **Contrast**: We listed contrast as a design strategy for singling out individual parts. Contrast is also highly effective in creating different experiences as one moves along a sequence. Changes of scale or

Figure 7.20: The strategy of clear intersection relies on the disclosure of the point or edge where adjacent parts connect. In the example below, the solidity of the bottom half of the wall, combined with the transparency of the top half, reinforce the separation between the two areas while simultaneously revealing their relationship.

Figure 7.21: The strategy of visibility works by maximizing the extent of what is seen from a particular space. Openness and strategic placement of tall elements are key components to make it work.

lighting levels (subtle or abrupt) help to break down sequences into discrete parts with unique characteristics, thus making the sequence more memorable and legible. Once again, contrast of scale is a commonly used and effective way of making sequences readable and memorable (Figure 7.23).

3. **Route Markers**: Route markers are design elements, distinguishable treatments, or objects placed at intervals along a route. Their presence helps to increase the awareness of movement in the observer. By marking spots along the length of a trajectory, the awareness of the experience of movement is increased. As one passes and recognizes another marker, one is reminded that one is in motion. The elevation sequence shown in Figure 7.24 shows a repeating architectural element marking regular intervals of a route.

The Whole

Understanding the whole is the most difficult level of order to grasp, especially in large or complex projects. The problem is that we never see the entire space at once. Sequences may be long and difficult to remember, and we may never actually move through the entire space. Understanding the whole is not always necessary. Sometimes it is sufficient to understand where you are in relation to where you

came in, or where you are in relationship to the exterior. Nevertheless, the more users have a fairly clear mental picture of the total environment they're in, the more at ease they will be. We suggest four design strategies to facilitate legibility at the overall project scale:

1. **Repetition**: As the name implies, this strategy relies on the repetition of parts or approach. Repetition of parts occurs when perceptible units such as space modules are used repeatedly in some kind of regular pattern. Repetition of approach involves the repetition of sequences or arrangements of multiple parts. In the latter case, the sequence or arrangement acts as a unit, and it is the unit that gets repeated throughout the space (Figure 7.25). Repetition is helpful because it reinforces patterns and can help us make accurate predictions about spaces we haven't visited based on what we have seen. Yet it must be used with caution, as too much repetition can be disorienting.

2. **Consistency**: Consistency of approach helps users decipher patterns by reinforcing their assumptions as they attempt to figure things out. It is, similar to repetition described above, a strategy that also relies on the recurrence of a pattern. Consistency, however, does not require repetition of units. All that is

Figure 7.22: This corridor is an example of gradation. The different widths can help visitors remember whether a particular space is near the narrow or wide end of the corridor.

Figure 7.23: A good strategy to make a sequence memorable is the use of contrast. Whether achieved by the alternation of open and closed spaces in plan or by the alternation of low and tall spaces, as shown, the contrasting spaces are marked and remembered.

Figure 7.24: This example shows the use of route markers to provide regular points of reference along a long route.

Figure 7.25: Repeated patterns help users get acquainted with the modules used to assemble their project. In this example, a basic arrangement is repeated throughout the project.

required is continuity of intent. An example of this would be a long wall with a gradated use of color, slowly becoming lighter as one moves on. After a minute, one could assume that the wall color will continue to get lighter ahead. Consistency of approach provides users with consistent clues that they can use to make reasonable generalizations.

3. **Visibility**: As we have stated before, it is seldom possible to see entire projects at once. We form our mental idea of the whole by combining perceptions of the various individual spaces. This usually requires some educated guesswork on our part as we try to figure out relationships between spaces we have not experienced together.

For example, say you visit a certain unfamiliar building one day and visit three spaces. A day later you go back and enter through the same door. This time, however, you visit three different spaces. On day three you go to the building once again, but this time you enter on a different side of the building. From this information, we can assume that you are familiar with the three spatial sequences experienced. Beyond that, we can speculate that you have some idea of how the spaces adjacent to the entrance used on the first two days relate, since both were close to the same entrance and, therefore, to each other. That's as much as we can claim you know. You are most likely to be clueless about how the sequence of spaces from the third day relates to

the previous two, since there are no spaces in common. Now, suppose the last space of each of the three sequences shared the common characteristic of terminating at a balcony overlooking a central atrium space where you can see from one to another (Figure 7.26). All of a sudden, the relationship between them would be clarified and even the relationship of the three sequences might start to make sense.

The principle of visibility works by providing certain spaces or vantage points from which multiple spaces can be seen. Examples include multistory spaces and other large spaces that allow us to see many spaces and/or features at once, providing instant information about how spaces relate to one another and relate to their position within the whole.

4. **Points of Reference**: The strategy of points of reference works by providing spaces or features that can be seen from multiple parts of a project, thus providing useful markers for orientation. The strategy is somewhat similar to visual scope, but instead of relying on a large space from which a lot can be seen, it relies on common spaces or features that can be seen from different vantage points. Although all spaces providing visual scope also serve as points of reference (since they can be seen from various vantage points), not all points of reference are vantage points. Spaces that provide visual scope are large, show a multitude of spaces at once, and thus make spatial relationships readily understood; spaces serving as points of refer-

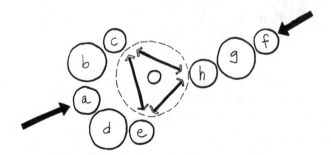

Figure 7.26: A central space connecting spaces (c), (e), and (h) visually would help visitors understand the relationship of the three sequences (a, b, c), (a, d, e), and (f, g, h). Large central spaces from which you can see many areas at once are often used to achieve the strategy of visibility.

Figure 7.27: With the strategy of points of reference, views from different areas converge on a common space, object, or plane. In this example, the space and object are centrally located, although they are not large.

ence, although connected visually to several areas, don't necessarily reveal the relationship between areas (Figure 7.27). Points of reference can be isolated efforts supplied by the designer to help users understand the project or important strategic places around which project parts are organized.

Space Composition and Order

One of the most important variables in the perception of space is **legibility**, the extent to which space is readable. If there is some unifying organization tying a project together, and if we are allowed to see enough of the project parts and how they go together, sooner or later we will be able to understand the whole. Two factors affecting legibility are the clarity of individual parts and the relative complexity of the spatial composition. Projects can be more or less legible depending on how we arrange their open and enclosed areas to allow more or less visibility. Enclosed spaces are often seen as masses or objects in space. Open areas are the spaces surrounding the enclosed spaces. We turn our attention now to different effects derived from their composition.

As discussed previously, it is while walking through the corridors and aisles of a project that we truly experience its spaces and sequences. The result is a storylike spatial experience composed of recalled information, unfolding information, and anticipated information. In projects consisting of mostly enclosed spaces, little information is revealed as we travel through corridors and we have limited visual access to the enclosed rooms we pass by. It may be impossible in some of these projects to get an idea of the whole. At the very least, however, we should feel oriented in relation to the point of entry, the sequence of the path,

and the location of our destination. In open projects, we enjoy much greater visual access to a project's parts and features. Because we see more at once, we become better acquainted with the whole and can rely more on accurate real-time impressions and less on our memories.

Below, we look at some examples of how the composition and placement of enclosed spaces affects the resulting spatial patterns and our sense of orientation. Among the variables are the number, size, and arrangement of the open and enclosed areas, the legibility and integrity of the bounding planes, and the use and arrangement of partial-height partitions or of furnishings that obstruct our ability to see beyond.

Enclosed Spaces with Closed Corridors

The spatial experience of projects consisting of enclosed spaces is limited to the experience of enclosed corridors and individual rooms. It is difficult for visitors not familiar with these projects to get a sense of the whole since these projects are partitioned so much. Corridors usually offer no useful clues to help the user know where he or she is. Institutional and office buildings often have these characteristics. Guest room floors in hotels also tend to be this way. Figure 7.28 shows four diagrammatic floor plans as examples. Figure 7.28a shows a circulation loop, a common occurrence in institutional buildings. There is no visual access to rooms on either side of the corridor or to the exterior. The only points of reference serving as orientation cues are the point of entry to the loop, the location of doorways leading to specific rooms, and the signage that identifies the occupants of the suites. Even with those clues, it is easy to lose one's sense of orientation in these corridors. Figure 7.28b–d shows variations of linear arrangements. It is also difficult in these examples to get a real sense of orientation. In Figure 7.28c, users don't even know they are moving diagonally because they have no sense of the configuration of the floor's boundaries. Even when they find out about this relationship they can never experience it directly from the corridor. Only when inside a room or suite can they really see both the diagonal orientation of the front wall and the straight exterior wall. In Figure 7.28d, one experiences walking on a curved corridor, but, once again, from the corridor, one has no sense about how it is oriented to the building's perimeter.

Figure 7.28: It is hard to find points of reference for orientation in totally enclosed corridors. The examples here show a full loop corridor (a), a straight-run corridor (b), a diagonal corridor (c), and a curved corridor (d). Despite their configurational differences, these corridors share the quality of low imageability.

Figure 7.29: Closed corridors that change directions facilitate orientation by breaking the corridor into segments and providing a specific tangible point of reference at the intersection point. Configuration (a) is a simple example of this. The other three options add features to enhance legibility. Configuration (b) features an expanded intersection point. Configuration (c) features different shapes for the two segments. Configuration (d) brings the intersection point to the exterior perimeter.

Figure 7.29a–d offers a different situation. In these four examples the corridor changes direction near the center, therefore establishing a useful point of reference. Without looking at doors or suite numbers you can conceptualize the corridor into three parts: the first leg, the transition point, and the second leg. In Figure 7.29b the transition point is articulated slightly and given more importance, thus becoming more memorable. In Figure 7.29c each leg of the corridor has a unique configurational character, making it possible to distinguish each leg by its shape: the straight one and the curved one. There is less room for misinterpretation when explaining to someone which leg of the corridor you were on at a given time. Figure 7.29d is similar to Figure 7.29a except the transition point occurs all the way at the perimeter window, thus increasing its impact and offering a welcome sense of orientation in relation to the exterior. In this instance it becomes possible to see where you are in relation to the neighborhood outside.

As with the examples shown in Figure 7.29, it would be possible to design corridor systems with not two but three legs. The legs of the corridor and their intersections would become identifiable locations and have the potential to enhance the user's sense of sequence and orientation. The only potential danger with this approach is that too many offsets can confuse more than orient. Therefore, corridor segments should be kept to a reasonable number. For very large and complex projects it is

Figure 7.30: In large complex projects it is counterproductive to use too many corridor segments. After a certain point they confuse more than they inform. The corridor system here shows one alternative approach to achieve differentiation. The number of corridor segments is kept to three while nodes are added at intersections and at the midpoint of the circular segment to provide markers that facilitate further differentiation.

desirable to use other design strategies, such as to create points of reference within each leg instead of adding more corridor segments. Figure 7.30 offers one idea.

Open Spaces with One Enclosed Mass

Visual disclosure is ampler in open spaces. This makes them easier to understand. Figure 7.31a–c shows three diagrammatic plans of open spaces with one single free-standing mass of enclosed spaces. In all three, the perimeter wall is left untouched, thus making it possible to grasp the totality of the open space when walking around it. Notice that it is necessary to move around to see the whole space. The location of the floating mass in all three cases is such that the entire space is not visible from a single vantage point. The character of the open areas is different from case to case. The fact that the solid masses in Figure 7.31b and c are closer to one side improves the

Figure 7.31: The simplest example of a solid element within an open space consists of a freestanding single mass within the space. Here are three examples of this arrangement. In example (a) the mass is centered in space; in examples (b) and (c) the mass is pushed to one of the sides. The floating mass is readable in all three examples, although the spaces around the mass in examples (b) and (c) become different from one another and are, thus, easier to differentiate.

Figure 7.32: In these three examples, a single solid mass is attached to the boundary. Space legibility is simple in all three. The resulting configuration of the open space varies. In examples (a) and (c), the resulting open space is U-shaped but has different proportions. In example (b), the resulting open space is a simple L-shaped configuration.

Figure 7.33: These three examples feature two freestanding masses each. The masses are centered in both directions (a), pushed to one of the long sides (b), and pushed up toward one of the short sides (c). Although similar to the examples in Figure 7.31, these configurations are slightly more complex due to the increased number of parts (one added mass and one added space sandwiched between the two masses).

Figure 7.34: Offset masses in space increase complexity and make the space configuration slightly harder to decipher.

legibility of the space, making it possible to distinguish between the narrow sides and the wider sides.

Figure 7.32 a–c shows three diagrammatic plans similar to the ones we just saw except, in these, the solid mass is attached to the perimeter. The effects are similar to the previous ones except the attachment to the perimeter wall system breaks its continuity, thus making the extent of the outer boundary somewhat ambiguous. In these cases, users are forced to make some assumptions, or actually investigate the existing conditions by going into the enclosed spaces to figure out the perimeter beyond the enclosed mass. In terms of overall orientation within the open space, the task is actually simplified since the open areas are easier to read with the mass moved away from the center.

Open Projects with Multiple Enclosed Masses

We now turn to examples having not one but multiple solid masses in space. One inevitable result of having more parts is an increase in spatial complexity. Even the simple configurations shown require more investigation than before to get a sense of spatial understanding. Figure 7.33 a–c shows three diagrams of plans with two freestanding masses each. The arrangements are similar to the ones in Figure 7.31. The same general observations made there apply here, but now the number of subspaces is greater and more walking around is necessary to assess conditions.

In Figure 7.34 a–c we further complicate things by offsetting the pairs of masses. In Figure 7.35 a–c the masses

Figure 7.35: These three examples show masses of different sizes offset in space. The resulting open spaces vary widely.

Figure 7.36: These three examples feature masses attached to the perimeter. Configuration (a) features three simple rectangular masses. Configurations (b) and (c) mix rectangular and L-shaped masses, adding some complexity. In these cases, due to the obscuring of the boundary, the principal clues used for legibility are the resulting configurations of the internal spaces. The examples with the most visual continuity tend to be the clearest.

Figure 7.37: Five single but irregular freestanding masses are shown here. Despite the complexity of some of the shapes, the fact that they are single masses assures a reasonable degree of clarity. The example featuring two equal sides (b) can be somewhat disorienting as far as distinguishing where you are at any given time. Masses with no equal sides offer greater differentiation among sides.

are offset and of unequal sizes. Notice that the shapes we have used in our examples are simple rectangular ones. With compound or irregular shapes, spatial complexity is even greater and the task of understanding the space more challenging.

Spaces with Partial Obscuring of Boundaries

As we saw above, arrangements in which the perimeter boundary has an exposed, simple, and uninterrupted shape tend to be easier to read than those in which the configuration of the boundary is interrupted by attached masses. We will focus here on a few exampl es where a substantial portion of the perimeter boundary is claimed by masses of enclosed spaces. Figure 7.36a shows an example with three rectangular masses of different sizes claiming three of the four corners. Notice the irregularity of the remaining network of open spaces.

Figure 7.36b and c show examples that utilize L-shaped

masses. In these examples, the resulting open space configurations are even more complicated and difficult to read, although the relatively good shapes of the open spaces make them understandable as a system of linked spaces (even if the greater totality is unclear). The central space and the two partial cross-axes of the configuration in Figure 7.36b make it simpler to understand than the configuration shown in Figure 7.36c. This last one results in a network of open spaces producing three spaces with a couple of narrow corridor-type spaces joining them. These conceptualizations are much easier to make when we see the floor plan from above. In real spaces the twists and turns have a disorienting effect, and it takes much longer to figure things out.

Spaces with One Irregular-Shaped Mass

Irregular-shaped masses can enrich or confuse, depending on their legibility and the characteristics of other building components around them. Figure 7.37 a–e shows five diagrammatic examples of plans having one irregularly shaped mass in the middle. Differences include the regularity of the offsets and the treatment of the different sides.

These examples are oversimplified to make a point. The geometry of the central mass helps to differentiate one side from the others. It is possible also to have masses with similar sides and use some other design elements to make sides read differently from one another. Nevertheless, the impact of masses in space is quite powerful and makes them a principal variable to use for differentiation.

Let's turn our attention now to examples where the internal mass is rotated at an angle in relation to the bounding planes. The principles at work are the same as those discussed above. Namely, the use of uniform or consistent patterns, and the deliberate differentiation among physical characteristics of the sides, will make it easier for users to understand their environment and feel oriented in it.

Figure 7.38a–c illustrates three examples with a single rotated mass floating in the center. In these examples all sides form unique spatial configurations between the mass and the perimeter. Every side becomes unique. This creates the challenge of having to distinguish between, and form mental maps of, unique irregular shapes. As can be seen in the diagrams, the arrangements themselves are rather simple; we are just dealing with one object inside one container. The object's shape is irregular, however, and its relationship to the container is further complicated by the fact that the two are not parallel. Nevertheless, as soon as the observer realizes that the mass is one continuous uninterrupted object, the mystery is solved and the observer can enjoy the richness of the composition.

Let's now look at one useful variation of these mass-in-space studies: the regular mass with superimposed accent. Many projects don't have the kinds of curved, offset, or angled masses we have been showing as examples. Instead, they have ordinary simple rectangular masses. Sometimes the superimposition of portions having unique form characteristics helps to improve imageability. For one thing, the mass becomes more memorable. Additionally, better distinction between sides is possible, and the unique part becomes a strong element that serves as a point of reference, acting as a landmark.

Figure 7.39a–c shows three examples that have similar effects, although using different geometries and compositions. Whatever the design vocabulary used (classic or contemporary), and whether the approach is subtle or bold, this technique can effectively increase the imageability of otherwise plain and featureless masses in a project and identify important destinations.

The Shape of the Boundary

Interior projects take place inside given compartments in buildings that have particular geometric characteristics. The actual boundary may be readable as such, as in the

A   **B**   **C**

Figure 7.38: These three examples feature single, irregularly shaped, freestanding masses. The spaces created are dynamic and complex. Configuration (a) features an L-shaped mass positioned diagonally. Configuration (b) shows a mass with one straight and one curving side. Configuration (c) features a composite shape composed of a square and a semicircle. Flowing shapes (b) tend to be easier to read as a continuous mass, while masses with offsets require more walking around for verification.

A   **B**   **C**

Figure 7.39: The three examples feature simple rectangular masses with asymmetrical superimposed forms protruding from them. Example (a) shows a diagonally oriented rectangle coming off the main straight one. Example (b) shows a fan-shaped mass superimposed over the main rectangle. Example (c) shows a curvilinear mass coming off the corner of the main rectangle. All these protruding masses become distinct, if not dominant, parts that stand out and are remembered.

case of an office building with glass windows around the entire perimeter. At other times it is only partially revealed. There may be two sides exposed to the outside, for instance, while the other two may be adjacent to interior spaces, thus resulting in walls that blend in with the rest and are unrecognizable as boundary walls. The legibility of the boundary is important to our sense of orientation. While we may be able to get around based on an understanding of the route system, it will be nearly impossible to get a clear mental picture of the whole if we don't get a reasonable sense of the boundary. Understanding the extent of the container housing the project helps us understand the project from the outside in.

So far we have looked at examples having simple rectangular perimeter boundaries. We have also assumed that the entire outside perimeter is readable as the boundary. Next, we look at more complex boundaries. Figure 7.40 shows two examples of a complex boundary. The freestanding masses in Figure 7.40a are simple in shape and arrangement. Still, the resulting spaces between them and the perimeter are varied and irregular due to the complex shapes of the boundary. Here we see the reverse of the effects we saw in the examples of simple boundaries with irregular interior masses. Figure 7.40b shows the same perimeter, but this time the internal mass is more complex.

Figure 7.40: The two examples below feature irregularly shaped perimeter configurations. In example (a), the interior consists of two simple staggered masses. In example (b) there is only one mass, offset on the diagonal perimeter side and diagonal on the stepped perimeter side. This avoids the high complexity that would result if the stepping walls on both perimeter and mass were on the same side.

Open Spaces with Partial-Height Elements

So far we have focused on full-height boundaries and internal masses. In other words, we have dealt with masses whose walls go all the way to the ceiling plane, creating a complete visual separation between one side of the wall and another. A very different effect is achieved when tall, yet not full-height walls are used to separate different areas. While a separation is achieved between both sides of the partition, the implications for orientation are different. With partial-height walls, even when they are high enough to obstruct the view straight ahead, one can see the ceiling plane continuing above, an important visual cue. Noticing this, one instantly knows that the condition is merely a break within the same container, and not the end of the space, that both sides of the partial wall are inside the same boundary, an important orientation clue. Figure 7.41 shows a plan and a perspective view illustrating this phenomenon.

The compositions formed by a project's enclosing boundaries, the masses in it (whether freestanding or attached), and other view-obstructing interior elements establish what we see when we move around a project. Results will vary in levels of complexity and clarity, depending on the arrangement. A great part of our sense of order or disorder of a project will be determined by how these compositions are handled. Designers need to devote enough attention to arranging these elements to improve the sense of order and legibility.

Order and Complexity

It is impossible to separate the issues of order and complexity. They go hand in hand. Order is possible, and necessary, at all levels of environmental complexity. More complex environments require more order; simpler ones can get by with less. This brings up the issue of appropriate levels of order. In this chapter, and throughout this book, we have been advocating the importance and necessity of order in interior environments. Does that mean that all projects need to be crystal clear?

The answer is no. Total order can result in boring environments. Total order would mean total regularity without differentiation. Imagine a large project laid out with total and unyielding regularity. It would become as disorienting as a project lacking order. As the layout in

Figure 7.41: These drawings show the effect of partitions that block the view ahead but do not extend to the ceiling. The user's sense of the whole is disrupted less than it is with full-height partitions, because the continuity of the ceiling plane is visible.

Figure 7.42 demonstrates, the optimal level of order for a given project will lie somewhere between the two extremes of perfect order and total chaos.

Appropriate levels of order need to be considered in relation to the project's size, program, and users. Large projects of many interrelated units serving the visiting public, for instance, need more order than smaller projects for familiar users. Some projects may have two levels of order: a clearer one for strangers who visit, and a more challenging one for those who spend time in them daily.

Even in projects that cater to the visitor, it is often unnecessary to reveal the entire order right away by providing instant clarity and disclosure. In fact, it could be argued that order that requires some effort to discover is more rewarding than order perceived without effort. Designers can utilize a more complex order or manipulate the level of disclosure of a simple arrangement to make the order harder to decipher.

Are we saying now, after arguing so strongly for order, that some disorder is actually desirable? Not quite. What we are saying is that complex or not-so-clear order is sometimes appropriate. The key is that there has to be a system or principle of organization behind the arrange-

Figure 7.42: Excessive regularity is as disconcerting as disorder. Notice how this floor plan lacks differentiation. It is spatially monotonous and lacks instinctive clues useful for orientation. Users must count modules and workstations to orient themselves.

ment, and it should be possible, with more or less effort, to figure it out. As long as these two ingredients are present, the designer has a multitude of possibilities to manipulate order to fit the circumstances.

Order is indeed an important and far-reaching concept in the design of interior environments. The topic thus does not end here. Chapter 8 will continue this discussion and address ways to manipulate the levels of order and clarity to produce interest and enrichment. Chapter 10 will address the issue of resolution of form to achieve perceptual order.

People demand a certain degree of clarity in the environment. The optimal degree of order for a given environment varies depending on the people involved and the specific circumstances. It is unrealistic to attempt to understand order without considering factors such as variety and complexity. In fact, a great deal of research has focused on complexity and the degree of preference associated with stimuli of different levels of complexity. Here, we briefly discuss a few basic aspects of this research with a special focus on a framework developed by Rachel and Stephen Kaplan involving complexity and other environmental attributes.

Amos Rapoport has summarized some of the findings of complexity-related research as follows:

1. Animals and humans prefer complex patterns in the visual field.
2. There is an optimum preference range, and both simple visual fields and chaotically complex visual fields are disliked.
3. Complexity can be achieved through ambiguity (meaning multiplicity of meanings and not uncertainty of meanings), through rich and varied environments, and through environments that unfold and reveal themselves gradually.

Daniel Berlyne was one of the pioneers of complexity research. His area of research was animal behavior, with a special emphasis on curiosity and exploratory behavior. When Berlyne started his investigations, the prevailing view about animal motivation emphasized the fact that animals act to satisfy basic needs, such as food and sexual gratification. But, as Ray Crozier explained, Berlyne observed that much behavior was driven by motivations other than the satisfaction of specific needs. He observed that a great deal of behavior was driven by the desire to explore novel situations and events.[1] Based on this insight, Berlyne conducted research and developed theories about exploratory behavior in humans. He suggested that the pleasure derived from works of art could be related to arousal level. He chose to express this in terms of arousal because states of arousal, from sluggishness to high alertness, can be detected and measured objectively.

According to Berlyne, "a work of art is regarded as a stimulus pattern whose collative properties, and possibly other properties as well, give it a positive intrinsic hedonic value."[2] Much of his research focused on his collative variables, named *collative* because they require one to combine the effects produced by them. The variables were ambiguity, complexity, novelty, and surprise. *Hedonic value* is a technical term for pleasure or enjoyment. Berlyne's findings corroborated some existing notions of aesthetics that posited that pleasurable effects are produced when there is a balance between simplicity and complexity, or between order and variety.

In simple terms, Berlyne's findings established that increases in ambiguity, complexity, novelty, and surprise increase one's level of arousal. Thus, scenes of, say, high complexity can be said to have a high arousal potential. He proposed, and his research demonstrated, that hedonic value will increase as the arousal potential of the stimuli (for example, the complexity or novelty of the environment) increases. However, the increase in pleasure will not continue indefinitely. It will reach a peak and then start to decline when stimuli produce uncomfortably high levels of arousal. Figure C7.1 shows the result as an inverted-U curve, known to psychologists as the Wundt curve. What this means is that people prefer moderate over either low or high levels of ambiguity, complexity, novelty, and surprise. They want some stimuli but not too much, with the optimal level varying somewhat from person to person.

Figure c7.1: Berlyne's inverted-U curve showing the effects of arousal potential on hedonic value.

Source: Copyright ©1994 by Ray Crozier. From *Manufactured Pleasures*, by Ray Crozier, Manchester University Press, Manchester and New York, 1994, p. 63.

In an effort to remove distracting associations with known figures and shapes, Berlyne and his colleagues used randomly generated nonsense images for their experiments, as opposed to images of real art or environments. Another researcher, Joachim Wohlwill, later performed similar studies with works of art and photos of outdoor environments. While the results of his research produced the inverted-U relationship, Stephen Kaplan noted that in the case of the outdoor environment, stimuli were relatively weak and the results failed to reach an acceptable level of significance.[3]

Fueled by, among other things, a conviction that the actual content presented by real environments has an important effect on how much people like them, the Kaplans started conducting research of their own concerning environmental preferences. First, they compared preferences of natural and man-made environments. Natural environments were uniformly preferred over their built-environment counterparts. Due to the high variation in preference from scene to scene and a somewhat inconsistent performance of complexity as a predictor, the Kaplans suspected there had to be other predictors of environmental preference. After some analysis, they came up with three other variables.

They noticed that the most preferred scenes featured either a trail that disappeared around a bend or a brightly lit clearing partially obscured from view by foliage in the foreground. In both types of cases, the scene appeared to promise new information if one moved deeper into it. These characteristics were adopted as a variable and labeled *mystery*. Another variable was devised as a result of the realization that scenes varied in the degree that their elements "hung together." Scenes where the elements did not hang together were difficult to grasp and were generally disliked. They named this variable *coherence*, referring to "the ease with which the information in the scene can be organized into a relatively small number of chunks."[4] The fourth and final predictor in their framework was concerned with the perception that it was possible to predict and remain oriented in space as one wandered deeper into the scene. It was called *legibility*, after Lynch's term with a similar meaning.

What these four variables share is the fact that they all provide information that users can utilize to make sense of the environment. The Kaplans divided the information

offered by the variables into two categories: understanding and exploration (Figure C7.2). The degrees of coherence and legibility afforded by the environment assist in its understanding. Coherence can be determined within a single scene. As the Kaplans explained, "A coherent scene is orderly; it is organized into clear areas. People can readily discern the presence of a few distinct regions or areas, and those make it easier to make sense of, or understand, a place."[5] Legibility requires anticipating characteristics of the rest of the space based on a present scene. It requires that some features in the environment be distinct. Featureless environments possess low legibility; however, environments with a strong sense of hierarchy and distinctive features make the reading of their organizing structure easier.

Complexity and mystery, in turn, are related to exploration, although in different ways. The exploration associated with complexity is stationary, visual exploration, as when you visually scan an intricate pattern to explore its contents and relationships. The exploration associated with mystery is more ambulatory. A scene rich in mystery tends to draw you in with the promise of additional information.

It is interesting to note that the Kaplans do not subscribe to the view that too little complexity is boring and too much is overwhelming. They attribute this view to a confusion between coherence and complexity and believe that these two variables act together and influence each other. It is possible, for example, to have acceptably high levels of complexity as long as the organization of the parts is coherent. Conversely, a scene with even moderate complexity can overwhelm if its parts are disorganized or lack coherence.

Unlike other areas of research, this is one where research specifically geared to interior environments has been conducted. Separate studies conducted by Suzanne Scott in relation to interior environments confirmed some of the Kaplans' assertions. In an open-ended study aimed at identifying visual attributes related to preferences in interiors, Scott confirmed preferences for environments that are complex, exhibit strong legibility, and possess some degree of mystery.

A separate study by Scott aimed at testing the effectiveness of complexity and mystery as predictors of interior preferences also found positive correlations between these two variables and preference. As stated by Scott, "The strength of the positive correlations observed between complexity and preference and mystery and preference offer rather convincing evidence supporting the contention that people prefer more involving settings."[6] The study also found a fairly strong correlation between mystery and complexity scores and suggests that "these are not independent qualities and that manipulation of physical design characteristics contributing to perception of one may also contribute to perception of the other. For example, subdividing a larger setting to increase its complexity may simultaneously provide screening devices that introduce mystery."[7]

This study also contributed to a better understanding of the physical characteristics that produce complexity in interiors as well as the influence of the exact nature of the view beyond on perceptions of mystery. In addition to confirming that the number and variety of the elements present in a scene are related to perceived complexity, the study also suggests that composition or pattern of elements in a scene as well as its spatial geometry (volumetric shape and internal articulation) are important contributors to environmental complexity. In terms of mystery, the study provided an insight into the fact that the exact content of the view beyond is likely to influence the degree of preference expressed for the scene. In the study, correlations between mystery and preference were greater when the qualities offered by the view beyond were considered preferable, thus pointing out that the content of an upcoming space is at least as important as the evidence that the space lies beyond and can be accessed if one ventures farther into the scene.

The two quoted studies by Scott demonstrate the frequent correlation of research conducted in different fields. In this case, cognitive models of preference, born of studies of natural and urban landscapes, were also found to be useful to explain preferences in interiors. It is important to note, though, that there are slight, sometimes important differences between one discipline and another. Thus, preferences indicated for nonsense random patterns, natural scenes, urban scenes, buildings, and interior spaces, despite their commonalties, will also exhibit nuances specific to the scale and discipline involved.

The application of these findings is not clear-cut and presents some challenges. In an office setting, for instance, it may be desirable to have a relatively low level of complexity so that people can concentrate. Yet, a case can be made for a relatively high level of intricacy in such an environment since people spend so much time in it day after day. Higher levels of complexity can enrich such an environment by making it possible for the regular user to discover new things from time to time, as happens when one reads a good book for a second and third time.

1. Ray Crozier, *Manufactured Pleasures: Psychological Responses to Design* (Manchester, UK: Manchester University Press, 1994), 61.
2. Ibid., 61.
3. Stephen Kaplan, "Aesthetics, Affect, and Cognition: Environmental Preference from an Evolutionary Perspective," *Journal of Environment and Behavior* vol. 19, no. 1 (Sage Publications: 1987), 6.
4. Ibid., 10.
5. Rachel Kaplan, Stephen Kaplan, and Robert L. Ryan, *With People in Mind* (Washington, D.C.: Island Press, 1998), 14.
6. Suzanne Scott, "Complexity and Mystery as Predictors of Interior Preferences," *Journal of Interior Design* vol. 19, no. 1 (1993): 31.
7. Ibid.

CASE STUDY

One Strong Design Manipulation and a Memorable Route Help Achieve Interest within an Established Order: APCOA/Standard Parking

DESIGN FIRM: MEKUS STUDIOS

Figure CS7.1: Floor plan showing manipulations of the central zone.

The APCOA/Standard Parking Office is a 37,000-square-foot facility housing two parking giants that merged into one. The design provides good examples of the transformation of a simple scheme by the inflection of a single area and the design of a strategic circulation route.

The project consists mostly of enclosed rooms. The only open space of significant size is the open-plan area on the west side of the floor. The totality of the floor is never perceived at once, and a mental image of the project is attained only after one has moved through the entire floor via its corridors. The general circulation scheme is a simple loop around the floor with an additional major cross path through the elevator lobby.

Despite the simplicity and straightforwardness of the basic scheme, we can see how the form manipulations performed around the center radically transformed it (Figure CS7.1). The central portion of the interior mass is rotated approximately ten degrees and extended outward. The resulting mass is articulated as if it were a separate superimposed part, yet one that is still integrated with the orthogonal interior loop. It becomes the main focal mass of the space, transversing the elevator lobby and extend-

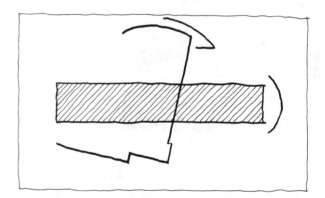

Figure CS7.2: Conceptual parti diagram.

ing in both directions to transform an otherwise ordinary office space into a dynamic composition.

The parti diagram (Figure CS7.2) shows an abstract, simple representation of the project's floor plan. The orthogonal basic grid provides an easy-to-understand organization and, thus, establishes order. The rotated central mass provides diversity and interest. The elevator lobby, reception area, main conference room, two secondary conference rooms, break room, and several support rooms all assume dynamic, irregular shapes.

Figure CS7.3: The diagonal line and offset at the elevator lobby to reception area route, as well as the curved forms on the north end, add dynamism to the project.

The shapes and subdivisions produced by the rotated mass and its articulations also create an interesting interplay of obstructed and unobstructed interior vistas. The twists and turns experienced as one moves around the facility make the perception of the simple plan organization a bit more challenging and rewarding (Figure CS7.3).

Three important aspects of the rotated mass reinforce each other and make this zone the heart of the project: its location at, practically, the geometric center of the plan, its distinct orientation and shape, and the important functions it houses. Because it is at the center of the space and contains the elevator lobby and entry/exit sequence, everybody who visits the floor experiences the rotated mass and can always get oriented in relation to it.

Its unique axis of orientation, its protrusions into the corridors at both ends, and the distinct shapes it adopts at both ends (circular on the north, angled and stepped on the south) make it a recognizable, prominent, and consequently memorable mass on the floor. This mass is prominent not only as a backdrop to other activities around it but also as home to some of the key communal functions of the office and, therefore, an important destination that draws people and activity.

The central rotated mass acts as a divider of space, helping to break down the scale of the floor into well-defined and easily recognized neighborhood areas with comfortable proportions. Particularly clear and successful are the two corner neighborhoods on the east side of the floor. These feature clear and definite entry points, clear edges to separate them from adjacent areas, and short L-shaped corridors to keep the relative distance from end to end manageable and adjacencies strong.

Another interesting aspect of this project is the incorporation of a special tour route to conduct "moving marketing presentations." Prospective customers are taken around designated portions of the office in the process of the tour, thus making the marketing experience interactive and locomotive. The success of the marketing tour is due to the skillful integration of strong anchor destinations with memorable events and in-between channels of moving that reinforce the main selling points without "stealing the show."

Propelled by the movement-inducing dynamic qualities of the rotated central mass, the tour starts in the reception area, where prominent displays of projects and parking structure graphics are featured (Figure CS7.4). After a short walk through corridors that feature samples of parking garage graphics and materials and vivid colors, one arrives at the tour's principal node, a semicircular space that features specialized displays set into a wood-paneled wall (Figure CS7.5). Two turns later, one reaches the main diagonal cross-corridor leading back to the starting point. Along the route the clients can catch a glimpse of the displayed computer room, which serves as the brain for the administration of all the facilities under APCOA/Standard Parking's management. One of two conference rooms becomes the final destination for further talks (Figure CS7.6).

Figure CS7.4: Displays of projects and parking structure directories are prominent features of the reception area, the starting point for the marketing tour.

Figure CS7.5: One of the highlights of the marketing tour is the semicircular wood-paneled node on the east side of the floor.

Figure CS7.6: The comfortable and elegant conference rooms provide a fitting destination after the marketing tours.

REVIEW

Summary

One of the major contributions a designer makes is endowing the built environment with order. Environmental order manifests itself in different ways: order related to proper fit, order related to visual harmony, and order related to spatial orientation.

Designers should strive to provide more than just neat and functional organization, and provide an overall structure based on sound organizing principles. Interior environments are experienced sequentially, one space at a time. Sometimes, what appears clear on paper while looking at a floor plan is hard to figure out as we move about in built space. Three factors that help facilitate the understanding of interiors are identity, structure, and meaning. Environments strong in order have easily identifiable main components, a systematic structure derived from an organizing principle, and meaningful destinations.

The ten place elements introduced in Chapter 3 play important roles in providing environmental legibility and order. Notable are the role of arrival spaces, paths, nodes, and landmarks. To feel oriented inside buildings it is necessary to understand components at various hierarchical levels: parts, groups, relationships between parts, sequences, and, finally, the whole. Many design strategies are available to make these various components stand out clearly so they can be understood and remembered. By making individual parts and groupings recognizable, their points of intersection visible, their sequences memorable, and the structure of the whole comprehensible through the proper provision of environmental information, designers bring order to the projects they design.

A crucial aspect related to legibility and order is the composition of the masses and spaces of a project. Predominantly enclosed projects with closed corridors are the most difficult to understand due to the lack of visual accessibility. Open spaces are easier to decipher. Nevertheless, it is possible to design predominantly open projects of great complexity. The number, size, placement, orientation, and shape of masses and the complexity and level of disclosure of the boundary all combine to produce spaces of different levels of complexity and readability.

Order is possible at all levels of complexity. In general, the more complex a project is, the greater the need for order to help users feel oriented. Optimal levels of order will vary from project to project depending on their scope and users. The level of order established and the level of difficulty involved in understanding it are factors controlled by the designer. If appropriate design choices are made, the level of order achieved will help orient users in space by facilitating their understanding of the environment, its place within the larger context, and their position within these environments at any particular time.

1. Bernard Leupen, *Design and Analysis* (New York: Van Nostrand Reinhold, 1997), 25.
2. Stanley Abercrombie, *Architecture as Art: An Esthetic Analysis* (New York: Van Nostrand Reinhold, 1984), 147.
3. Christian Norberg-Schulz, *Genius Loci* (New York: Rizzoli International, 1980), 19.
4. Romedi Passini, *Wayfinding in Architecture* (New York: Van Nostrand Reinhold, 1992), 45.
5. Pierre Von Meiss, *Elements of Architecture* (London: Van Nostrand Reinhold International, 1990), 110.
6. Kevin Lynch, *The Image of the City* (Cambridge: MIT Press, 1960), 8.
7. Ibid., 9.
8. Passini, 111.
9. Ibid., 120.
10. Von Meiss, 31–52.

Chapter Questions

1. Name three examples of order related to fit.
2. What is meant by architectonic order related to visual harmony?
3. What are the main concerns of order related to orientation?
4. Describe how interior environments are experienced.
5. Name and define the three factors that facilitate understanding and orientation in interiors.
6. How can domains and centers contribute to order?
7. Why are arrival spaces so important for orientation?
8. How can paths be used to supply order?
9. How do nodes and landmarks contribute to order?
10. Name and define four design strategies to facilitate understanding of project parts.
11. Name and define four design strategies to facilitate legibility of groupings.
12. Name and explain two design strategies to clarify the relationships between project parts.
13. Name and describe three design strategies to increase awareness of motion and sequence in interior environments.
14. Name and explain four strategies to help users understand a project as a whole.
15. What effect does attaching masses to the perimeter boundary have on legibility and orientation?
16. Why does it sometimes make sense to design freestanding masses with no equal sides?

Exercises

1. Select an important space, a *center*, of a past or present design project and determine three design strategies to make it more memorable inside and outside.
2. Sketch two ways to make an *arrival space* enhance the user's sense of orientation.
3. Sketch three *paths* with different levels of disclosure to the rest of the project.
4. Design two versions of a vibrant *node* for any project type.
5. Design one memorable *landmark* for an interior project.
6. Make a part (mass or space) of one of your projects stand out by using one or more of the strategies discussed in this chapter.
7. Sketch two ways of using a *datum* to group parts of one of your past or present design projects.
8. Select a prominent space from one of your past or present projects and expand its level of *visibility* toward other interior areas. Sketch the result.
9. Sketch two *sequences* of past or present projects using some of the strategies we discussed to make them legible and useful for orientation.
10. Design one idea using the concept of *points of reference* to facilitate orientation in interior projects.
11. Sketch two ideas to increase the imageability of closed corridors in a compartmentalized project.
12. Sketch two ideas (one formal, one casual) to group all the solids of a past or present project within one (freestanding or attached) mass.
13. Sketch two ideas (one formal, one casual) similar to the ones above using not one but two masses.

CHAPTER 8
Enrichment

INSTRUCTIONAL OBJECTIVES

- Explain the need for both environmental stimulation and environmental stability.

- Present general principles to enrich interior spaces.

- Show ways to incorporate meaningful events along circulation routes.

- Present strategies to enhance the formal qualities of the path itself.

- Show ways to design the views within and beyond the path.

- Suggest a framework for the enrichment of personal experience while stationary.

My house is practical. I thank you, as I might thank Railway engineers, or the Telephone service. You have not touched my heart.

—*Le Corbusier,* Towards a New Architecture

THE INTRODUCTORY QUOTE by Le Corbusier reminds us of the need to address a key, and sometimes forgotten, function of design: to enrich, to touch the human heart. The commitment to find ways to do this is what distinguishes a designed solution from an engineered solution. This chapter addresses ways to make projects more than engineered, functional solutions.

In Chapter 7 we discussed the role of order in design. Regularity and clarity make interior environments easier to understand, satisfying our inherent need for making sense of the world. However, too much order can be monotonous. We also need variety and interest in our environment. One of the challenges for the designer is achieving an adequate balance between these seemingly conflicting needs. In reality, order and enrichment are highly intertwined and form part of a single puzzle. Expression is also a piece in this puzzle, but it will be covered in the next chapter. These different variables are presented in separate chapters to facilitate understanding of their unique contributions. In real projects, they are usually explored simultaneously while different design ideas are being considered.

In this chapter we first discuss the role of enrichment in the design of interiors. The rest of the chapter presents ways of making projects and our experiences in them richer. The strategies are broken down into three categories: general enrichment strategies, enrichment while in transit, and enrichment while stationary.

ORDER AND ENRICHMENT

We concluded our last chapter by saying that too much order can be as undesirable as too little order. The optimal level of order for a project must fall somewhere between those two extremes. Order makes a project visually agreeable and understandable. Order involves repetition and follows rules based on a predetermined principle of organization. It offers constancy and predictability. We quickly become familiar with highly ordered projects.

The human mind values predictability and constancy in the environment, but it also seeks novelty and variety. Opinions about how much and what kind of the above qualities are optimal can be quite personal. They can vary from project to project and from designer to designer. Furthermore, the potential approaches and combinations used to produce order, novelty, and variety are limitless. It is possible to achieve a desirable balance of these qualities with alternate design solutions quite different from each other.

Let's start by examining how reducing the degree of regularity can enrich a project. Consider an alternate version of the highly regular project presented in the last chapter in Figure 7.42. Suppose you had the same programmatic needs to fulfill but wanted to add some novelty and interest within a similar design vocabulary of rectilinear forms. Just by manipulating the placement of the solid modules, as shown in Figure 8.1, the project acquires enough variety to alleviate its severe sense of repetition. The project is now inherently more interesting and has more differentiation between zones, even though the parts are still highly repetitive.

Let's take it a step further. Suppose you were concerned with the experience of moving through the project and wanted to make it even more interesting. Figure 8.2 shows the solid modules of the same project arranged to provide various different experiences as one moves from one end to the other. Although the movement is basically straight throughout for most of the length, the two offsets and their placement divide the floor into three zones with two transitional areas between them.

Finally, suppose you wanted to enrich the daily experience of each worker as perceived from his or her desk. You might then arrive at something like what is shown in Figure 8.3. The typical worker, regardless of location, now has an identifiable sense of place that provides a focus for the area and anchors users in space. If the solid masses

Figure 8.1: The simple act of moving some of the solid masses of the floor plan presented in Figure 7.42 produces a more interesting design.

Figure 8.2: This arrangement seeks to enhance the circulation experience. The project's masses have been rearranged to increase variety and interest. Sometimes one is walking between a mass and an open space, other times between two masses, and still others between two open spaces.

Figure 8.3: Depending on their desk location, workers in this facility have one or more masses close by that act as anchoring devices and internal focal points.

Figure 8.4: This arrangement is similar to the one in Figure 8.3 but provides an even stronger sense of containment and group territory.

viewed from there had some special surface articulation or wall treatment that was pleasant to look at, the experience would be further enhanced. Figure 8.4 shows a similar example with an even stronger sense of definition and containment, especially in the interior zones.

Each of the manipulations mentioned in our example above enriched different aspects of the project. The modifications performed in Figure 8.1 gave the project, in general, an increased level of interest due to the additional variety. Users and visitors could still sense order and harmony throughout, but without the excessive original regularity. The simple modifications increased the level of spatial articulation and complexity, but modifications were done in such a way as to provide relief and engage the mind without confusing it.

The modifications performed in Figure 8.2 made the act of moving through the project more interesting. Now, in the process of traveling from one point to another, users encounter meaningful intermediary events that enrich the journey. The modifications in Figures 8.3 and 8.4 make it possible for users, while working at their desks, to engage a bit more meaningfully with their internal surroundings. Instead of interior masses being just rooms, they now perform the additional duties of anchoring adjacent open

areas and providing beneficial focal points on which to rest the eyes.

Are these kinds of interventions necessary? Not really. Projects can be functional without them. Are they desirable? Of course they are. They enhance the experience of the people using the space. Some designers give more consideration to these matters than others. It is important that you develop your awareness and skills to perform these kinds of manipulations to make your projects more enriching.

A Case for Project Enrichment

The success of most interior projects relies more on function than anything else. As we said earlier, the context of the project and the requirements of the program give a project its fundamental form. Response to these alone determines the size and location of the different areas of a project. However, response to function alone will rarely produce the best form. Form has to be dealt with in its own right, respecting the placements and adjacencies dictated by the context and program, but following its own agenda to produce experiential desirable qualities. It takes conscious and intentional effort from you as the designer to provide more than good function and pleasant aesthetics.

It is common for design to be limited to the functional and the artistic. Designers put a lot of effort into resolving the way things work and the way they look. What we are proposing here is that design should be just as concerned with the way things are, the way they are arranged, and the effect these design decisions have on those who experience them. You may think of this dimension as the poetic dimension of projects.

Architecture is unique among the arts in that people operate within its structures most of the time. Designers, as part of their craft, have the responsibility to determine the spaces and sequences of buildings. In doing so, they have the power to create experiences that seduce and stimulate or to downplay physical aspects of the building in order to provide a barely noticeable background to the theater of life. This is a remarkable power. While an attractive appearance is always desirable, we remind you that even visually plain projects can possess poetry in their composition.

Achieving qualities and experiences that engage the user and enrich his or her experience requires designers to adopt a separate agenda concerning these issues. These qualities and experiences rarely occur without a conscious desire to produce them. They require the designer's commitment to seek them out and work on them so they occur seamlessly without neglecting or disturbing the other requirements of the project. It may become necessary for you to negotiate between the various requirements and agendas of the project in order to balance them satisfactorily. This will often require compromise. For example, you may occasionally have to consider moving a room a couple of spaces down from its optimal functional position in order to achieve a more desirable experiential or compositional effect. These types of decisions are sometimes difficult and are not always possible. They need to be con-

sidered on a case-by-case basis and require proper insight and input from the users and design team alike.

So, your task is to manipulate the required physical parts of the project in order to achieve more evocative effects and meaningful encounters within it. Is this really possible, you may ask, with the kind of strict and limiting programs designers have to work with? It's seldom simple. It often requires an approach where project parts perform double functions. A wall may be the enclosing plane of a room needing privacy and also the canvas for an experientially rich corridor on the other side. The resulting configuration of the wall, therefore, may be a compromise that works for both of these intentions.

Another approach used sometimes is the incorporation of spaces and events not required by the program to enrich the experience of users. The enlargement of an important intersection to create an energetic node and the addition of small niches for people to gather in are examples. Of course, the addition of space to a program is a sensitive matter requiring proper justification in the eyes of the client. It is often impossible to add additional square footage to a project, and whatever amenities are desired have to be planned skillfully within the physical size constraints of the project.

Intentionality

The effect the interior of a building has on its users is produced by a combination of factors, some having nothing to do with the environment itself. In Chapter 2 we explained how the nature of the occasion, the people involved, nearby activities, and other similar factors affect our experience. Even when we consider building aspects only, the resultant effect is produced by an interplay between a number of elements we perceive simultaneously at different levels, many of them subconsciously. The spatial character, the order of spaces, the furnishings, the materials, the colors, the sounds, the lighting, the artwork, the details, and the specific combination of all of the above act in unison and produce an overall effect on us.

It is impossible to separate form from meaning. Most everything in the environment elicits associations that conjure certain connotations and levels of personal response. Certain aspects of design stimulate more symbolic associations than others. Specific design styles, materials, and graphic representations (artwork and photography, for instance) usually have strong associations with specific attitudes and ways of being. Other aspects are more neutral and harder to label. We tend to experience these as they are, for what they offer or present to us, without much symbolic interference. In this chapter we will focus on formal rather than symbolic aspects of form. Symbolic aspects of design are addressed in the next chapter.

Designers need to consider some important questions in order to formulate a personal philosophy regarding the extent to which they allow themselves to manipulate design for effect. For instance, how does one go about manipulating space to increase the level of engagement between users and their environment? Is it even right to perform somewhat arbitrary manipulations for the sake of effect? To what extent is well-intentioned artistic license a right or privilege of the designer?

Personal positions related to these questions are likely to vary. Some designers favor straightforwardness over cleverness, some favor simplicity over complexity, some like the realistic and pictorial over the abstract and obscure. Whatever your personal position may be, it is important that you are clear about it and pursue it consistently within each project. Design manipulations for effect may sometimes come across as superficial. It is therefore imperative that all interventions are well thought out and considered carefully before implementation. Many seemingly good ideas are better left undone if they will lose their impact and seem foolish after their novelty wears off.

Stimulation and Stability

Having issued the above warnings, we maintain that it is worthwhile to manipulate project forms, spaces, and elements to increase their richness and enhance the users' experience. The rest of this chapter addresses specific attributes and strategies for your consideration. We will start by introducing two opposing human needs that you must understand before embarking on the task of manipulating projects for enrichment. They are stimulation and stability.

Stimulation

We have said that optimal qualities of the visual field lie somewhere between total regularity and total disorder; the exact levels depend on the particular realities of each project. Despite our need to perceive order and the sense of orientation and satisfaction that comes with it, we also have a desire to experience environmental stimulation. An efficient, functional, and orderly environment that does not stimulate will rarely satisfy. People need some level of stimulation.

Optimal levels and kinds of stimulation are relative. A nightclub, for instance, demands much more stimulation than a hotel guest room. In the nightclub, the combination of design features, colors, lights, loud music, and interesting people produces a very high-load environment. This, we recognize, is appropriate for the project type. The hotel guest room, in contrast, other than being cheerful and welcoming, needs to be a good place to unwind and relax. Therefore, bright blinking lights, extravivid colors, and loud music are not likely to be appreciated.

Stability

Although we make the point that some level of stimulation is healthy for all projects, some projects, or parts of projects, benefit from less environmental stimulation. Spaces where repose, peacefulness, and concentration are desirable don't want to be highly stimulating. Hospital rooms, for example, need to be pleasant in a quiet, non-agitating way. Stable places can be evocative and powerful in some ways, but should not be visually loud. Areas of mental activity requiring high concentration, such as private offices in some work facilities, should be conducive to concentration without much distraction. Areas meant for relaxation, such as the hotel guest room mentioned above, usually need to be subdued more than stimulating. Keep in mind, however, that the desire for subtle and subdued qualities doesn't necessarily mean the elimination of all stimulating features.

Part of the challenge of design is determining the appropriate level of stimulation and the means of achieving it. Understanding the effects of these two fundamental, and opposite, forces will help you make judgments about the correct balance of the stimulation/stability spectrum for a specific project. In the rest of this chapter we discuss attributes and strategies that help make projects engaging. They can all be handled in ways that provide more or less stimulation and can, therefore, be utilized in both high-load and low-load environments.

Enrichment in Building Interiors

In Chapter 2 we analyzed the basic events of the building experience. Starting from the approach to the building, we described the process of arriving, waiting, proceeding to, and arriving at the target destination within the facility. In Chapter 3, we presented a related set of project parts labeled the place elements. Some of these, such as arrival spaces and destination spaces, relate directly to the various rituals of the building experience. By thinking of the basic events of the building experience and the places where they occur, we can gain awareness of opportunities to enrich the experience of users. Below, we address a few of the place elements especially apt for enriching design manipulations and point out some instances in which to use them.

The arrival space gives visitors their first impression of a project. Whatever message that is to be communicated to the user begins here. Additionally, this space represents an important transition from the space immediately outside, and between itself and the rest of the facility. Among the design variables available for manipulation in order to provide opportunities for engagement are the overall impact of the space, the level of visual disclosure to other spaces in the facility, and the freedom of movement from the space.

Waiting involves anticipation. It sometimes induces a state of heightened awareness as we anxiously wait for someone to rescue us and take us to our real destination. Other times, the act of waiting supplies a few minutes between tasks during which we can have a chance to unwind. For some, the close proximity to other people can be uncomfortable. Waiting areas offer opportunities to provide engaging graphic or verbal information about the entity housed in the facility (whether a corporation, a health-care facility, or a restaurant). They are also good places to add elements of visual relief.

The circulation spaces of a project present great opportunities to engage the user with building elements as well as with the rest of the facility. The design of the main corridors is one of the most important design factors of many projects. Unfortunately, corridors are often not given the attention they deserve. If properly orchestrated and articulated, the circulation experience can delight, entice, and provide engaging sequences.

Destination spaces, you may recall, are the spaces where we usually do what we came to do in the facility, be it work, eat, study, socialize, or shop. When we engage in our target activity, the building and its interiors and elements take a secondary, supporting role. The actions in these spaces may focus on paperwork, food, books, people, or merchandise, among many possibilities. Even in these spaces, where the facility, like a good butler, should be unobtrusive except to provide utilitarian assistance when needed, there are opportunities for enrichment. Design manipulations can enhance users' abilities to focus on the task at hand, connect with adjacent surroundings, and find momentary relief in well-conceived and well-placed views and vistas.

GENERAL ENRICHMENT STRATEGIES

Below, we present a number of enrichment strategies. For convenience, we have grouped them into three categories: general enrichment strategies, enrichment strategies for users while in transit, and enrichment strategies for users while stationary. The first group can be exercised anywhere within the project, either throughout or in select areas. The second group is specific to circulation areas. The third group is closely associated with areas where we spend time doing something while stationary, such as destination spaces and waiting areas.

Variety

The relatively simple manipulations performed in Figures 8.1 through 8.4 at the beginning of this chapter show the profound effect of variety in projects. Although the organization of the project in the various schemes remained relatively formal and regular, the modifications provided relief and interest. In projects where parts are not repetitive, there is a natural occurrence of variety. In projects that feature repeated parts, it is up to the designer to provide enough variety to avoid monotony and make the project more challenging perceptually. Sometimes all it takes is a few basic shifts, as seen in the examples mentioned above. Other times a greater degree of variety and differentiation may be desirable. In those cases, variety becomes complexity.

Complexity

Environmental complexity has been a well-researched topic in studies of environmental preference (see Capsule #7: "Complexity, Order, and Other Environmental Attributes"). Research indicates that people tend to prefer higher levels of environmental complexity up to a certain point, beyond which any increase produces discomfort. That critical point varies from individual to individual. Design features to add complexity can be anything from lines on a wall to the heavy articulation of surfaces, ornamental features, or multiple and varied objects in space.

The relationship between complexity and order has also been studied. Environments high in order have been found to tolerate higher levels of complexity than those with less order. Therefore, the number and kind of elements in a space and their specific arrangement go hand in hand and work together. Complexity is rewarding because it stimulates the brain. Complex orchestration of parts requiring some mental effort to decipher is stimulating as long as the effort required is not overly taxing. There is a sense of accomplishment in understanding arrangements that challenge our mental faculties.

Environmental complexity occurs at many levels and can be produced a number of ways. The surfaces of enclosing planes and other elements (such as columns) can be articulated in increasingly complex ways. The number and arrangement of masses and objects in space can be manipulated to achieve increasing levels of complexity. Also, the treatment and orientation of project components (floors, walls, furnishings, and so on) can be treated as different layers and arranged in contrasting ways to achieve complexity. We examine them in more detail below.

Surface Articulation

One important way you can provide environmental complexity is through the articulation of the enclosing planes. The degree of complexity can be minimal, just enough to provide some interest, or it can be substantial, enough to challenge our senses and even overwhelm us. One simple way to provide subtle articulation is by **modulation**, the subdivision of any element, such as a surface, into smaller components or modules that, in turn, add up to the whole. Modulation on surfaces usually relies on the

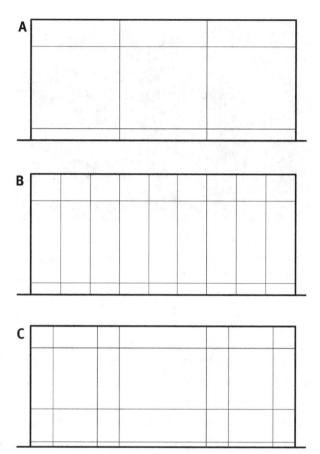

Figure 8.5: The three elevations shown are examples of modulation using lines. The level of intricacy can be minimal (a), moderate and regular (b), or moderate and irregular (c).

use of regulating lines. Thus, a simple and featureless wall can acquire a sense of texture by the addition of lines produced by either molding strips or reveals.

Figure 8.5a shows a simple wall subdivided by the use of lines. Although the level of complexity achieved is minimal, the modulation of the wall is enough to give it some interest. The lines have to be placed so that a good sense of scale and proportion is achieved. Otherwise, the attempt to enrich will do more harm than good. Figure 8.5b shows the wall modulated into an increased number of equal parts. Although the result produces a degree of richness, the composition is not very interesting. The modules of the wall in Figure 8.5c feature an irregular rhythm, thus resulting in a more varied and complex arrangement incorporating a sense of hierarchy. If the material used is wood or stone, their graining and veining would supply still another level of richness due to

Figure 8.6: This corridor in a corporate facility utilizes horizontal, vertical, and angled reveal lines on the walls and columns, thus giving some articulation to otherwise featureless architectural elements.

Figure 8.7: Pattern and lines applied to floors and ceilings also increase relative complexity and supply richness. The orderly arrangement of the floor pattern makes it rich without seeming overly complex, despite the intricate pattern.

their subtle patterning. Figure 8.6 shows an example of the use of surface modulation in an office facility.

The example in Figure 8.7 shows modulation on both the floor and ceiling. Here, the modules are smaller in size and larger in number than in the previous wall example. There is some complexity. The floor tiles are arranged in a repetitive pattern, and this makes the composition easy to understand despite the variety of tiles. In fact, it is possible to keep adding layers of complexity to a composition such as this and keep it within acceptable perceptual levels if the parts are arranged in some perceivable pattern. The ceiling composition shown here is nonhierarchical and repetitive. The end result is increased textural richness at the ceiling plane.

Modulation can also be accomplished by **surface relief**. With this technique, alternating parts of a surface advance or recede to create differentiation. The result is similar to the one created by lines, but, in the case of relief, the sense of depth is manipulated to create more pronounced effects. Notice how the composition shown in Figure 8.8 uses depth to provide a sense of articulation to the wall unattainable with just lines.

Spatial Composition

Complexity can also be attained by the composition of elements in space. By manipulating the disposition of architectural and interior elements in the visual field you can produce interesting and rich compositions. Factors that play a part and can be manipulated are the number of parts and their size, shape, and arrangement. While the

Figure 8.8: Surface relief provides modulation three-dimensionally. In this rotunda space, instead of mere lines or reveals, the effect is accentuated by deeper recesses and protrusions on the walls and ceilings.

number of parts is often dictated by the program, such as the number of tables in a restaurant's dining area or the number of display fixtures in a retail store, it is possible to manipulate the amount of architectural articulation

Figure 8.9: Spatial complexity adds richness and interest. A sense of complexity is accomplished in this office through the playful interplay between wall, ceiling, and floor elements.

around them to increase or decrease the overall level of complexity. Figure 8.9 shows two views of an office facility where curves and angles are used to create a stimulating environment of some complexity.

The size and shape of the various objects in the visual field also enter the complexity equation. Groups of similarly sized and shaped objects will be fairly uniform and perceived as simpler than the same number of objects with different sizes and shapes. Grouping objects by similarity of size or shape will produce a greater sense of order and, thus, allow more variation. Figure 8.10 shows a simple example illustrating this principle. Two groups of workstations are arranged somewhat randomly in Figure 8.10a, and grouped according to similarity in Figure 8.10b and 8.10c.

A way of providing ordered complexity when dealing with parts of different sizes or shapes is by using pattern. If a harmonious pattern is established and it is easy to see, then the arrangement can be successful despite the variety among the objects. See Figure 8.10b, which shows an example of this using a variety of furniture workstations arranged in a simple pattern (by size), producing a simple composition despite the use of parts of different sizes.

Arrangement is important in manipulating complexity. You can make a simple group of a few components more interesting by using an irregular spatial composition. Conversely, you can control the complexity produced by a

Figure 8.10: The level of perceived complexity is affected by the way in which different pieces are arranged. Groupings that mix unequal elements (a) tend to be more complex than those where similar parts are grouped together. Where unequal elements are grouped together, simplicity and harmony can be achieved if they are grouped to form a pattern, such as a progression from smaller to larger (b and c).

collection of many disparate parts by utilizing more regular arrangements. Even projects that have immense inherent density and variety of parts can be controlled by the use of pattern and regularity.

Figure 8.11: In this example, the floors, ceilings, enclosing walls, and furnishings are treated independently and given different orientations to produce a more complex arrangement.

System Overlapping

One unique way to produce complexity in the interior environment is to think of different spatial components as layers that can be manipulated independently of each other. You can think of a project as consisting of the following systems: the enclosing boundary, the floor plane, the interior walls, the ceiling plane, the furnishings, the building structure, miscellaneous objects in space, such as suspended elements and fixtures, and details. All these systems overlap with one another to produce the final composition. A perfectly ordered arrangement would have all these systems aligned neatly in parallel or perpendicular relationships to one another. When some of these systems are rotated laterally in relation to the others, an interesting, more complex effect is produced while maintaining a sense of order, as shown in Figure 8.11.

This technique can be used in subtle ways by performing slight rotations (or other kinds of variations) and by the alteration of a few systems. It can also be used in ways that produce extreme complexity by rotating all systems so they each have different orientations.

Novelty

Another enriching factor in the environment is novelty. Novel shapes and arrangements attract our attention and engage our minds. Novelty goes beyond mere variety. The novelty can be due to the uniqueness or the unconventionality of the approach taken. In any case, the novel approach is different from the norm. As with any of the other variables, the degree of application can vary from subtle to extreme. A space can be slightly unique or highly unusual.

Spatial novelty can be produced by the nature of individual masses and elements in space and their shapes, as well as by their combination into specific arrangements having novel effects. In general, regular shapes, usually rectangular, and uniform rectilinear arrangements are considered the norm, the conventional default approach we customarily see. Almost any design deviating from these approaches has the potential for being novel and attracting our attention if done skillfully.

Figure 8.12: One of the ways to achieve novelty is by making the shape of space itself unusual and different.

Figure 8.13: Architectural elements with playful shapes are novel and increase the interest of a space, as the overhanging curved soffit does here.

A

B

C

Figure 8.14: Surfaces such as elevation compositions can be treated in unusual novel ways. A simple elevation requiring a door and a window (a) can be composed in different, even highly unusual ways (b and c).

Examples of novelty include unusual shapes of architectural elements (Figures 8.12 and 8.13), unusual treatment of specific visual elements, such as openings and elevations (Figures 8.14 and 8.15), and unusual arrangements in space, such as the effect produced by taking otherwise normal arrangements to an extreme, as in the case of extreme geometry and rhythm (Figure 8.16).

Boldness

Boldness, a specific kind of novelty, requires its own category. It relies on exaggeration to make something stand out in the environment. Often associated with boldness of treatment, such as surface treatment, it can also be expressed spatially. Accomplishable in interiors by exaggerated applications of anything from color to light to texture, when related to space it usually involves the exaggeration of shape or scale, making them much more intense than normal.

Examples of boldness include the exaggeration of a shape to an extreme, the use of very bold color, and the use of exaggerated, imposing form, as shown in Figure 8.17. Boldness of scale involves the exaggeration of size. While large spaces can be associated with grandiosity, large masses are more effective at achieving boldness because of their heaviness and their figural character. They become almost defiant. It helps if they have some

Figure 8.15: The nonorthogonal orientation of this storefront window creates a novel effect.

Figure 8.16: A simple arrangement, such as the staggering of masses, can stand out as different and novel if handled severely. In this example, the insistent and regular repetition of the idea makes it stand out.

degree of verticality and detachment from surrounding walls. Being able to see the entire mass as a freestanding object in space helps to accentuate its massiveness.

Tension

A strategy that is sure to engage the mind, and the emotions, is the use of deliberate tension in the environment. The goal is to create a situation of temporary tension in order to heighten the user's emotions. Long-term exposure to environmentally tense spaces can be detrimental and should be avoided. Short-term exposures of appropriate intensities can be enhancing, especially when part of a sequence that eventually provides welcome relief.

Tension can be produced by overtaxing the senses with extreme levels of the already discussed conditions of complexity, novelty, and boldness. High levels of these conditions can actually be appropriate in high-load environments like nightclubs, some retail applications, especially those targeted for the youth, and short-term high-load settings, such as some restaurants. On the other hand, environments such as workplace and institutional settings do not normally tolerate these conditions.

Two additional strategies to provide enrichment through tension are the use of intentional visual discord and intentional compression. Visual discord is equivalent to dissonance in music. It requires intentional incongruity. Its intensity and extent have to be carefully considered in order to avoid highly negative reactions. The technique is inherently risky, as many people will not appreciate any deliberate attempts to produce disharmony. Additionally, intentional discord can easily be confused with lack of design skill.

Tension through compression can be successfully applied in selected points along a route or sequence by the deliberate compression of space to produce a tightening effect. The tightening can be sudden (Figure 8.18a) or gradual (Figure 8.18b). Its duration can be just an instant

Figure 8.17: The protruding curved wall is highly unconventional and somewhat playful.

Figure 8.18: A common way to produce tension is by the compression of space. The five examples shown to compress space along a route achieve different levels and durations of tension.

A

B

C

D

E

(Figure 8.18c) or longer (Figure 8.18d). Finally, relief can come suddenly or gradually (Figure 8.18e).

Ambiguity

The use of ambiguity to engage users relies on the presentation of mixed messages in order to confuse and/or challenge the mind. Instead of a crystal-clear and consistent message, a muddled one is presented. This is another tricky strategy requiring good judgment and skill for success. American architect Robert Venturi argued for the value of ambiguity in design in his classic book, *Complexity and Contradiction in Architecture*. He noted: "An architectural element is perceived as form *and* structure, texture *and* material. These oscillating relationships, complex and contradictory, are the source of the ambiguity and tension characteristic to the medium of architecture. The conjunction 'or' with a question mark can usually describe ambiguous relationships. Is it a square plan or not? Are they near or far? Big or small?"[1]

Examples of ambiguity in interiors include an almost perfectly symmetrical elevation—with enough inconsistencies to provoke the question: Is it symmetrical or not? (Figure 8.19)—and a corridor utilizing a forced perspective to make it seem longer than it actually is, provoking the question: Is it a short or long corridor? (Figure 8.20).

All these instances of ambiguity may or may not be justifiable. In general, they are more justifiable when they are a result of the inherent complexities and contradictions of a project. They can be questionable when they are arbitrary, although there are times when they may serve a worthwhile purpose. There may be some usefulness, for instance, in making a corridor seem longer than it actually is to exaggerate and enhance the sense of transition between two areas of a facility.

Pictorialness

As modern design has evolved, we have grown accustomed to environments that are complex and more abstract than in the past. There is greater tolerance and demand for the less literal and the more cerebral. The pictorialness, symmetry, and straightforwardness of the past are no longer dominant. Nevertheless, well-composed pictorial project parts still continue to engage and delight many of us. Not everything has to be complex, novel, or ambiguous to be enriching. In fact, many people still prefer the straightforward to the overproduced or ambiguous. Although pictorial compositions lost favor with the emergence of the more abstract modern movement during the twentieth century, they did not disappear. Well-composed pictorial elevations, often formal and symmetrical, are still a joy to look at. They engage our minds and make us appreciate them. The same is true for the well-composed detail, be it a column or a railing. Whether simple and serene

Figure 8.19: Ambiguity can be used playfully, such as in these two house elevations by Robert Venturi that appear to be symmetrical; elements in each break the perfect symmetry.

Figure 8.20: Illusions, such as the use of a forced (exaggerated) perspective here, are also ambiguous. The corridor will seem longer than it really is, and a user may wonder why it feels so deep when it really isn't.

Figure 8.22: Intensifying use to create vital areas of high energy produces enrichment by use. Activity, sounds, and movement themselves become the agents of variety and complexity.

Figure 8.21: Well-composed pictorial spaces and elevations have delighted for centuries and are still appropriate today. Here are two straightforward, formal, symmetrical elevations.

or more active through articulation, it is still a source of delight (Figure 8.21).

Activity Manipulation

One final general strategy for enrichment involves not the kind of manipulation of building elements for effect presented in the examples above but the strategic placement of certain functional areas that become instruments of enrichment by attracting people. Examples include spaces whose vitality results from a concentration of human activity and spaces that foster in us a sense of special meaning because some specific opportunity has been thoughtfully provided.

A specific example of the first case above is a space, such as a node, located strategically in such a way that it is impossible to get around the building without going through it. Because of its centrality, it is likely to have constant traffic and activity. Furthermore, if some strategic function can be located within or adjacent to that area, acting as a magnet, then not only would people pass by, some would stay. This may elicit images of the urban plaza with cafes around it. It is not that different, although the scale and specific functions are likely to vary in interiors. In these cases, the vitality and energy of the people themselves enrich the space and

Figure 8.23: This student area in an academic building is usually filled with people. The increased level of activity makes the space one of the most energetic and vital in the entire building.

attract others to join in. It has nothing to do with the composition of elements for effect and everything to do with the strategic placement of functions to maximize the impact of human presence.

These kinds of spaces can be most successful in public or semipublic areas not requiring high degrees of privacy or tasks requiring concentration. Applications are possible in restaurants, stores, hotels, some areas of office projects, and within the major circulation routes of most projects (Figure 8.22). In Figure 8.23 the heavy use of a student area endows it with much vitality.

An example of spaces that foster in us a sense of special meaning because of the kind of opportunity they present for a given use is a well-placed, small-scaled space off a main route or major space, where one or two persons can sit to talk, work, or just rest. We are talking, of course, about the art of designing the small human niche, cultivated by some designers but unknown to many. These spaces are seldom included in the program of requirements supplied to the designer at the onset of a project.

Figure 8.24: Small off-the-path spaces where users can step off and feel grounded, yet still be in the middle of things, provide enrichment.

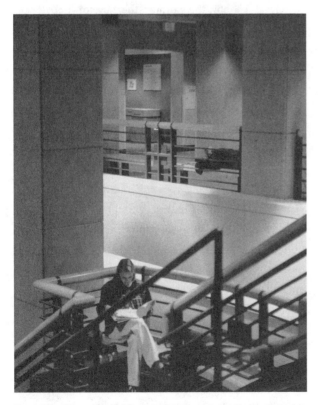

Figure 8.25: This pocket off to the side of a stairway is a perfect example of the thoughtful use of off-the-path yet connected spaces.

They are provided by thoughtful designers who understand the nature of people and their desire for small intimate spaces in certain settings that provide a comfortable place to step into without losing connection to the greater totality beyond. Figure 8.24 shows an example of one of these spaces. Figure 8.25 shows a similar example but that one occurring along vertical circulation or one of the stair landings.

ENRICHMENT WHEN IN TRANSIT

There are many opportunities to create enrichment in a project's circulation spaces. People are usually between tasks when in transit. During those times people can be highly receptive to environmental stimulus. It is while moving that we truly experience what has been called the fourth dimension of architecture, seeing the physical environment changing and emerging as we move through space. All projects have circulation spaces, some more formal or explicit than others. Enriching projects have engaging circulation routes.

Below, we consider the path or corridor as a vehicle for enrichment. We'll look at the effect of sequences, the qualities of their components, and their capacity to engage us in them and the rest of the project.

Sequence

A good part of our experience inside buildings takes place as we move through space. Our perception of space while moving is especially important because the physicality of movement and the goal-oriented nature of most walking episodes produce a state of alertness that helps us absorb more of the surroundings.

Moving through space offers the potential for exploration, providing variety and distraction. Whether through a trip to the coffee room at the office, a trip to the restroom in a restaurant, or a side trip while shopping, we welcome opportunities to take a break and look around. Sometimes these trips are meant as a break; other times they are necessary. In any case, they provide the benefit of providing an opportunity to explore the environment around us.

Regardless of the degree of urgency and our level of familiarity with the environment, just about every trip we take within a given environment offers an exploratory experience. This can occur at different levels. We can discover the spaces of a new environment as we move through it, and we can also notice qualities and details we hadn't noticed before in familiar territories. Additionally, the unfolding human drama often seen from the path is like an ever-changing theater stage, full of interest and surprises.

Exploration can be actual exploration of unfamiliar territory, but it also refers to the kind of exploration we do when we visually scan, say, a wall with intricate pattern and detail. In the latter case, the brain is engaged in the exploration of a complex composition and is challenged to make sense of it. Therefore, it spends a few seconds taking it all in and trying to understand it. Assuming there is some engaging complexity and a well-composed arrangement, we are likely to be not only momentarily entertained but also delighted. If we think of the path as a vehicle for enrichment, we can consciously plan it in ways that increase the perceptual richness it offers. This section will give you some ideas.

Designing the circulation system of a project requires taking into account the kind of movement different segments are required to facilitate. Movement in buildings is not always leisurely or recreational. In fact, it is rarely so. Most movement in buildings has a specific purpose and destination. We move with resolve to reach our destinations, often so preoccupied that we barely notice the environment around us. In cases of emergency or extreme rush, we actually run, and anything we encounter on our path is an obstacle. In those cases, the only image we welcome is that of the door or passage leading to our destination, be it a space inside or the door leading to the exterior.

Environments require efficient movement. Most movement inside projects will have a fair amount of resoluteness. Therefore, while we want to still provide experiences along the way, these should not be so distracting or indirect as to be annoying or, worse yet, dangerous. Any attempt to enhance the experience of users while moving should not slow people down excessively. Emergency egress paths, especially, need to be clear and direct for

Figure 8.26: A typical trip to many destinations, such as the clinic shown here, involves a sequence featuring distinct experiences.

obvious reasons. But even clear, efficient paths can provide opportunities to slow down and step aside.

People's main concern while moving along a route (with some exceptions) tends to be their final goal or destination. If the journey is long, it may include several subgoals or intermediate arrival places. When visiting a clinic on an upper floor of a multistory building, for instance, we arrive first at the front door, then in the building lobby, the elevator lobby, the elevator, the elevator lobby of the target floor, the entrance outside the destination clinic, the reception area of the clinic, and, finally, the examination room (Figure 8.26).

If unfamiliar with the above environment, we may, at any given time, not be able to think beyond the next intermediate destination, moving in chunks from one to the next until we arrive at our real target destination. All the transition points become the salient locations that will be mentally recorded and remembered during subsequent visits. Those locations may very well have special design features that, when traveling more leisurely, users will notice and appreciate. After all, transitions force the user to slow down or stop, setting up, potentially, a moment of enough conscious awareness for an aesthetic experience.

Many routes will lack the natural transitions presented in our clinic example above. In those cases, it is up to you as a designer to find ways to break up the route and provide meaningful events along the way, especially for long routes. Here is where you can put on your movie director hat and plan the route in ways that produce enriching experiences.

Events along the Route

Think of the route's sequence as a story line with plots, subplots, and one or more climaxes. To do this, keep in mind that we tend to move from goal to goal until we reach our destination. It is those goals that often stay in our minds. That's where your planning of the nodes, centers, and landmarks of your project can become a factor, and make a positive contribution, turning ordinary circulation systems into experiences full of events.

A sequence can be made engaging by transitions along the trajectory and by the presence of distinct events along the way. Transitions can be changes in direction or transitions in the physical character of the path. Figure 8.27 shows an example of a route featuring some changes in the path's direction and configuration. Figure 8.28 illustrates how changes in the physical spatial character of the path provide a story line in themselves.

Other potential distinct events are the centers, nodes, and landmarks along the route. Figure 8.29 shows a fairly linear and potentially uneventful route sequence enhanced by the incorporation of strategically located nodes.

Other possible events along the route are surprises (or rewards), whether anticipated or not. These are often in the form of enriching encounters with meaningful objects, details, and views. These may come as total surprises or be anticipated destinations hinted at prior to reaching them.

Qualities of the Path Itself

In addition to having an engaging sequence, the circulation route can be enriching by virtue of its inherent physical qualities. Despite their typological similarities, paths can have distinctive characters. Let's examine the components of a prototypical path. Most path segments are, basically, similar. They tend to be long, narrow spaces. We normally travel along them in linear fashion. As we move, we see the

Figure 8.27: Altering the shape of the path can make it dynamic and exciting. The zigzagging effect combined with the diagonal line in this corridor makes the last leg quite stimulating.

Figure 8.28: Segments of a sequence can be defined in section, as shown here. Different heights and the distinctiveness of the central section makes the experience of moving through this circulation sequence exciting and memorable.

Figure 8.29: The use of some of the place elements we have discussed in the book, most notably, nodes and landmarks, along circulation routes is an effective way to accentuate certain points. In this example three nodes establish distinct, recognizable points along the path.

Figure 8.30: A view from a typical corridor is long and narrow, featuring some defining side boundaries, a view straight ahead, and perhaps views of adjacent spaces.

Figure 8.31: The level of openness or enclosure of a corridor greatly affects its character and psychological length. Enclosed corridors that are self-contained can get uncomfortably long (a). Corridors with openings provide visual relief to adjacent features and activities and don't seem as long and tedious (b).

sides of the path obliquely, from the near parallel relation of our line of vision to them. There is some view, planned or unplanned, at the end of the corridor that we see straight ahead and some distance away. As we move along we may, depending on the specific situation, see adjoining spaces beyond the corridor (Figure 8.30).

Our job is to make the path special. Once we have a basic path outlined on our preliminary floor plan we may ask the questions: Are the visible components of the path engaging in and of themselves? Should they be? To what extent? Answers to these questions will inform the direction we take. Aspects that can be controlled and enhanced include the shape of the path and the qualities of its enclosing surfaces.

Figure 8.32:
Intersections and intermittent spaces help relieve the perceived length of corridors by breaking up their linearity.

The Shape of the Path

Despite the recurring configuration inherent in the typology of the path, as described above, there are a few variables that give paths different characters. These are length, degree of enclosure, height-to-width proportions, and configuration in both plan and section.

Paths come in different lengths. Many of these are perceptually comfortable, but others get to be too long. Acceptable lengths vary depending on the height-to-width proportion of the path, as well as the degree of lateral enclosure and the articulation of the side walls. In general, enclosed corridors with solid side walls on both sides will seem longer than those connected visually to adjacent spaces, especially if the side walls are flat and plain (Figure 8.31).

One way of keeping long paths within acceptable length limits is to break them up into smaller segments by the addition of intermittent spaces, such as cross-corridors (Figure 8.32), or by offsets in the path or enclosing walls (Figure 8.33).

Figure 8.33: A strategy to alleviate long corridors is to offset the path at some point before it starts to seem too long. This breaks the path into subsegments.

Figure 8.34: Modulation on the side walls enriches the formal visual qualities of a corridor by the addition of rhythm, pattern, and texture. Vertical planes or protrusions, whether straight (a) or angled (b), provide relief and add interest.

At a more subtle level, vertical and horizontal articulations on the side walls, ceilings, and floors affect the perceived length of a path. Figure 8.34 a and b shows the effect of side wall articulation on two corridors of equal length. Articulation or pattern on the ceiling and floor planes can also have an impact on the perceived depth. In general, lines along the length of the corridor will make it appear longer than lines perpendicular to it (Figure 8.35).

Although the level of enclosure around a corridor is somewhat dictated by the privacy and enclosure needs of the spaces adjacent to the path, there is some room for manipulation. In terms of enclosure, paths can be fully enclosed, partially enclosed, or fully open. They can also be a combination of these pure conditions. The principle of variety is a handy one to use when designing paths. To the extent that the program will allow flexibility, it is a good idea for you to design paths that offer variety through contrast.

Figure 8.35: Lines and pattern on the floor and ceiling planes also add texture. Similar to the case of side walls, lines along the length of the corridor (a) will make it seem longer. Lines across the corridor (b) will have a shortening effect.

Figure 8.36: The experience of moving through corridors can be enhanced by the use of variety and contrast. These examples show a corridor with alternating open and closed sides (a) and a similar corridor with overlapping walls resulting in smaller openings (b).

This can be achieved by contrast between the two sides of the path or by contrast between successive segments of the path (Figure 8.36).

Another important contribution of the enclosing planes is their role in determining the relative autonomy of the path. A path with no barrier on one side has the potential of blending with it. It can read as an extension of the adjacent space, or it can read as a distinct path if some differentiation is provided by the ceiling and floor planes. Whether through level changes or through a change of finish, the treatment of the two important horizontal planes can change the feeling the path has in relation to the adjacent spaces. This is one case where the design can result in clear autonomy, clear affiliation, or an ambiguous condition where one may question whether it is a corridor or a continuation of the adjacent space. Figure 8.37 shows examples of both a path with little architectural differentiation (Figure 8.37a) and one where the ceiling helps to accentuate the distinction between the path and its adjoining space (Figure 8.37b).

Height-to-width proportions of paths, like their length, impact the way we perceive and experience them. Some proportions feel better than others. Different combinations will produce paths that can be categorized as tall, normal, and low-height corridors. All three have their appropriate applications. The one to be careful with is the low-height path. Despite the nice intimate scale it can provide, it can also be quite uncomfortable if it gets to be too long. Figure 8.38 shows examples of tall and low-height corridors.

Figure 8.37: The ceiling and floor planes are important elements in the determination of perceived autonomy of a path. Example (a) reads as one space where the edge defined by the furniture establishes an aisle. In example (b) the path reads as a distinct, well-defined corridor due to the ceiling treatments.

Despite the predominance of the path with parallel sides, due in part to its inherent economy, there are other possible plan configurations. While these normally require more space, they add dynamic qualities and produce path segments of great interest. Figure 8.39 provides just two of many possible examples. You should master these and other similar ones and try to use them where sensual or dynamic qualities are needed.

Similar manipulations are possible in section. Most corridors consist of parallel, plumb side walls and a flat ceiling plane above, but this is by no means the only configuration possible. While some of the possibilities can violate the sense of what is considered normal, some of them will be appropriate at times. Your repertoire of

Figure 8.38: Corridors come in different heights: Both tall (a) and short (b) corridors have their proper applications.

Figure 8.39: Corridors do not have to always consist of parallel walls. There are times when it is possible, and desirable, to make corridors dynamic by the modification of one or both sides. These two examples modify only one side to achieve dynamic results.

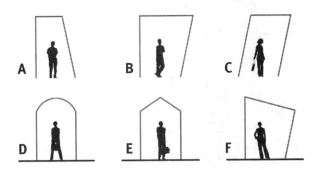

Figure 8.40: Most corridors tend to be boxy in section. There are times when the geometry can be changed for effect by changing one side wall (a and b), changing both side walls (c), changing the shape of the ceiling (d and e), or a combination (f).

corridor sectional configurations should include a wide range of possibilities, from the articulated to the unconventional. Figure 8.40 shows some examples.

Qualities of Enclosing Surfaces

The treatment of enclosing surfaces affects the level of interest of a path and should be carefully considered. Included are the side walls or screens, the floor plane, and the ceiling plane. Design variables to consider include modulation, spatial texture, and pattern. Modulation can be used on any of the enclosing planes alone or in combination. A rhythm of vertical elements on one or both of the side walls, a subdivision of the ceiling plane into units through articulation, and the use of pattern via modular flooring materials can all be used to modulate surfaces (Figure 8.41). The subdivision of paths through modulation endows them with a sense of strong rhythm that can be rather attractive if well executed.

Figure 8.41: Modularity on the side walls and floor (a) or on the ceiling (b) give corridors a nice sense of richness through articulation.

The articulation of paths does not need to always result in distinct modules. In some cases a reduced approach will provide a pleasant rhythm without a feeling of strong subdivision. Rhythm along one of the dominant surfaces can be quite engaging and afford the path a nice sense of spatial texture (Figure 8.42).

Figure 8.42: When the modules used are smaller and feature additional line work or pattern, the result is a greater sense of spatial texture.

In addition to the kind of articulation shown in the previous examples, simple elements such as openings on the side walls and cross-corridors form part of the overall path composition and contribute to its sense of variety, rhythm, and texture.

Manipulation of Disclosure

So far, we have talked about the role of events along the path sequence and the inherent qualities of the path in providing experiential richness. A third way paths engage us is by manipulating the kind, degree, and rate of disclosure of spaces and features within and beyond them. Equally important is how the path affects the overall spatial composition when seen from adjacent spaces, that is, when looking into the path while being outside of it.

The View at the End

One of the most noticeable aspects of any path is the view straight ahead. Depending on the arrangement, it may or may not be possible to see the final view at the end of the path from a given point in it. In paths that zigzag or meander, the end is often blocked from view until one arrives at the last leg of the path. In straight paths we see the view at the end. Except for the portion of a side wall immediately next to us at any given time in our trajectory along the path, nothing is likely to be as strong as the view at the end, whether we are conscious of it or not. Even if we are still at a distance, we are looking at it head-on. Figure 8.43 shows examples of framed views.

Figure 8.43: The framed view at the end is an important strategy used in many corridors (a). Variations include the framed exterior view (b), the framed piece of artwork on the wall (c), and the important room at the end (d).

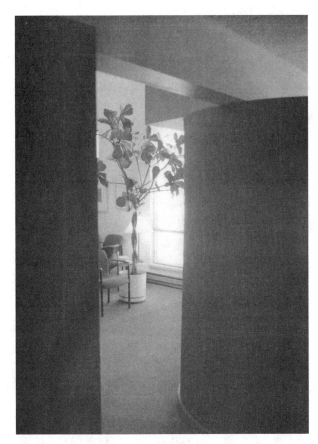

Figure 8.44: Prospect is the view seen beyond the corridor. Consideration needs to be given to the placement of elements seen in order to produce an enticing view.

becomes necessary to consider the view of the wall seen from the adjacent space. The wall needs to work as both a side wall of the corridor and a wall segment seen as a vista from the adjacent space.

Prospect

Prospect is the framed view we see at the end or beyond the turn. It serves as somewhat of a focal point, except its composition is not necessarily a framed termination. In the case of prospect, we see what lies beyond, say a wall of an adjacent mass in the distance. You could think of prospect as a carefully composed partial view of something beyond. Because what is seen beyond has a degree of visual prominence, it requires careful attention to make the resulting view at least adequate. Unfortunately, the view at the end of many interior corridors is the default result of whatever happens to be beyond, with no effort to control it. While not every view at the end of a path needs to be treated with special accent pieces, every ending view should be designed to produce agreeable, if not engaging, results. Figure 8.44 shows an example of a prospect view that is not quite a focal point but has been carefully arranged to produce pleasing results.

What is revealed at the end is important and requires proper attention. Possible strategies to consider include the strategic use of focal points, prospect, and enticement.

Focal Points

The use of focal points can be an effective strategy to enrich users' experience in circulation areas. Focal points usually occur at the end of the view ahead. These views are carefully framed. Possibilities include a view to the exterior or space beyond, a piece of artwork, or some well-placed evocative object, such as a flower vase on a shelf, perhaps set into a well-proportioned niche on the wall.

While the side walls of a corridor are usually seen obliquely and not straight ahead, there are conditions when we may see a side wall or a portion of it straight ahead. This occurs in cases where one of the two sides is open to the adjacent space, allowing a straight-ahead view from these spaces toward the wall. In these cases it

Enticement

In addition to careful, focal compositions of the views at the end of the path, and sensitively composed views of what lies beyond, it is also possible to design arrangements that lead the moving person in a desired direction. This is usually achieved through the use of arrangements with directional properties, the use of arrangements that disclose what lies ahead only partially, and the use of powerful elements that attract at the ends. Diagonal arrangements and circular configurations favoring one direction are effective in this regard (Figure 8.45). It is possible to increase the level of attraction of the view at the end by arousing people's sense of curiosity. Circular shapes and compelling distant views (because of their composition, boldness, brightness, and so on) arouse our curiosity and draw us toward them. See Capsule #7, "Complexity, Order, and Other Environmental Attributes," for a discussion of mystery.

Figure 8.46: Openings along side walls of corridors connect us visually to adjacent spaces. Their arrangement can be straightforward and rhythmical (a) or rhythmical in pairs (b), among others.

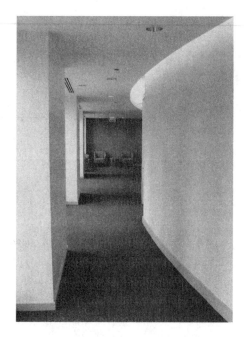

Figure 8.45: Compositions can be arranged to entice and attract. Curved walls allow partial views beyond that arouse our curiosity and make us want to move forward.

The View Beyond the Path

While in many cases the view at the end of the path may be dominant, lateral views to adjacent spaces also form an important part of the circulation experience. Views to adjacent spaces reveal other spaces of a facility and provide orientation, distraction, and, sometimes, entertainment. How much is revealed depends on the required level of connection or separation needed and the intentions of the route designer. In areas not requiring total separation there is room for interpretation and manipulation. The variables of disclosure and access discussed in Chapter 4 come into play here.

The process of designing corridor walls and points of entry from the circulation into the spaces is somewhat automatic and driven by functional needs. However, there are sometimes opportunities to perform manipulations for effect. Two important design strategies to create engaging routes are the manipulation of points of visual connection to adjacent areas and the manipulation of the correspondence between visual and physical access.

Points of Visual Connection

Most circulation spaces in individual interior projects afford some degree of visual connection to adjacent spaces. Sometimes the extent of the view continues to the outdoors in the form of external views. Visual connection from the circulation area to adjacent areas is desirable; however, caution must be exercised because total continuous connection can be as monotonous as total separation. The optimal level lies somewhere in the middle. Partial visual connection is gratifying, since it provides relief from the enclosure of the corridor. It is possible to create a playful pattern of "now you see it, now you don't" between the corridor and adjoining spaces to stimulate users' minds and enrich their experience.

While a balanced mix of visual separation and visual disclosure in itself is likely to result in generally agreeable arrangements, it is possible to have an even greater impact through the strategic placement of the openings providing the visual connection. If a certain opening between a corridor and an adjacent space coincides with a point along the route where visual relief would be desirable, the overall impact is likely to be greater. If openings between the corridor and adjacent spaces are rhythmic or gradated, the result will have an increased level of playfulness and engagement (Figure 8.46). If the visual connection is framed strategically to reveal a particularly special view of the adjacent space, then the impact is going to be stronger. In short, it is not enough to only provide connections. The actual arrangement of the openings requires careful thought and consideration if the effect is to be truly enriching and poetic.

We have seen how the placement of the points of visual connection between areas is crucial to the overall orchestration of the corridor. Also important is the degree of physical connection afforded. Any given connection can range from a narrow glimpse through a small opening

Figure 8.47: It is possible to perform playful orchestrations between open and solid portions of side walls. The play of openings in a mostly solid wall (a) and the play of solids in a mostly open boundary (b) are two examples.

Figure 8.48: The view from adjacent spaces back to the corridor should be planned carefully. Possibilities include the framed view toward a focal piece (a), the aligned view with an intersection (b), and the prospect view of a corridor segment without any focalization (c).

to a full view of the adjacent space. It is possible to use uneven rhythms such as the glimpse, glimpse, wide-view sequence shown in Figure 8.47a. The opposite is possible in predominantly open corridors. Instead of locating openings, you deal with solids, such as column, column, wall (Figure 8.47b).

The placement, size, and arrangement of openings from a corridor require careful consideration if you want to provide enriching experiences. Every situation needs to be looked at individually and analyzed carefully to arrive at optimal balances between separations and connections and to enrich the experiences of those moving in them.

In addition to internal views, views from the corridor to the exterior are enriching when they occur. These can be lateral views at a distance, immediate lateral views, or views at the end of the corridor. These views can be panoramic or carefully framed views that look in a particular direction with something beyond as a focal point. Exterior views have the effect of extending the perceived space horizontally. They can provide a great amount of relief, not to mention a sense of connection to the external context. In some cases, circulation routes may even be located along the perimeter of a building to provide external views all along the way.

As important as the view from the path to an adjacent space is the view from that adjacent space back to the path. The composition of the framed view back toward the path should be given proper consideration and not left up to chance. Figure 8.48 shows three of many possible arrangements. Figure 8.48a and 8.48b create focal points, one terminating the view in a piece of artwork on the wall and the other extending it into the gateway to a corridor centered on the framed view. Figure 8.48c shows a view without a dominant focal point, but one that has been thoughtfully composed to make the framed view rewarding.

Correspondence of Visual and Physical Access

The design of visual access points in relation to the actual point of entry to an area presents some interesting opportunities to provide enriching experiences. In projects where a clear and efficient path is necessary, either because of a project's particular use or the population for whom it is being designed, correspondence between visual access and physical access will be important and, generally, will be the norm. In such cases, ambiguity and tension are not likely to be appreciated. Even in some of those cases, however, it may be useful sometimes to see a view of the destination before having to make a decision about heading toward it or not.

In cases where more playfulness can be tolerated, it is possible to manipulate the relationship between visual disclosure and physical access to an area in order to create either a sense of anticipation or intentional tension. Figure 8.49 shows an arrangement featuring a view on axis with the circulation of an area, yet requiring the person to go around the corner to enter the space and connect to its path. Figure 8.50 shows an example where several views of the area are presented to build anticipation before arriving at the eventual entry point. These types of manipulations are not appropriate in all cases. They are to be used only in areas of projects where they will be appropriate and, even then, only in moderation.

Figure 8.49: Interaction between visual and physical access to a space can be manipulated to increase anticipation. Here, the user sees the internal corridor leading to his destination but has to walk around a corner to enter the space leading to the corridor.

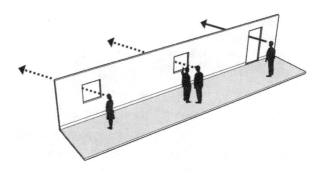

Figure 8.50: A simple way to produce anticipation is to provide visual access a few times before the entry point can be reached.

CAPSULE | Safety versus Opportunity

One of the main themes of human behavior and, consequently, of the design of places for people, is the duality of exposure and withdrawal. British geographer Jay Appleton devised a theory that provides much insight into these fundamental human necessities. Called prospect-refuge theory, it was conceived to help understand human appreciation of the exterior landscape. The theory is a specific application of habitat theory, which Appleton explains as follows:

All this leads to the proposition that aesthetic satisfaction, experienced in the contemplation of the landscape, stems from the spontaneous perception of landscape features, which in their shapes, colours, spatial arrangements and other visible attributes, act as sign stimuli indicative of environmental conditions favourable to survival . . . "Habitat theory" thus asserts that the relationship between the human observer and the perceived environment is basically the same as the relationship of a creature and its habitat. It asserts further that the satisfaction which we derive from the contemplation of this environment, and which we call "aesthetic," arises from a spontaneous reaction to that environment as a habitat, that is to say as a place which affords the opportunity for achieving our simple biological needs.[1]

Prospect-refuge theory can be generally exemplified by Konrad Lorenz's account of the advantage afforded by the point between enclosure and openness found while taking a walk in the forest. He states: "Before we break through the last bushes and out of cover on to the free expanse of the meadow . . . we reconnoitre, seeking, before we leave our cover, to gain from it the advantage which it can offer alike to hunter and hunted—namely to see without being seen."[2] Both the hunter and the hunted need strategies to fulfill their goals and protect their best interests. The hunter's strategy involves putting himself in a position to maximize opportunity. He must approach his prey as close as possible without getting noticed.

The strategy of the hunted involves assuring safety. It requires having a place inaccessible to the pursuer and putting himself in a position to, if needed, reach that place before being prevented by the hunter. To accomplish this, the hunted will have to be in a position where the hunter will not see him or, if visible to the hunter, one that will give him enough time to react and reach safety. In both cases, as Appleton points out, "it is in the creature's interest to ensure that he can see his quarry or predator, as the case may be, without being seen, and the achievement of these conditions becomes a first objective which renders more likely the achievement of the second, to catch or to escape."[3] Obviously, familiarity with the environment would give either hunter or hunted an advantage, as it would potentially increase the number of routes for attack or escape.

According to the theory, environments whose characteristics are perceived to offer the ability to see without being seen tend to be aesthetically more satisfying. During primitive times, more than now, the ability to see and the ability to hide were both necessary for survival. Appleton suggests that humans carry those evolutionary tendencies within them even though they have long evolved from a primitive existence when hunting and protection against hostile tribes were prevalent. He calls the unimpeded opportunity to see *prospect* and the opportunity to hide *refuge*.

One may question the magnitude with which these programmed tendencies really influence our aesthetic judgments and preferences for places. After all, life in most of the civilized world is relatively safe from antagonistic hunters. We also have to acknowledge that in certain types of situations people want to see and to be seen, such as at the type of bar or cafe where people go to socialize. Nevertheless, and excluding the obvious application to settings high in crime or terrorism, prospect-refuge theory still offers wonderful insights into some fundamental traits of human behavior. People's tendencies to approach or avoid a place, after all, depend as much, if not more, on who is present rather than on the issue of environmental load discussed in a previous chapter.

At an even more fundamental level, the issue of prospect and refuge brings us back to the topic of existential space, discussed previously in Capsule 3, "A Phenomenological View of Space and Dwelling." There, we described the notion of center at the heart of human dwelling in contrast to the beyond, conceptualized as paths and domains away from the center. Just these three existential space-elements serve to articulate the basic and most fundamental duality of existential space, between the "here" (what is familiar and safe) and the "there" (what lies outside and involves exposure and risk). These correspond to all kinds of dualities frequently found in design, such as open-closed, sheltered-exposed, and private-public.

With prospect-refuge theory we start addressing the important role of the environment in influencing interactions between people by the positioning of places and the visibility between those places. It is important for a person to be not only at his or her safe and familiar center but also in a strategic position to see who is coming and have a chance to react by welcoming or hiding, as well as to know who is outside and have a chance to decide whether to use the front or back door. Likewise, someone on a path approaching a place can strategically scope a scene and make decisions about whether or not to enter and which way to go depending on the potential opportunities or threats presented by it.

Potential application of prospect-refuge thinking is found in many types of settings, some more than others. Public settings where people spend time, such as restaurants, cafes, and clubs, present some of the best opportunities to use prospect-refuge thinking. At a cafe, a preference for prospect is likely to dominate. People will want exposure to see and be seen, although it would be wise to have a few tables in the back for those seeking less exposure. At a restaurant, people may prefer a table that affords some anchoring—in other words, a refuge. Depending on circumstances, they may opt for one visually accessible from the rest of the space (reducing the sense of refuge but increasing prospect) or one tucked away, allowing them to see without being seen, thus providing both prospect and refuge. A good practice is to provide a variety of tables with different degrees of privacy and exposure, so people can choose one that fits their particular needs at the moment.

For a quiet, intimate dining experience, the emphasis is definitely on refuge. In fact, the desire for prospect may be limited. Through careful zoning of areas, positioning of tables, and use of local lighting (e.g., individual candles at tables), it may be possible to create an atmosphere in which each table feels like an oasis, even though it may be just a couple of feet from an adjacent table.

Prospects and refuges occur at different scales. A town on a hill may be a refuge (familiar and secure) from which you may enjoy views of the prospects beyond. Within the town, the house represents another level of refuge, having views from the windows that connect with prospects beyond. Within the house, the personal bedroom represents yet another scale of refuge and the chair tucked away in the corner still another. We can see how the concept of refuge has many similarities to that of center in existential space.

Figure C8.1 Wright's Fallingwater is one of many houses designed by him that exemplify the concepts of prospect (openness, view, opportunity) and refuge (enclosure, protection, safety) in built environments.

Frank Lloyd Wright was a master of the art of providing a good balance between prospect and refuge. In *The Wright Space*, Grant Hildebrandt applies prospect-refuge theory to analyze Wright's residential designs. In relation to the preferred landscape dispositions of prospect and refuge advocated by Appleton, Hildebrandt writes, "The houses Wright designed after 1902 almost all held an extraordinarily rich array of these analogies, at several hierarchical levels—and did so through a complex and repetitive composition of elements unique to him in his time."[4] The overall structure of Wright's houses was based on a principle involving a strong and protective center from which the house grew outward toward infinity. Many of his houses emanated from a central hearth space that anchored them in space and symbolized the center of centers. While the houses obviously had bounding walls, they provided open vistas that extended the actual perceived space infinitely (Figure C8.1).

The organizational structure was just the beginning. As Hildebrandt pointed out, the occurrences happened at several hierarchical levels, providing opportunity and choice. He explained: "The degree of refuge or of prospect is subject to infinite variety and can be manipulated by the occupant at will simply by moving to the condition he wishes to enjoy at any moment. We move around, we take our pick, we suit our mood. And when our mood changes we know there are other spaces in the house that can suit the new mood too. That Wright was able to provide not only a rich array of these conditions, but also a range of choice with regard to them, is an extraordinarily important legacy of his work."[5]

Suggested Exercise

List a few places you have been that afforded both good prospect and refuge. Discuss them in one or several groups. What were the circumstances? What design features contributed to the perceptions of refuge? To what extent was one able to see without being seen?

1. Jay Appleton, *The Experience of Landscape* (New York: Wiley, 1996), 62.
2. Ibid., 52.
3. Ibid., 64.
4. Ibid., quoting Grant Hildebrandt, *The Wright Space* (Seattle: University of Washington Press, 1991), 250.
5. Ibid., 253.

ENRICHMENT WHILE STATIONARY

Although it is true that we see more of a given interior environment while we walk around, it is also true that we spend most of our time stationed in the destination spaces of the facility, be they important or ordinary. It is in these spaces that people do what they came to the building to do. The tasks performed there become the main thing and the environment assumes the secondary role of quiet facilitator. Given an adequate amount of space and acceptable ambient conditions, people manage to do what they need to do. Conditions, however, can be taken to higher levels of function and perceptual enrichment.

Many of the general strategies discussed earlier in this chapter come into play here. There are several enrichment strategies specifically applicable to places where people are stationary while performing a task. In general, we would like to suggest that a complete task experience consists of the task at hand in a grounded setting that provides opportunities to connect with nearby surroundings and allows episodes of relief on demand. A way of illustrating this with an everyday example is the experience of food preparation in a residential kitchen. An enriching experience would include a spatially well-defined kitchen with a layout that facilitates the various tasks of food preparation while providing visual access to other parts of the house (to connect with adjacent activities and the comings and goings of family members) and to the outside through a well-placed window (to enjoy the view but also to monitor a young child playing outside). If, in addition to all this, it also had a couple of focal points on which to anchor the view occasionally (one internal and the other external), the kitchen would offer quite a range of enriching features beyond mere functionality and good looks.

Facilitating the Task

Facilitating a task requires providing appropriate conditions. Spatially, these include appropriate levels of space, privacy, and connection to related functions. Once these basic needs are met, the next level of facilitation occurs at the proxemic scale of the furnishings and objects in the space (the table in the restaurant or conference room, the individual desk at the office, and so on). When it gets to the task itself, the selection, composition, and arrangement of these objects in space becomes dominant. Other relevant factors, such as complementary lighting and pleasant materials and finishes, are also important. Many of these go beyond the possible contributions of spatial design.

There are, however, contributions to be made at the spatial scale. The location, size, and arrangement of the spaces housing these functions will have an impact on the overall experience. An intimate scale may enhance the experience at the restaurant table, a well-proportioned room of comfortable volume will enhance the experience at the conference room table, and a quiet space of adequate size may facilitate the work done at the desk in the office. Additionally, users are more likely to be satisfied if they have a physical connection to the greater whole of which their space is a part, and if opportunities are offered to take occasional brief breaks by focusing momentarily on well-planned views and focal points. We discuss these various types of contributions under the headings of grounding, connection, and relief below.

Grounding

The tasks people perform in buildings involve interactions with things and other people at the material level and data and ideas at the nonmaterial level. In our restaurant example the main focus is on the table, with the plates, glasses, silverware, and, of course, the meal itself taking center stage. If we have company, they are also likely to be a primary focus of the experience. Behind all this is a certain mood that will vary from restaurant to restaurant. The decor and lighting will provide much of that mood. How each table is grounded will affect the individual experience from each table.

Grounding refers to the manner in which a space, or part of a space, is defined in the total environment in ways that make one feel anchored in space, as opposed to drifting in space. People like to feel grounded. An example of this in a restaurant environment is the reassuring experience of being next to a column or side wall rather than feeling like you are floating in the middle of a large room. The concept of containment introduced in Chapter 4 comes into play here. Also important is our relative location in relation to the vertical elements, corners, and edges of the space. Sitting along a defined edge, next to a column, or in a corner generally offers good grounding experiences (Figure 8.51).

In large rooms, even though the external envelope may provide only four corners and four edges, it is possible to subdivide space internally to create more corners and edges. Compare the two plans shown for a restaurant in Figure 8.52. The one in Figure 8.52a has a large internal zone with floating tables that don't feel grounded. The

Figure 8.51: Good grounding can be achieved by proximity against an edge (a), a column (b), or a corner (c).

Figure 8.52: Designers often create internal edges and corners to create grounded, well-defined spaces. In this example, the floating tables (a) find better grounded locations where edges and corners have been added (b).

Figure 8.53: Accommodations that help us feel grounded in a restaurant include the table against the window wall (a), the booth (b), and the table along a low wall or railing (c).

one in Figure 8.52b shows the same space subdivided to create more edges and corners inside, thus adding opportunities for feeling grounded. Figure 8.53 shows views of well-grounded tables in restaurant settings. Grounding is important in all types of projects. Other than restaurants, projects such as office spaces (especially those with large areas of open workstations), stores, and hotel lobbies will benefit from having spaces that are well grounded.

Connection

Even if we sometimes appreciate isolation when we need privacy to concentrate and perform certain tasks, we also value the ability to stay connected with our surroundings, not only because of our inherent interest in human activity but to know what's happening around us, who is coming and going, and when we need to be on alert. For that reason, it is often desirable to have some degree of connection between areas. That way, people in a restaurant can see other tables and areas beyond, people in an office can see adjacent workers, and people in a hotel lounge can see people in the adjacent lobby. Even though these types of connections are often desirable, deciding when to provide connections and how much to provide are tricky design issues, since the optimal degree of connection to adjacent areas will vary from project to project, from department to department, and from individual to

Figure 8.54: Visual connection to adjacent spaces provides stimulation and useful information. It is especially satisfying to find protected spaces from which to look out or down into space, like the space from which this photo was taken in a restaurant.

individual. Having too much connection can be a real annoyance to anyone not desiring it.

People love to watch other people. In settings such as cafes, teahouses, and even the theater, the social aspect of seeing and being seen is an integral component of the overall experience. Exchanges of stares can be open and candid or they can be discreet. Sometimes we feel especially at ease when located in strategic spots that allow us to look at people around us without being noticed, such as when we look down from a strategic location higher up (Figure 8.54).

Another type of desirable connection is to the outdoors. In addition to providing relief, visual connections to the outside give people valuable information about the approximate time of day, weather conditions, and other external contextual conditions. Figure 8.55 shows a good example from a cafe setting.

Relief

In addition to providing valuable information, the kinds of connections described above also provide relief. The visual openness to the adjacent areas allows for expansion of vision and mind, providing beneficial mental breaks. In this section we discuss another means of providing relief: the use of relief features seen from stationary points.

Views to adjacent areas and the exterior allow the eyes and the mind to expand outward and experience relief. Also useful are focal points where views to framed features are provided. These can be both external and internal. With external foci, the strategy consists of framing specific views that may have special meaning due to their significance, beauty, or other associational qualities. Examples include framed vistas of important monuments, natural or landscaped features, or areas of special vitality based on their use. Well-placed furnishings in relation to existing windows can sometimes make an ordinary view an extraordinary vista.

While many designers provide focal points in circulation areas, others neglect the art of providing internal features for people to focus on from their stationary locations. People in places such as waiting areas, office cubicles, and lobbies need spots they can focus their attention on from time to time to give their eyes and minds a rest. Examples include artwork (both flat and sculptural), intricate detailing of architectural and decorative elements, and all types of accessories. Figure 8.56 shows an example of a bar in a hotel lounge providing an internal focal point. In office situations they often need to occur high up on a wall or on the ceiling so people can see them from their stations without having to stand up. Figure 8.57 shows an example of this condition and the importance of the often-forgotten upper portions of walls.

Figure 8.55: Visual connection to the exterior provides interest, information, and relief. This cafe features built-in tables along the front window.

Figure 8.56: Providing internal relief is a neglected art. This bar in a hotel lounge provides not only a destination but an internal focal point, providing relief.

Figure 8.57: In some interior settings, like this open-plan office setting, it is important to consider the view above the furniture walls. In this example, the enclosed offices beyond feature colorful accent panels at the tops of their walls.

A Case of Unconventionality: The Doane Pet Care Company Headquarters

DESIGN FIRM: VOA

The Doane Pet Care Company Headquarters was an unconventional corporate office project full of freedom and wit. The program consisted of the consolidation of multiple groups into a single facility in Brentwood, Tennessee. The principal goal of the client was to improve communication and interaction between teams. In terms of a general approach, the client wanted a free-form parklike concept. That's exactly what they got from VOA, the selected design firm.

Looking at the floor plan (Figure CS8.1), one immediately gets a sense of looseness and freedom. The paths defined by the curvilinear central cores meander in flowing, naturalistic fashion (Figure CS8.2). The office areas are predominantly wide open, just like an open field in a park. For the most part, enclosed rooms are assembled in one of the four free-form core masses that divide the project into two mostly open sides. Only one department in the space is walled off from the rest of the project and this was necessary due to the confidential nature of its work. Other than that, the few enclosed spaces are placed strategically to subdivide open areas into units of perceptually comfortable proportions.

Characteristic of the space is the absence of orthogonal planning. Architecturally, there are very few instances in which partitions meet at 90 degrees. Even adjacent systems furniture clusters are rotated in relation to each other, thus creating unique and unusual spaces between them. This is clearly not your textbook design project. The irregular nature of some of the leftover spaces and skewed relationships between adjacent pieces would surely upset many design instructors intent on stressing the "proper way" of doing design. Yet here

we have a real corporate project designed by a top firm pushing the limits of conventionality. This project serves to illustrate that while most clients might still prefer conventional designs, others need more environmental interest and demand designs that go beyond the ordinary to produce stimulating and interesting environments.

In addition to the unconventional geometry of the floor plan, the design provides enrichment through its innovative and nonpretentious approach to detailing and furniture selection. The fencelike serpentine screens behind the reception area (Figure CS8.3) and break/work table (Figure CS8.4) and the elliptical shallow floating ceiling planes are examples of innovative and playful detailing. Similarly, the furniture creation and selection approach exemplified in those two illustrations and Figure CS8.5 for the reception desk, the waiting area banquette, and the casual break/work table and stools further convey an innovative and rather humble approach, considering it is a design for a corporate headquarters project. A final illustration of the project's playful detail is the way the two walls are joined above the opening (Figure CS8.6).

Figure CS8.1: The freedom of the parklike office landscape is readily apparent from the floor plan.

Figure CS8.2: Much of the circulation occurs along meandering, curving paths.

Figure CS8.3: A fencelike serpentine dividing screen behind the receptionist and wood fins at the reception desk add texture to the project.

Figure CS8.4: Additionally, the elliptical shallow soffts display subtle articulation and a sense of playfulness.

Figure CS8.5: The waiting area seating and reception desk display innovation and a casual approach.

Figure CS8.6: The joint of the two segments of wall coming together is another example of the playful approach to detailing employed throughout this project.

EIGHTEEN ALTERNATIVES TO THE CARPET BORDER

There is a tendency among many designers, especially but not exclusively among novices, to resort to the same solution when attempting to add interest to the floor (usually the carpet) of a room such as a conference room. That solution, "the proverbial carpet border," is usually manifested by a band around the room. It comes from a tendency many people have to always put a frame around things. Our aim here is to give you some alternatives to this common but limiting tendency.

Figure C8.2a–i: Basic carpet borders: rectangular band (a), rectangular band with accent on four corners (b), band with angled ends (c), dark rectangle on light field (d), field of aligned squares (f), light rectangle on dark field (g), progressively shorter stripes (h), random squares (i).

Figure C8.3a–i: Alternatives to borders: wide band along long side (a), wide band along short side (b), combination of a and b (c), corner diagonal field (d), sweeping curve (e), undulating curve (f), corner diagonal with stripes (g), sweeping curve with circle and uneven stripes (h), undulating curve with diagonal stripes and accents (i).

Figure C8.2a–c shows three common variations of the proverbial carpet border: the simple band around the room (Figure C8.2a), the band with accents on the corners (Figure C8.2b), and the band with hexagonlike ends (Figure C8.2c). These are simplistic and not very sophisticated but show a desire to add pattern to an otherwise homogeneous flooring. Our first three alternatives are shown in Figure C8.2d–f. Their aim is still to define a rectangular area centered in the room, but they accomplish it by using different means: defining the desired area by a rectangle with a contrasting color or value (Figure C8.2d), with a field of stripes (Figure C8.2e), or with a field of squares (Figure C8.2f).

Figure C8.2g–i, in turn, provides three variations to the ones just presented. In Figure C8.2g the colors or values are reversed to accentuate the perimeter instead of the rectangle. We recognize this may be considered another case of the proverbial border. Figure C8.2h is similar to Figure C8.2e, except the shape defined by the lines is no longer a rectangle (one side progresses diagonally). In Figure C8.2i, the squares, unlike the regularly spaced ones in Figure C8.2f, are fragmented from a regular and dense center to a dispersed perimeter.

The approach to our design challenge is handled differently in Figure C8.3. The six alternatives shown here are variations on a common theme. These do not attempt to define a rectangular area in the space. The approach here is irregular and asymmetrical. In Figure C8.3a, a wide strip is provided along one of the long ends of the room. Figure C8.3b is similar, but the strip is along one of the short sides. Meanwhile, Figure C8.3c features a combination of the previous two, having strips along one long and one short side with a contrasting intersecting area at the corner. Figure C8.3d–f features more irregular approaches using diagonal (Figure C8.3d) and curvilinear (Figure C8.3e and C8.3f) shapes. Notice the differences between the two curvilinear solutions. The different radii and orientation of the curves produce quite different effects.

Figure C8.3g–i provides three more variations. They become more complex. These add a layer of shapes on top of the patterns shown in Figure C8.3d–f. The added shapes clearly become figures on a two-toned field. Figure

Figure C8.4a–c: Patterns that go beyond the borders: angled rectangle (a), curve (b), diagonal (c).

Figure C8.5:
The checkerboard pattern.

C8.3g adds a series of stripes. The two other solutions add uneven stripes and a large circle (Figure C8.3h), and diagonal stripes and points (Figure C8.3i).

Finally, Figure C8.4 shows an entirely different approach. Here, the conception of the context is expanded. The area to which a pattern is applied is no longer confined by the boundaries of the original space (even if they are walls). The resulting shapes within the room (or space) are a segment of a larger pattern that continues beyond the space. This is a powerful design device useful to unify spaces in projects where it is okay to go beyond the borders. The variations shown are three of the many possible. Figure C8.4a shows what appears to be one end of a rectangle. A segment of a curve is shown in Figure C8.4b. In Figure C8.4c, a diagonally shaped strip starts narrow inside the room and moves out, while getting progressively wider. Notice that in these cases it is not necessary to complete (i.e., close) the shape. By just showing enough of it, the mind can read the shape. These applications work best when it is possible to see the shape continuing from one side to the other. Therefore, in cases where the two sides are separated by a wall, it is a good idea to use glass or have an opening near the point where the inside and outside meet so the effect can be perceived.

NINE ALTERNATIVES TO THE CHECKERBOARD PATTERN

When it comes to a modular pattern with tile, nothing is as popular as the checkerboard pattern. While not an unattractive pattern, it has become the default pattern for many designers. Creating patterns with tile is one of the most enjoyable and, potentially, creative design activities possible. It is necessary, however, to move beyond the checkerboard pattern. The possibilities are endless. Here are nine ideas for starters.

Figure C8.5 shows the well-known and widely used checkerboard pattern. You are likely to be familiar with it. Contrasting tiles are alternated horizontally and vertically to create a textured field. A popular alternative to the checkerboard pattern is one that places diamonds (or diagonal squares) at the intersections of tiles. These can be placed at every intersection (Figure C8.6a) or at wider intervals (Figure C8.6b). These two patterns, like the checkerboard, normally occur uniformly throughout—that is, the entire area is treated the same.

Patterns created with tiles do not necessarily have to be uniform throughout the entire area. Nor do they have to be of the alternating type (black tile, white tile, black tile). It is possible to create lines with tiles by placing several tiles next to each other on a contrasting field. These can be simple uniform bands, as shown in Figure C8.6c,

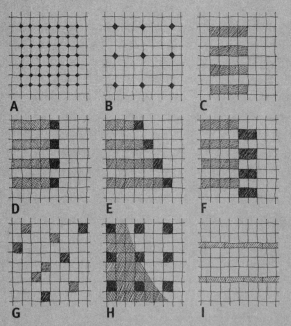

Figure C8.6a–i: Alternatives to the checkerboard pattern: diamond (or inverted square) at each joint (a), diamond (or inverted square) at wider spacing (b), even parallel bands (c), even parallel bands with accents at ends (d), uneven parallel bands with accents at ends (e), even parallel bands with short accent bands at in-between spaces (f), random squares (g), evenly spaced squares over two-toned field with curve (h), bands of contrasting width and finish (i).

or they can have accent pieces at the ends, as shown in Figure C8.6d. The next two patterns show variations of this idea. In Figure C8.6e the length of the strips vary, getting uniformly longer to create a diagonal slant. In Figure C8.6f, the accent pieces at the ends are two tiles wide and they are shifted to occur on the in-between strips.

A random pattern is used in Figure C8.6g. In a random pattern, accent tiles are placed as if they had been sprinkled on the floor from above. The density can vary. Accent tiles can have a prominent presence or be sparse. Also, the density does not need to be uniform throughout. This strategy relies on a painterly eye to achieve good results. The pattern in Figure C8.6h shows two things. First, it is possible to spread apart a uniform pattern of squares. When you do that, they read more as figures than the background. The other thing that takes place in that pattern is the division of the background into a light and a dark zone that meet along a curved line.

Finally, Figure C8.6i illustrates the fact that you are not required to keep the same tile module throughout. Although the field probably needs to be composed of uniform pieces for practicality, accent bands can be of a contrasting size. It is even possible to use contrasting finishes of the same color tile (or stone) for subtle differentiation. A layout that uses narrow bands of a roughly textured stone against a smoother field of larger tiles can be quite pleasing. The subtle tone-on-tone effects produced by the variations between the two sizes and finishes can produce a restrained, elegant effect.

One last note: Remember that just because the majority of tile and stone available commercially is 12" × 12" does not mean that you have to accept this size as a given. This is one example where optimal practical size does not equal the optimal perceptual size. While the 12" square module looks fine in some applications (mostly residential), the module looks out of scale in many commercial applications where an 18" × 18" or 24" × 24" module would better complement the scale of the space. Similarly, many instances call for the use of smaller modules such as 8" × 8", 4" × 4", and small mosaic tiles. In some projects it is even possible to have the installer cut tiles to a custom size. You may, for instance, want to use rows of 12" × 3" strips. In that case, the installer (or factory) would cut 12" × 12" pieces into four strips to meet your specifications. Cutting tiles requires additional labor and expense

and is, obviously, out of the question for low-budget projects. However, it is done frequently on high-end projects.

SIX VARIATIONS OF THE EYE-LEVEL DECORATIVE TILE BAND

The eye-level decorative tile band has limited applications but is seen frequently in places such as public restrooms and hallways. It usually occurs in places with a field of tile, although it can also be set into a drywall wall as an accent. It is another example of the type of application that gives designers a chance to create meaningful expression, and yet they often resort to simplistic solutions. The application requires some length of uninterrupted wall (Figure C8.7). Although it is normally placed somewhere around eye level, there is no reason it couldn't be treated as a focal feature on the upper section of walls in cases where the wall is seen from a distance.

Figure C8.8 shows three examples of simple patterns. Figure C8.8a, the checkerboard, is well known and needs no elaboration. It is not the most imaginative pattern but it is playful in a simple way and serves to engage the mind. Figure C8.8b and C8.8c have certain similarities. They both use a repeating pattern spaced regularly. The

Figure C8.7: Elevation of band on the wall.

Figure C8.8: Checkerboard band (a), four corners plus center (b), cross pattern (c).

pattern itself fits in a square defined by nine tile spaces (three vertical and three horizontal). Figure C8.8b consists of four corners and a center. Figure C8.8c consists of a top, bottom, left, and right. These patterns, although not very imaginative either, are seen frequently and provide some interest along the band.

We recognize that designers seldom have much time to devote to such tasks as designing tile patterns; however, it is possible to achieve interesting effects with little additional effort. Five reminders shall serve to multiply the patterns you can do quickly:

1. Not all accent pieces have to be of the same color or value.
2. You can combine pieces to create lines.
3. Rhythm intervals can vary.
4. You can combine pieces to create a contrasting background.
5. You can combine the horizontal and the vertical.

Figure C8.9a features a simple pattern featuring a rhythm of aligned short light lines and dark points. It is not complex, yet it displays the ability of the designer to think in more than one modality simultaneously (points and lines). The pattern shown in Figure C8.9b highlights a background band by using a contrasting tone. It also shows an example of a simple irregular interval of accent pieces (alternating single and paired accent pieces). Figure C8.9c features long lines and paired dark

Figure C8.9: Line, square, line (a), contrasting with irregular intervals of single and paired square (b), line, pair of squares, line, plus vertical bands (c).

accent pieces. In this pattern, vertical bands intersect the horizontal band. The exact location of vertical bands would have to be determined to suit the circumstances of the application. They can occur regularly or at strategic locations. Our example shows them coinciding with the locations of the paired accent pieces.

These are just a few possibilities to get you started. Using the five reminders above, it is possible to create many different combinations of background, lines, and points using different lengths, tones, and intervals. Give them a try.

REVIEW

Summary

While projects need regularity and order to be perceptually clear and satisfying, they also need to be rich and stimulating. Humans need both stability and stimulation. It is necessary, thus, to achieve a balance between these two seemingly opposing forces. Providing a sense of enrichment in projects requires the commitment of the designer. Enrichment is possible and desirable in any space of a project, particularly in arrival spaces, waiting areas, circulation spaces, and destination spaces.

General enrichment strategies are applicable anywhere in a project. These include the use of variety and complexity. Project complexity can be achieved via complex surface articulation, complex spatial compositions, and complex system overlapping. Other enrichment strategies include the use of novelty, boldness, and tension.

Two somewhat opposite general enrichment strategies are ambiguity and pictorialness. Ambiguity is produced when an arrangement has more than one possible interpretation. Pictorialness relies on the careful composition, articulation, and framing of harmonious, straightforward spaces and surfaces. General enrichment can also be produced by manipulating the use of space in ways that concentrate human activity in certain areas.

Some of the most enriching experiences in interior spaces occur while people move around along the circulation route. Sequences can be like stories, with plots, subplots, and climaxes. The shape of the path itself can be a source of enrichment. The length of the path and its configuration, proportions, and degree of connection all play a major role in the character of the path. Also crucial is the articulation and modulation of the side walls, floor, and ceiling.

What we see from the path becomes part of the total experience. The view at the end of a path and the view along a path to adjacent spaces are important considerations. Opening size and placement can be orchestrated in stimulating ways. The level of correspondence between visual access and physical access can also be manipulated to delay gratification and produce tension, followed by relief.

In addition to facilitating the tasks people perform in buildings, designers have an obligation to provide enriching environments in a project's destinations. Enrichment strategies in these cases include providing proper grounding, connection, and relief.

1. Robert Venturi, *Complexity and Contradiction in Architecture*, 2nd ed. (New York: Museum of Modern Art, 1977), 20.

Exercises

1. Think about past or current design projects you have been involved with. What attempts to enrich experience have you tried to use? Has there been a pattern to your use of enrichment strategies? What?

2. Name three specific design strategies you would use to enrich the following spaces:
   - an arrival space
   - a waiting area
   - a corridor segment
   - a design studio space

3. Draw a plan or axonometric of a highly regular and modular space (see, for example, Figure 7.42 in Chapter 7), and perform at least one variation to make it more varied and interesting.

4. Think of one of your projects. Name three ways you could increase its level of complexity.

5. Take a single important elevation from one of your projects. Draw three complex variations of it.

6. Draw one space and one mass using the principle of novelty.

7. Draw a mass and an elevation using the principle of boldness.

8. Draw three corridor segments using compression to create tension followed by relief.

9. Draw one spatial arrangement featuring intentional ambiguity.

10. Draw a pictorial version of the elevation used in Exercise 5 above.

11. Take a circulation sequence from a previous project. Modify it as necessary to incorporate some meaningful events along it.

12. Take a circulation segment from one of your projects and explore different treatments for the side walls, floor, and ceiling to achieve different effects.

13. Pick one of your projects with several corridors. Draw a focal point at the end of one of the corridors.

14. Pick one of your projects with several corridors. Draw an enticing composition at the end of one of the corridors to attract people by making them curious about what lies ahead.

15. Draw a corridor sequence incorporating various views of the destination space prior to getting to it in order to build anticipation.

16. Pick a past or current project. Design an internal focal plane or mass on which to occasionally rest the eyes in order to take a break from the task at hand.

CHAPTER 9
Expression

INSTRUCTIONAL OBJECTIVES

- Introduce the concept of expression as an integral part of design.
- Explain some of the factors affecting design expression and interpretation.
- Present two different kinds of architectural meanings and how they work.
- Explain how design features can express fundamental aspects of humanity.
- Explain how contextual factors can be expressed in design.
- Discuss ways in which design properties and assemblies can be expressive.
- Discuss the expression of two basic aspects of design related to programmatic necessities.
- Explain how identity is expressed in design.
- Describe the many variables that affect identity.
- Explain how the mode of self-presentation affects the way expression is manifested.
- Explain the roles of the designer's personal style, attitudes, and preferences on expression.

"Architectural expression" is a wide term covering not only the outward manifestation of the inner purpose of the building, i.e. the characteristics of the building programme, but also questions of manners, of the personal equation of the 'ego' of both client and architect, and of the claims of materials and structure to be expressed for their own sake, either directly or by implication.

—Howard Robertson, Modern Architectural Design

S O FAR WE HAVE elaborated on important design tasks, such as conceiving appropriate organizational structures, establishing order, and providing enrichment in design projects. Our next topic, expression, is particularly important because it permeates and colors all of these other aspects of design. In the process of determining which kind of structure, what kind of order, and which enrichment strategies to use for a particular project, the designer has to decide what type of expression the project should have. Structure, order, and enrichment need to be customized into a unified response to the particular realities of the project. The qualities thus embodied will give the project particular meanings appropriate to its unique realities. The project will then attain a presence similar to that of a living organism, with a distinct personality of its own.

Should a given project be a self-conscious, elegant, subtle, and self-disclosing one, perhaps even with a few metaphoric allusions thrown in for the enjoyment of the connoisseur? Or should it be self-conscious, extremely elegant, even pompous, with straightforward boldness and no intellectual games? The possible qualities attainable through design expression and their combinations are countless. The possibilities appropriate for a particular project are narrowed down by the specifics of the project but still leave ample room for interpretation. What are the possibilities, and how does one decide among them?

Mastering the art of determining appropriate expressions for projects and then executing designs that incorporate those expressions successfully is one of the goals of design. Some aspects of expression are straightforward and objective, although much of expression in design is highly personal and subjective. This chapter presents some of the ways design expression can be manifested in your projects. It is difficult to give precise rules about how to incorporate specific expressions in design, much less

about which one is appropriate for a particular project, because project details vary widely from case to case—what's appropriate in one case is not in others. We suggest some of the possibilities and, hopefully, provide some insight about the factors to consider when making decisions about project expression.

EXPRESSION IN DESIGN

Every design expresses something, whether intentionally or not. It tells us something about the character (real or desired) of those who use the space, the attitude toward the context in which the project occurs, and the preferences and design tendencies of both the designer and the user group. Designs, like people and their belongings, embody ways of being and acting. Particular expressions are chosen and approved by clients because they help convey, materially, who they are or aspire to be. The interior design of a place can embody the particular essence of the group using it.

Expression

The particular expression adopted for a project is usually pervasive and, thus, seen throughout the project. Nevertheless, specific expressions can also be localized, occurring only in certain parts of a project. A project or portion of it may express desired emotional qualities (joy or somberness), attitudes of the client (conservatism or innovativeness), specific intentions (a desire for a heightened sense of entry and arrival), and the status of the owner (powerful and successful, or emerging and upcoming). The room in Figure 9.1, for instance, strongly communicates information about the character of its owner.

The particular project being designed and its context, owners, programmatic needs, and designers all contribute

Figure 9.1: The particular characteristics of interior spaces communicate the attitudes and beliefs of the people who own them. The treatments in this room give us clues about the character of its owner.

Source: *Here of All Places*, by Osbert Lancaster (John Murray Ltd., 1958).

to the final expression. The self-image and personal intentions of both the owner and the designer are particularly important, as we will see.

Interpretation

Communication in design, in many ways, operates the same way as other types of communication. It involves the sending of a message by the sender and the reception and interpretation of the message by a recipient. The built environment, due to its physicality, is always present in very tangible ways and, therefore, is always up for interpretation. Every aspect of a design is open to interpretation, whether intended or unintended. A design message may even be accidental. An example of an intentional message is a project designed with a formal layout, classic forms, overpowering volumes, and rich materials to convey a sense of dignified power. An example of an unintentional message is the inaccessibility of an important public area of a building (due to careless design or legitimate design constraints) resulting in the perception (erroneous but understandable) that you are intentionally being discouraged from going there. An example of

an accidental message is the unplanned effect caused by direct sunlight penetrating a project in some magnificent way at certain times of the day. The designer may be praised for orchestrating such a powerful and inspiring combination of forces when he or she was really not consciously trying to produce it.

Design as a language communicates through **formal properties** and **symbolic content**. Particular arrangements created by the specific forms used constitute the formal properties of the project. The meanings conveyed by these properties, as well as the materials, finishes, furnishings, and accessories used, constitute the symbolic content. Whatever associations are derived from them are likely to vary from culture to culture, from group to group within a culture, and from person to person within a group. Despite the variety of interpretations, however, there tend to be similarities of interpretation among people from the same group. In general, people from a particular culture or group share certain attitudes, values, and physical vocabularies related to building forms, physical symbols, and so on. This may make it easier to communicate through design with users from a homogeneous group that share similar views. In such a case, it is more likely that specific forms and symbols employed are interpreted similarly by the users.

Another highly influential factor affecting how people interpret the built environment is the background of the person or group doing the interpretation. Given average conditions, people tend to develop visual affinities with certain environments they encounter during their formative years. For example, a typical restaurant in a rural area may be simple and rustic, and one in downtown New York City may be artsy and pretentious. Someone from a rural area may feel more at home entering the restaurant shown in Figure 9.2a while an urbanite may prefer the one in Figure 9.2b.

A person's cultural literacy also has a significant influence on how they interpret the physical environment. We can expect different interpretations from a person with minimal design literacy and a person who makes a living as a designer. A client trained in the arts is more likely, for example, to appreciate nuance and subtlety, abstract gestures, and historical allusions. Someone else may not care much for any of these attributes.

Figure 9.2: These two restaurants would carry different appeal for people from different backgrounds based on their relative level of exclusivity.

Figure 9.3: Some very basic architectural expressions carry profound existential connotations. Stairs, those utilitarian devices that transport us from one level to another, embody the act of ascending, a powerful symbolic act.

Even among people of similar design literacy levels, interpretations can be quite personal, often colored by the lens through which they look at a design. The historian, the art critic, the designer, and the technical person will all tend to assign greater value to different aspects of a design depending on their particular areas of knowledge and interest. To complicate matters further, it is not uncommon for people from similar backgrounds and areas of knowledge, such as, say, two design critics, to have opposing views about a particular design and to defend their respective points of view passionately.

Furthermore, as design philosophies, fashions, and trends change over time, interpretations and meanings will change too. What is valued today may not be appreciated tomorrow, and vice versa. Expression and interpretation in design are, indeed, very subjective and unstable matters.

Interpretation and Meaning

In order to understand the dynamics of expressing meaning through design and the way those meanings are perceived and interpreted, it is useful to distinguish between two types of meanings: those that are understood spontaneously and those that are learned through convention. **Spontaneous meaning** can be conveyed through literal iconic signs or through inherent expression. These are understood directly, without training. Iconic signs utilize literal representations of the desired meaning, as when a building for an automobile corporation is shaped like a car.

Inherent expression relies on the spontaneous symbolism associated with the formal qualities of objects or compositions and what these represent. Spontaneous symbolism, Rudolf Arnheim explains, "derives from the expression inherent in perceived objects. To be seen as expressive, the shape of an object must be seen as dynamic. There is nothing expressive, and therefore nothing symbolic, in a set of stairs or a staircase as long as it is seen as a mere geometrical configuration. Only when one perceives the gradual rising of the steps from the ground as a dynamic crescendo does the configuration exhibit an expressive quality, which carries a self-evident symbolism."[1] Arnheim is referring to the symbolic meaning of ascending and the deep connotations it carries (Figure 9.3).

Most associations we make in our efforts to interpret the environment are not spontaneous and natural but learned associations, acquired by convention. We have said that **learned associations** between symbols and meanings can vary widely from one culture to another. This fact helps to explain the different interpretations made by groups from different cultures of the same symbols. The same phenomenon occurs between different groups and subgroups of the same culture who learn to perceive and give meaning to certain aspects of the physical world (symbols) in particular and consistent ways. Charles Jencks speaks about differences in **visual codes**. People from different backgrounds, upon looking at the same design, will use different codes (based on learning and culture) for its interpretation. Buildings that incorporate various codes can be seen as having opposing meanings: "the 'harmonious, well-proportioned pure volume' of the modern architect becomes the 'shoe-box' or 'filing cabinet' to the public"[2] (Figure 9.4).

How is a designer to proceed, you may wonder, if there is no certainty about whether the meanings and values

Figure 9.4: Interpretations of design works vary according to the point of view of the person doing the interpreting. The pure volume that provides so much pleasure to the modernist designer can be seen as a lifeless filing cabinet by the general public.

you intend to communicate through the expressions of your design will be understood and interpreted correctly? What kind of expression is best? How concrete do our expressive messages need to be? There are no right or wrong answers to these questions. Opinions vary among designers and critics. Of the two critics mentioned above, for example, Arnheim advocates going beyond arbitrary convention, allying design intentions "with features of more basic, spontaneous expression."[3] He adds that "the most powerful symbols derive from the most elementary perceptual sensations because they refer to the basic human experiences on which all others depend."[4] Arnheim warns, "The use of identifiable subject matter (such as, literal, pictorial, iconic signs) as a component of architectural shape may interfere with a building's spontaneous symbolism because of the concessions its dynamics must make to the shape of that subject matter." He notes that "Eero Saarinen's TWA air terminal might soar more purely if it looked less like a bird."[5] Arnheim, thus, prefers elementary symbols that are perceived naturally and are associated with basic human experiences.

Jencks is in favor of iconic signs, which "speak with exactitude and humour about their function. The literalism, however infantile, articulates factual truths . . . and there is a certain pleasure (which doesn't escape children) in perceiving a sequence of them."[6] Unlike Arnheim, he praises the literalism of Saarinen's TWA terminal (Figure 9.5): "The TWA terminal in New York is an icon of a bird, and by extension, of aeroplane flight. . . . Here the imaginative meanings add up in an appropriate and calculated way, pointing towards a common metaphor of flight—the mutual interaction of these meanings produces a multivalent work of architecture."[7] Looking at architectural components as words, and these in turn as signs, Jencks points out the predominance of conventional symbolic signs over natural ones: "Most architectural words are symbolic signs;

Figure 9.5: The birdlike form of Eero Saarinen's TWA terminal in New York carries meaning beyond its sculptural articulation.

certainly those that are most potent and pervasive are the ones which are learned and conventional, not 'natural.'"[8] For Jencks, the symbolic sign learned by convention is clearly the dominant one.

Vehicles of Expression

The rest of this chapter will present some of the types of expression that can be manifested in a design project. Selecting which ones are embraced and given preference and which ones are ignored is a matter of personal preference and will vary from designer to designer. Beyond personal preferences, the requirements and context of a project will also suggest pertinent expressions for the specific project. The best way for you, as the designer, to be prepared is to have an awareness of the possibilities, become familiar with different ways to execute expression, and develop the ability to diagnose a project to discover what particular type of expression is most fitting. Keep in mind that it is often possible and desirable to communicate with different groups at different levels on any given project. In fact, projects with multiple meanings acquire multiple levels of validity and have the power to delight many audiences.

When it comes to architectural expression, the entire spectrum of the physical environment comes into play. Successful designs have a sense of coherence among all their layers and, as a result, communicate clearly. In these cases, all (or most of) the elements reinforce each other to produce a consistent and powerful expression. In other cases, there can be multiple meanings operating simultaneously and even sending different messages. This may work as long as there is a recognizable sense of hierarchy and balance. The basic vehicles of expression are layout, space, surface, detail, furnishings, and accessories. These are elements that can be manipulated by the designer.

Layouts require many decisions about the placement of functions in relation to the context and to one another. They establish who goes where and who is next to, or far from, whom. They communicate messages about status, hierarchy, relationships between different groups, the degree of constraint or freedom throughout the project, and so on. The two simple office plans shown in Figure 9.6 show different attitudes about hierarchy. Figure 9.6a shows

Figure 9.6: The size and placement of functions project attitudes about the hierarchy of an organization. These two plans reflect two different organizations, one (a) more hierarchical than the other (b). Hierarchical levels are embodied in corner offices, other perimeter offices, interior offices, and general workstations.

a strong hierarchy, with large corner offices, medium-sized perimeter offices, and small interior offices. The plan in Figure 9.6b is much more democratic, with same-sized offices located away from the perimeter and open office areas given exposure to the outside.

Space and its articulation communicate stylistic approach, hierarchy level, and degree of conventionality. Surfaces communicate stylistic approaches and preferences. Through the use of composition, pattern, texture, material, and color, designers can create combinations that communicate an infinite number of expressions. Figure 9.7 shows a view of a prominent civic building interior with generous volumes, strong architectural shapes, and well-articulated surfaces. The next layer of expression is the detail. Details can be shaped in many ways and can incorporate materials and colors that convey a myriad of different expressions. Compare, for example, the two railing systems shown in Figure 9.8. Each different expression has its own unique character.

Furnishings, whether chairs, desks, tables, or display cases, can also have variations in shape, materials, colors,

Figure 9.7: Shapes and surface character contribute much to the architectural expression of this civic building.

and trim, conveying widely different styles and meanings. The many stylistic and material choices make it possible to achieve almost any desired look. Beyond furnishings, accessories are usually specified by the designer. These include items like desk accessories for work settings and the tablecloths, china, candleholders, and silverware in restaurants. Accessories, like most furnishings, are manufactured products that come as they are, and are generally not changed by the designer. Nevertheless, as with furnishings, there is a wide range of styles available, which makes it possible for designers to specify accessories congruent with the desired design expression of the project. The lounge space shown in Figure 9.9 illustrates the important contribution of furnishings and accessories to the character of a space.

In addition to the above, there are also elements of expression not controlled by designers. These are also part of the total picture and contribute considerably to the visible expression of a project. They include the people in the setting, their attire, and the type of language used.

Figure 9.8: Particular expressions are manifested through the detailing of architectural features. These railing systems manifest different characters.

Although the designer usually has no control over these elements, it is important to have an awareness of them as part of the total picture and realize the fact that designers do not control every single element of expression.

Figure 9.9: Furnishings and accessories contribute greatly to the overall expression of a space. These highly functional and decorative interior design elements come in many styles to suit the particular expressions desired by the designer. Notice the influence of the chairs, tables, plants, planters, and decorative railings and light fixtures in this room.

TYPES OF EXPRESSION

There are many types of expression, and designers have great latitude in determining what types of expression to emphasize consciously for a given project. These are not just personal whims but represent the designer's responses to the specific qualities of the project and the client. Once these intentions are clear, it is up to you as the designer to decide how to best achieve the desired expression. Below we discuss different types of expression grouped into six classifications: expression of universal human experiences, expression of contextual factors, expression of formal design properties and assemblies, expression of programmatic necessities, expression of identity, and designer's personal expression.

Expression of Universal Human Experiences

Certain expressions found in the built environment operate at a very basic level by revealing to us simple fundamental aspects of our own humanity. Arnheim talks about "the symbolic overtones of practical life"[9] and explains that works of architecture make symbolic statements that convey relevant human qualities and situations. "We speak of 'high' hopes and 'deep' thoughts, and it is only by analogy to such elementary qualities of the perceivable world that we can understand and describe non-physical properties."[10] Thus, elements such as verticality, depth, and the like can be utilized to evoke some of these human associations. Whether attempts to evoke some of these abstract qualities will be perceived consciously by users is questionable. Some users, because of their training or sense of intuition, will be more conscious of them. Others may sense these qualities subconsciously. Expressions in this category are most effective when the function expressed is asserted strongly for emphasis. Among the possible expressions in this category are the following three dualities.

Ascending/Descending

Ascending is associated with improvement, moving toward better things, even toward the sublime. Heaven is always up, as are the offices of the top-ranking officials of a corporation. The act of ascending, thus, can be a very symbolic act. One climbs a few steps up to get to a special

Figure 9.10: The act of descending carries powerful symbolic connotations that may vary depending on the particular occasion and arrangement. This descending path leads to a somewhat mysterious, cavelike environment.

location, such as a king's throne. Descending can carry connotations of moving deeper into the earth, where one can find security and protection, or perhaps the intriguing, obscure, and unknown. Figure 9.10 shows a downward view toward a mysterious-looking lower area.

Other than with the main staircases in some buildings, gestures of ascending and descending are not widely used these days because of increased sensitivity toward accessibility. Nevertheless, many old buildings still possess great examples of subtle and not-so-subtle level changes that express the functions of ascending and descending in ways that emphasize their metaphoric overtones.

Constraint/Freedom

Another aspect with strong symbolic connotations is the relative degree of constraint or freedom allowed by a given space or project. These are usually related to programmatic requirements, but the way they are treated can carry deep symbolic connotations. People form perceptions in response to the level of overall space available around them and also the degree to which the space permits them to move about at will.

We have talked before about how the use of contrast can be a powerful tool to heighten the awareness of specific qualities. In this case, moving from a tight space to a generous one can emphasize the sense of freedom the larger space affords, and vice versa. Similarly, progressing from a confining and inflexible system of corridors to an area that offers many travel choices and the freedom to pursue them can surely heighten the sense of freedom given by the latter space.

Admittance/Rejection

As in the previous example, the duality of admittance/rejection is usually dictated by programmatic requirements. Here, too, you can find opportunities to emphasize either the admittance or rejection aspect of the equation. Admittance refers to the degree of welcoming offered by a particular arrangement. Admittance presupposes connection and openness between spaces while rejection prevents admittance, either by mere discouragement or by absolute denial.

Rejection usually involves some kind of barrier to prevent passage. The solidity of the wall, the number and character of points of connection between the two sides, and the level of control at those points can send clear messages about how welcome one is to come in. Even more fascinating is the handling of admittance. Admittance has many levels. It ranges from reluctant tolerance, as when a manager reluctantly admits a street person to his fast-food establishment, to eager invitation, as in the case of a store desperate for customers, looking for ways to entice and attract them. When it comes to admittance, it can be allowed (reluctantly or indifferently), encouraged (enthu-

Figure 9.11: The gateway, or portal, is one of the most powerful ways of expressing admittance. These three portals of stores in the same complex are representative of the variety possible within the portal idiom.

siastically), or demanded (aggressively). The three storefronts shown in Figure 9.11 feature portal-like gateways that highlight the point of entry into the respective stores, thus encouraging admittance. Notice the different expressions of the same basic idea of welcoming.

Expression of Contextual Factors

Oftentimes, the contextual forces related to a project not only influence some of the design decisions but actually acquire a dominant form of expression. These forces can be historic, cultural, regional, or related to current norms.

Historic Expression

Many interior projects occur in older buildings or neighborhoods having distinct design features typical of the time when they were built. In many cases the style adopted for a project is congruent with the style of the building. Examples include literal, carefully researched restorations, where every aspect is reproduced as it was originally; renovations, where the basic character of the original style is preserved without getting overly literal; respectful rehabilitations, where new functions going into old buildings respect the character of the original style without feeling an obligation to mimic what was done originally (Figure 9.12); and historical re-creations, where new projects are designed in an older, historical style (Figure 9.13).

In these cases, stylistic approaches from the historical period in question are either incorporated into the

Figure 9.13: Historical re-creations manifest historical expression on new construction. In these cases, a new environment is inspired by an older design style, as shown in this old-world setting in the lounge of a new hotel.

Figure 9.12: Respectful rehabilitations retain elements that convey the historic expression of a place without subjecting the vocabulary of the new design to the same stylistic constraints.

Figure 9.14: Forms based on ethnic traditions, such as the pointed and ornate arches in this restaurant, contribute to the expression of culture.

project or taken as points of departure for the development of new designs. Depending on the project, these may be applied in pure form or expressed abstractly to retain their original essence. **Historic expression** can be pursued at all or just some levels of the design spectrum (from layout to the selection of accessories). Historic expression requires knowledge of the design aspects particular to the project's historical period and the related design expressions that go with it. Lacking this, the designer is in danger of conceiving and executing a historical expression inaccurately.

Cultural Expression

Whenever a project has a strong and specific cultural component based on its location or the nature of its users, the project may need to reflect design expressions from the culture in question. Most cultures have recurring design characteristics one can draw from literally, such as arches and sombreros traditional in Mexican architecture and culture. Even more challenging is when the designer is attempting to interpret aspects of a culture in a nonliteral way, like designing a Mexican restau-

rant without cacti, sombreros on the wall, or the colors of the Mexican flag.

As in the case of historic expression, **cultural expression** can incorporate the entire spectrum of design elements or just select ones. Figure 9.14 shows ethnic forms used in a Middle Eastern restaurant setting.

Regional Expression

Regional expression can vary due to regional cultural differences or to regional topographical differences. In the United States, for instance, certain regions possess strong subcultures with unique characteristics and particular visual affinities. One such region is the Southwest, where the strong presence of Mexican and Native American people and culture has created a unique visual style associated with it.

Topography and location also affect the visual character of a region as well as the materials used for construction.

The arid topography of the Southwest makes the visual uniqueness of the area even more pronounced. Projects done in this region are likely to reflect this expression and incorporate adobe construction and unique regional shapes, as the exterior and surroundings of the church shown in Figure 9.15 illustrate.

Current Norms and Conventions

Design occurs within a certain set of cultural norms and conventions prevalent at the time. The German word *zeit-*

Figure 9.15: Some regions, such as the Southwest, possess strong regional character due to topography, ethnicity, and other factors. The view shown here is unmistakably typical of the region.

Figure 9.16: Every period in history has its own prevailing stylistic norms and conventions. Modernism was characterized by a simple austere machine aesthetic (a). Some designers operated within the new conventions but gave them a more organic feel (b).

Source: *Here of All Places,* by Osbert Lancaster (John Murray Ltd., 1958).

geist is often used to describe the spirit of the time. Some periods in history have enjoyed consistent and widely accepted rules, while others have been characterized by disagreement and change. Whether you, as a designer, adopt the prevailing design tendencies of your time or take a different view becomes your prerogative. Individual designer positions will be dealt with a little later. For now, it is sufficient to say that some projects, especially during times of stylistic transition and progress, can become conscious efforts to express the new spirit of the time. During the reign of modernism, for instance, the desire was to incorporate the machine aesthetic, using it as a metaphor of the industrial progress of that time. Designs became streamlined and devoid of decoration. Although many designs started looking alike, there were still various ways of interpreting these prevailing tendencies. For instance, Figure 9.16 shows cartoonish versions of two different interpretations of modernism. This points to the fact that, even during times of specific prescriptive design norms, there is room for individual interpretation based on personal philosophy or the realities of the project and its context.

Expression of Formal Design Properties and Assemblies

Designers have much control over the treatment of design elements. Shapes, textures, thicknesses, colors, and lights can be emphasized or deemphasized at will to create particular forms of expression. These design properties are objective and tangible. They can be manipulated as part

A

B

Figure 9.17: Certain physical characteristics of the environment can be accentuated and highlighted for their own sake, like the emphasis on the texture of this wall.

Figure 9.18: The function of support can be expressed in many ways. One of them is through the treatment of supporting columns. A normal-looking arcade, for instance, can be transformed through the use of slender columns spaced close together (a) or the use of fewer but heavier columns (b).

of a greater design strategy of expression or for their own sake. For example, the texture of a wall could be accentuated to create a rich and evocative surface (Figure 9.17). It can become expressive and possess a strong character without having to symbolize any meaning beyond the desire to be rich and textural. This type of expression is akin to the idea of enrichment discussed in Chapter 8; the treatment doesn't carry any conscious symbolic meaning beyond the richness produced by the special treatment. Conversely, you may choose textured surfaces on a project in order to symbolize a cave or fortress.

In addition to manipulating specific design properties for effect, you can also manipulate composite design assemblies. These assemblies, as a whole, produce parts of the design that fulfill and express specific functions. Examples include the functions of support, shelter, and connection. These basic functions can, if desired and deemed appropriate, be emphasized or deemphasized to produce specific effects. A greater number of columns spaced closely together would exaggerate the function of support. Fewer but oversized columns would accomplish the same effect with a different feel (Figure 9.18). A floating ceiling canopy over a space in a high area tends to accentuate the function of shelter (Figure 9.19). Emphasizing a connecting path through the treatment of the floor reinforces the idea of connection between two points (Figure 9.20).

Figure 9.19: The floating overhead canopy shown reduces the scale of the defined area below and, thus, gives it a greater sense of shelter.

Figure 9.20: The function of connection can be highlighted by emphasizing the threshold between the parts being connected. Highlighting a connecting path by differentiating the floor material is one way to emphasize connection.

Expression of Programmatic Necessities

The programmatic requirements of a project dictate the basic configuration a project takes. Here we discuss two basic aspects of the programmatic realities of a project that help to shape its basic spatial expression and give it overall character. These are the degree of openness of the spaces and the degree of connection between them.

Openness/Closedness

In Chapter 4 we elaborated on issues of spatial definition, containment, encapsulation, and so on. Choices made regarding layout and spatial definition, largely in response to the program, give spaces distinct characters in terms of their degree of openness, spatial definition, and encapsulation. In the past, there was not much choice. Due to structural limitations, projects were mostly subdivided into compartments bound by load-bearing walls and connected via doors and corridors. Luckily, we have more choices today. A project's degree of openness is one type of expression easily apprehensible on most projects. The openness, or compartmentalization, of a project will quickly tell us information about the level of privacy users require and whether people operate individually or in groups. These visual cues immediately tell us something about the nature of the project and how it is structured and organized. It may be composed of a few large spaces, of one large space and a few small ones, or of many small spaces. Openness, of course, can refer to the overall feeling of openness in a space, which is the result of spatial volume, light levels, and density of components, among other factors. Compare, for example, the different degrees of openness in the two restaurant spaces shown in Figure 9.21.

Connection/Segregation

The way in which different spaces are connected to one another reveals much about the nature of an entity and the way it operates. Connections between main parts, as well as between subparts, tell us about their level of autonomy, as well as about the levels of flow and admittance desired between parts of the project. Are the spaces rel-

Figure 9.21: Openness can be manifested through the freedom produced by generous and/or uncluttered spaces, as well as by the perceptual freedom produced by taller spaces. These two restaurant spaces are approximately equivalent in size, yet (a) expresses more openness than (b) due to its more generous height and less dense table arrangement.

atively open to one another or are they encapsulated by full walls on all sides with small punched holes providing restricted access? Both the level of physical access and the degree of visual disclosure between separate areas are involved. This aspect is related to openness/closedness. The two work hand in hand, the first one referring more to the general character of spaces and the second one to the nature of separations between them.

IDENTITY

Perhaps the most exciting and vital design expression of a project is the visual expression of its identity. **Identity** refers to the embodiment, in tangible ways, of the qualities that distinguish a particular person or group. You can think of it as the physical manifestation of the entity's personality. This identity may be real or ideal. A simple example to understand the interaction of real versus ideal identities would be the case of a person shopping for a car. Let's suppose this person is a conservative, middle-class man but thinks he is hip and likes to project an image of wealth. If this person were to select a car that expresses his perceived self-identity, he would most likely select an expensive sports car. If others were to select the car on his behalf, relying on objective perceptions, they would probably select a less expensive, conservative car.

In determining what identity to reflect, there is sometimes a fine line between reality and fiction, between what some entity really is and what it wants others to think it is. As a rule of thumb, designers are more like public relations professionals trying to show their clients in the best possible light than journalists trying to disclose them objectively.

There are many factors that contribute to a project's personality and, therefore, many considerations that have to be made to decide how to externalize identity. The topic of identity and its expression in design is complicated and sensitive.

Understanding individual identity and knowing how to give it expression through design can be challenging. Projects where the client is a single individual are the simplest, as there is only one identity to reflect; however, most interior projects are designed for more than one person. When you design for a couple, the design task becomes slightly more challenging except, of course, in those rare cases where the two individuals have very similar identities. Designing projects for larger groups becomes even more challenging. The good news is that, in reality, a designer does not attempt to address every identity involved. This would be a futile effort. In these projects you design for the identity of the group, not the individual. Large corporations have their own collective identities, and most stores, restaurants, hotels, and nightclubs cater to very specific publics, making the task of design more targeted. Below we address the topics of individual identity and group identity.

Individual Identity: Personality and Self-Image
Much research has been done over the years in the fields of marketing and consumer behavior to understand people and what factors influence their consumption patterns and preferences. These efforts have looked at individual variables such as personality, self-concept, and personal lifestyle. An individual's identity is related to his or her personality, loosely defined as the patterns of thoughts, emotions, and behaviors that characterize the individual. Personality, in turn, is comprised of those specific combinations of traits that are innate in the

individual and are, therefore, consistent and predictable. Raymond Cattell and his team of trait-theory researchers, for instance, developed a group of 16 traits that can be helpful in suggesting corresponding characteristics of the built environment:

Reserved versus outgoing
Serious versus happy-go-lucky
Shy versus uninhibited
Trusting versus suspicious
Practical versus imaginative
Unpretentious versus polished
Conservative versus experimenting
Relaxed versus tense[11]

While personality may address relevant aspects of an individual, it may be difficult for a designer who has just been hired for a project to determine a client's true personality. The information offered by clients is usually based on their self-image, which is their own assessment of who they are. This is also tricky. Research suggests that people have not one but multiple selves. Some of the self-images identified in the consumer behavior literature are—

Actual self-image, or how people actually see themselves.
Ideal self-image, or how people would like to see themselves.
Social self-image, or how people feel others see them.
Ideal social self-image, or how people would like others to see them.
Expected self-image, or how people expect to see themselves at some point in the future. This one tends to fall somewhere between the actual and ideal self-images.[12]

Understanding the existence of multiple selves is important to designers because, among other challenges, designers need to know which of the client's self-images to address.

Associated with the self-image of any individual is a group of products and material objects that support and communicate that image. According to the image congruence hypothesis, individuals actively seek those products and places that correspond to their self-image.[13] The props and settings individuals use to define themselves become extensions of self. Russell Belk describes four levels of extended self: individual, family, community, and group.[14] Included in the family level, for instance, are the individual's residence plus its furnishings and objects. The house is, in fact, one of the most important aspects of self-identity. Personal collections are also important extensions of self, as they represent the person's judgment and taste. A person's close attachment to neighborhood and town at the community level can also be a strong aspect of his self-image. Finally, included at the group level are an individual's attachment to specific social groups, which often comprise consumer subcultures that influence many of the individual's consumer choices.[15]

Ultimately, the self-image of an individual manifests itself outwardly as a particular lifestyle. The person's way of life, money-spending habits, use of time, interests, and opinions are all part of that lifestyle. The concept of lifestyle has proven more useful to marketers than isolated traits and other aspects of personality in their efforts to correlate people and their preferences related to consumption (including the consumption of houses, furnishings, and all the stylistic variables that go with them). Lifestyle is a compounded concept influenced by factors such as demographics, social class, reference groups, cultural environment, and family.[16] Lifestyles have been studied systematically and some generalized segmentation models have been developed, such as VALS and VALS2, developed by the Stanford Research Institute. VALS2, for instance, classifies the American public into eight distinctive segments.[17] While such classifications are useful to marketers, their usefulness to designers is minimal due to the relative broadness of the groups.

Factors Affecting Identity and Its Expression in Interiors

One of the designer's tasks is to make sense of the client's image and seek a corresponding expression through design. This expression is made visible in many different ways through the materials used, the style used for the interior architectural elements, the furnishings selected, and the detailing of the project. Choices made regarding the design of the project will address the following questions: Should it be conservative or innovative? Should it be pompous or down to earth? Should it be classic or modern? What is the most appropriate expression for this client and this particular project?

Among the motives that drive consumers to formulate their self-images and related product constellations, Eric Arnould, Linda Price, and George Zinkhan highlight five that marketers often use in their promotions. These help explain some of the factors that influence the determination of expression in interior projects.[18]

The Achievement Motive is defined as "the drive to experience emotion in connection with evaluated performance," and its followers strive for achievement and recognition. Expressions of achievement include luxurious and expensive environments and other material symbols that convey high status.

High status, in turn, relates to things like having a high rank in an organization, a high social standing, and wealth. While high rank and social standing are reflected through symbols associated with power (such as getting the corner office), it is wealth that really serves to communicate achievement and having "made it." People of high status usually seek environments that reflect their status. They shop and dine in places where the status expressed by design is consistent with their own. Likewise, people aspiring to high status often commission designs that reflect such a level of success. Conversely, one can have a rich client with few pretensions who prefers to downplay his or her success and communicate a sense of restraint.

While admittance to the prestigious private clubs of the privileged may be reserved for those that meet certain status qualifications, admittance to prestigious restaurants and stores is more public, and most of us can enter these places as long as we dress and behave appropriately. In fact, many people enjoy going to expensive shops and restaurants for an occasional splurge. Conversely, it is possible to make an economically priced restaurant or store appear classy and exclusive so it will attract both economy-minded and image-conscious high-class patrons.

Exclusivity due to status is expressed through the use of expensive materials, furnishings, accessories, and merchandise. In a store, it is likely to be expressed by expensive merchandise, sophisticated finishes, upscale graphics, and low merchandise density. In a restaurant, low-level intimate lighting, tablecloths, and fancy dinnerware and china are symbols of exclusive establishments (Figure 9.22).

The Power Motive "is defined by the drive to have control or influence over another person, group, or the world at large."[19] Ways to show power include the display of prestige possessions (e.g., fancy cars, expensive watches, and prestigious offices and furnishings), formal and intimidating environments (home or office), and the possession of impressive real estate (such as having the corner office with the best view and greatest square footage). Office layouts, in general, say much about a company's attitude related to power. How those in power decide to position themselves and everybody else becomes an important factor. Are groups mixed or are they arranged by status level? Are the arrangements democratic or hierarchical? Who gets the perimeter offices with windows? Who has the corner offices? Are there certain places accessible only to the powerful few, or is every part of the facility accessible to all? Are some areas fancier than others, or is the level of finish and detail consistent throughout the facility?

The Uniqueness/Novelty Motive: While some people strive to fit in (integration), others prefer to stand out (differentiation). Consumer behavior researchers distinguish between dogmatism and innovativeness. A person who is dogmatic tends to think rigidly and to have an intolerance for new ideas.[20] Innovativeness, in contrast, refers to the tendency to seek novel things and situations. Highly dogmatic people are closed-minded and "more likely to choose established, rather than innovative, product alternatives."[21]

This motive relates to what we could call progressiveness related to design. Putting it in terms closer to designer lingo, progressiveness is a measure of how conservative or innovative someone is. In general, the younger generation will tend to be more progressive than older generations. Youngsters tend to have a taste for the new, different, and, sometimes, radical. Older adults, on the other hand, generally pay less attention to the latest fads and tend to be, in general, more dogmatic. There is, however, a range of progressiveness within every age group. Every age has innovative people who defy conventions and conservative ones who stick to traditions.

A challenging situation arises when the progressiveness level of the client differs from that of the space visitor. The person who owns the space (e.g., a store or restaurant) may

Figure 9.22: Projection of status is an important component of group membership. Restaurants range from inexpensive and unpretentious to expensive and exclusive. Low-level lighting, tablecloths and cloth napkins, and fine plates and silverware are usual indications of exclusive, status-conscious restaurants.

be highly conservative but the prevailing audience that supports the establishment may be creative and innovative. In this case, the owner may choose to cater to the tastes of the patrons. In most cases, as we will see later, the owner targets a specific kind of crowd and tailors the level of progressiveness of the facility to cater to that specific market segment. In general, conservative projects rely on proven, conventional, and straightforward forms and compositions. Progressive projects defy convention and utilize novel forms, finishes, and compositions. The storefronts shown in Figure 9.23 portray two levels of progressiveness, with 9.23a being more conservative and 9.23b more progressive.

The Affiliation Motive is defined as "the drive to be with people."[22] Unfortunately, alienation and detachment have been some of the byproducts of societal progress and development. As a result, people are often driven to seek ways to connect with others, especially with people with whom they share certain affinities. Common backgrounds and interests bring people together. Similarly, environments that are friendly and welcoming may serve to invite strangers to join in and feel at home.

Figure 9.23: Some environments project innovativeness while others project conservatism. This applies to all building types, regardless of age group, status, or background. The two stores shown convey different degrees of progressiveness.

Motivated by affiliation needs, many people identify with, aspire to, or may be associated with membership in specific economic and social groups. Their participation integrates them with and differentiates them from other consumers. Factors involved include class, ethnicity, caste, religion, gender, and age.[23] Retail corporations are particularly conscious of these differences. Through careful market research, they determine specific market segments and develop specific strategies (including design strategies) to cater to very specific clientele. Projecting an image consistent with the characteristics of the group will validate and reinforce the self-concept of the group members and send messages to outsiders in an effort to invite and attract compatible members.

People can also feel bound together as groups based on a common contextual background. Whether due to shared culture, subculture, or geographic location, these com-

monalities establish bonds and mutual understandings and affinities that find expression in the built environment. One can generalize that people of the same nationality will feel at home in environments reflecting traits from their culture, that people from the coast will enjoy the presence of water, and that people from the woods will enjoy dense vegetation. These are, of course, generalizations, and designers are warned to check and confirm them.

When designers try to project an image of a certain contextual background for, say, a theme restaurant, they rely on the typical visual symbols of the context being targeted. We have previously discussed cultural and regional common contexts. Other common backgrounds affecting membership are those established by occupation, neighborhood, membership in special interest organizations, and so on.

Related to affiliation needs is the idea of friendliness. Some people and organizations, by innate personality or by calculated intent, project feelings of warmth and friendliness. Others project a sense of coldness, sobriety, and impersonality. In either case, their built environments typically communicate those traits. In some cases, it may be necessary to compensate to make the prevailing tendency more fitting with the requirements of the enterprise. For example, an overly friendly client may choose to tone down the friendliness aspects of his built environment in order to project a more professional image. Similarly, a cold, impersonal organization may choose to have a cheerful and friendly environment in order to compensate for its lack of grace. In general, public projects such as clinics and service centers want to be welcoming and friendly, while private and exclusive ones, such as a private and confidential government entity, may want to convey coldness and distance, at least up front, to discourage intrusion by outsiders.

Friendliness is often expressed by openness, cheerful colors, and a general sense of admittance. Many designers and clients make conscious efforts to produce reception areas that are friendly and inviting, as the one shown for an office in Figure 9.24.

The Self-Esteem Motive refers to the need to maintain a positive view of the self. It is often expressed as an appeal to "be and express yourself."[24] Individuals with high self-esteem are likely to express themselves confidently to blatant arrogance, will affect the character their spaces take: assertive, upright, and distinguished or pompous and pretentious. Other people and organizations give less importance to matters of pride, even if they possess self-pride. In these cases, the environment is likely to express a sense of restrained success or even tasteful humbleness. These combinations are likely to produce slightly different design expressions. The ability to capture the exact level of pride comes with practice and is a trait of the accomplished designer.

Pride can be exhibited through elegant and sophisticated designs that project success or through details and accessories that speak of the success, sophistication, and status of the client. To some, displaying treasured possessions and accomplishments is a way of expressing pride (Figure 9.25).

Sophistication and Taste

Clients have a wide range of aesthetic sensibilities. Characteristics of aesthetically discerning clients include the ability to intuitively sense good composition (proportion and balance), to appreciate nuance and subtlety, to understand and appreciate abstraction, and to distinguish and appreciate special artistic content. In general, discerning clients will be more in tune with the sensibilities of the designer and appreciate, sometimes demand, sophisticated design efforts. The not-so-discerning client is likely to prefer more ordinary solutions. Note that good taste is not indicative of preference for a particular style or design approach. In fact, different levels of aesthetic sophistication are possible within any style, from traditional to contemporary. The two spaces shown in Figure 9.26 are examples of tasteful designs using two radically different styles.

Expressions of sophistication sometimes carry a degree of pretentiousness. A barbershop, for instance, usually makes no attempt to look sophisticated. It is quite content being ordinary and straightforward. An exclusive hair salon, on the other hand, often makes a conscious effort to look sophisticated and even pretentious.

Figure 9.25: Displaying the sense of pride of owners and users can be accomplished in different ways. One of the ways of expressing pride is through display of treasured possessions, accomplishments, and hunting trophies.

Source: *Here of All Places*, by Osbert Lancaster (John Murray Ltd., 1958).

through their environments. One way they may express themselves is by showing a sense of pride.

Some people and organizations like to project a sense of pride through the design of their built environment. The level of pride, which can range from mere self-confidence

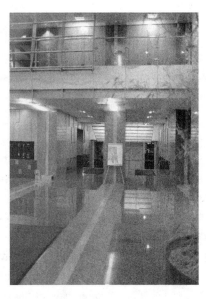

Figure 9.26: Sophisticated expression can occur in any kind of project, regardless of style, as shown in these two scenes from very different projects.

Muddy Waters: The Issue of Taste

We know that tastes vary widely and that part of the designer's training aims to cultivate a sense of good taste. Good taste, however, is a very relative thing. Arnould, Price, and Zinkhan define *taste* as "the making of judgments based on ideas of beauty, order, and arrangement."[25] They explain how "taste is part of the social world and helps consumers find their place in the world."[26] In fact, one of the most important and personal aspects of expression is taste. It acts as a form of cultural capital, giving individuals membership in certain groups and excluding them from others. In many ways, taste defines who we are. People even intentionally adopt certain tastes, with all their accompanying objects and activities, in order to signal membership in a certain group (e.g., museumgoers, wine tasters, and so on).[27]

In an effort to sort different patterns of taste, Herbert Gans identifies five taste cultures. He is careful to avoid making value judgments about them. In fact, he argues that each taste culture is valid and real. Factors that contribute to a person's choice of taste culture include age, class, religion, ethnic and racial background, regional origin, personality factors, and place of origin.[28] Gans posits that the major source of differentiation between taste cultures and publics is socioeconomic level or class, adding that "among the three criteria sociologists use most often to define and describe class position—income, occupation, and education—the most important factor is education . . . not only schooling but also what people learn from the mass media and other sources."[29] As a designer, your task is to recognize a client's taste preferences while acknowledging your own. Then you must come up with the corresponding modes of expression. The five taste cultures are:

High Culture: This culture differs from others in "that it is dominated by creators (such as designers)—and critics—and that many of its users accept the standards and perspectives of creators. Users in this culture tend to either look at culture from a creator perspective (thus, embracing the nuances of, in our case, design), or merely be interested in the output from the creators, but not necessarily in their methods. Members of this culture are almost all highly educated people of upper- and upper-middle-class status, employed mainly in academic and professional occupations. . . . The culture's standards for substance . . . almost always place high value on the careful communication of mood and feeling, on introspection rather than action, and on subtlety, so that much of the culture's content can be perceived and understood on several levels. . . . Since the culture serves a small public that prides itself on exclusiveness, its products are not intended for distribution by the mass media. . . . High culture . . . perceives itself as setting aesthetics standards and supplying the proper culture for the entire society."

Upper Middle Culture: "This is the taste culture of the vast majority of America's upper-middle class. . . . They do not find high culture satisfying . . . but prefer a culture that is substantive, unconcerned with innovation in form, and uninterested in making issues of method and form a part of culture. . . . As a result, upper-middle culture is far less 'literary,' and art and music (and design) are much less abstract than in the case of high culture."

Lower Middle Culture: "Numerically the dominant taste culture and public in America, it is comprised of middle- and lower-middle-class people in the lower-status professions. The aesthetics of lower-middle culture emphasize substance: Form must serve to make substance more intelligible or gratifying. . . . Lower-middle art continues to be mainly romantic and representational, shunning harsh naturalism as well as abstraction."

Low Culture: "This is the culture of the older lower-middle class, but mainly of the skilled and semiskilled factory and service workers. . . . Low-culture publics are still likely to reject 'culture,' and even with some degree of hostility. They find culture not only dull but also effeminate, immoral, and sacrilegious. . . . The aesthetic standards of low culture stress substance, form being totally subservient, and there is no explicit concern with abstract ideas or even with fictional forms of contemporary social problems and issues."

Quasi-Folk Low Culture: "This taste culture is a blend of folk culture and of the commercial low culture of the pre–World War II era, which catered to audiences who were just emerging from ethnic or rural folk cultures at the time. It is the taste culture of many poor people . . . many of them rural or of rural origin and nonwhite. Data about quasi-folk low culture are scarce, but it seems to be a simpler version of low culture. . . . Because this culture is almost entirely ignored by the mass media, its public probably has retained more elements of folk culture than any other."[30]

Gans makes a few qualifications regarding his taste cultures. First, the descriptions exaggerate the extent to which cultures and publics are cohesive and bounded systems; they are analytic rather than real aggregates. Second, many people regularly choose from more than one culture and, thus, can be classified as being in more than one public. Although most people probably restrict their content choices to one culture or to two adjacent ones, everyone occasionally chooses from a much higher or lower culture. Third, upward straddling sometimes involves explicit status motivations, as when people choose from a higher culture for status-seeking purposes or to encourage cultural mobility on the part of their children. Fourth, high culture has more influence than either the size or the status of its people would suggest. While high-culture standards are explicit and to some extent even codified, the standards of the other taste cultures are rarely discussed and taught and are, thus, implicit, uncodified, and for all practical purposes invisible. Fifth, standards from all taste cultures include criteria for bad content as well as good. People from high culture have more explicit standards, have been trained to make judgments based on those standards, and often have critics supporting their judgments. Other taste cultures lack explicit standards, the training to apply them, or a body of published criticism. The difference between those in high culture and those in the lower cultures is in the amount of aesthetic training, but this does not justify assuming a difference in aesthetic concern.[31]

Self-Presentation

The expressions manifested in a design include not only the basic content being expressed (tradition, glamour, and so on) but also a certain tone or approach. These have to do with the chosen mode of self-presentation. Variables include the levels of conformity, explicitness, and strength used in the process of giving expression to a client's image.

Some research conducted on interpersonal self-processes has focused on self-presentation, or impression management. Self-presentation approaches vary widely. Some people, for instance, are high self-monitors; they are concerned that their behavior is consistent with their conception of what the appropriate, or expected, behavior is in a given situation. They want to fit in and will tend to do what's in and acceptable. Others are low self-monitors; they are more concerned with being themselves and less with whether their behavior matches that of other people. This group makes little effort to conform to trends and other kinds of expectations. In general, high self-monitors are more concerned with image and are self-conscious while low self-monitors give more importance to pragmatic matters.[32] Below, we discuss some variables related to self-presentation and individual preferences.

Figure 9.27: Environments, depending on their use and nature, have a preferred load-level range. The three restaurants shown vary in load level from low (a), to moderate (b), to high (c). As can be seen from these examples, one of the main factors affecting load level is the density of objects and accessories in the space.

Load Level

The issues of order, complexity, and environmental load have been introduced already. Any project has a desirable range of adequate load level, depending on the nature of the project and its users. Projects range from highly stimulating to calming environments. In some cases, such as a nightclub or a relaxation spa, the desired load levels will be self-evident. In other cases, the designer has to probe further to determine the client's preference. Since we have already discussed this variable, we will simply reemphasize that clients and projects, due to personality and other factors, will have preferences regarding load levels, and those preferences need to be understood and addressed by the designer. Notice the different load levels of the three restaurants shown in Figure 9.27.

Abstraction

Not everyone appreciates abstraction, something many designers love to employ. Some people prefer more straightforward and literal compositions that look like something familiar. Projects with highly abstract compositions will not please them. On the other hand, straightforward, simple projects will not please people who enjoy ambiguity and abstraction. The more traditional client will demand flowery carpet borders and landscape scenes for their artwork; the more modern one will frown at such choices. Designers need to understand the preferences of their clients in this regard and design accordingly. Figure 9.28 shows two storefronts, one that is more symmetrical and pictorial and another that is more abstract.

Figure 9.28: Compositions can vary widely in their degree of abstraction. Some can be pictorial and literal (a) and others, more abstract (b).

Ambiguity

Another variable is a person's tolerance for ambiguity. People who can tolerate ambiguity often welcome it. Those who cannot tolerate ambiguity may find it threatening and undesirable. Ambiguity-intolerant people will avoid highly complex situations as well as situations containing contradictory information.[33] Consequently, we can see that expressions of identity will want to be clear and straightforward for some clients, while for others they may be complex and ambiguous.

Humor

This variable is concerned with the level of seriousness a client wants to project. Although related to friendliness, it does not always have to be consistent with it. A warm, friendly enterprise may also have a serious tone while a cold, impersonal one may exhibit a slight bit of humor, even if dry. Depending on the desired intentions, the environment can be straightforward and serious or may tolerate humor through the use of unlikely objects, funny artwork, and so on. In general, humor is produced by the incorporation of unexpected content, be it through space and form or furnishings and accessories. Figure 9.29a shows the clever use of props, in this case stuffed animals, to give a children's clinic a humorous and friendly tone. Figure 9.29b features a retail space with a Volkswagen vehicle in the display area. This unconventional approach contributes to the playful and humorous character of the store.

Formality

Related to both friendliness and humor is formality. Despite the general notion that warm, friendly people have a sense of humor and are more casual, other combinations are entirely possible. It is not uncommon to project warmth and friendliness in a formal environment or to have humor and formality, or seriousness and casualness, coexist harmoniously. A formal environment is produced by straight, symmetrical, rigid, and static arrangements. An informal or casual environment is associated more with asymmetrical, irregular, dynamic arrangements. A formal environment is also characterized by uprightness, seriousness, and stiffness, while a casual environment is relaxed and pliable. Compare the levels of formality of the two storefronts shown in Figure 9.30.

Figure 9.29: Humor has useful applications in the design of some environments. This children's clinic uses stuffed animals to liven things up and reduce the fear of its patients (a). The store incorporates a car with the merchandise to produce a humorous surprise (b).

Figure 9.30: Arrangement, materials, shapes, and content all contribute to formality. The store in (a) is relaxed and casual; the store in (b), serious and formal.

Figure 9.31: Expression can be loud and bold. The gigantic wristwatch suspended from the ceiling of this clock store is a rather bold statement.

Intensity

Another important variable affecting self-presentation is the intensity used to express a project's character. It is a potency measure and is related to levels of extraversion and intensity. Like the other factors discussed above, the type of presentation used will depend on the personality of the client and the requirements of the project. Intensity is related to and affects all the other variables, as every client preference will be colored by the intensity with which those variables are expressed. A client may like to show off success in a big way or may rather keep a low profile despite the success. An extroverted client may desire an office painted with bright, bold colors. On the other hand, a mellow restaurant owner may prefer a mellow kind of expression (except in cases where a high-load environment is more appropriate for a high-energy restaurant that caters to a young crowd). A useful way to talk about intensity in design is through the concepts of boldness and subtlety.

Boldness

Boldness is high intensity. Visually bold environments are intense and extroverted. Expressions of achievement, power, uniqueness, and other preferences are presented forcefully with little restraint. If part of the environment is to be off-limits to certain people, for instance, the barrier will be huge and there will be no confusion about the message. If the company is successful, you may expect to see exuberance. If the client is progressive, innovation will be expressed in no uncertain terms. If the users have a sense of humor, the place will surely make you laugh. If a group has preferences for, say, sensual form and complexity, expect to see unabashed curves and a very intense and complex environment. Of course, the designer is likely to help a bold client tone down a few items to achieve a healthy balance, but, if left untamed, this group would go all out and express all of its bold predispositions forcefully and loudly.

Boldness can be achieved many different ways, including the incorporation of high complexity, bright lighting, accented contrasts, strong colors, bold graphics, and unusual forms and furnishings. The gigantic wristwatch suspended from the ceiling in Figure 9.31 is an example of intentionally using bold props for expression.

Subtlety

Subtlety relies on restraint. Visually subtle environments express themselves in quiet ways. By subtlety, we don't mean lack of expression. In these cases preferences and predispositions are communicated without boasting. Success may be expressed without being ostentatious, traditionalism may be shown without getting too literal and stuffy, warmth may be shown without excessive use of warm colors.

A project may have subtle expression due to the personality of its users, or it may be a conscious choice made to fit the project. Subtlety is often influenced by the designer. Taken to an extreme, subtlety can become minimalism, although subtlety implies intricacy handled delicately rather than simplicity and absence of expression. Subtlety is characterized by slimness, the use of soft colors, soft lighting, low contrast, and overall restraint. Obviously, there is a lot of ground between exaggerated boldness and pure subtlety, and many projects find their comfort zone somewhere in the middle. Notice the restrained character of the two office scenes shown in Figure 9.32.

Formal Properties

Under the heading of formal properties we group a number of miscellaneous stylistic aspects related to expression. These preferences are usually the concern of designers

Figure 9.32: Opposite to boldness is subtlety, characterized by light-handedness and restraint, as shown in the design of these two office environments.

Figure 9.33: Client and designers prefer some shapes to others. Additionally, some shapes are more appropriate in certain projects than others. Curvilinear shapes always make an impression. Three applications of curves are shown: one on an entry canopy (a), one on a glass wall (b), and one on a floor pattern (c).

(creators) since clients, except the most sophisticated, are more concerned with other aspects of design, such as utility and comfort, and rarely get into this level of concern. Nevertheless, choices made about formal properties are often part of the designer's attempt to capture and express the essence of a client's identity.

Figural Character of Spaces, Masses, and Objects

The ways in which space and its elements are shaped and assembled can have different resulting characters. Some compositions flow, while others are choppy. Depending on the character of the client and the desired expression, some design arrangements will be more suitable than others. Important factors include the shapes used, the perceptual weight of elements, and the character of the compositions.

Shapes

The shape of interior space can take many configurations. These are most apparent on the shape of walls, the configurations of lines and patterns on two-dimensional surfaces (walls, ceilings, and floors), and the shape of furnishings and their components. Designers make conscious choices about the character of the shapes in their projects. A certain project may call for straight lines, others diagonal lines, others tight curves, and others smooth, sweeping curves. Curves often carry connotations of flair and sensuality, straight lines of straightforwardness and formality. Figure 9.33 a–c shows applications of curvilinear shapes on a ceiling, wall, and floor plane.

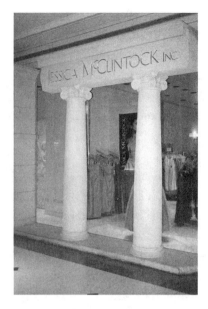

Figure 9.34: An important consideration in design is the perceptual weight of parts and elements. The columns supporting this entry portico seem relatively heavy, but they make the desired statement.

Figure 9.35: Weight is also an important consideration in the proportions chosen for trim. The three storefronts shown display various degrees of trim heaviness, ranging from very heavy (a), to moderate (b), to light (c).

Weight

Perceptual weight is another important formal property. It refers to the light- or heavy-handedness of design elements. Applications may include the size of vertical supports or the proportions of trim, column bases, and other elements. Some projects call for a "light" feel, while others need a "meatier" look. A good example is a column and its proportions. Notice the relative heaviness of the columns shown in Figure 9.34. Consider now the trim of the three storefronts shown in Figure 9.35.

Composition

In addition to shapes and weight, the actual design composition plays a significant role in determining the figural character of spaces, masses, and objects. The size, number of parts, and arrangement of subcomponents impacts the final appearance of a given composition. To give a project its proper expression, a designer may ask the following questions: Should a certain composition be broken down into a few large pieces or many smaller pieces? Should parts be assembled seamlessly, or should they read as individual pieces on the same background?

Figure 9.36 shows the composition of two elevations. Figure 9.36a features just a few large pieces, while Figure 9.36b shows the same wall divided into a greater number of smaller pieces. Notice the difference. Now look at Figure 9.37, which shows the same elevation shown in

9.36b fragmented into separate individual sections. Notice the specific look it takes. In recent times, an increasing tendency of many commercial designers influenced by the modern movement has been to use fewer, larger parts and extend them all the way to the ceiling plane, as shown in Figure 9.36a.

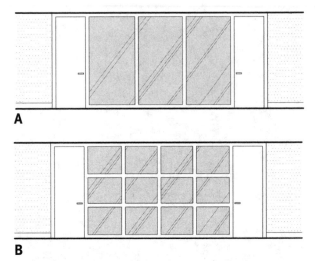

A

B

Figure 9.36: Different compositions convey different expressions. The wall composition in (a) features a few full-height parts and produces a subtle, uncluttered elevation. The composition in (b) features greater modulation and produces a richer, more complex effect.

Figure 9.37: Compositions can look like an overall piece that has been subdivided, such as the two elevations shown in Figure 9.36, or they can look like individual parts that have been brought close together to form a group. This elevation is similar to the one in Figure 9.36, but this time it is fragmented into distinct individual parts and has a very different feel.

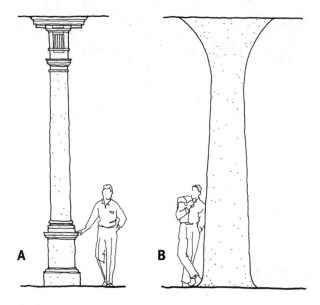

A   **B**

Another related composition issue refers to the method of construction used to shape form. Some elements look like they were carved from a single piece; others appear to be composed through the assembly of many pieces arranged into a single composition. Compare the two columns shown in Figure 9.38. The column in Figure 9.38b is made up of one piece that has been shaped. It is pure as it is and consists of only one part. It can be changed only by "carving" it further. The character of the column in Figure 9.38a is quite different. It is clearly composed of parts that have been assembled together in a specific arrangement. Each part contributes to the whole but also reads as a distinct part that can be changed independently.

Material Palette

A highly influential aspect of projects is the choice of the material palette. Materials have an immense impact on the expression of a project. Possibilities and variations are countless. We will focus here on one particular kind of differentiation among material palettes to illustrate the point: the distinction between natural material palettes and manufactured ones. Natural material palettes use wood, stones, and natural textiles and give a more organic, or natural, feel. Manufactured palettes use materials such as metals, plastics, and glass and give a more industrial look. Some designers favor one approach over the other, while some combine the two successfully. Choosing one or the other will produce radically different looks and project very different expressions. These material expressions can be found mostly on walls, frames, doors, trims, and furnishings. Notice the different feel of the three scenes in Figure 9.39 based on their material palette.

Ornamentation

One final important category is the attitude toward ornamentation. Today, many designers see applied decoration as fake and unnecessary; however, many designers and clients enjoy ornamentation, and some projects demand it. Each project and client has a specific character, and many times the use of applied ornamentation will be the most fitting approach for a project.

Figure 9.38: Objects, masses, and planes can look like assemblies achieved by the careful combination of many parts (a). They can also look like plastic-type objects that are shaped from a single piece (b).

Figure 9.39: Different materials carry different expressive connotations. Note the different effects produced in the three environments shown by virtue of their materials. The materials range from textiles and painted drywall (a), to wood paneling and granite floors (b), to steel and glass (c).

Many designers take a different approach and utilize inherent detailing and carefully selected accessories, artwork, and finishes to give projects the richness once supplied by applied ornamentation, shunning away from applied embellishments. Figure 9.40 shows a carefully detailed contemporary coffee bar and a more ornamental, yet restrained, drinking water fountain in a niche.

Figure 9.40: Ornamentation, although still used, has been substituted by detailing. Ornamentation implies applied decoration, while detailing implies intrinsic form. The approach used carries specific connotations and stylistic inclinations. The modern detailing approach used for the coffee bar design (a) is quite different from the ornamental drinking fountain (b).

GROUP IDENTITY

So far, our discussion of identity has focused on personality traits, self-images, and preferences of individuals, both in general and as clients. It is not difficult to think of groups and organizations that would have some of the same self-images and personalities as those discussed. Now we shift our attention to group or collective identity, referring to the identity of larger enterprises. The development of these identities into expressive environments relies strongly on the design concepts adopted for the projects, as we discussed in Chapter 6. Examples include the image that corporations adopt and the identity of establishments that cater to specific publics such as shops and restaurants. Below we look at corporate identities, restaurant and retail identities. A capsule in this chapter takes a specific look at branding.

Corporate Identity

Not only individuals have a sense of self. An organization also has a sense of self, an identity. As Nicholas Ind explains, such identity is unique and "is formed by an organization's history, its beliefs and philosophy, the nature of its technology, its ownership, its people, the personality of its leaders, its ethical and cultural values and its strategies. . . . It is not something cosmetic, but is the core of an organization's existence.[34] During these times of increased diversification and globalization, companies are becoming decentralized and, consequently, losing their sense of cohesion. For these companies, now more than ever, it is essential to find a common identity. Ind explains:

> Corporate communication is the process that translates an identity into an image. This is a vital part of the process because a corporate identity, if it is to have any value, has to be communicated to employees, shareholders and customers alike. Without communication the values and strategies of the organization will not be understood or owned and the company will not have any clear sense of identity.[35]

While corporate communications cannot turn a poor company into a success, it can "convey a consistent and credible message of what a company is, what it does and how it does it, by trying to control the messages it transmits."[36] Wally Olins states that corporate identity is concerned with four major areas of activity:

1. Products and Services: What you make or sell
2. Environments: Where you make or sell it, the place or physical context
3. Information: How you describe and publicize what you do
4. Behavior: How people within the organization behave to each other and to outsiders.[37]

The identity mix of product-based companies is dominated by the product, how it feels, what it looks like, what it costs, how it works, and so on (e.g., Apple and Nike). Some companies, in turn, have identities dominated by environments (e.g., Hilton or Marriott), and it is the places themselves that come to mind and dominate our impressions.

Many identities are communication-led. Often associated with generic products or commodities, these otherwise anonymous and undifferentiated products are brought to life through information techniques, especially advertising. This is how a product like Coca-Cola,

Figure 9.41: Vidal Sassoon was an early pioneer in the use of identity programs. The company's program, which included hair products, lively unisex salons, and friendly staff, still thrives today.

"a maroon fizzy liquid of—some would say—no intrinsic interest of merit,"[38] became a global success. Finally, there are service-based organizations that depend on how their people behave for their success (e.g., a police force). In practice, the identity of a company is a mix of all four areas of activity, even if one area dominates.

Olins explains how Vidal Sassoon was an early pioneer of the successful use of identity programs, utilizing all the classic identity tools to exploit a commercial opportunity in the 1960s. The products were the styling of hair and the hair-care products required for hair maintenance; the environments were the open, lively, unisex salons; the information was the cleverly devised publicity, advertising, and public relations used to heavily promote the business; and the behavior was the relaxed, informal, and friendly atmosphere created by the staff working in the salons (Figure 9.41).

Shops and Restaurants

Our main interest here, though, is in the environment component of the identity matrix, because it is there that interior designers make their main contribution. In the retail and restaurant markets, the role of the facilities is crucial. The identity of restaurants is closely linked to the restaurant concept, something that is chosen intentionally by the owner and his consultants. Restaurants try to project a total image to appeal to their chosen market, whether defined as families or executives, formal or informal, inexpensive or pricey. Here again, various factors work together to create the total image: location, layout, decor, menu, operational style, the appearance of the staff, the background music, and, of course, the actual food and its presentation. The image produced is most successful when it is vivid, clear, and easily remembered.

A great example of a strong concept with a strong sense of identity is the Hard Rock Cafe. The original, in London, was conceived to offer economical American food in an energetic environment that celebrated rock music, past and present. The concept caught on and spread to other major cities. Decorations consist of memorabilia from rock stars, from Bowie to Hendrix, from Presley to Madonna. Apparel and memorabilia for sale help to propagate the image.[39]

In restaurants, every detail contributes to the total image and experience: Materials, color, form, space, light, uniforms, napery, glassware, flatware, china, and menu graphics constitute the stage setting and the props. The staff and clientele are the actors. At the Chart House restaurants, servers are dressed in attractive Hawaiian shirts and dresses. Their natural nautical decor, warm woods, and privileged locations next to water complement the total experience.[40]

Retail stores, like restaurants, cater to well-defined markets and rely on strong concepts to convey their identities. Millard Drexler of the Gap explains the importance of an easy-to-recognize identity: "It was critical, not only to our image but to our success, that the customer get an immediate visual sense of what the store stood for. . . . Today, the Gap's philosophy is to have an easy, simple-to-shop, very pointed assortment of clothing with color as an emphasis."[41] Their stores, merchandise, and advertising are clean, simple, and uncluttered.

The Pea in the Pod store in Dallas was conceived to cater to the pregnant woman "who had any sense of style." The philosophy of the store is to provide pregnant women high-quality and stylish clothing in a high-service kind of environment. The stores are designed "to have the sparkle, ease, and light of one's own home . . . an architecture not to interfere with the clothing, but to create a feeling of comfort in an understated way, so that the customers would not even be aware of why they felt comfortable." Also important was the goal of creating "architectural touches that were consistent with our customers' own personal environment and socioeconomic level."[42]

Catering to a specific age group and socioeconomic status is an important consideration in the design of many shops and restaurants. Shops, accordingly, will project an image sensitive to the affinities of the target group. This is especially pronounced when it comes to fashion, where every store will project an image that will attract the intended audience by catering to their age and status. The visual symbols used through the architecture, signage, graphics, and merchandise project an image that caters to a specific group, be it children, teens, young adults, adults, or mature adults. Looking at the two stores shown in Figure 9.42, one gets an immediate sense that the store in Figure 9.42a caters to a younger crowd than the store in Figure 9.42b.

Specific expressions can be manifested through design. In some cases, these expressions cater to the members of a particular group while sending messages to others that the place is not for them; however, many environments are intentionally designed in such a way that everyone can feel at home. Some types of projects, such as clinics and some public buildings, even demand it. If done with sensitivity and skill, these can be attractive, genuine, and successful. If not, they can be as bland as food that tries to cater to all tastes.

Figure 9.42: Particular treatments and images can project qualities that are congruent with the affinities of specific age groups. This is particularly evident in the world of retail, where some stores cater to a young crowd (a) and others cater to a more mature crowd (b).

Think of big powerful brands and what comes to mind? Coca-Cola, Microsoft, Nike, Apple—just to name a few. Big powerful brands have existed as long as the media that has disseminated their message. Behind them have been the megaworlds of advertising, radio, and television. Why, all of a sudden, would the world of architecture and interior design enter the world of branding? For years the powerful brands have relied upon clever copywriters, graphic artists, and other ad makers. Why are designers, all of a sudden, claiming some ground in this competitive arena? What do we have to offer? Let's first go back and try to understand how branding became such a powerful phenomenon.

While the idea of bolstering product names through the media was widely acknowledged as important, the focus of manufacturers was, until recently, on the production of goods. Yet, all that changed in the mid-1980s. As Naomi Klein explains, the immense growth in the wealth and influence of multinational corporations in the recent past has been triggered by "a single, innocuous idea developed by management theorists in the mid-1980s: that successful corporations must primarily produce brands, as opposed to products."[1] As the Nikes and Tommy Hilfigers claimed and proved, the secret was to produce not goods (those could be made cheaply overseas) but images of their brands. There was no need, they reasoned, to have oversized corporations full of employees and things, when the real secret was owning the least, having the fewest employees on the payroll, and producing powerful images.

One company who had success with the newfound secret was The Body Shop. During the recession of the late eighties and early nineties, The Body Shop started an aggressive growth campaign in the United States, opening 40–50 stores a year. As Klein relates, "It pulled off the expansion without spending a dime on advertising. Who needed billboards and magazine ads when retail stores were three-dimensional advertisements for an ethical and ecological approach to cosmetics? The Body Shop was all brand." Also expanding during this time without spending much in advertising was Starbucks, the coffee chain. Pretty soon Starbucks was everywhere,

from the airport terminal to the airplane cabin, to the corporate boardroom, to the strategic downtown corner, "incorporating marketing into every fiber of its corporate concept—from the chain's strategic association with books, blues, and jazz to its Euro-latte lingo." The new companies had transcended the old routine of splashing logos on billboards. "Here were two companies that had fostered powerful identities by making their brand concept into a virus and sending it out into the culture via a variety of channels: cultural sponsorship, political controversy, the consumer experience and brand extensions. Direct advertising, in this context, was viewed as a rather clumsy intrusion into a much more organic approach to image building."[2] Starbucks knew about the importance of establishing emotional ties with customers. As Starbuck's CEO Howard Schulz once expressed, the people who line up for Starbucks aren't just there for the coffee: "It's the romance of the coffee experience, the feeling of warmth and community people get in Starbucks stores."[3]

In the brand builders' vision of success, products are presented "not as commodities, but as concepts: the brand as experience, as lifestyle."[4] Now instead of presenting Brand XYZ as a product, it is presented as "a way of life, an attitude, a set of values, a look, an idea." Consequently, Nike's mission "is not to sell shoes but to *enhance people's lives through sports and fitness* and to *keep the magic of sports alive.*" Likewise, IBM is not about selling computers but "*selling business solutions,*" Swatch is not about watches, it is about "*the idea of time,*"[5] and McDonald's is not about selling burgers, it is about "*convenience*" and "*fun.*"[6]

For a brand to work well it has to speak to its audience in some way, representing a desired lifestyle or a unique service it aspires to experience. More than ubiquity, visibility, and function, brands are now more about "emotionally bonding."[7] Their personalities communicate the brand proposition to their target audiences through design. A brand can be designed to be old-fashioned and traditional, glamorous and romantic, or, in the case of the Virgin brand, "fun, wacky, impulsive, and irreverent."[8] Being responsible for giving form to brand ideas, designers have to be able to think of a brand as a person and then ask questions, such as: If you were a shop or a restaurant, what kind of shop or restaurant would you be?

Helen Vaid classifies brands into two broad categories: corporate and consumer brands. "Corporate brands usually relate to a company itself . . . but can also be used broadly to describe services offered to other businesses (rather than to consumers). Consumer brands, on the other hand, relate to the physical products or services that the company offers to its (noncorporate) customers."[9] She also classifies brands by industry, as follows:

Service brands deal with not an object but a performance. The impression made by a particular airline during a typical air-travel experience is a good example.

Retail brands offer great opportunities to designers, as they require special environments that offer unique and engaging experiences. "The various aspects of interior design—graphics, layout, display systems, color schemes, fascias, signage, and even sounds and smells—all have to be considered, planned, and created for a given floor space, but still within the boundaries of the overall brand design."

Consumer product brands are the most commonly and heavily branded. Included here are many familiar product brands, such as Wheaties, Pepsi, and Sony.

Industrial product brands deal with products intended for businesses, not consumers.

Commodity brands are used for commodity goods (generic goods such as toothpaste, oatmeal, and bananas). Despite the lack of differentiation between these generic products, their branding campaigns influence our perceptions of their apparent desirability and influence our choice of brands such as Colgate, Quaker, and Chiquita over their competitors.[10]

Now we come back to the earlier question. Why has the world of branding become so important to architects and interior designers? Or, why are architects and interior designers so important to today's brand-

ing efforts? After all, as Eleanor Curtis puts it, "Can the interior spaces and hanging rails really inform the customer about the brand?"[11] A common-sense reply is the argument that good design helps clients stand out in an oversaturated, crowded business world. Nancye Green explains: "Today, it is clearer to all marketers that the real threat to dominance in any single market segment is the difficulty of establishing, and then maintaining, relationships with empowered customers in a world of abundant choices, shifting distribution channels, and powerful new retail formats."[12] Today, the need to promote a message of being distinctive in order to stand out is essential for survival. Good, attractive design by itself is often not enough, though. Businesses must go further and establish an emotional bond with their clients by creating strong and engaging brands their clients can buy into.

As Curtis explains, in regards to fashion retail, "Today, in our all-consuming, all-pervading culture, when we purchase a product we are buying into the brand. The building, the logo, the advertising, the fashion model, even the shop assistants, in addition to the clothes and accessories themselves, all tie-up this thing called 'image' or brand. In a sense, buying into this is like buying into a club membership. A customer will identify with a brand that reflects his or her tastes and will gravitate towards those names, reinforcing his or her self-image, just as one becomes a member of a club."[13] She goes on to explain what architecture can add to the overall image the customer has already bought into. One of architecture's contributions, according to Curtis, "is in the all-encompassing nature of the built form: the store is more than just products and may say something about a way of doing, a way of being, or a way to organize. . . . The design of a space can represent our social background, our income, our cultural values, our age, our aspirations."[14] Otto Riewoldt reiterates, "Brands signal our membership of an 'in' group. They are the tools with which we build status. They ensure we belong and give us security. Brands build emotions, promise happiness and provide kicks. This decisive paradigm shift has taken place on the emotional plane of the brand experience."[15]

"Brandscaping," as Riewoldt explains, "the three-dimensional design of brand settings—is all about forging backdrops for experiences with a high entertainment value."[16] While advertisers may get a few seconds on the air or a two-page spread, designers of environments "can formulate and shape narratives, drawing on the dimensions of space and time, to weave together the breadth of elements necessary to build a totally immersive experience."[17] The quality of the brand experience is founded on direct interaction and a very specific kind of encounter. "We are not talking about virtual non-experiences in the no-mans-land of the internet, but about concrete encounters in real locations, where the world of the brand is staged and enacted. Here we can experience the manifestation, the messages and the emotions of the brand in company with the products themselves, in unadulterated, unusual, and unique style. . . . By staging the brand experience in flagship stores, shop designs or entire theme parks, companies communicate the image of the brand and imprint a characteristic atmosphere on the customer consciousness."[18]

Interior design, in fact, has become one of the most powerful tools for creating the brand experience by stimulating emotions, sensory experiences, and, ultimately, sales. "Sensory experiences are instant, potent and capable of influencing buying decisions in both the long and short term," states Vaid. In place of traditional retail, now there's "the 'art of shopping,' which is less about purchasing and more about creating all-embracing experiences of a brand."[19] Extreme examples include the shrinelike Niketown stores and Disney, one of the first to create a microcosmos reflecting a brand.

Julian E. Markham, author of *The Future of Shopping*, believes design innovation is key in today's rapidly changing and competitive marketplace. Today, Markham writes, "it's no longer enough to do it well, you also need to do it new. . . . A new age of innovation is in progress. The key words are 'surprise,' 'delight,' and 'surpass.' . . . Architecture and spatial design have become major elements in retail presentation. Their place in the overall scene and promotion of the retailer, the merchandise and the message is a delicate balance of complementary aesthetics, seduction, and comfort."[20]

Sociologist Gerhard Schulze explains the way some of these "experience settings" act as "backdrops to happiness, providing a brief experience, a short sensation of happiness," where the customer becomes a character in the play. The most important thing becomes to engage the customer, "not to sell the product but to generate a fascination with the brand: to get the customer to identify with the world of the brand, creating a brand awareness and providing it with a deep-set emotional anchor."[21]

Riewoldt believes the balance between familiarity and surprise is also critical. "As actors, customers must encounter familiar aspects and be able to find their way around by recognizing landmarks or layouts, but at the same time there must be exciting new elements for them to experience. In brandscaping, architecture and interior design are the stage that provides a setting for ever changing scenes. As the immediate environment of the brand experience, salesrooms and shopping centers themselves take on brand character. Down to the finest detail of interior design, they are geared to transmit a message that translates design into emotional impact."[22]

Branding has indeed become an important topic in the lives of many architects and interior designers. Green puts it in perspective: "This kind of brand-building is the topic du jour, and what is specially compelling is that we are now critical members of the brand-building team. Today, we have the chance to bring to the table more than design expertise. We can be true partners in giving life to brands and in building relationships with customers through deeply engaging experiences. We have a tremendous opportunity: our domain is extraordinarily rich and uniquely powerful."[23]

As a critical member of the branding team it is the designer's responsibility to learn how the interior design medium can create the kinds of sensory experiences required to consummate the emotional bonding so critical to the branding experience. It is also important to understand the interplay between the interior design medium and other messages conveyed by other media. As Riewoldt stresses, "The design of the retail environment must merge with the brand image down to the finest details. Expressiveness, the purposeful use of characteristic forms, and calculated elements of surprise combine to make an integral whole."[24]

Green concludes, "We are not simply designing stores and restaurants and shopping malls . . . we're impacting the total relationship between brand and customer. We are creating the *experience* of the brand."[25]

Exercise

Below we present paired photographs of well-known brands from different retail niches. Discuss in class your perceptions of these brands, addressing the following:

1. How would you describe the *brand idea* in a short statement?

2. How would you describe the *brand experience* in a short statement?

3. How is one brand different from the one it is paired with?

4. Invent a third brand in each of these market segments. What is the idea? What is the brand experience like? What kind of physical environment would best support the brand?

A

B

A

B

A

B

1. Naomi Klein, *No Logo* (New York: Picador, 2000), 5.
2. Ibid., 20.
3. Ibid., 20.
4. Ibid., 21.
5. Ibid., 23.
6. Helen Vaid, *Branding* (New York: Watson Guptill, 2003), 13.
7. Ibid., 8.
8. Ibid., 36.
9. Ibid., 30.
10. Ibid., 30–33.
11. Eleanor Curtis, *Fashion Retail* (West Sussex, U.K.: Wiley, 2004), 14.
12. Nancye Green, "Creating the Brand Experience," *Interiors Magazine* (May 1998): 241.
13. Curtis, 14.

14. Ibid., 14–15.
15. Otto Riewoldt, ed., *Brandscaping: Worlds of Experience in Retail Buildings* (Boston: Birkhauser, 2002), 8.
16. Ibid., 7.
17. Green, 241.
18. Riewoldt, 8.
19. Vaid, 82.
20. Julian E. Markham, "E-tail and the Increased Importance of Retail Innovation," in *Fashion and Architecture*, ed. Helen Castle (London: Wiley-Academy, 2000), 25–26.
21. Riewoldt, 10.
22. Ibid., 11.
23. Green, 241.
24. Riewoldt, 79.
25. Green, 241.

Designer's Personal Expression

Every project's expression, however indicative of the realities of the program, context, and client's identity, is also an expression of the attitudes and beliefs of its designer. All the kinds of expression discussed up to this point, after all, get filtered through your own judgment and you ultimately decide what gets expressed and how strongly. Additionally, as the designer you carry a responsibility to the profession, and your decisions are made within the context of a set of current norms in design. Both timeless principles and current trends affect the design climate in which designers operate. There are also personal tendencies and beliefs held dear by individual designers. All these affect the ultimate expression of a project.

Below we look at three major factors that affect the kind of expression designers choose for a project: the designer's personal style, attitude about current design norms, and use of symbolic expression.

The Designer's Personal Style

All designers have particular design tendencies and a certain design range within which they like to operate. For some the range is broad, encompassing diverse ways of designing, while for others it is quite narrow. Many designers develop distinct styles that become their signature style. People who share affinities with that style will seek them out to be their designers. Some designers operate within strict modernistic principles of simplicity and austerity, while others are more flamboyant and decorative.

Designers, like clients, have specific preferences and predispositions. They will, consciously or not, try to influence the project to arrive at an expression within their own range of preferences. The final expression the project takes is usually a combination of the expressions agreeable to both client and designer. When clients seek designers whose style is compatible with their own tendencies, the bargaining process becomes a much smoother one. Many clients either don't feel comfortable making or don't have time to make choices about expression and look to their designers to take charge and get the job done.

Other than style, per se, designers can endow projects with particular expressions based on their personal attitudes about composition, materials, and construction approach. They can also express their own convictions about materials and their use. Some will prefer natural materials, while others will choose man-made ones. Some will strive for a highly crafted look and others for a very artsy look.

When it comes to craftsmanship, some designers believe that it is important to reveal the way design elements are put together for all to see and understand. American architect Louis Kahn, for example, was known for designs that revealed the structure of a building in its many details. This approach carries with it the additional burden of having to resolve every detail clearly so they can be displayed, understood, and appreciated. Many designs express exquisite detailing and craftsmanship. These attest to the great skill of the designer who conceived and worked out the details and, in many cases, to the skill of the individuals who built them.

Another important aspect of design for which designers develop personal convictions is the issue of honesty of expression. This involves questions, as Robertson said, "of architectural 'deceit' or 'honesty,' and of the borderline between legitimate make-believe and trickery."[43]

The Designer's Attitude about Current Design Norms

All design occurs within a given artistic climate of the time. At any time, certain tendencies and trends will be in vogue, and designers often feel compelled to go with the flow and design of the current trends. This is not always the case. The design profession, not unlike music and the other arts, has its share of rebels who enjoy going against the tide, either for the sake of noncompliance or because they genuinely disagree with the trend. Instead of adopting the current style, they ignore it or even mock it. Frank Lloyd Wright was one of them.

While it is essential that you recognize the current design trends at any one time, you are not obligated to abide by them. If you dislike a current design trend, cultivate whatever you believe is the correct approach; just do it with care and skill.

The Designer's Use of Symbolic Expression

Many architectural and interior designers like to go beyond the basic expressions of a project. They do so through the use of often sophisticated symbolism, metaphoric expressions, and similar devices. All these are legitimate in design but must be used with skill, restraint, and

Figure 9.43: Sometimes the shapes, proportions, and materials used can reinforce the character of the products associated with a place. Compare the heavier approach of the fur store (a) to the lighter feel of the lingerie store (b). Both approaches seem to fit with the character of their merchandise.

Figure 9.44: The functions or products associated with a given enterprise can be manifested in many ways. One effective approach is the use of straightforward displays that feature the function or product in question.

Figure 9.45: Forms and materials can be expressive of the products and functions associated with a given enterprise. This example shows the clever use of fluid forms and glass to capture the feel of water, the name and theme of the store.

caution, because often these clever design expressions go unnoticed by most people. If the level of symbolism or abstraction is too high, most people will fail to make the desired associations between symbol and meaning. Nevertheless, these techniques can be useful and meaningful in projects whose users or public share common meanings and symbols. In these cases, allusions to common symbols, historic events, or important people can be understood and appreciated by all the insiders familiar with them. Possible gestures include the placement of a given function of particular symbolic importance in the center of the project, or the orientation of the main circulation spine of a project on axis with the original location of the company three blocks away.

Another way designers try to endow projects with meaning is by responding and giving expression to the essence of the product or service associated with a given entity. The expressive characters of the two storefronts in Figure 9.43 fit the nature of the merchandise sold in them. The graphics, geometry, and massing of the fur store are appropriately heavy while the same elements in the lingerie store are much lighter and delicate. Figure 9.44 shows an example of a straightforward shoe display in a corporate environ-

Figure 9.46: Props are often effective in reinforcing the products and functions associated with a given entity. In this example, the forms, logos, and signs of the store are reinforced by the presence of a well-known Warner Bros. character.

ment celebrating the product associated with the company. In Figure 9.45 the designer expresses the essence of the company's name and products by emulating the fluidness of water through the forms used. Finally, Figure 9.46 is an example of the use of humorous expression by the integration of one of the main characters associated with Warner Bros., in this case Daffy Duck.

Any long-lasting intellectual or artistic pursuit requires an ideology, a framework of principles and ideas that explains and justifies our actions and gives them direction. An artist today needs a personal ideology in order to accomplish original work. We build our ideology using pieces we gather throughout our lives from parents, teachers, books, friends, other artists, and most important, from our own thoughts and experiences.[1]

Designers usually start their careers with a vague and loose ideological framework consisting largely of borrowed ideas. That is fine. As they gain experience, though, they start to develop more precise personal beliefs that they express in their designs. As Cesar Pelli points out, "In order to do significant work, however, we need to reinterpret and modify shared ideas and make them part of a personal body of thoughts. The more we develop our individual position, the more we move away from that of our peers."[2]

In this piece, we expose you to beliefs expressed by four influential design thinkers. They are excerpted from proclamations committed to writing by them at particular points in time. To become a great designer, you will need clarity and consistency of approach. This requires having, at any one time, a set of personal convictions that helps you decide, for each project, which is the right path to take from among all the design approaches possible for that project. The intent of this piece is as much to present four different ways of thinking about design approaches as it is to encourage you to initiate your own personal ideology.

VENTURI ON COMPLEXITY AND CONTRADICTION

In 1966, the Museum of Modern Art published Robert Venturi's *Complexity and Contradiction in Architecture*, a highly influential manifesto that critiqued the shortcomings of modern architecture. In it, Venturi attacks the reductive tendencies of modern architecture and the pure, but boring, designs it produced. He thought architecture had to get up to par with science, poetry, and visual art and acknowledge complexity and contradiction.

"I like complexity and contradiction in architecture," Venturi's manifesto begins. "I do not like the incoherence or arbitrariness of incompetent architecture nor the precious intricacies of picturesqueness or expressionism. Instead, I speak of complex and contradictory architecture based on the richness and ambiguity of modern experience, including experience which is inherent in art."[3] He points out not only the inherent complexity of life but also the increasing complexity of buildings and their programs. How could anyone try to simplify, he wonders, that which is inherently complex?

"The doctrine of 'less is more' bemoans complexity and justifies exclusion for expressive purposes."[4] Here Venturi condemns the practice of selectivity in determining which problems to solve. One can be selective in how one approaches problems but shouldn't select which problems to approach. Isn't one supposed to tackle them all? "Mies's exquisite pavilions have indeed had valuable implications for architecture, but is not their selectiveness of content and language their limitation as well as their strength? . . . Such forced simplicity is oversimplification. . . . Where simplicity cannot work, simpleness results. Blatant simplification means bland architecture. Less is a bore."[5] This doesn't mean that one cannot strive for simplicity. But, according to Venturi, "aesthetic simplicity . . . derives from inner complexity,"[6] and he goes on to demonstrate how the Doric temple achieves apparent simplicity through real complexity. He is obviously referring to resolved complexity.

Venturi also favors contradiction in his aim for vitality as well as validity. He explains: "I like elements which are hybrid rather than 'pure,' compromising rather than 'clean,' distorted rather than 'straightforward,' ambiguous rather than articulated, perverse as well as 'impersonal,' boring as well as 'interesting,' conventional rather than 'designed,' accommodating rather than excluding, redundant rather than simple, vestigial as well as innovating, inconsistent and equivocal rather than direct and clear. I am for messy vitality over obvious unity."[7] He strives to produce an architecture that "evokes many levels of meaning and combinations of focus: its space and its elements become readable and workable in several ways at once."[8]

Contradictory levels of meaning involve paradoxical contrast, and the level of ambiguity varies. Something can be closed, yet open. Venturi prefers "both-and" to "either-or" and the finer distinctions it permits. He also advocates the "double-functioning" element, which performs multiple functions related to use and structure, as opposed to "both-and," which emphasizes double meaning.

"An architecture of complexity and contradiction," he stresses, "does not mean picturesqueness or willfull expressionism. If I am against purity, I am also against picturesqueness. False complexity currently counters false simplicity."[9] Complexity must arise out of the program and the structure of the whole and not from just the desire to be expressive. In the end, he assures, "an architecture of complexity and contradiction has a special obligation towards the whole: its truth must be in its totality or its implications of totality. It must embody the difficult unity of inclusion rather than the easy unity of exclusion. More is not less."[10]

GRAVES ON FIGURATIVE ARCHITECTURE

Michael Graves, another critic of modernism, rejects the lack of character of modernism. His humanistic architecture is representational and suggestive, relying on articulation, color, and historical references. He distinguishes between building (the practical aspects of architecture) and architecture (the symbolic representation of culture and its myths).

"The poetic form of architecture," he explains, "is responsive to issues external to the building, and incorporates the three-dimensional expression of the myths and rituals of society. Poetic forms in architecture are sensitive to the figurative, associative, and anthropomorphic attitudes of a culture."[11] Graves strongly believes in architecture's duty to register society's patterns of ritual and condemns the nonfigural abstract geometries of the modern movement.

While acknowledging the practical physical side of architecture, he reminds us "that the components of architecture have not only derived from pragmatic necessity but also evolved from symbolic sources." A defender of the integrity of an element's anthropomorphic and figurative meanings, Graves expresses dismay at modern architecture's audacity to transform the window from an element that helps "us make sense not only of the landscape beyond but also of our own position relative to the geometry of the window and to the building as a whole"[12] to disorienting window walls. He advocates the use of thematic and figural aspects of design. Associations can be made with natural phenomena (ground as floor), and anthropomorphic allusions (column as man).

Figurative architecture assumes "that the thematic character of a work is grounded in nature and is simultaneously read in a totemic or anthropomorphic manner."[13] Thus, a wall, similar to the window that helps us understand our size and presence in the room, fulfills both pragmatic and symbolic functions. Its tripartite division (wainscot, body, soffit), while not intended to imitate man, helps to stabilize the wall relative to the room, an important secondary function.

Modern architecture lost its sense for figural void, the form of space. Amorphic, continuous space, such as in Mies's Barcelona Pavilion (once again) "dissolves any reference to our understanding of figural void or space." Such space is "oblivious to bodily or totemic reference, and we therefore always find ourselves unable to feel centered in such a space. This lack of figural reference ultimately contributes to a feeling of alienation in buildings based on such singular propositions." It is crucial, Graves concludes, "that we reestablish the thematic associations invented by our culture in order to fully allow the culture of architecture to represent the mythic and ritual aspirations of society."[14]

PORPHYRIOS ON CLASSICAL ARCHITECTURE

Another critic of modernism, Demetri Porphyrios also attacks the scenographic and eclectic tendencies of postmodernists and instead advocates authentic classicism. "The aim of modern eclecticism," he points out, "has been to look at historical styles merely as communicative devices, as labels and clothing. Style itself was seen as having no natural relationship to the tectonics of building." He criticizes "the pluralism that sprung out of an age of conciliatory culture, widespread visiting of the beliefs of all countries and all ages, accepting everything without fixing any part, since truth is everywhere in bits and nowhere in its entirety."[15]

While modernism showed, and not concealed, the elements used to construct a work of art, "postmodernist works show themselves for the contrivance they are, but in doing so they also state that everything else in life is a contrivance and that simply there is no escape from this. Hence the self-referential circularity of the postmodern quotation and the extreme fascination with parody and metalinguistic commentary."[16]

Porphyrios believes the metalinguistic attempts of the high-tech branch of postmodernism resulted in buildings that are "only make-believe simulations of high-tech imagery."[17] Meanwhile, the postmodern classicists rely on parody. "They favour playful distortion, citation, deliberate anachronism, diminution, oxymoron, and so on. Ultimately, this is yet another make-believe cardboard architecture."[18] The third group of postmodernists criticized by Porphyrios are the deconstructionists who "loudly reject such ideas as order, intelligibility, and tradition. Architecture is supposed to become an experience of failure and crisis. And if crisis is not there, well then, it must be created."[19] While these three versions of postmodernism are different, they all share a similar scenographic view of architecture.

His view is that of a classicist. Classicists, he explains, "adopt the theory of imitation. Art, it is argued, imitates the real world by turning selected significant aspects of it into mythical representations. . . . Similarly, a Classicist would argue architecture is the imitative celebration of construction and shelter qualified by the myths and ideas of a given culture."[20] Contrary to the mute realism of modernism, "what makes classical architecture possible is the dialogic relationship it establishes between the craft of building and the art of architecture. Our imagination traverses this dialogic space between, say, a pergola and a colonnade, and establishes hierarchies, levels of propriety, and communicable systems of evaluation."[21]

While many designers tend to value what is new and different, Porphyrios suggests that the contribution of an architect "lies in what he/she chooses to borrow."[22] He sums up his view: "Architecture has nothing to do with 'novelty-mania' and intellectual sophistries. Architecture has nothing to do with transgression, boredom, or parody. It has nothing to do with parasitic life, excremental culture or the cynical fascination with the bad luck of others. Architecture has to do with decisions that concern the good, the decent, the proper . . . Surely, what constitutes a proper life varies from one historical period to another. But it is our responsibility to define it anew all the time."[23]

AN ARCHITECTURE OF REALITY

The final view presented is by Michael Benedikt. He, like Porphyrios, condemns postmodernism's insistence on communicating superficially through architecture. Instead of the return to classicism, though, Benedikt advocates an architecture that relies on "the real" for effect. He speaks of moments when reality produces an "unreasoned joy" due to the "simple correspondence of appearance and reality" and "the evident rightness of things as they are." During those moments "the world becomes singularly meaningful, yet without being 'symbolical.' Objects and colors do not point to other realms; signs say what they have to and fall silent. Conventional associations fall away. . . . We are not conscious of reference, allusion, or instruction."[24]

Benedikt calls those privileged moments "direct aesthetic experiences of the real" and suggests that "in our media-saturated times it falls to architecture to have the direct aesthetic experience of the real at the center of its concerns."[25] He questions the view that for something to be meaningful it has to "say" something, that reality has to be "read like a book or deciphered like a code for its messages."[26]

He compares the allusion, reference, and symbolism in postmodern architecture to "the much-discussed process in postmodern literature where the . . . dizzying self-reflection on and in the literary act are typical"[27] and poses the question of whether a building's meaning should be "fabricated with building-parts by the architect . . . by any process analogous to the way writers construct worlds and meanings with words in literary fiction." Of course not, he says. "We count on buildings to form the stable matrix of our lives, to protect us, to stand up to us, to give us addresses, and not to be made of mirrors."[28]

"Real architecture is architecture especially ready—so to speak—for its direct esthetic experience, an architecture that does not disappoint us by turning out in the light of that experience to be little more than a vehicle contrived to bear meanings. . . . Real architecture is, then, architecture in which the quality of realness is paramount. And here, with realness, is how the idea of reality can best enter the realm of architectural discourse. Like 'proportion' or 'scale,' like any number of qualities ascribable to architecture good and bad, 'realness' becomes an attribute of buildings that can be pointed out and discussed, can be found lacking here, present in greater degree there . . . and so on: in short, realness becomes an observable quality amenable to some level of conceptual formulation."[29]

Benedikt concludes: "While it may be argued that ironic poses and movie-set history, allegories and recondite allusions, reflect most accurately and properly our information- and entertainment-oriented culture, they can also be seen as a defeat: a sliding of architecture into the world of television. For it can be argued equally well that an architecture that stands against, or in contrast to, the culture-wide trend to ephemeralization and relativism—as a kind of last bastion of dumb reality and foil to it all—constitutes the more appropriate, timely, and potentially esthetic response."[30]

These four views are personal, sincere, and different. They represent the thinking of these designers at a certain point in time. Whether we agree with them or not, they affirm a position, an ideology, a strong belief. A personal ideology gives direction to our work. In developing a personal set of core beliefs, and in facing the many design decisions that require judgment and reflection, it is good to bear in mind two questions proposed by Cesar Pelli: The first one—Is it correct?—seeks to find out whether the solution satisfies external expectations. The second question—Is it right?—seeks to find out if the solution is helping or harming people and surroundings. As Pelli explains, it is relatively easy to find out what are the correct options. These are constantly being defined for us. "But we have to seek the 'right' direction for ourselves, using our own internal compass."[31]

1. Cesar Pelli, *Observations for Young Architects* (New York: The Monacelli Press, 1999), 196.
2. Ibid., 196.
3. Robert Venturi, *Complexity and Contradiction in Architecture* (New York: The Museum of Modern Art, 1977), 16.
4. Ibid., 17.
5. Ibid., 17.
6. Ibid., 17.
7. Ibid., 16.
8. Ibid., 16.
9. Ibid., 18.
10. Ibid., 16.
11. Michael Graves, *Theorizing a New Agenda for Architecture*, ed. Kate Nesbitt (New York: Princeton Architectural Press, 1996), 86.
12. Ibid., 87.
13. Ibid., 88.
14. Ibid., 89–90.
15. Demetri Porphyrios, *Theorizing a New Agenda for Architecture*, ed. Kate Nesbitt (New York: Princeton Architectural Press, 1996), 93.
16. Ibid., 93.
17. Ibid., 94.
18. Ibid., 94.
19. Ibid., 94.
20. Ibid., 95.
21. Ibid., 95.
22. Ibid., 96.
23. Ibid., 96.
24. Michael Benedikt, *For an Architecture of Reality* (New York: Lumen Press, 1988), 4.
25. Ibid., 4.
26. Ibid., 8.
27. Ibid., 12.
28. Ibid., 14.
29. Ibid., 30.
30. Ibid., 64.
31. Pelli, 194.

CASE STUDY
Western Detailing at El Dorado Grill

DESIGN FIRM: LINVILLE ARCHITECTS

The El Dorado Grill provides a good example of the role of detailing in interior projects. El Dorado is a high-end, southwestern-themed restaurant and it is the details, both of the existing building space and of the added interior components, that give the place its character. Our focus here, hence, is on the development and resolution of the details.

The restaurant is housed in a charming old warehouse with exposed brick walls, wood floors, and rustic ceiling rafters. After seeing the project site early on, Ed Linville, the project designer, recognized its inherent character and, as he put it "surrendered to it," thus leaving it pretty much intact except for some necessary cleaning. The existing natural wood in the space had the kind of golden glow that Linville wanted to incorporate in the project. This also allowed him to use contrasting, deeper colors to achieve the required level of richness, articulation, and formality.

El Dorado features a detailing approach that reinforces the southwestern theme in a refined, subtle way. Among other things, it includes a backdrop wall behind the bar with a western scene etched in glass, a host station featuring cowboy imagery, a mesa-inspired wall mass housing the fireplace, banquettes with saddle-inspired leather upholstery, and a custom-designed light fixture inspired by a Native American drum.

All these detail ideas started as rough doodles on paper. Figure CS9.1 shows rough preliminary sketches of saloon doors and the Native American drum fixture. Figures CS9.2 and CS9.3 show early conceptions of the banquette and fireplace, and of the background wall behind the bar, respectively. These ideas were next subjected to a process of further evaluation and refinement.

Finer levels of detail were addressed in each subsequent step. These started as freehand drawings done to scale, as shown in Figure CS9.4 depicting the backdrop wall behind the host station. You can see how definite treatments, materials, and motifs started to emerge; however, once Linville started to consider a detail idea seriously, he began drafting it hardline. This forced him to make precise decisions about dimensions and proportions and helped to accelerate the process of resolution.

Proportions, materials, motifs, and small details were resolved during this stage of detailing. Figure CS9.5 shows the development of the banquette, with brass tacks, Mexican concho medallions, a leather headrest, and the El Dorado logo incorporated into the design. Similarly, the imagery, shapes, and proportions for the bar and its backdrop wall were carefully laid out, as shown in Figure CS9.6.

Figure CS9.1: Loose early sketches of saloon doors and drum light fixture ideas.

Figure CS9.2: Early sketches of banquette and feature wall behind the bar.

Figure CS9.3: Loose sketches of banquette designs and miscellaneous details.

Figure CS9.4: Development drawing of host station and background wall.

Figure CS9.5: Development drawing of banquette design.

Figure CS9.6: Development drawing of feature wall behind bar.

Figure CS9.7: Finished details of host station and background wall.

Figure CS9.8: Finished detail elevation of fireplace front.

The details went through one more stage of refinement and resolution when they were drafted in final form for incorporation in the construction documents. These are documents the contractor will prepare his own shop drawings from, so all the information for each part of the project, including the details, needs to be accurate, precise, and resolved. It may be that they were fully resolved in the preceding stage and are only drafted in final form during this one but, quite often, last-minute matters are decided or changed at this time. In other words, if something has not been previously resolved because it either was overlooked or left for later, this is when to address it. Figures CS9.7 through CS9.10 show some of the final details for the host station, fireplace, booths, and drum fixture. Notice the precision and level of detail. These drawings, and other similar ones not shown, tell the full story about these creations. The designer considered these walls and objects from every angle and made decisions about form, shape, proportion, articulation, materials, colors, accents, and so on, as if he were designing the products themselves.

Figure CS9.9: Finished details of banquette.

Figure CS9.10: Finished details of drum light fixture.

Figure CS9.11: View of host station area.

Figure CS9.12: View of fireplace front.

Figure CS9.13: View of banquettes.

Figure CS9.14: View of drum light fixture.

Details are sometimes subjected to some tweaking during the pricing and construction stages. Then they get built. Although you as the designer would have a pretty good idea of what they are going to look like, it is really after they are built that you can enjoy seeing the fruit of your creation. Hopefully, the effect is the one intended.

Figures CS9.11 through CS9.14 show photos of the details discussed above after the project was completed and occupied for some time. It's amazing that these features and objects, now part of the tangible and real world, all started as rough doodles on a piece of paper. Yet, here they are for all the restaurant's visitors to experience and enjoy.

REVIEW

Summary

Designed environments embody the qualities of the people and organizations that inhabit them. Previously discussed design aspects such as order and enrichment are treated in particular ways to give the project its unique personality. These expressions communicate messages whose meanings vary widely from culture to culture, from group to group within a culture, and from person to person within a group. These meanings are based on associations, some spontaneous and others learned by convention.

Designers can give expression to all aspects of design. They control most of the elements that go into a project, such as layout, space, surface, detail, furnishings, and accessories. There are, however, other factors contributing to expression that are beyond the control of designers, such as the people who use the space and their attire, language, and so on.

Expression works at many levels, and there are many types of design expression. Among them are expression of universal human experiences, expression of contextual factors, expression of formal design properties and assemblies, and expression of programmatic necessities.

The expression of identity is one of the most important and challenging. Identity is like the personality of a project and is determined by the client's character and preferences. Factors such as the client's self-image (and the motives informing that image), its basic taste culture, and its preferred ways of self-presentation all act together to determine the expressed identity.

Designers' own personal attitudes, convictions, and preferences are also expressed in projects. Three factors that affect the kind of designer expression manifested are the designer's own personal style, his or her attitude toward current design norms, and the designer's use of symbolic communication.

1. Rudolf Arnheim, *The Dynamics of Architectural Form* (Berkeley: University of California Press, 1977), 210.
2. Charles Jencks, *The Language of Post-Modern Architecture* (New York: Rizzoli, 1984), 42.
3. Arnheim, 208.
4. Ibid., 209.
5. Ibid., 211.
6. Jencks, 46.
7. Ibid., 46.
8. Ibid., 4.
9. Arnheim, 209.
10. Ibid., 208.
11. John Mowen, *Consumer Behavior*, 2nd ed. (New York: McMillan, 1990), 190.
12. Leon G. Schiffman, L. Lazar Kanuk, *Consumer Behavior*, 4th ed. (New Jersey: Prentice Hall, 1997), 137.
13. Mowen, 195.
14. Russell Belk, "Possessions and the Extended Self," *Journal of Consumer Research* 15 (1988): 139–68.
15. Michael R. Solomon, *Consumer Behavior: Buying, Having and Being*, 4th ed. (New York: Prentice Hall, 1999).
16. Eric Arnould, Linda Price, and George Zinkhan, *Consumers*, 2nd ed. (Boston: McGraw-Hill / Irwin, 2003), 437.
17. Schiffman et al., 70.
18. Arnould et al., 272–75.
19. Ibid., 273.
20. Mowen, 183.
21. Schiffman et al., 127.
22. Arnould et al., 274.
23. Ibid., 476.
24. Ibid., 275.
25. Ibid., 324.
26. Ibid., p.325.
27. Ibid., p.325.
28. Herbert J. Gans, *Popular Culture and High Culture: An Analysis and Evaluation of Taste* (New York: Basic Books, 1974), 70.
29. Ibid., 70.
30. Ibid., 75–94.
31. Ibid., 118.
32. Arnould et al., 414.
33. Mowen, 191.
34. Nicholas Ind, *The Corporate Image: Strategies for Effective Identity Programmes*, rev. ed. (London: Kegan Page, 1992), 19.
35. Ibid., 24.
36. Ibid., 25.
37. Wally Olins, *Corporate Identity* (Cambridge, MA: Harvard Business School Press, 1990), 29.
38. Ibid., 33.

39. Donald E. Lundberg and John R. Walker, *The Restaurant: From Concept to Operation*, 2nd ed. (New York: Wiley, 1993), 22.

40. Ibid., 27.

41. Vilma Barr and Charles E. Broudy, *Designing to Sell: A Complete Guide to Retail Planning and Design*, 2nd ed. (New York: McGraw Hill, 1990), 172–73.

42. Ibid., 178.

43. Howard Robertson, *Modern Architectural Design* (Westminster: The Architectural Press, 1932), 99.

Chapter Questions

1. Which two types of meaning were introduced in this chapter? How are they different?

2. Within the spectrum of the physical environment and its parts, which components can the designer affect and use to give expression?

3. Which three dualities did this chapter introduce as expressions of universal human experiences?

4. What are four types of contextual factors affecting expression?

5. Which two dualities did this chapter present as basic determinants of the project's programmatic necessities?

6. Could you explain the concept of identity as presented in this chapter?

7. What five motives that influence consumers and their product constellations were presented in this chapter?

8. Name and explain five of the eight variables presented in this chapter under self-presentation.

9. What are the differences between high self monitors and low self monitors related to self-presentation?

10. Which aspects of designers' personal expressions were presented in this chapter?

11. Name two examples of spontaneous associations.

12. Name two examples of associations learned by convention.

13. Name one example of constraint/freedom as it relates to the expression of universal human experiences.

14. Name one example of admittance/rejection as it relates to the expression of universal human experiences.

15. Name a situation that would be appropriate for the manifestation of historic expression.

16. Name a situation that would be appropriate for the manifestation of cultural or regional expression.

17. Discuss with your classmates the dominant design norms and conventions of our times. What are they and how are they changing?

18. Discuss what kinds of environments would be appropriate for individuals or groups driven by the following motives. Be as specific as possible.
    a) the achievement motive
    b) the power motive
    c) the uniqueness/novelty motive
    d) the affiliation motive
    e) the self-esteem motive

19a. Which characteristics would your design for a social club have for the following target audiences, based on Gans's taste cultures:
    a) a high-culture audience
    b) an upper-middle culture
    c) a lower-middle culture

19b. Identify a prototypical building in your city or region that would fit each of the three cultures.

20. Describe your idea of an environment at each end of the range (from high to low) of the following modes of self-presentation:
    a) load level
    b) abstraction
    c) ambiguity
    d) humor
    e) formality
    f) intensity

21. Describe your current tendencies in relation to the following formal properties of design:
    a) shapes
    b) weight
    c) composition
    d) material palette
    e) ornamentation

22. Vidal Sassoon was mentioned as an early example of a company with a strong identity program, integrating its products, services, graphics, physical environment, and advertising into a cohesive total identity message. Name three companies in your community (large or small) that similarly combine these elements into a successful identity message.

23. What are your current design tendencies? Which others would you like to develop?

24. How would you use symbolism in a retail application?

25. How would you use symbolism in a restaurant application?

PART FOUR
COMPLETING THE DESIGN

CHAPTER 10
Resolution

INSTRUCTIONAL OBJECTIVES

- Emphasize the importance of achieving resolution in design.
- Show various stages of the resolution of floor plans.
- Discuss the process of refining the design of surfaces and details.
- Show several ways to manipulate scale for effect.
- Explain important peculiarities about the use of symmetrical compositions.
- Discuss ways of achieving balance with asymmetrical compositions.
- Explain how to use continuity to achieve unity.
- Explain how to use repetition to achieve unity.
- Explain how to use gradation and dispersion as vehicles for unity.

In any worthwhile activity we see what we do with two different sets of eyes. In the midst of doing we give all of ourselves to our labors in constructive sympathy. We are one with our work. A moment later, we look again at what we have done and judge it as if from outside ourselves, with as critical and detached manner as we can muster. We redesign again and again, trying to satisfy our inner demands, though in architecture time is limited and we can rarely please ourselves fully.

—*Cesar Pelli,* Observations for Young Architects

O RDER, ENRICHMENT, AND expression are seldom pursued individually, one at a time. We have isolated them in order to talk about them individually and facilitate their understanding. The three relate to, and affect, one another. Efforts to address the issues related to these three variables start early in the design process. They are subsequently developed and refined. These efforts take place as part of the overall effort of producing a fitting and functional design.

Design exploration usually starts with rough ideas early on. These are converted into design drawings in order to be visualized, analyzed, and judged, and, if adopted, these preliminary, rough ideas are adjusted and refined later. Before the design of a project is finalized, the many ideas, and corresponding physical elements, need to be developed and resolved. Parts need to be adjusted, relationships fine-tuned, and details given final form. Additionally, the designer needs to step back, look at the entire project as a whole, and make necessary adjustments to ensure proper cohesiveness.

This chapter is about the process of working out and completing design ideas to fully resolve the many design problems associated with a project, achieve visual harmony, and produce a unified creation. The first part of the chapter will address some peculiar aspects of the design process and discuss what it takes to produce synthesis. Next, we will discuss the process of resolving the project from floor plan to the more detailed compositional aspects of form. Last, we will address the designer's responsibility to produce environments that are perceptually harmonious and unified.

DESIGN SYNTHESIS

The design process seldom occurs in linear fashion. Except for the smallest and simplest of projects it is uncommon to arrive at an optimal and fitting solution from a single attempt, refine it in linear fashion, and then send it to the contractor ready to build. Most real-life projects are much more difficult to solve than that. They require an ongoing cyclical process of commitment and testing followed by evaluation and adjustment. With every cycle of response and feedback, the designer commits to some aspects of the solution, modifies some, and discards others. With every step the designer aims at a higher level of resolution concerning function and the other aspects of design we have been discussing. Figure 10.1 shows a diagram of the process. It is like a spiraling helix, moving cyclically from one stage to the next and incorporating successful ideas as they are developed and additional insights gained during previous stages.

Starting from the ideation stage, it is necessary to commit to and test comprehensive design ideas based on your current understanding of the design problem. These comprehensive ideas, as William Kleinsasser explains, act "like rehearsals before a game, serve as hypotheses or

Figure 10.1: Within each stage, the design process should incorporate complete cycles that achieve synthesis to a level appropriate to the stage. Every stage should produce a tangible outcome derived from the understanding of the project at that stage, culminating in the thorough and complete project solution at the end of the resolution phase.

probes out there . . . they will preview the whole and generate better proposals."[1] Each such cycle should include a design scheme developed to a level appropriate to the stage of the project and devote some time to analyze and evaluate the scheme in order to assess its merits and get a greater understanding of the project. These cyclical evaluations need to generally address three things: the appropriateness of the overall design approach being taken, the way particular aspects of the approach are working, and the way the design problem definition is evolving.

During the early part of the design process, as we saw in Chapter 6, the majority of the effort goes into developing an organizational structure that will give the project unity and direction. Alternatives have to be closely scrutinized and run through one of the review cycles. Once an organizational structure has been determined appropriate, it has to be tested to see if it works with the particular requirements of the program, the geometry of the space, and other such realities of the project. After determining that the concept will work, the attention can shift to particular, more detailed aspects of the design solution and to efforts to maintain the integrity of this organizational structure as the design goes through modifications. At every step of design it is important to examine the current understanding of the problem for accuracy and breadth since it will tend to shift and come into clearer focus as one gets more information, which invariably leads to a better understanding of the project and its potential solutions.

The problem definition stage is itself cyclical. It starts with a rudimentary understanding of a complex design problem. The problem is redefined into subissues or components, which in turn produce a better understanding of components and relationships. While addressing these, new subissues continue to surface. The more you keep working on the design solution, the more layers of information and nuance rise to the surface, changing and refining your definition of the problem and the way you think about the project.

Resolution of the Plan

Resolution starts with the floor plan. Plans go through a number of revisions, starting with the first attempt to translate the organizational concept idea into a floor plan and culminating in the final plan. Plans have to be resolved in order to satisfy two basic goals: maximizing the quality of the overall design approach and resolving the many pragmatic and practical issues throughout the plan. Throughout the design process you have to constantly question your current design direction to ensure that the solution is basically a good one and that the many parts of the plan work well. Figure 10.2 shows the development of a student's floor plan for an office project from conception through design development. Figure 10.2a shows the initial organizational concept diagram. Figure 10.2b and Figure 10.2c show the plan at two intermediary stages. Figure 10.2d shows the final solution with the plan fully resolved. After spending

Figure 10.2: This series of floor plans for an office project shows different stages of resolution, starting with the original organizational concept. This plan was particularly challenging to solve because of the geometry imposed by the concept. It was deemed workable, and the designer succeeded in planning it out. The organizational diagram (a), an early transposition of the program's specific requirements to the plan (b), a developed but not totally refined plan (c), and the final version of the plan (d) are shown.

time with the design idea, the student was convinced that the challenging geometry being attempted would work. It took, however, many adjustments and some compromises to make it all work in the end.

Figure 10.3: Shown are three of the many studies drawn by one student trying to resolve the area around the main reception area of an office project. One of the main issues was resolving the circulation to the town commons and the rest of the space.

Once the organizational concept has been successfully translated into a floor plan, you can focus on fitting all the requirements of the program more exactly, eliminating wasted space, and, in general, adjusting the plan with greater precision. Even after you have fit in all the requirements, there are often troublesome parts that require ongoing efforts to resolve. Especially tricky are those areas that seem to have a domino effect such that, upon fixing one area, you manage to ruin the previously successful adjacent area. Figure 10.3 shows several variations developed by a student in the process of resolving one area of the floor plan for an office project.

Refinement beyond the Plan

In addition to the plan, the three-dimensional and other detailed aspects of the project also need to be developed and refined. Their resolution should occur in hierarchical fashion. As basic levels of design are determined and committed to, new and higher levels of detail can be addressed. That way, less time is wasted resolving details of preliminary ideas that may be discarded later. Surfaces and details are among the aspects to be addressed in detail after the plan is in place. Surface refinement includes such tasks as developing the composition of elevations by adjusting, adding detail, and articulating the planes.

In addition to elevations, details also need development and refinement. Basic ideas are studied and developed to produce well-executed final details. Figure 10.4 shows the development for a custom-designed pendant light fixture in a restaurant. Figure 10.4a shows the original conceptual ideas. Figure 10.4b and Figure 10.4c show the details resolved and drawn with great precision.

Figure 10.4: Original details are resolved in stages. The sequence shown for a pendant light fixture started with loose conceptual ideas (a) and was transformed into full construction drawings (b and c).

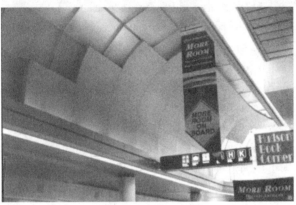

Figure 10.5: Special articulations, such as the ones shown for these two ceilings assemblies, require proper study and resolution.

Many designers give much importance to the articulation of the ceiling plane, an aspect that also requires resolution. The ceiling provides important contributions to the definition of space, the determination of scale, and the provision of expression. In the past, ceilings were often treated with elaborate decorations that made them extremely rich and expressive. Today, ceilings tend to be much simpler. However, it is possible to position and articulate the ceiling planes overhead in ways that make them both effective in defining space, as well as a vehicle to add texture and relief to projects. Figure 10.5 shows two ceiling views, illustrating the great latitude of articulation possible.

SIZING AND BALANCING PROJECT PARTS

In Chapter 7 we introduced the different kinds of order needed in a design project. One of these had to do with matters of perceptual correctness. It is what we call architectonic order and involves tasks such as the proper

placement of elements in a composition, their proper size related to other elements, and the proper spacing between them. Proper composition is an obligation of design. The craft of design involves the creation and disposition of so many physical parts that the resulting environments have a significant visual impact. Designs, once built, are presented to the world at full scale. The look they take becomes our physical environment. When you design, you determine the look of the environment. That is no small responsibility.

Aesthetic and stylistic approaches vary from designer to designer and from project to project. A design may have more or less aesthetic merit. It may or may not be high art. Nevertheless, regardless of the stylistic direction you choose for a project and the amount of art you inject into it, you have an obligation to produce good compositions. This is where the basic principles of design that you have studied in your design fundamentals classes come in handy.

It is assumed that you have been exposed to the basic elements and principles of design in previous courses. Here, we will elaborate on the principles that are the most crucial to the resolution and refinement of designs. Three aspects deserve special attention: scale, proportion, and balance. They are essential to achieve harmony. If these three design attributes are conceived and executed correctly, the product is more likely to be a harmonious-looking environment, one where the elements will be in accord with each other. They will fit together, look right, and form a cohesive unit. This, of course, is easier said than done.

So basic are these concerns to design that they have been featured prominently in all the treatises on architecture and design, starting with Vitruvius's *Ten Books on Architecture*. In addressing the fundamental principles of architecture he refers to the "order which gives due measure to the members of a work considered separately, and symmetrical agreement to the proportions of the whole."[2] He goes on to discuss three essential concepts to good composition: arrangement, eurythmy, and symmetry.

Figure 10.6: Resolution requires the proper disposition of parts, subwholes, and wholes. In this example the single column is an element complete in itself. Paired with another column, and with the addition of a pedestal below and entablature above, another whole unit is formed. The addition of a symmetrical entryway, flanked by two of the previous units, forms yet another whole unit. Finally, two of these latter units, with the addition of a central grand entrance, form the lower portion of a complete facade. All of these subparts need to be resolved individually and also as components of the entire totality.

Arrangement includes "the putting together of things in their proper places and the elegance of effect which is due to adjustments appropriate to the character of the work."[3] It is concerned with the project's agreeable composition at the overall scale. He notes that it requires both reflection and invention.

> Reflection is careful and laborious thought, and watchful attention directed to the agreeable effect of one's plan. Invention, on the other hand, is the solving of intricate problems and the discovery of new principles by means of brilliancy and versatility . . .
> **Eurythmy** [emphasis added] is beauty and fitness in the adjustment of the members. This is found when the members of a work are of a height suited to their breadth, of a breadth suited to their length, and in a word, when they all correspond symmetrically.[4]

This refers to the agreeable scale and proportion of units in and of themselves.

> **Symmetry** is a proper agreement between the members of the work itself, and relation between the different parts and the whole general scheme, in accordance with a certain part selected as standard.[5]

Note that Vitruvius's concept of symmetry refers to the agreeable relationships among the units or parts that form a composition and not to the use of symmetrical compositions.

These three aspects of design are related and part of a logical continuum that works at different scales, starting with one part and its relation to itself and the human body, then the combination of that part with others to create a group or subassembly, followed by the combination of subassemblies to produce, say, one level of an elevation, then the combination of levels to produce the entire elevation (Figure 10.6).

Translating Vitruvius's concerns into more familiar terms, we can then discuss three highly interrelated design aspects previously mentioned: scale, proportion, and balance.

Scale and proportion are two of the basic design fundamentals students learn about early in their design education; however, intermediate and even advanced students often struggle with these aspects of design at a basic level. Needless to say, scale and proportion need to be resolved for a project to be successful.

Scale

Scale in design refers to the relative size of a space, object, or element in relation to some other part. That other part can be adjacent spaces, the immediate space where the element is housed, the human person, or other objects and elements in the space. The kind of scale we are talking about, although related to size, does not refer to the actual size of things, such as when we talk about a large-scaled complex, meaning a large project.

Scale is influenced by use and custom. Thus, its appropriateness is also judged relative to the kind of space being evaluated and the type of activities that occur in it. Our judgments are also influenced by the preconceived ideas we have of similar elements based on what we have experienced in the past. If we are talking about a church, because of its use and symbolic importance, the scale is likely to be grand. If you ask a group of people from diverse backgrounds just how grand the church should be, their answers will tend to vary depending on whether they are used to grand cathedrals or small parish churches. Which one is more appropriate for the occasion will require the judgment of the designer and the users associated with the project.

In order to become competent using interior architectural scale, you need to understand how scale varies depending on the reference unit used for comparison. Additionally, you must understand the use of scale at two different levels. First, you need to learn to design straightforward projects that handle scale in a customary and agreeable way. In this kind of project, things are sized in a responsive and fitting manner. There are no other intentions other than providing good, appropriate scale. Beyond this, it is also possible to manipulate scale for effect. We discussed some of this in relation to spatial level in the section on spatial size in Chapter 4. In this chapter we expand on the topic and present different ways of manipulating scale for effect, taking into account the role of other factors in the space. We will start, however, with a presentation of the basic relationships affecting scale in interior environments.

The Size of Things in Relation to Humans

Of all the relationships concerning scale in interiors, none is more important than the relationship of space and its components to the human figure. This is especially true for the profession of interior design, a profession that specializes in the interaction of humans and environment at the proxemic scale. Height and depth dimensions of interior components, for instance, are governed by the size and reach of the persons using them. Acceptable ranges fall somewhere between some ideal dimension for the application and the outer acceptable limits. Scale decisions in relation to the human body affect the design of wall openings, privacy panels, cabinetry, furnishings, control devices, and so on. Proper dimensions for many different applications are usually well documented in reference books. A word of caution: While sizes and dimensions given in standard reference books are usually adequate, it is important to take into account the kind of population being designed for and make adjustments accordingly.

Figure 10.7: The chair (a) designed by Frank Lloyd Wright is intentionally much taller than is needed. A lounge chair (b) is quite different. It is meant to embrace and comfort.

A **B**

Special groups, such as young children, the elderly, and the physically disabled, have unique needs that the standards may not specifically address.

The sizes of objects do not always have to be the customary sizes people are used to. In some cases they can be manipulated in relation to the human body for effect. The size of a chair, for instance, can be exaggerated to increase definition, as the extra-tall chair in Figure 10.7a shows, or to create a feeling of comfort, as shown in Figure 10.7b. Door hardware can be oversized to accentuate the physicality of turning the handle to open the door and gain access. It can also be minimized, to create a more delicate and refined experience. Do keep in mind that, in spite of the desired effect, the increase, reduction, or other scale manipulation has to satisfy the basic function it addresses, be it seating or opening, as in the examples above.

In addition to these types of functional items, there are other kinds of design elements involving scale that have a less immediate, yet insistent effect on the human beings using a space. A door, for example, as long as its height is adequate to provide proper clearance for normal individuals, can be relatively short. It can also be much taller than it needs to be. When it comes to doors, we can use a door that barely provides clearance (as long as it meets code), one that provides comfortable clearance with some room to spare, or one of monumental height (Figure 10.8).

Everything we physically use in a space, from doors to furnishings to objects, relates very closely to the human body. Although they all have optimal sizes, dimensions can be somewhat adjusted for effect as long as the resulting size falls within an acceptable functional range.

A   B   C

Figure 10.8: The three openings here show three distinct scales: minimal (a), comfortable (b), and grand (c). Each relates to the size of the human figure differently. Opening (a) is oppressive and uncomfortable, while (c) is generous to the point of excess.

Relation to Application

Also important is the size of things in relation to their application, as mentioned in our example about the appropriate scale for a church. Depending on the type of activity a space is designed for, its scale may need to be grandiose, normal, or intimate. While the scale of palaces, churches, and prominent civic buildings will tend to be monumental, the scale for certain areas in exclusive candlelit restaurants or the seating areas off a main corridor (Figure 10.9) will often need to be small and intimate.

Relation to Element Type

Objects, such as building components, furnishings, and accessories, belong to their respective typological families. Windows, doors, tables, chairs, artwork, and plants are familiar objects for which we have preconceived mental images based on our previous encounters with them. Although the exact stylistic image that comes to mind when we think of any of these items will vary slightly from person to person based on background, the essence of the mental picture will be quite similar. Part of that image is the relative size of the object and its usual overall dimensions as well as the usual dimensions of its parts. These establish a mental point of reference. Variations toward a larger or smaller version will constitute a change of scale.

Most design-related items are available in a range of sizes. Commercial-grade doors, for instance, although they tend to be of relatively uniform width, come in many heights. The relatively low 6-foot-8-inch doors used in residential construction are rarely used in com-

Figure 10.9: The scale of this seating area off a main circulation space has been intentionally reduced to make it more intimate and inviting.

Figure 10.10: In addition to judging interior elements in relation to the size of the human body, we also make judgments in relation to the customary size of the components. This door is tall compared to most other doors we encounter.

mercial projects, where taller doors are usually preferred. Thus, one can choose very tall doors like the one shown in Figure 10.10. Tables, although their height does not change much, come in a variety of widths, lengths, and shapes. Other items, such as art objects and plants, come in many sizes, and designers can choose among them to suit the scale needs of the project. Although these are related to the scale of the object in relation to the human body as previously discussed, here the distinction is that a judgment is made using the customary size of the object as a reference, such as when one says, "That chair seems odd; it's too small."

Relation of Space to Entire Project

As we saw in Chapter 4, the spaces of a project can vary much from project to project in their shape, size, and character. Within a single project, the predominant spaces may set an overall scale constituting a point of reference. Consequently, if their scale is generally consistent, any major scale deviations will be noticeable. "Aha," someone might say upon seeing a room with a more generous scale than the rest, "something important must happen here."

Relation of Contents to Space

Once inside a specific space, the objects in it will have an important relationship to the overall space and its architectural features (doors, windows, columns, and so on).

Among the important components are the furnishings, equipment, and accessories of the space. The correspondence between these objects and the space can be complementary or discordant to create a desired effect. In the first case you may use oversized furnishings, fixtures, plants, and artwork to fill the volume of a large space (Figure 10.11). Conversely, you may use small furniture, fixtures, and artwork in a small space to make it feel comfortable (Figure 10.12). These cases can be seen as examples of balanced and appropriate correspondence between objects and space.

The opposite approach would be to accentuate the largeness of the first space by using normal-sized furniture in it. These manipulations usually require a good eye and judgment in order to avoid making the disproportion seem like a mistake.

One final example of the relationship of the scale of objects to that of the space can be illustrated by the various effects produced by different arrangements of artwork on a wall. A wall can be equally filled (proportionately) with different possible combinations of artwork by varying the number of pieces and their size. Different combinations

Figure 10.11: There is an important scale correspondence between a room and the objects in it. Rooms with a large volume often require large-scaled furnishings and accessories (as shown) to look right.

Figure 10.12: In contrast to large rooms, small rooms almost demand small-scaled furniture and accessories. Otherwise the largeness of these objects can dwarf the room and make it perceptually uncomfortable.

Figure 10.13: The scale of a space can be affected by the size of the objects in it. In this example, the artwork on the three segments of wall shown varies. The effect produced by one large painting is different from the effect produced by a series of smaller works.

can have approximately equal proportions of artwork-to-wall ratios, but produce very different effects. Figure 10.13 shows three wall segments in a corridor, one of them having one large painting filling the wall, one having three medium pieces, and one having many smaller pieces covering approximately as much wall space as the large paintings. The feel of the applications is quite different, all due to the size and number of pieces used.

Relation of Contents to Other Contents

The last scale relationship we will discuss is that of the objects in a space. Among the objects are the ones we referred to above (furnishings, plants, and artwork) as well as others such as fixtures, doors, cabinetry, and hardware. In general, the relative size of all these elements needs to be complementary so that everything works together. If the tendency is toward largeness, then everything should be oversized and vice versa. It is possible, though, to purposefully work with more than one scale for effect. Everything may take a normal scale except for, say, the artwork on the walls, or some special details, or some architectural elements, which may be oversized for effect.

One important characteristic of space worth noting here is the way the natural scales of things (some small,

Figure 10.15: Not all objects of the same type need to maintain the same scale. In this dining table example, one of the end chairs is intentionally made larger to dominate and communicate the hierarchy at the table.

Figure 10.14: Real environments, especially complex ones, are often comprised of many scales working together and complementing each other. A good space will normally progress harmoniously from the largeness of the overall space to the in-between scale of objects in it, and the smallness of accessories and utensils around, as shown in this view.

Figure 10.16: In this dining table by Frank Lloyd Wright, not one but all the chairs are tall. Additionally, there are four light fixtures of similar height integrated into the corners of the table. The purpose here is to produce a sense of enclosure around the table to make it feel contained and intimate.

some medium, some large) complement each other and the richness that this multiplicity of scales produces. In Figure 10.14 we can distinguish among a variety of scales, ranging from the largest (the spatial volume) to the smallest (the silverware on the table).

Approaches to Scale

Resolving scale is a part of all interior projects. The approach taken may be straightforward, using normal scale appropriately to achieve harmony, or involve manipulation for effect. The criteria for judging the success of any attempt consist of two basic questions: Was the approach used appropriate? Was its execution done well?

The straightforward approach to scale is simple in intent. Its execution, of course, requires good aesthetic sense. The goal is quite simple: to size everything in the space to look in scale. With this approach, all layers of space and objects are treated in a complementary fashion and the approach kept consistent throughout.

The approach involving manipulation has many possible applications, as we have hinted at with our examples above.

Yet, it can be harder to produce successfully. Scale manipulations are an important device at the designer's disposal, and it is important that you learn how to perform them. In general, you manipulate scale to create a focus, establish dominance, define space, or produce tension. You create a focus by making the size of the desired element different (usually larger) so it stands out by contrast, like the chair at the far end of the table in Figure 10.15. Similarly, you can increase the size of any one type of item, be it the furniture or the artwork, in order to establish dominance or help define space. Figure 10.16 shows a design by Frank Lloyd Wright for a dining table setup in which he increased the height of the chairs surrounding the table to contain the area and make it more intimate. In this example he also used four special light fixtures at the corners to help define the area further. Other effects can be accomplished by the manipulation of scale, such as the creation of tension by the intentional and balanced juxtaposition of elements and objects of various sizes. This is hard to achieve and carries a great risk of looking wrong. Nevertheless, a skilled designer can accomplish it without adverse effects.

Proportion

Proportion is also concerned with the size of elements as well as with the size of the leftover spaces between them. With proportion we look at elements in relation to the composition of which they are a part. Pertinent issues are whether the dimensions of the individual pieces, and the spaces in between, are appropriate given the dimensions of the overall composition. This was an issue of great concern during the Classical and Renaissance eras, when the size and spacing of columns were considered at length in order to produce agreeable compositions for temples, palazzos, churches, villas, and so on. Figure 10.17 shows the correct proportions of columns and the spaces between them for the composition of an Ionic colonnade according to Palladio. Similarly, there were prescribed optimal proportions for the other orders of columns, for room proportions, and so on.

A more pertinent example to interior work today, and also related to the interplay of solids and voids, is the pro-

portions of openings on a solid wall. Figure 10.18 shows two arcades, one with many smaller arches and the other with fewer, larger ones. As you can tell, the issue of scale is also involved here. Notice the proportions of the arched openings in relation to one another, the spaces in between, and the space above them.

Figure 10.19 shows a similar example. This time we have a wall with punched penetrations. Notice the progression of adjustments from the elevations shown in Figure 10.19a–c. They get progressively more refined, and the one shown in Figure 10.19c looks the most appropriate. The heights of the openings seem to work well in relation to their width and the height of the overall wall. The widths of the spaces in between also seem to have a good relation to the size of the openings.

Although proportion is associated mostly with two-dimensional compositions, it is also relevant in the third dimension. Let's look at two examples. If we look at two variations of the depth dimension of pilasters we notice that there is an important relationship between the depth of the pilasters and the width of the in-between spaces. Depending on the width of the in-between spaces, some column depths will work better than others (Figure 10.20).

Now, let's examine a freestanding mass in an open space. Depending on the height of the space and the amount

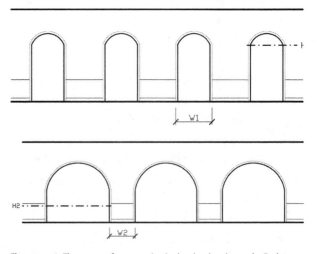

Figure 10.17: During the Renaissance, architects such as Palladio developed rules of correct proportioning for the different classical orders. Palladio's proportioning for Ionic colonnades is shown here. The basic dimension used was the diameter of the column. All other dimensions were developed using this basic dimension as a reference.

Figure 10.18: The concern for proportion is closely related to scale. Each type of scale has its own set of agreeable proportions. In the two arcades shown here, the types of arches used establish very distinct scales. In this case the height of the arches and the amount of solid wall above them are similar. They seem to work well in both cases. In order for them to work, though, notice how both the cutting point of the arch on the sides and the width of the solid portion of the wall between the arches are different in each case.

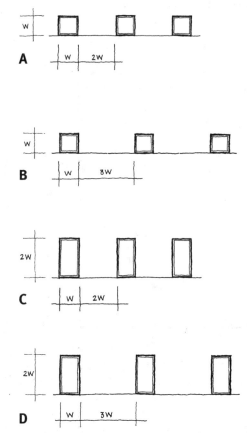

Figure 10.19: Any two-dimensional surface with multiple features needs to be studied proportionally. This example shows three proportional studies for openings on a wall. The size of the openings, the space between them, and the remaining space above and below are all considered. In these examples, the openings in (a) have too much space between them and the ones in (b) seem a bit oversized. The openings in (c), as well as their placement and spacing, are the most successful of the three.

Figure 10.20: The proportions created by the depth of elements needs to be considered carefully. This example shows the relation of the spacing of pilasters to their depth dimension. The height, of course, is also critical to the study; however, for the sake of this example we exclude its consideration. In general, shallower pilasters will tolerate tighter spacings [compare (a) to (c)] and deeper ones will demand wider spacings [compare (b) to (d)].

of space around the mass, different dimensions of the mass will look more correct than others. Figure 10.21 shows two variations of this situation. The mass in Figure 10.21a is wide and short, while the one in Figure 10.21b is slender and taller. Its slenderness and extra height seem more appropriate for this space given its height and tight dimensions.

What is the formula? The truth is, you don't need one. You can develop an eye for proportion; however, if you must rely on formulas, there are some formulas you can use. You have probably already heard about the golden mean, the Fibonacci Series, and the Modulor. These can be used to devise well-proportioned rectangles and other shapes. They have been used extensively to compose architectural plans and elevations throughout the years.

Figure 10.21: The size, shape, and placement of objects in space need to work proportionally. In this example, the proportions of the freestanding mass in (a) don't work well. The passageway feels tight, and a lot of empty space is left above it. The tall and slender floating mass in (b) has better correspondence to the proportions of the space.

Figure 10.23: Le Corbusier's Le Modulor system was derived from the proportions of the golden mean and the proportions of the human body. It addressed all kinds of proportions, from those of small objects to those used at the town-planning scale.

Figure 10.22: This basic drawing shows the proportioning system prescribed by the golden mean. The proportions are such that the ratio of segment a to segment b is the same as that of segment b to the entire length of a + b.

The golden mean is a mathematical system of proportion devised by the Greeks, who applied it not only to buildings but also to sculpture and the design of small objects and details. The basic ratio of the golden mean is that produced when a line is divided into two unequal segments such that the ratio of the smaller segment to the larger one is the same as the ratio of the larger one to the entire line (Figure 10.22). The proportions of the golden mean are universal and can be found in flowers, vegetables, and other examples from nature. They have also been adopted by architects and designers from Palladio to Le Corbusier.

The Fibonacci Series is named after a famous Italian mathematician of the thirteenth century, Leonardo Fibonacci. The proportions of the series are very similar to those of the golden mean. The series consists of the addition of consecutive whole numbers in a series such that the sum of any two sequential numbers equals the next number in the sequence. This produces a series of whole numbers as follows: 1,1,2,3,5,8,13,21,34, and so on. Similar to the golden mean, with this series, if you have a line of, say, eight units of length and divide it into two unequal sections of three and five units, respectively, the ratio of the short segment (three) to the long one (five) is

equivalent (approximately) to the one between the long one (five) and the total length (eight).

The Modulor was a proportional system devised in the twentieth century by Le Corbusier based on the golden mean and the dimensions of the human body (Figure 10.23). It is derived from the division of an average human height into segments of ratios based on the golden mean. He found the derived proportions useful in determining heights of spaces and fixtures and other anthropomorphic relationships.

Although such proportional systems are helpful in providing some basic guidelines to follow, it is wise to avoid the obsessive use of mathematical formulas for two reasons. First, it will make your design process stiff and mechanical. Second, it will not always produce satisfactory results. Not even these three well-known proportional systems will work satisfactorily all the time. The golden mean, despite its wisdom, was considered to produce monotony if applied strictly. For that reason, it became necessary to perform intuitive corrections in order to produce more satisfying proportional results. Similarly, some critics believe Le Corbusier's best work was produced when he relied less on mechanical means and more on artistic intuition. In matters of proportion, thus, it is helpful for you to develop a good intuitive sense through practice and criticism.

In addition to the examples presented above, issues of proportion arise in cases where you have two-dimensional patterns on surfaces. Whether the variety is achieved by different materials or different colors, the same principles apply. You stand back and look at the proposed composition and start telling yourself: The red strip needs to be wider and moved to the center; the blue squares are too small, and so on. This kind of analysis, though, gets into the issue of balance, our next topic, so we will elaborate there.

Balance

The resolution of both scale and proportion in a project requires the achievement of proper balance. These three factors—scale, proportion, and balance—are closely intertwined. **Balance** in design refers to the visual equilibrium of elements in a composition. It is affected by the size, shape, and placement of the parts of the composition. The goal is to produce an assembly of parts that looks right, a composition that is harmonious. The principle of balance applies to both two- and three-dimensional compositions. Two-dimensional compositions are seen as planes composed of parts, such as in an elevation or patterned floor. These are called pictorial compositions because, especially when seen in elevation, they are experienced as pictures before our eyes.

Three-dimensional compositions are perceived differently. Here the element of depth comes into play, so not only do we see things to the left, center, and right, but objects and elements are also in the foreground, middle ground, or background. These form a more complex kind of composition that incorporates, among other things, the changing apparent size and location of things as one moves about the space.

A project's two- and three-dimensional compositions need to be balanced if they are to appear harmonious. In talking about balance it is customary to divide compositions into two broad categories: symmetrical compositions and asymmetrical compositions. We will use these two widely recognized distinctions to organize our discussion.

Symmetrical Compositions

Symmetrical compositions employ equivalent, usually identical, elements mirrored on either side of a central vertical axis. We are all familiar with symmetry. For many centuries, the only acceptable way to compose was using symmetry. Symmetry is pervasive in our world. Not only are humans composed symmetrically but so are many of our creations, like cars and many of the other machines and pieces of equipment we make. There seems to be a natural tendency toward symmetry in design. Many novice designers cannot seem to get away from it. This may be due to the fact that it is easy to use symmetry and it achieves a good level of success in relation to the effort exerted.

There is nothing wrong with using symmetry. Symmetry is a well-tested approach to composition with many successful examples from various epochs and places. It is when the designer starts to impose symmetry on every aspect of every design, whether it is called for or not, that the tendency becomes problematic. The goal of a designer is to determine when symmetry is appropriate and to learn how to execute it properly.

Symmetrical organizations carry connotations of logic and formality. Combined with the proper materials and details they can also express elegance and dignity. Ideal applications include formal, traditional, and dignified projects, such as government buildings, churches, and courthouses. On the other hand, symmetrical organizations are stable and static and, therefore, can be dull. The obvious way in which the elements of the built environment are presented through symmetry provides limited perceptual challenge to the observer and, therefore, has limited interest. Symmetrical compositions, however, offer an instantly perceived equilibrium and a strong figural whole seen against the background of everything else around them. As such, they are easy to read as a unit and, if framed properly, can acquire magnetic qualities that attract the eye.

There are several important considerations when composing symmetrical arrangements. Four particularly relevant ones are the location of the focus ahead, the relationship between the central axis and the approach, the level of intricacy of the composition, and the purity of the symmetry.

The focal point of symmetrical compositions is usually along the central axis. The center of a composition is normally differentiated, often emphasized (Figure 10.24). Whether a framed view to the outside, a piece of artwork, or a formal arrival space, central foci tend to make symmetrical compositions particularly powerful. They frequently give the ceremonial feeling of walking straight toward a meaningful destination. Another

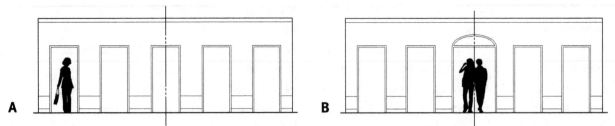

Figure 10.24: Strong symmetrical compositions rely on a strong center and two flanking sides. Of the two elevations shown, elevation (a), while symmetrical, reads more as a series than a static symmetrical composition. Elevation (b) is anchored by the emphasis of the central archway.

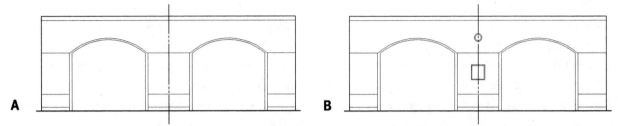

Figure 10.25: Symmetrical compositions with a featureless center are not very strong (a). Even if the flanking sides are intended to be dominant, there has to be something at the center. The small, nondominant accent pieces shown in elevation (b) give a better sense of balance and resolution.

Figure 10.26: The center of symmetrical elevations tends to act like a magnet. The center of elevation (a), despite not being emphasized by size or treatment, works here because there are only three parts to the composition. By mere placement at the center it achieves dominance. The center in elevation (b) is even more magnetic. In addition to its central position, the central archway is emphasized further through size dominance. Elevation (c) does not work. While symmetry will work adequately with an equal element at the center, it will not work well with a same-type element that is weak. It looks like a mistake. Strangely enough, if the element, while maintaining its basic character, gets reduced to a detail or nonequal accent, it works fine (d).

approach possible is the placement of two strong, symmetrical elements on either side of the center. If nothing is provided at the center, the composition may sometimes seem incomplete. Even when the center is not dominant, good symmetry relies on having something, even if only a detail, featured at the center (Figure 10.25). The composition goes from having two parts to having three (tri-partite) by the addition of something in the middle. In fact, tripartite compositions are among the most used and most successful kinds of symmetrical compositions.

In scenarios where the center is equal to the sides its power isn't as strong, because there is no clear sense of hierarchy, except for the one established by position. In cases of only three equal elements (Figure 10.26a) the

A

B

Figure 10.27: Both these possible elevations in a corporate conference room work well. Elevation (a) features a dominant central niche with local symmetry and two flanking sides with the entry doors. Elevation (b) features a pair of dominant doors at the center with two smaller niches at the sides.

composition can work. Magnetism will be strongest when there is a dominant center, as shown in Figure 10.26b. The one approach that always tends to look wrong is the placement of a weak element at the center, as shown in Figure 10.26c. A smaller element at the center, however, can work if it's read as a detail, like the small central window in Figure 10.26d. Figure 10.27 shows two tripartite symmetrical elevations of a wall that might be found in a corporate conference room. The one in Figure 10.27a features two lateral entrances, while the one in Figure 10.27b has a central entrance. They both feature niches with casework and artwork. Notice their different effects and the local symmetries in each of their three sections.

A factor of considerable importance is the correspondence between the central axis of the composition and the approach toward, or along, it. In cases where one moves toward a symmetrical composition, the effect is heightened by having a path, symmetrical itself, centered along the central axis of the composition. This achieves a strong formal, stately, and ceremonial effect. If used in the right circumstance, it can be quite powerful (Figure 10.28). Up to the twentieth century, symmetrical compositions of walls and symmetrical approaches to them were carefully orchestrated to achieve centrality and maximize the effect of the composition as seen from a one-point perspective. A different approach would be to have symmetrically arranged paths flanking the central space of the approach, thus creating two lateral approaches toward the end wall (Figure 10.29). In this case, while the mind recognizes the arrangement as perfectly symmetrical, one is unable to experience it perfectly as one starts to move to one of the two sides around the central circle in order to approach the wall.

A whole different effect results when one walks not toward the symmetrical composition but rather along it, in parallel fashion. In this case the view of the composi-

Figure 10.28: Whenever a symmetrical composition, such as a wall, is approached via a central, symmetrical path, the overall effect of the composition is strengthened. This adds formality and a literal sense of walking toward the center.

Figure 10.29: Whenever a symmetrical composition, such as the one here, is approached laterally and not centrally, the effect is different. The composition shown, while allowing visual access from the center, forces people to approach the end wall from one of the two sides.

tion is oblique, and one only experiences the full effect if one happens to stop when reaching the center and turns 90 degrees to face it. Where there is not enough distance to stand back and perceive the symmetrical composition, the compositional effort is wasted, as it will not be seen as intended. Symmetry is meant to be seen from the front. In cases where spaces are narrow, as in corridors, it is best to rely on other compositional techniques dealing with sequence, such as the use of rhythm, instead of symmetry (Figure 10.30).

Figure 10.30: Symmetrical compositions are meant to be seen straight on. Using a symmetrical composition for a wall along a narrow corridor as shown here would be counterproductive since the symmetry would never be well perceived. In a case like this, a composition that addresses sequence and progression would be more appropriate.

While simple symmetrical compositions may lack interest, complex ones can be quite engaging. Complex symmetrical compositions that have secondary symmetries and different lateral and vertical relationships provide richness and variety and can be quite stimulating despite their static nature. The elevation composition shown in Figure 10.31 progresses from a simple idea to an elaborate composition. The addition of layers of articulation shown in Figures 10.31b and c make the elevation come to life, endowing it with sufficient intricacy to attract, engage, and delight the eye.

Symmetry does not always have to be perfect. While most symmetrical compositions tend to be pure, with both sides mirroring each other identically, it is possible to have imperfect symmetry by having inequalities between the sides in such a way that symmetry is apparent, but, upon further scrutiny, what is on the right is not exactly what is on the left (Figure 10.32).

Asymmetrical Compositions

Asymmetrical compositions are more a product of the twentieth century. Their use increased with the advent of modern architecture and the free-flowing plans introduced by the likes of Frank Lloyd Wright and Mies van der Rohe. Wright rejected the formality and rigidity of classical architecture and favored more natural and organic approaches to planning. He described the emerging composition attitude as follows:

Figure 10.31: Although symmetrical compositions tend to be static, they can certainly be stimulating. This example shows the transformation of a simple symmetrical composition into a highly articulated creation. The simple idea of the arched openings in (a) is enriched by the modulation of the arches, and the addition of columns with capitals and pedestals between them (b). The composition is elaborated further in (c), where more detail is added and surfaces are enriched by the addition of relief.

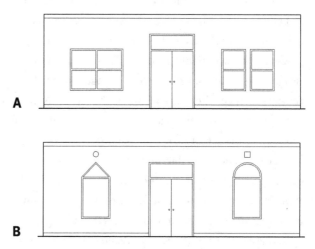

Figure 10.32: Symmetry does not always have to be perfect. These two elevations show symmetrical compositions that, despite their apparent symmetry, are not quite the same from side to side. In elevation (a), the side window is broken into two units on the right side even though it still looks close enough to its counterpart on the other side. In elevation (b), the pediments over the two side windows and the ornamental motifs above them are shaped differently.

Modern architecture rejects the major axis and the minor axis of classical architecture. It rejects all grandomania, every building that would stand in military fashion heels together, eyes front, something on the right hand, and something on the left hand. Architecture already favors the reflex, the natural easy attitude, the occult symmetry of grace and rhythm affirming the ease, grace, and naturalness of natural life.[6]

Asymmetry, like symmetry, applies to both spatial organizations and pictorial compositions. Figure 10.33 shows two equivalent spatial compositions, one symmetrical and the other asymmetrical. They both feature one reception area, two small utility rooms, two main spaces, and one meeting room in the back. Notice the difference between the two approaches, the symmetrical one being rigid, formal, and ceremonial, and the asymmetrical one being freer and more dynamic.

Asymmetrical compositions achieve balance through the careful placement of different elements of varying sizes and proportional weights. They avoid the kind of side-to-side repetition employed in symmetrical planning. For instance, a mass on one side may be balanced by a group of carefully placed elements of a different size and shape on the other side. Asymmetrical balance relies more on a painterly eye than on specific rules. It requires greater skill and control by the designer but can produce very satisfying results. Figure 10.34 shows two successful office reception area scenes composed asymmetrically.

One of the characteristic effects of asymmetrical compositions is their tendency to be more casual and informal than symmetrical ones. They work best in compositions having no symmetrical components. Figure 10.35 illustrates the difficulty of imposing asymmetry on elevations with strong symmetrical components. The doors in Figures 10.35a and b establish fairly strong symmetrical traits that are hard to counteract without moving them. The results are ambiguous compositions with a mix of symmetry and asymmetry.

Asymmetrical compositions work best when there is nothing located at the center or equally spaced on either side. They tend to also be more dynamic and engaging than symmetrical ones if executed properly. Figure 10.36 shows two elevations equivalent to the two symmetrical ones shown in Figure 10.27. Notice how different these are, much less formal and static. Asymmetrical compositions can also have some level of formality, as shown in Figure 10.37.

Figure 10.33: Similar to the composition of elevations and other two-dimensional planes, the overall layout of spaces can also follow symmetrical or asymmetrical approaches. These two space layouts show a symmetrical (a) and an asymmetrical (b) composition in a suite consisting of a reception area, two small utility rooms, two main general spaces, and one meeting room. Note the different effects produced by the two approaches.

Figure 10.34: Today's design is full of examples of asymmetrical compositions. Two office reception areas are shown here. Both are well balanced. The horizontality of the sofa on one side and the verticality of the display on the other create balance in (a). The central chair in the foreground and the flower arrangement in the background serve to produce some secondary interest and act as a pivot point. In (b), the reception desk on one side is balanced against the prominent painting on the other. The sharp vertical line just to the right of the center of the composition serves as a visual break point on this composition. The flowers, once again, serve as a secondary point of interest.

Figure 10.35: It is difficult to impose asymmetry on arrangements containing strong symmetrical properties. Of the two examples shown with given locations for the doors, elevation (a) is particularly difficult to resolve due to the powerful symmetry imposed by the doors. The resulting elevation is ambiguous and weak. In elevation (b), despite the power of the centrally located pair of doors, the fact that it is just one element makes it easier to incorporate into the asymmetrical composition. Even so, there is something strange about an asymmetrical composition with a principal component perfectly centered.

Figure 10.36: Asymmetrical compositions work best with nothing centered. These two elevations are equivalent to the two shown in Figure 10.27, except they are not symmetrical. Compare the two approaches and notice the different effects produced.

While the path shown has a formal side of uniformly placed rhythmic elements, the opposite side supplies contrast with its planar, nonrhythmic treatment. There is a level of formality produced by the composition of the left side, while the contrasting right side counterbalances and softens the rigidity of the overall effect.

Another way of having some degree of formality in an asymmetrical composition is by the alignment of regulating lines (Figure 10.38). While there is no identical repetition from side to side, the regularity produced by the alignments helps to give a somewhat formal sense of order. Alignments can be at the edges of elements (Figure 10.38a) or through their center lines (Figure 10.38b). Height alignments are particularly useful devices to achieve balanced compositions. The regularity produced in Figure 10.39 by the consistent alignment of elements in relation to the window wall's horizontal lines gives this elevation a sense of resolved equilibrium.

In contrast to orderly asymmetry are totally free compositions having no repeated parts and no alignments

Figure 10.37: Despite their relative informality, asymmetrical compositions can still be arranged in ways that elicit formality. The asymmetrical path shown here has unequal elements on either side. The presence of a regular colonnade on the left side gives it a sense of decorum and formality, even if a casual one.

of any kind. The result of such an approach is increased informality and dynamism. Needless to say, this approach requires a very refined eye and some patience to achieve an appropriate level of balance. The elevation shown in Figure 10.40 uses this approach and still achieves a sense of equilibrium and harmony.

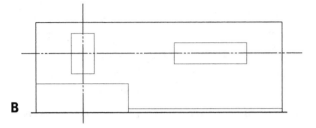

Figure 10.38: Components of asymmetrical compositions can have strong geometrical relationships. This can be achieved by the use of alignments. These can be edge alignments, as shown in elevation (a), or center line alignments, as shown in (b). These alignments add regularity to the composition.

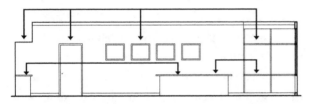

Figure 10.39: A strategy often used to create strong relationships in compositions, either symmetrical or asymmetrical, is the alignment of regulating horizontal lines. These are often derived from existent components in the shell space. In this example, horizontal lines established by an existing window wall are used to establish the heights of the door, the bench, and the artwork. Additionally, the heights of the cabinetry and the underside of the artwork are also coordinated. These relationships help create a consistent unified overall effect.

Figure 10.40: Free asymmetrical compositions can work without repeated elements or alignments of any kind. They rely on a painterly eye and, if done properly, can have very satisfying results.

Unifying the Whole

Ultimately, the totality of a project has to come across as a unified whole, seemingly conceived by a single mind having a clear and cohesive design plan. No matter how complex a project is, the obligation is there to solve the "whole." As Robert Venturi expressed it years ago:

> An architecture of complexity and accommodation does not forsake the whole. In fact, I have referred to a special obligation toward the whole because the whole is difficult to achieve. And I have emphasized the goal of unity rather than of simplification in an art "whose . . . truth [is] in its totality." It is the difficult unity through inclusion rather than the easy unity of exclusion.[7]

Unity

Unity in design is accomplished by composing elements in such a way that they appear to be one entity. In order to achieve unity, all the components of the interior must relate to each other and the overall approach of the project. The result of a unified project is a sense of connectedness, relatedness, and coherence. With unity the project becomes one and reads as a whole. Consider the following explanation:

> The word "unity" means oneness. Of course, no actual oneness exists, unless you get down to the single cell organism or the atom. . . . When we speak of unity we do not mean this kind of oneness. We are referring to the putting-together of things, the composing of things, the combining of things into a group to which we can then attribute the quality of oneness.[8]

Unity occurs at different levels. Within a project, unity needs to be addressed at the level of individual scenes, such as rooms, and at the level of the entire project. Any given part of a project, when seen individually, should look visually unified in itself. It doesn't necessarily need to be complete within its boundaries, yet frequently it will be. We will explain the distinction later in the section on how to produce unity and wholeness. Beyond the individual scene or room, the project as a whole needs to achieve a quality of oneness. As one moves from space to space, one should get the feeling that all the spaces and parts are components of the same entity.

How the project relates to the building in which it is housed may sometimes be an important consideration. Many times there is no relationship, and, as soon as one enters a space from the building's public corridor, it appears as though one has entered a totally different world. Such is the nature of a great number of interior projects. There are times, however, when, because of the nature of the building or the project, the designer tries to produce some unity between the qualities of the building and those of the project. The attempts can be subtle, as when using regulating height lines originating in the building spaces outside the project or when repeating motifs of the building within the project. The unification can sometimes be stronger, such as a project that adopts the general feel and detailing of the building, as in some historical buildings, or in cases where the building and the interiors are designed concurrently by the same designer.

There are specific strategies used to achieve unity. The two key aims are similarity and continuity. Any composition, whether contained and static or free and sequential, needs both these qualities to achieve unity. We will first discuss unity in single spaces and later talk about achieving unity from one space to the next so as to unify the entire project. For the study of unity within a single scene, we rely here on some useful concepts articulated previously by Pierre von Meiss.[9]

Unity within a single scene relies on similarity, proximity, common enclosure, consistency of approach, or complementary composition. **Similarity** can be due to the repeated use of elements sharing similar characteristics such as form, size, material, color, and detailing. **Proximity** fosters unity by clustering elements close enough to produce distinct groups that read as unified clusters. **Common enclosure**, whether by surrounding walls, overhead planes, floor platforms, or background datum walls, also serves to unify a scene. **Consistency of approach** is also paramount. Whatever the approach taken, it has to be consistent throughout to make it clear that the scene was created by the same hand. If it's a scheme relying on high contrast, then look for the use of high contrast throughout; if it's a scheme emphasizing horizontality, then look for the consistent use of horizontal elements.

Unity within a space can also be achieved through good **complementary composition**. By this we mean the skillful integration of complementary, not similar, elements to form a unified whole. This approach can be harder to achieve as it requires a painterly eye and good aesthetic sense. With this approach it's the complementary nature of the components that gives the space unity. There is no repetition. Colors can be combined with their complementary opposites, horizontals can mix with verticals, rough can mix with smooth, and light can mix with dark.

When it comes to the unity of the project as a whole, the task takes on new challenges. Now the task becomes to achieve unity from one space to the next, and the next, and so on. The ultimate goal is for the entire project to read as one. For this to happen there has to be, first and foremost, clarity of concept. As stated by Eugene Raskin: "Clarity of concept is the inescapable basis of unity."[10] At this point we refer you back to Chapter 6, where we discussed concepts. You may recall our distinction between organizational concepts and character concepts. Both of them come into play here. Organizational concepts give the project physical structure. The project becomes a cohesive system based on some logic appropriate to its needs. Although the structure is seldom apparent all at once, especially in larger projects, eventually, as one navigates the project and becomes acquainted with it, the structure, if well conceived, begins to make sense (Figure 10.41). This gives the project spatial and structural unity. While the organizational concept supplies structural unity, the character concept gives it visual unity. Whatever design

Figure 10.41: The unity of an overall project begins with a cohesive scheme. This oversimplified example illustrates how, if there is some underlying structure, even one not readily apparent initially, it will contribute to a sense of overall unity that sooner or later will be understood.

approach is taken, stylistic and otherwise, has to be continued throughout.

Unity of the overall project is complicated by the fact that one cannot see the various spaces of projects all at once. Most projects, except the very small, are comprised of multiple spaces that one experiences as one moves through them. In some cases, especially in open, flowing plans, you can see clearly from one space to the next and see whatever continuity links the designer has provided. In other cases, where passage from one space to the next does not allow visual connection, you have to rely on memory to tie the spaces together and perceive whatever unity there is. A good example of this is the case where you are transported from one space to another space via an elevator ride. When you arrive in the second space your only way of establishing visual continuity is to remember what the first space was like. These important distinctions establish the basis for providing unity at the overall project level. Two useful strategies to achieve overall unity are continuity and repetition, as discussed below.

Continuity

Continuity in a project means that there is a continuation of treatments from one space to another, thus linking different parts of the project visually. This can be accomplished through consistency or extension. **Consistency** simply requires treating elements, approaches, and finishes consistently from space to space. An example is the consistent use of forms and wall finishes from one space to the next (Figure 10.42). Another example is the consistent employment of a thematic idea throughout the project. Themes can create strong links between spaces by acting as a thread that weaves through the entire project, thus holding it together. Themes can be abstract constructs, held together by consistency of meaning, such as an ethnic restaurant utilizing symbols of the appropriate culture, or more direct architectural themes relying on consistent form or approach.

Extension refers to the practice of extending elements from one space to another. Examples include the continuation of a pattern from one room to the next (Figure 10.43) and the extension of horizontal lines from space to space, providing a common thread throughout the project (Figure 10.44). Another example of extension, this one using spatial features, would be extending either the floor or the ceiling plane to serve as the unifying element between two adjacent spaces, while the other plane (either ceiling or floor, whichever is not the unifying element) varies from space to space (Figure 10.45).

Consistency and extension are similar but not the same. Consistency means the repeated and sustained application of an overall treatment (often materials and finishes) with or without interruptions. The key factor is that the treatment is consistent and sustained throughout. Extension means the continuation of certain elements from one space to another, even if the approach is not sustained throughout the project. A variation of extension is **overlapping**, where a certain element (wall, floor, or ceiling) is extended from the space in which it originates to overlap with the adjacent space, thus creating a strong link. In this case, two spaces share a common area defined by the extended, overlapping element. However, it is a limited extension. It does not continue but achieves enough overlap to tie the two spaces together. Figure 10.46 shows examples of overlaps produced by ceiling extensions (Figure 10.46a) and wall extensions (Figure 10.46b).

Figure 10.42: Consistency is paramount to achieve a sense of unity. In this example the consistent use of forms, wall finishes, shapes, and fixtures all contribute to unity.

Figure 10.43: The extension of a pattern from one space to another helps to bridge spaces and contribute to a feeling of unity between spaces. There is more than consistency of approach here. The pattern is continued, by extension, from one room to the next.

Figure 10.44: Not only can horizontal lines be used to regulate the heights of elements in space, as shown in figure 10.39, they can also be expressed literally through the use of reveals, moldings, or surface relief. When used, they become an element that can be extended from space to space to help foster a sense of unity.

Figure 10.45: The ceiling and floor planes can contribute much to unity between adjacent spaces. This applies to adjacent spaces seen simultaneously. Example (a) shows a consistent, extended floor pattern unifying two contiguous spaces that are broken up by a change of ceiling height. In this case the floor is the unifying element. Example (b) shows the opposite. Here, the ceiling is the unifying element, while there is a break of continuity between the two spaces defined by a dividing wall and a change of floor pattern.

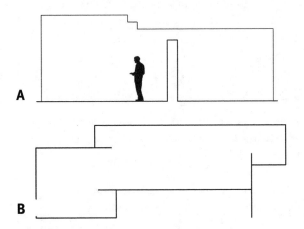

Figure 10.46: Another approach to unity is to link spaces by the use of overlapping elements. Example (a) shows an overlap at the ceiling plane. Notice that it is not continuous, like the one shown in Figure 10.45(b), but partial. Example (b) shows the use of overlapping walls extending from one space to the next, producing a similar bridging effect between spaces.

Most projects rely on consistent treatments among their spaces for unity. Other than using the same finishes throughout the project, possibilities include consistent shapes, colors, details, scales, patterns, and textures. Consistency does not require identical treatments from space to space, just consistency of approach. If, for example, color is being used to unify various spaces, the actual shade of the color may vary from space to space as long as there is some consistency of the hue. Or, if there is a mix of colors in some geometric pattern on the wall, the next space can have a different mix of the same colors and a slightly different geometrical pattern, as long as the basic characteristics are retained.

Repetition

Repetition is different from consistency and extension. It happens when some element, such as a particular motif, occurs over and over again. The recurrence may or may not be consistent throughout. In some cases it may occur throughout, although in others it will occur only selectively. In instances of selective recurrence it is important that it recurs often enough to be recognized as a pattern. Repetition is different from extension because extension implies uninterrupted continuity. With repetition the repeated element appears and reappears from place to place, more like a stamp that gets stamped in one room and then another than a line that extends between spaces. Figure 10.47 shows three rooms unified by the repetition of the anchorlike wall details and the suspended light fixtures. The repeated element may be identical from one place to the next or just similar, as long as the similarity is recognizable. It may also be either literal or thematic. In the case of a thematic repetition, the one element only needs to tie in with the rest through its theme, not its visual appearance. Thus, in a seafood restaurant, an anchor in one room, a hanging marlin in another room,

Figure 10.47: Repetition is a powerful unifying strategy. This example shows the repeated use of intermittent decorative wall motifs and suspended lighting fixtures to produce a consistent look among the three spaces shown.

and a sail in a third room would provide thematic repetition without being visually similar.

Repeated elements can be details, accessories, motifs, plants, artwork, furnishings, and so on. Repetition can be especially effective in instances where there is not much visual connection between the spaces of a project. In these cases, as we have said, the observer relies on recall to make linkages between spaces. The repeated appearance and reappearance of similar elements stimulates recall in the perceiver's mind and serves to increase the sense of unity among the spaces.

Special approaches to the use of repetition include gradation and dispersion. With these approaches, equal elements are not repeated over and over but are transformed as they move from one space to another. **Gradation** involves the gradual transformation of an element or characteristic. To apply gradation to color, for instance, its hue, value, or chroma would gradually be changed as the color progresses through the space, becoming more or less pure, light, or saturated. Other examples include the gradual modifications of lighting level and spatial or furniture density. Key to the application of these techniques is the use of a consistent stylistic approach to anchor the variety produced by the gradation. This plus the recognition of a pattern that continues from one space to the next generally provides the necessary level of consistency to achieve unity between the different areas involved.

Dispersion is a special application of gradation where the transformation of an element is less regular. It involves the increase or decrease of density in a planned but somewhat random fashion. It can be especially effective when applied to floor patterns or as a technique of repetition with motifs or materials. To understand the principle of dispersion, try to visualize what would happen if you dropped a large container of marbles on a hard floor. They would bounce around and be dispersed throughout the floor. After the bouncing ceases you would find that a large number of pebbles end up concentrated close to the point of origin, a moderate number end up some distance away, and a few take such bounces that they actually end up quite far from the point of origin. Although the general pattern of this result is predictable, the exact way the pebbles choose to go is not. You can repeat the procedure several times and the result is always different.

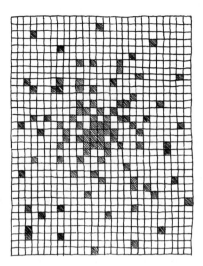

Figure 10.48: This floor pattern illustrates the use of dispersion. The pattern is more concentrated at its center. From there it moves outward in random fashion and becomes less dense to the point where it becomes faint, eventually disappearing.

Figure 10.49: This longitudinal section through a space shows the strategy of dispersion used with wall applications, in this case wood. The first space is the most prominent and features wood paneling throughout. As you move into the space the paneling is reduced to a wood band. As you move even further into the space, the wood band becomes a wood medallion that occurs selectively from that point on. The presence of wood, though reduced, never disappears, thus contributing to the sense of unity of the project.

You can use this technique to design patterns that vary in regularity and density, creating areas of high concentration of a pattern, followed by areas where the pattern is dispersed, becoming quite faint and infrequent in some places. Although the presence of the pattern is reduced as you move away from the area of high concentration, it never disappears, thus serving as a unifying motif (Figure 10.48). Similarly, you can use this technique to maintain some continuity of special finishes in a project. You could, for instance, have one or two areas with a high concentration of upgraded finishes and fixtures followed by areas of less concentration of the same finishes. Instead of completely eliminating the use of the special treatments, they are just reduced. Thus, the wood paneling becomes a wood band and, later, a recurring small wood

Figure 10.50: In this example the strategy of dispersion is applied to a floor. As in the wood paneling example in Figure 10.49, the first room is a prominent space and features a marble floor throughout. The marble floor gets reduced to marble borders in the next room. Eventually, it is used only at the thresholds between major spaces. Here again, even though the amount of the high-end finish is reduced as one moves farther into the space, it never goes away, thus contributing to the unity of the project.

motif (Figure 10.49). Similarly, the marble floor becomes marble borders, and, later, marble thresholds at key junctures (Figure 10.50).

Avoiding Dullness

Unity, similar to order as discussed in Chapter 7, relies on regularity and repetition. As with the goal of order, a warning is appropriate: Too much uniformity may produce dullness and monotony. These desirable qualities if taken to the extreme can have undesirable consequences. True, it can be argued that monotony is better than lack

of unity, or order, or balance; however, it is best to address both of these dualities and seek both unity and interest, order and stimulation, balance and dynamism. Amid the consistency and regularity there has to be variety, contrast, and a sense of hierarchy. These need to be achieved while maintaining unity and order and, certainly, have to find equilibrium.

Finally, while interest and enrichment are produced by incorporating elements that provide variety, contrast, and hierarchy, you should be cautioned that these worthwhile goals don't justify the excesses often produced by designers in the name of enrichment. Though complexity is desirable in design, its opposite, simplicity, is also a valuable quality. True competence requires learning how to design with an economy of means so you can produce the richest expression with the fewest strokes and elements. While this may appear simple due to the reduction of the number of parts, it is not so. Remember the quote from Venturi where he refers to "the difficult unity through inclusion rather than the easy unity of exclusion."[11] We are not advocating minimalism, just the elimination, or at least reduction, of nonessentials. Even with a simple approach, you still have an obligation to engage the mind and stimulate the human spirit.

CAPSULE | Visual Harmony in Figural Composition

The issue of visual harmony is central to the goal of resolution. Not many people have attempted to study the issue of architectural form in depth. One of them is Ralf Weber, who, in *On the Aesthetics of Architecture*, concentrates on the role of form in the experience and judgment of architecture.[1] This valuable book offers many insights about architectural form. Here we summarize some of Weber's contributions to the issue of visual harmony related not to space but to the solid elements in space. These are highly relevant to the art of composing interior environments. We separate this brief summary into the topics of centers, perceptual weight, vertical elements, hierarchy, and figure/ground articulation.

CENTERS

The perception of order depends, among other things, on the impact of the various perceptual centers in a composition. These can be dominant or subordinate but in all cases act as some kind of visual focus. The dominant visual area of any display is the visual center of gravity, which is determined by the distribution of the principal centers and their perceptual masses. Additionally, areas of high contrast, areas along symmetry axes, areas along the vertical axes of shapes and larger composite patterns, patterns with strong figural characters, concave and enclosed shapes, heterogeneous elements within homogeneous arrangements, and areas of high contrast attract the eye and establish perceptual centers exerting more or less influence (Figure C10.1).

Centers are also induced by the contours of a configuration, and it is possible to make some generalizations about the location of fulcrums in simple shapes. The single perceptual center of a square or a circle, for instance, is at the geometric center. Vertically elongated shapes pull the perceptual center upward. Not all shapes, however, enjoy a strong perceptual center. It is hard, for instance, to establish a precise perceptual center in elongated shapes, whether vertical or horizontal, exceeding a ratio of 1:2.

Consciously planning the centers of a composition is important. Their location and interaction play a crucial role in establishing order and determining its dynamic character.

PERCEPTUAL WEIGHT

The dynamic character of a pattern is also affected by the perceived heaviness of the various parts of the configuration. Perceptual weight is affected by size, tone, levels of articulation and regularity, location, and direction. Larger, darker, articulated, or regular shapes generally carry more

Figure C10.1: Building with clear perceptual center.

Figure C10.2: The treatment and placement of the cylindrical shapes in this building give them perceptual weight.

perceptual weight than their opposites. Likewise, shapes that are isolated, placed somewhere in the periphery (instead of in the center or along a major axis), or vertically oriented assume greater visual weight (Figure C10.2).

VERTICAL ELEMENTS

To perceive space, the body favors orthogonal localization. The horizontal and the vertical, thus, provide the framework for stability as well as for the apparent dynamic properties of a composition. The vertical dimension, however, is more significant for figural segregation than the horizontal. Particularly important is the role of the vertical axis of symmetry in the perceived stability of a figure. The highest degree of perceived stability is attained when figures are symmetrical, both horizontally and vertically, and the main direction extends horizontally. The perceptual stability can be increased further by interlocking such a configuration with vertical shapes placed at the axis of vertical symmetry (Figure C10.3). Configurations where the orientation of the shape's main dimension and its axis of symmetry coincide are perceived as dynamic, such as in the case of a vertically symmetrical, tall and slender building, which appears to move upward. This is further reinforced by the natural tendency of the eyes to move upward faster than they move downward.

Perceptual dynamics in a composition are produced by the interplay between vertical and horizontal elements. Elevations with main centers aligned horizontally appear

static. Perceptual stability will increase when the main perceptual center is located above the actual center of balance. Vertical elements stop horizontal visual scanning and help to anchor vision. Horizontal arrangements can be enhanced, for example, by a strong vertical accent at the position of the main focus. It is also useful to utilize vertical elements to

Figure C10.3: The vertical center on this otherwise horizontal and symmetrical facade gives this building a sense of stability.

Figure C10.4: The hierarchical organization of this facade allows a high level of complexity without being overtaxing.

demarcate the axes along which the individual centers of a pattern are aligned.

HIERARCHY

Hierarchical arrangements that create subordinate groups and subgroups allow sustained perceptual arousal without overtaxing perceptual capacity. They permit a high absolute complexity while maintaining a moderate level of perceptual complexity. The hierarchical arrangement of perceptual centers in a composition is, thus, generally desirable. Weber points out two crucial factors: The first factor is the need for both a distinct overall fulcrum and distinct centers for each of the subordinate component groups. The second factor is the need for an organization of a subordinate type at the highest levels where small parts form larger patterns, which in turn are grouped to form a larger group, and so on (Figure C10.4).

Perceptual hierarchy demands that each of the groups and subgroups of shapes of a composition should be identifiable as discrete perceptual wholes. A clear compositional center in each group helps in this regard. Ideally, the point of the shape's equilibrium coincides with the perceptual focus (visually strongest) of the configuration. Distinct foci can be created by the use of heterogeneous shapes, contrasting sizes, rhythms or symmetries, and contrasting tones, colors, or textures, among other devices.

When a composition, say, an elevation, is subdivided nonhierarchically into equal parts, and these exceed the maximum number of elements that can be perceived at once (between five and seven), the result is monotonous. This condition can be improved by using a rhythmic alternation of different elements and by the incorporation of foci, such as an overall central vertical symmetrical axis. In a composition of similar elements, a strong

focus can also be produced by articulating one of the shapes using tone, texture, or color. Yet, the simplest way of creating a strong overall focus is by using a shape that is either different or scaled differently. The effect of a single heterogeneous element is normally so strong that it can easily center an otherwise homogeneous arrangement, catalyzing an otherwise monotonous appearance.

There are several advantages to organizing the various centers of attraction in a composition hierarchically:

- A subordinate arrangement of parts allows the visual segregation of a distinct fulcrum, whereas a coordinate (nonhierarchical) arrangement results in similar and competing perceptual dominance.
- Hierarchical arrangements permit greater absolute complexity without leading to an equally high degree of perceptual complexity. The organization of parts into groups complies more readily with the demands of wholeness in a complex configuration, thus allowing a more complicated arrangement of shapes to emerge.
- In a hierarchical organization, there is a clear difference between various levels of scale, that is, between the sizes of the individual entities in relation to the whole. Consequently, there can be a greater number of levels without resulting in visual chaos.
- Hierarchical organization allows similar elements to be grouped into larger shapes instead of simply fusing with the overall pattern.
- Hierarchical organizations make it easier to achieve equilibrium of areas of interest when exploring perceptual centers.
- Hierarchical organizations allow a gradual decrease of scales in a composition, thus avoiding abrupt jumps from large scales to minute ones, which often result in low levels of stimulation.
- Compositions that are hierarchical but lack detail and articulation at the smaller subordinate levels also can result in low stimulus. The lack of microstructure leads to poverty of information.

FIGURE–GROUND ARTICULATION

An important factor in the analysis of the perceptual impact of corporeal form is the internal articulation of the spatial boundaries. Two of the most predominant properties of a composition's articulation are its textural appearance and the organization of component elements into figures and ground. The completeness of figure–ground organization largely determines the perceived orderliness of the composition. The distribution of contrast endows the shape with heterogeneous structure.

The parts of an elevation possess different visual dominance, and thus appear to advance or recede, resulting in multiple levels of perceived depth. The effect is due to the perceptual organization of stimulus patterns into figure and ground. Depending on the arrangement, some features will attain perceptual dominance or subordinance. The process of perception involves selecting stimuli and unifying them into perceptual figures that segregate themselves from a surrounding ground. Important to the formation of perceptual units is the function of the contour. Contours function as a boundary for enclosed areas, thus defining figures. The ground appears to continue behind the figure.

Other things being equal, Weber gives the following laws as determinants of figure–ground segregation:

- Orientation: Shapes whose orientation follows the cardinal axes form figures more easily.
- Proximity: Small areas dominate. Larger areas tend to become grounds.
- Closure: Fully closed shapes segregate more easily.
- Articulation: Areas with greater internal articulation will form figures more easily.
- Concavity: The concave side of a boundary will induce shapes more easily than the convex side.
- Brightness and Color: Brighter tones and hard colors segregate into figures more easily.
- Symmetry: The more symmetrical shapes will tend to form figures.

Figure–ground organizations vary. The possibilities can be summarized into five basic categories:

1. Unified ground—intervening spaces do not form figures: The negative spaces between or surrounding the primary shapes possess no, or only a weak, figural character of their own (Figure C10.5).
2. Unified ground—intervening spaces form figures: The negative spaces between the principal shapes assume their own figural character.

Figure C10.5: This facade is an example of a unified ground where the intervening spaces do not form figures.

3. Nonunified ground—duo-formation of shapes: As in a facade of a curtain-walled building subdivided into endless squares, distinction between figure and ground is impossible, and all shapes assume equal dominance.
4. Nonunified ground—intervening spaces form figures: Negative spaces form figures in their own right but do not result in duo-formations. The figural character of the negative spaces is weaker than that of the main components.
5. Nonunified ground—intervening spaces do not form figures: Intervening spaces do not assume a figural character. The negative spaces cannot group themselves, and the overall pattern appears unstable.

Although it is easy to relegate negative spaces to unimportant subordinate status, it is obvious that they impact the overall composition significantly and, therefore, deserve attention. When there is no clear distinction between figure and ground, or when the permeating order of the organization is locally violated, the result is perceptual ambiguity.

It is possible for both positive and negative spaces to assume a figural character. Grounds can take on a figural character by reducing it to narrow, regular shapes, as when a group of windows is spaced tightly, producing a pattern of strips between them that takes on the role of figure, thus creating a reversal effect between figure and ground.

---

1. Ralf Weber, *On the Aesthetics of Architecture* (Aldershot, England: Avebury, 1995).

CASE STUDY
Enriching a Project with a Straightforward Floor Plan: A Professional Services Firm

DESIGN FIRM: GARY LEE PARTNERS

This design for the offices of a professional services firm is a good example of how a project does not need to have an elaborate floor plan to be stimulating and provide an enriching experience. The client occupies six and a half floors in downtown Chicago. The office personnel consist predominantly of highly educated business consultants, and the nature of their work requires that they have private enclosed offices. As a result, private executive offices along the perimeter characterize the typical layout. The floor plate of the building is somewhat unique in that the major core elements are located at the two extremes, thus freeing up the center of the long rectangular floors.

The basic layout of the typical floor is efficient, orderly, and straightforward. Important strategic planning decisions include the location of team rooms at the four corners of the floor and the creation of a dominant communal zone at the center. This central zone features major break areas, conference rooms, informal meeting areas, and the internal stairs that connect all the floors (Figure CS10.1). The result is a floor plate with three magnet areas, a main one in the center and one at each end (Figure CS10.2). An inexperienced designer may look at the floor plan and consider it static and old-fashioned. However, when one understands the three-dimensional realities of the project its richness is revealed.

The surface articulation, thoughtful detailing, and carefully selected and placed artwork give this project abundant richness within its clean and crisp modernistic design vocabulary. Being a project of mostly enclosed spaces, it is experienced mainly through its corridors and individual rooms. The use of offsets, strong visual anchors at the ends via artwork, and a major break in the middle give the long east-west corridors plenty of variety and interest (Figure CS10.3). Variety in the type and level of lighting also help to articulate and differentiate the

Figure CS10.1: The cental interconnecting stairway and surrounding area is one of the principal nodes of the entire project.

Figure CS10.2: This unusual floor plan has the service cores at the two ends. The meeting rooms are at the four corners and the principal aperture is at the center.

Figure CS10.3: Offsets, visual anchors, and material variations break up the long corridors perceptually.

Figure CS10.4: Much consideration was given to the effects of lighting. The use of uplighting and vertical offsets with incorporated lighting behind translucent screens create dramatic effects and leave the ceiling plan uncluttered.

Figure CS10.5: Artwork placement was carefully planned at all levels of hierarchy, from commanding pieces at the ends of long vistas (a) to smaller pieces in series (b).

Figure CS10.6: One is frequently pleasantly surprised by framed vistas anchored by impressive artwork (a). Additionally, areas rich in comfort, such as the "club" shown in figure (b), provide employees with welcoming common areas away from their desks.

various elements and zones along these corridors (Figure CS10.4). Despite the predominance of perimeter offices, natural light and views are provided through planned apertures at the four corners, as seen in the background in Figure CS10.4, and the two ends of the central public area. The use of reflective stone flooring and translucent glass panels in these areas allow natural light to penetrate deeper into the interior space.

The materials palette is simple but rich, consisting of light-colored walls, French white ash millwork with a light natural finish, translucent glass panels, dark carpet, and black granite flooring in select areas. The dominant ends and central area are easily noticed from a distance due to the change in flooring material from carpet to polished stone. Artwork is featured as an integral part of design and plays an important role in the project, providing focal points of different sizes and intensity (Figure CS10.5).

Beyond the richly articulated corridors, the project also features exquisitely comfortable and pleasing gathering places. Figure CS10.6a shows a comfortable lounge area outside a conference room anchored by a great big painting on the wall. Figure CS10.6b shows the principal lounge space, known as "the club," whose furnishings, tactful lighting scheme, rich materials, and artwork help to make it special.

REVIEW

Summary

Successful design requires a cyclical design process involving successive, ever more refined solutions to the design problem. The ultimate goal in the end is total resolution of the project or full synthesis.

Resolution starts with the floor plan, which must evolve from the original organizational concept to a fully functional composition. In addition to making the concept work, the floor plan needs to be refined and resolved.

Proper resolution requires the achievement of harmony. Three crucial aspects of harmony are the appropriate use of scale, the skillful use of proportion, and the achievement of balanced compositions. Scale can be considered in relation to the size and proportions of human beings, in relation to the particular design application being executed, and in relation to learned expectation of size concerning the elements in a space. Scale can also be measured in relation to the size of the entire project, in the relation of specific contents to the space in which they are housed, and in the relation of certain contents to other contents in the space.

Proportion is concerned with the relationship of elements to the composition they are a part of. Balance is the third requirement for harmony. A composition is said to be balanced if all the components are in perceptual equilibrium. Symmetrical compositions have been used since antiquity. They feature two equal sides, mirrored on either side of a central vertical axis. Asymmetrical compositions are a more recent phenomenon. They are more difficult to balance than symmetrical ones. They can rely on some repetition and alignments to give them coherence or they can be totally free of repetition and alignment.

In addition to harmony, the other essential for proper resolution is unity. Unity occurs at many levels. It is useful to distinguish between unity within a scene and unity within an entire project. Unity within a scene relies on similarity, proximity, enclosure, consistency of approach, and complementary composition. Unity within an entire project requires a strong and cohesive organizational concept to provide a unified structure. Beyond structural unity a project needs to look consistent. This is done through the employment of continuity and repetition. Repetition strategies include consistent repetition, sporadic repetition, gradation, and dispersion.

To a great extent, harmony and unity rely on similarity and repetition; however, it is important to remember that harmonious and unified projects are not good if they are also dull and boring. It is necessary to provide enough variety to achieve a reasonable level of interest according to the type of project being designed. This calls for a calculated departure from the easy and predictable design tendencies toward regularity.

1. William Kleinsasser, "Synthesis 9: A Comprehensive Theory Base for Architecture" (1995), 255.
2. Vitruvius, *The Ten Books on Architecture* (New York: Dover Publications, 1960), 13.
3. Ibid., 13.
4. Ibid., 13–14.
5. Ibid., 14.
6. Frank Lloyd Wright, *In the Realm of Ideas* (Carbondale, IL: Southern Illinois University Press, 1988), 20.
7. Robert Venturi, *Complexity and Contradiction in Architecture* (New York: Museum of Modern Art, 1977), 88.
8. Eugene Raskin, *Architecturally Speaking* (New York: Reinhold Publishing, 1954), 25.
9. Pierre Von Meiss, *Elements of Architecture: From Form to Place* (London: Van Nostrand Reinhold International, 1990), 31–54.
10. Raskin, 32.
11. Venturi, 88.

Chapter Questions

1. Name two basic goals that need to be considered during the process of resolving the floor plan of a project.
2. Related to design, what is the difference between size and scale?
3. As a designer, you need to be able to use scale in two different ways. What are the two ways presented in this chapter?
4. Give an example of scale manipulation related to the human figure (other than the ones presented in this chapter).
5. Name an example of appropriate scale as related to design application.
6. Give an example of scale manipulation related to element type (other than the ones presented in this chapter).
7. Give one example of scale of content in relation to the space in which it is housed.
8. Name an example of scale of an element in relation to other similar elements in the space.
9. State some of the reasons presented in this chapter for the manipulation of scale.
10. Explain how proportion differs from scale.
11. Name the three well-known systems of proportion discussed in this chapter.
12. Does proper scale and proportion ensure good balance? Why or why not?
13. Explain why the focus ahead is important in the composition of symmetrical two-dimensional compositions of vertical surfaces.
14. What is the ideal placement of the approach path toward symmetrically composed elevations?
15. In what ways can complexity and intricacy be added to symmetrical compositions?
16. What would be a feasible way to produce an intentionally imperfect symmetrical elevation?
17. In what kind of instance is a symmetrical composition of elevations not fully perceptible?
18. Describe a way to produce formality in asymmetrical composition.
19. What compositional device would you use to increase regularity in an asymmetrical elevation?
20. Is achieving unity between a project and the building in which it is housed necessary?
21. What strategies can you use to achieve unity within a single scene?
22. In what ways can continuity be utilized to produce unity between different spaces of a project?
23. In what ways can repetition be used to produce unity between different spaces of a project?
24. Give some examples of how you might use the techniques of gradation and dispersion to foster unity in a project.
25. Why is excessive regularity problematic? What can you do about it?

CHAPTER 11
Modifiers of Interior Space

INSTRUCTIONAL OBJECTIVES

- Explain the role of lighting in creating mood.
- Explain the role of lighting in enhancing three-dimensionality.
- Describe ways in which lighting helps to create focal areas.
- Explain how lighting can help to animate sequences.
- Present how designers can respond to daylighting.
- Explain how designers can manipulate acoustical properties for effect.
- Suggest strategies to manipulate the thermal and olfactory environments.
- Explain the important role of furniture arrangements in dictating use patterns.
- Present the role of finishes in providing character and tactile experiences.
- Comment on the symbolic and associative powers of color.
- Explain the important role of detailing in providing specific expressions.
- Explain the effects of people and goods in the interior mix.

SPACE AND ITS ENCLOSING surfaces are incomplete by themselves. The task of design involves not only the creation of space but requires that space be properly revealed and enhanced through light, texture, pattern, and color. Referring to architecture in general, Simon Unwin makes a useful distinction between its **basic elements**, those that establish place, and what he calls **modifying elements**. "In their physical realization and our actual experience of them," he explains, "basic elements and the places they identify are modified: by light, by colour, by sounds, by temperature, by air movement, by smells (and even possibly by tastes), by the qualities and textures of the materials used, by use, by scale, by the effects and experience of time."[1] The focus of this chapter is on these modifying elements of space.

Light not only allows us to clearly see form and shape but it can also be used to accentuate forms, textures, and colors. Materials are chosen not only for their durability or economy. Beyond their basic properties they also possess unique personalities and characteristics that carry strong connotations and give space unique qualities. The meaning of materials is seldom neutral. Colors have immense powers of their own, and their qualities influence the totality of space. They are like a hypersensitive musical instrument whose effect is dependent on the skill of the performer. Results can be quiet and gentle or loud and aggressive, and they can also be painful.

It is not the intent of this chapter to cover any of these modifying elements in great depth. These are complicated subjects having their own extensive body of literature. The aim here is to review some of the contributions they make to the goals of providing order, enrichment, and expression in interior projects.

AMBIENT ELEMENTS

Ambient elements are environmental elements, such as lighting conditions, acoustics, thermal properties, and even odors, inherent in any work of architecture. Whether meticulously controlled or left to chance, they are always present and influence the way interior environments are experienced. They particularly affect the level of comfort of a space. While you may be aware of the importance of lighting in interiors, you may not have thought much about how the acoustic and thermal environments can be manipulated to enhance the experience of space users. In this section we look at lighting, acoustics, the thermal environment, and odors.

Lighting

You are surely aware of the importance of lighting in interiors and know some of the basic strategies for lighting interior space. Important considerations include having sufficient light levels for the needs of a space, avoiding glare, and selecting the correct light coloring. We will not focus on these practical matters here; instead, we would like to focus on aspects of lighting we consider important in the production of rich and expressive projects. Through thoughtful response to project needs and the manipulation of light, it is possible to heighten sensory experience and enhance the spatial experience.

We would like you to start thinking beyond supplying adequate light levels and an agreeable pattern of fixtures on the ceiling. Lighting, if used correctly, will help you to produce spatial crispness, create evocative surfaces, make objects more expressive, and achieve engaging sequences. Lighting can also be used to create drama and particular moods.

Light, Mood, and Use

The influence of lighting on the mood of a place is well known to most of us. Lighting can make its mood intimate, solemn, cheerful, or festive. One obvious variable is the brightness level of the light in a space. In general, brightly lit spaces will tend to be perceived as more cheerful and dimly lit spaces will be perceived as solemn or gloomy; however, dimly lit spaces, if accented with pools of light, can also be dramatic despite the overall low level of illumination (Figure 11.1). Our perception of the appropriateness of a particular brightness level depends on the case. A dimly lit office space is likely to be annoying, but so is a brightly lit nightclub. The difference between light levels that promote a feeling of solemnity and one of gloom, for example, is a delicate one. Typically, if a place does not seem illuminated enough for the type of activity that occurs in it, our perception is that someone made a mistake. If, on the other hand, a dimly lit space, despite the low level of light, seems bright enough to conduct the intended activities, and if the low level of light appears to correspond to a desirable mood, the perception will be one of proper fit (Figure 11.2).

In the case of the nightclub it is slightly different. There, one expects a low level of light. While lighting in, say, the dance floor can be busy and colorful with laser beams crossing in all directions, the general ambient light of the space has to be low or the application will seem wrong for the space. Interestingly, though, the same requirements would not apply to a dance hall for afternoon ballroom dancing. There, one would most likely expect a relatively high level of illumination.

Other factors contributing to the mood created by lighting conditions include the brightness of the light at the source, the size of the source, the number of sources, and whether it appears that the lighting scheme is complete. If a restaurant dining room features candles at the tables, we automatically perceive the intent for an intimate environment. We notice that lighting has been considered and addressed at every table, and we accept the low level of light. Furthermore, the bright and cheerful sparkle of the individual candles, however small, adds a certain life to the scene. By contrast, if the same restaurant featured only one large central ceiling fixture intended to

Figure 11.1: This restaurant scene, while relatively dark, gives a sense of theatrical drama because of the lighting effects produced by the spotlights.

Figure 11.2: The relatively low light level in this restaurant is intentional, resulting in an intimate and relaxed ambiance.

light the entire room, and if the level of light produced by that fixture was low to simulate the dimness of a candlelit space, the feeling produced would likely be one of gloom and inadequate lighting. It would seem like more fixtures were necessary, or that the wattage on the one fixture was too low.

One of the main factors used to judge the success of a lighting scheme is the function of the space and the relationship between the lighting scheme and the intended use. In addition to the issue of mood, lighting levels and quality of light are also important to the performance of the activities in the space. While a painter or a jeweler may need a bright studio of diffuse, evenly distributed light, a group having dinner may prefer an overall low level of light, with perhaps a dedicated, narrow-beam accent light over the table (for function and intimacy) and another accent light illuminating a piece of art on an adjacent wall (for drama).

Light-Enhancing Form

It's no secret that light helps reveal form. To reveal form it is more important to light surfaces than to light the air space. A room with moderate ambient lighting and well-lit enclosing surfaces (walls and/or ceiling) will appear to be brighter and better illuminated than one with higher ambient lighting but poorly lit enclosing surfaces. The illumination of the walls in the conference room shown in Figure 11.3 helps this interior room appear well illuminated despite the generally low level of light over the table.

Beyond just revealing form, light can also enhance it. When you have a mass in space, say a rectangular room,

its shape is perceived mostly by the lines that outline its shape and the different light values on the different planes. Compare the two drawings in Figure 11.4. Even though the receding perspective lines are identical in both cases, the level of value contrast between the different planes expresses their three-dimensionality differently. The object shown in Figure 11.4b is enhanced as a three-dimensional shape by sharper value contrast at the corner and the stronger shadows. This effect can even be emphasized, intentionally, by purposefully increasing the lighting level on one side to produce a greater value contrast.

Another similar strategy is the use of strong light coming from a consistent angle to produce strong shadows. We see the effect of such a scheme regularly outdoors, where the angle of the sun high above remains consistent in relation to the masses below. Consequently, the pattern of brightness, shade, and shadow remains consistent through the scene. Although the light sources inside are never high up enough to achieve this effect from a single source, the placement of a row of sources in relation to masses in space can achieve this effect, as shown in Figure 11.5.

Light has the capacity to accentuate textures. Surfaces and objects, whether a small sculpture, a detail, or a rough vertical surface, have particular characteristics based on the turns, twists, protrusions, and recesses in them. When these qualities are emphasized through lighting, their three-dimensionality becomes richer. It is the presence of highlight, shade, and shadow that make three-dimensional objects and surfaces come to life. Sidelighting usually works best to illuminate surfaces with texture or relief as well as sculptural pieces and details. It accentu-

Figure 11.3: Rooms, even if dimly lit, will appear livelier if their enclosing surfaces are well illuminated.

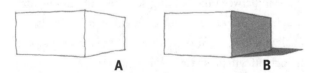

A   **B**

Figure 11.4: Lighting helps to enhance the three-dimensionality of objects and masses in space. The featureless room corner shown in (a) comes to life in (b) with the addition of sharper value contrast and shadows created by lighting.

Figure 11.5: By the consistent placement of light fixtures in relation to these two interior masses, it is possible to simulate the uniform patterns of shade and shadow produced by daylight outdoors.

A

B

Figure 11.6: Lighting helps to accentuate focal features. The central graphic in (a) and the display cases in (b) come to life as a result of the focused light falling on them.

ates the light and shaded spots created by the particular shapes and textures. In some applications it is necessary to add secondary (softer) lighting on the shaded side so it doesn't become too dark, unless a high contrast is intentionally desired. This rule of thumb, however, does not always work. In cases where the articulations or relief of a surface have a definite orientation, say a horizontal one, lighting from above (grazing) may be more successful in accentuating light, shade, and shadow.

One type of lighting approach that takes away from the three-dimensionality of objects and surfaces is straight-on lighting. Straight-on lighting tends to illuminate the object or surface too uniformly because of the lack of shade and shadow. This produces a washed-out, flat effect. For the same reasons, when illuminating an entire room or space, it is best to avoid uniform lighting from above if you are seeking textural richness. Uniform lighting from above produces almost no shade and shadow, thus creating scenes that are well lit but not very dramatic. Common examples of this phenomenon can be seen regularly outdoors, where the direct light at midday produces far less interesting results than the angular light in the early morning or late afternoon.

Light-Creating Foci

One common application of light is its use to establish or accentuate focal elements. It can achieve this by highlighting an existing focal object or by creating effects with enough magnetism of their own to become foci. Typical examples of the first application include the use of accent

Figure 11.7: Sometimes entire surfaces, such as the ceiling shown here, become focal points because of the bright light purposefully directed at them.

lighting on artwork or merchandise. In these cases, the focal object already exists. It has been located and framed perfectly, and all it needs is local accent lighting to make it stand out even more. Figure 11.6 shows two examples. In Figure 11.6a the accent lighting on the central graphic increases its effectiveness as a focus. The two jewelry display cases shown in Figure 11.6b feature internal lighting, which makes the contents shine brightly in contrast to the darker surroundings.

Brightness in itself can create a sense of focus. It is possible to light an entire plane (such as a wall or ceiling) to highlight it. In this case, the entire surface becomes a prominent feature of the space, such as the ceiling in Figure 11.7. Similarly, it is possible to illuminate a smaller surface brightly and, thus, convert it into a magnetic focal feature. This focal effect can be produced by the brightness

Figure 11.8: Focused brightness, especially when seen in relation to darker surroundings, always attracts the eye. In this example, the dark bottles placed against the bright background create a strong effect.

Figure 11.9: Space can be defined by light alone, as is done regularly in the theater. This space is created by the area defined by bright lighting seen against a contrasting dark surrounding.

Figure 11.10: The effect produced by the concealed uplighting in this example is cleaner and more dramatic than it would be if the light source were visible.

itself without the use of any other complementary features such as artwork. Whereas in the case of a single piece of art the lighting frames it closely, in the case of illuminating a surface, the lighting needs to cover the entire featured section evenly. A dramatic example of a brightly lit segment of wall is the bar display shown in Figure 11.8. The brightness of the backlighting, the contrast created by the darker bottles seen as silhouettes, and the brightness of the TV monitors above make this the focal point of the entire space.

It is possible to create not just a light surface but a **light space**. The resulting effect is somewhat more theatrical. In fact, it is commonly used in the theater. A light space is a volume of space defined by light, not by walls or solid elements. It is achieved by the use of bright lights with sharp cut-off angles within a very dark background. The result is a light shape defined by the pattern of light visible against the dark background (Figure 11.9).

Another important consideration about lighting, aside from the light itself, is the source. Light sources range from the totally concealed, which reveal only the light they produce (Figure 11.10), to fixtures that are seen and whose appearance makes a design statement either as a single object or a composition of several ones (Figure 11.11). Combinations of different sources are also common. One application seen regularly is the use of fixtures that are visible, but, because of their simple shape, moderate size, well-planned placement, and type of mounting (usually fully recessed), blend in and contribute positively to the space. Figure 11.12 shows two examples. Light

Figure 11.11: The numerous suspended light fixtures in the store in (a) are a prominent feature of this space. They have an assertive presence. Yet, their relatively high placement and their delicate proportions result in a balanced and pleasant composition. Similarly, the five suspended pendants in the bookstore shown in (b), despite their strong presence, are balanced and do not take over the space. Notice the different effects produced by the various sizes and number of fixtures in these two examples.

Figure 11.12: The fully recessed lights in these examples have a nonobtrusive presence. Their size, spacing, and flush mounting contribute to the balanced composition and help them blend in.

fixtures, as objects, are part of the overall visual composition we see, together with ceilings, walls, spaces, and other objects. Depending on the size, shape, number, and pattern of the fixtures, the two-dimensional composition created at the ceiling plane will take on a different character (Figure 11.13).

Light Animating Sequences and Projects

We have previously argued for the desirability of having engaging sequences in projects. We talked about these sequences in spatial terms, with space becoming progressively (or suddenly) narrower, wider, lower, or taller. Another way of achieving or reinforcing such variations is through lighting. A low corridor opening to a large volume may be dark in addition to being low. The space it opens up to may be bright in addition to being large (Figure 11.14). When the light level changes, the eye requires a period of adaptation to adjust to the new lighting condition. Once adjusted, the vision is stabilized. With this in mind, you can plan your variations to be sudden and radical for high drama or gradual for a mellower effect. The potential uses of lighting for special effects and engaging sequences should not be underestimated. As with other manipulative aspects of design, these attempts can be risky and, therefore, require proper execution for success. It is advisable to take courses in lighting and to collaborate

Figure 11.13: The design of lighting patterns on the ceiling requires that we revisit the basics of two-dimensional composition. Possibilities vary widely, depending on whether we use many small point sources (a), a group of a few large point sources (b), or rows of linear sources (c).

MODERATE | DARKER | BRIGHT

Figure 11.14: The addition of lighting effects to engaging spatial sequences can add drama to the experience. One of many scenarios is to highlight large volumes by brightness and make small passages darker, like caves.

Figure 11.15: The brightness of natural light is cheerful and inspiring. The glowing quality of this waiting area is due mostly to the brightness produced by the natural lighting that gets in through the skylight above.

Figure 11.16: In this scene at an airport we can see the effects of early morning natural light penetrating a space. On the left side, we see the dramatic effects produced by the long shadows from the columns. On the right side, close to the windows, we see the intensity of the light coming in.

with experienced and trusted lighting consultants until you learn to manipulate light for effect on your own.

Before we leave the subject of artificial light, we will suggest that the lighting in a project, because of its significance and extent, requires some planning of its own. Once the floor plan is decided, at least preliminarily, you can start formulating a lighting concept for the space. You can start defining the areas that require general light, the walls that need emphasizing, the focal points that require reinforcement, and the areas deserving special effects or detailing. In general, you should avoid rigid uniform lighting schemes throughout entire projects unless a specific circumstance calls for it. Although possibly well suited as a solution from an engineering point of a view, such a scheme would seldom produce the most interesting visual scene.

Daylighting

You may wonder why someone who designs interior spaces needs to be concerned with a light source over which he or she has no control. While it is true that you cannot control natural light, and while it is also true that the space in which you are to design a project is likely

to be existing (including the windows that let the light in), there are a few things you can do. The key is how you respond to given factors such as site exposure and the natural lighting characteristics of the site. Proper response will help you avoid potential problems on the one hand and take advantage of opportunities on the other.

While you cannot control nature and the orientation of the existing building where your project is housed, you can control where particular rooms and functions of the project go. Exposure to exterior natural light becomes one of the many criteria that affect where you place particular areas of the project (together with hierarchy, ease of access, heat, and so on). In a project with multiple exposures you have to decide who gets the morning light, who gets the afternoon light, who gets the side with the large windows, and who gets indirect, northern light. In some cases you can even have natural light coming from above. The cheerful mood of the waiting area shown in Figure 11.15 is due to the natural light it gets throughout the day via a large skylight above.

The rooms on the east and west sides of a project get direct, natural light in the morning and afternoon, respectively. If unblocked, light will penetrate deep into the space creating dramatic effects, or intolerable glare, depending on the nature of the spaces, their functions, and the arrangement (Figure 11.16). Rooms facing south will also get some direct light coming in, although the angle of the sun will be higher and the light won't penetrate as deeply. This light is bright and warm and is likely to be welcomed

Figure 11.17: The type of window coverings used affects not only the quantity and characteristics of the light coming in but also the nature of the exterior view allowed. The translucent screens in (a) let light in but block views to the exterior. The drapes in (b) filter light coming in but also allow filtered views to the exterior.

Figure 11.18: The rhythmic effects produced by the interplay of penetrating daylight and regularly spaced vertical elements often produce dramatic effects.

less in summer than in winter. Northern light, in contrast, is diffuse, never direct and, therefore, softer. Since some of it is reflected from the atmosphere, it is also bluish. This kind of light is good for rooms involving tasks requiring uniform, shadowless, and glareless lighting, such as art studios. In addition to decisions about the placement of rooms in relation to orientation, the placement of objects in the room in relation to incoming natural light is also important. Depending on the situation and specific conditions, the proper response may be putting a comfortable chair next to a window, or a desk looking away from it.

Other than the placement of spaces in relation to exposure, designers often have control over how light is blocked or filtered into the space by internal shades, screens, and other devices. Not only do screens and blinds satisfy practical needs such as keeping unwanted harsh light out, they also present opportunities to create special effects with light, ranging from the sensual effect of soft light screened through screens or drapes (Figure 11.17), to the creation of rhythmic effects with streaks and shadows through the use of intermittent columns or other vertical elements placed rhythmically (Figure 11.18). Related to this idea is the strategy of employing objects of particular shapes, sometimes in some sort of pattern, close to windows receiving direct light so that they will cast interesting shadows in the space.

In projects with bright spaces resulting from the presence of openings receiving natural daylight, designers have to make important decisions about how to treat the surfaces of the room and how to complement the natural daylight with artificial light. In rooms with dark surfaces and relatively small windows exposed to daylight, for instance, the light will not bounce around. When the

Figure 11.19: Designers have to control the relationship of incoming brightness and interior ambient brightness to produce acceptable conditions. The general darkness of this room intensifies the brightness of the light penetrating the room through the large window in the background, producing a glaring effect when you first enter.

sun is shining, the window areas will appear very bright and the dark wall surfaces, in contrast, will tend to appear quite dark (Figure 11.19). A fair amount of supplementary artificial lighting will be needed inside the room to produce an adequate and balanced level of lighting.

By contrast, if a room with a generous area of glass windows receiving natural light is finished with light surfaces, the incoming light will tend to bounce around and get distributed throughout the space. In this case, the entire zone close to the windows will be brightly illuminated naturally, with the drop-off occurring gradually deeper into the space. Here, fewer artificial light fixtures will be necessary to supplement the lighting, at least during the daytime hours.

Acoustics

Acoustics are an important component of our sensory environment; however, the use of acoustics for effect in interiors remains relatively unexplored. In design schools, students are typically exposed to practical acoustical concerns, such as how to control the transmission of unwanted sounds (i.e., noise) from one space to another, how to prevent unwanted echoes, and so on. Although these are important considerations of design that one should be familiar with, our goal here is slightly different.

We want you to increase your awareness of the sounds that make places unique and to learn about ways in which the acoustical properties of places can enrich the experiences in them. There are not too many types of sounds we hear in interior environments. Among these are the voices of people talking around us (far or near), the sounds of footsteps (loud or muffled), background music, ringing telephones, intercom systems, honking horns and sirens outside, the clicking sounds of glasses and plates at the table, the sounds of paper shuffling, and so on. These are the sounds of our daily lives. Some of them are more pleasant than others, and some of them can be controlled better than others. Although the categories are few, the variations and combinations are infinite.

Every type of place has its own recurring and expected sounds. In the office we hear phones ringing, people talking, receptionists answering incoming calls, and papers shuffling. In the restaurant we hear the sound of silverware, glasses, plates, human voices, and, often, background music. At the movies, the sounds of the screen dominate. At the library, we may hear the whispered conversations of people nearby. At the nightclub, there better be loud music! The job of the designer is to decide what is desirable and may need to be emphasized and what is bothersome and may need to be toned down or even suppressed.

As a designer, you have control over the zoning of functions, the way you place and construct barriers between spaces, and the way you use materials having distinct acoustical properties. Using zoning, barriers, and acoustical materials, loud areas can be located away from quiet ones, sound barriers can be used between adjacent areas, and the acoustical liveliness within any one given space can be manipulated. The zoning of functions and the construction of separating walls are fairly simple and straightforward design tasks. Trickier, and more exciting, is manipulating the acoustical properties of individual spaces.

Sound Properties of Individual Spaces

When it comes to the acoustics of individual spaces, the common tendency is to respond to concerns about loudness by adding absorptive materials to dampen the sounds. While there is nothing inherently wrong with this approach, designers commonly encounter two types of problems, both resulting from the indiscriminate overall application of the treatment. The first problem is that certain areas where sounds may not need to be muffled are muffled. The second problem is lack of environmental (in this case, acoustical) variety.

The sound in certain places doesn't need to be muted. Lively places need to sound lively. This applies to the casual restaurant or tavern, the sports bar, and the discotheque, among others. Beyond these overall environments, there are partial environments within other, less lively, settings that don't need to be severely muffled. Arrival areas, public corridors, and break areas in office buildings, healthcare facilities, and other such settings can benefit from a moderate amount of acoustic liveliness. The opposite is also true. Institutional settings, with all those solid, easy-to-maintain hard (and loud!) materials, can benefit from the incorporation of absorptive materials in some areas to reduce the sound levels. This increases local comfort by reducing loudness in those areas and also enhances the overall environment by providing variety between areas.

In order to manipulate the acoustics of individual spaces, the main acoustic concept you need to understand and know how to apply is reverberation. **Reverberation time** is the amount of time it takes for sound to decay in space. In environments having hard surfaces, sound will bounce around for a while and take some time to decay. In these spaces, sound will linger, sometimes producing an echo when it bounces back and forth between two parallel walls. In environments having materials that absorb sound, such as upholstered furniture, curtains, carpet, and acoustic ceiling tiles, a greater amount of sound will be absorbed. Consequently, it will decay rapidly, producing an acoustically muted space.

The other important variable related to reverberation, in addition to absorption, is spatial volume. The greater the spatial volume of a space, the longer the sound will be sustained. Therefore, for acoustically lively areas, think of volume and hard materials. If you need quiet rooms, use soft, sound-absorbing materials and smaller volumes. Since volume manipulations are often difficult to justify in common interior projects, you may often have to rely on manipulations of the levels of absorption.

The challenge of these seemingly simple acoustic ideas is knowing exactly how to apply them. What is the correct mix of volume and materials, for instance, if you want a moderately lively space? For the designer wanting to explore and experiment with these subtle and tricky aspects of design (and engineering!) it is advisable to work closely with an acoustic consultant until a reasonable amount of familiarity is attained. These types of manipulations, while worthwhile, are also risky. An unsuccessful attempt can have negative consequences and make a client quite upset. It is little wonder, thus, that the tendency is to stay within the safe norms and avoid taking unnecessary risks.

In general, your goal should be to let lively areas be acoustically lively, to ensure that the sound in areas needing quiet is dampened, and to strike an overall healthy balance, appropriate to the type of environment, between the two. With acoustics, as with space and lighting, environmental variety is desirable. The thing to remember is that you can use acoustics to help create experientially rich sequences. Imagine a space, a restaurant entrance for instance, that progresses acoustically in response to footsteps and other acoustic stimuli, from lively, high-

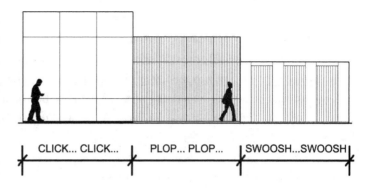

Figure 11.20: The sounds produced by materials can be an important contributor to dramatic experiential sequences. In this example, the flooring material of the individual spaces will accentuate or dampen the sound of footsteps. Additionally, the surrounding surfaces can heighten the effect by being more or less reflective or absorptive.

pitched tones, to lively and warmer (lower) tones, to a quieter muffled area as you enter the formal dining hall (Figure 11.20).

Other Environmental Factors

We will explore two other environmental factors briefly: the thermal properties of places and the olfactory properties of places. While these originate from sources over which you as the designer exercise relatively little control, certain manipulations are sometimes possible to enhance the overall effects produced.

The Thermal Environment

The control of the thermal environment falls under the domain of the mechanical engineer, not the interior designer or architect. The engineer's task is to design mechanical systems that will produce thermally comfortable environments. The problem with the typical solution is the same as with other engineered solutions, namely the tendency to treat entire projects uniformly, with no variety, producing projects of constant, unvarying temperature, humidity, and ventilation. Here we make the same case made for lighting and acoustics: Variety of environmental (in this case, thermal) conditions can make our experience of places richer. This advice comes with an important caveat, however: When it comes to the thermal environment, it is crucial to stay within the accepted comfort zone for that type of environment. Otherwise, the resulting discomfort will overshadow any gains from the variety of conditions produced and is sure to generate many complaints.

There are a few things designers can do to enhance thermal experiences in their projects. They require the assistance of the mechanical engineer. If you want to produce a space that is open and airy, a common request of clients, you could supplement your open space with a genuine airy experience. All you need to do is ask your mechanical engineer to supply extra fresh air ventilation to the room to account for the extra volume. While not always a justifiable request, where it can be implemented, it can result in a very comfortable interior environment because of the higher-than-normal volume of fresh ventilation.

It is sometimes desirable to manipulate the temperature in certain rooms for special reasons. A slightly cold conference room, for instance, will help to keep attendees awake during an early morning meeting. One thing you can do without the help of engineers is to complement the desired thermal character of the room (warm or cold) with materials, colors, and lighting having corresponding connotations. If the goal is warmth, use soft materials, warm colors, and yellowish lighting. If the goal is coldness, use hard, smooth materials, cool colors, and bluish lighting.

People generally enjoy spaces that provide comfort, especially warmth. One possible strategy, especially during climate extremes, is to create one important public space in a project that has very comfortable thermal properties (i.e., warmth in the winter and coolness in the summer). This could be a major break room or meeting room. This room would then become a popular destination and would acquire a special status because of the comfort associated with it. You could even make the sequence of getting to this area an experience in itself, using not only thermal properties, but also color, lighting, and acoustics to gradually build up the experience until you reach the epicenter of comfort.

The Olfactory Environment

Finally, we wish to say something about the way places smell. This is another variable where the potential interventions by the designer are limited. While certain materials, such as leather and polished wood, have their own peculiar smell, the smells in places are mostly a result of the goods and people in those places. Many places lack distinct smells, but certain spaces do have strong smells associated with them. These include restaurants, coffee shops, cookie shops, bakeries, soap and perfume shops,

flower shops, and even movie theaters. The desirable smells from these places are very much a part of their essence. Consequently, your task as a designer is to take advantage of these natural enhancers. This can be achieved by placing areas with particularly attractive smells in strategic locations in order to attract people, or simply delight passersby. Another possibility is to concentrate, even exaggerate the smells (often through mechanical means) in strategic places to make them acquire a magnetic effect. It is no accident that businesses like cookie shops direct the air from their kitchen exhausts into the public areas outside. Who, after all, can resist the tempting smell of a freshly baked cookie when it is directed at them?

INTERIOR DECORATIVE ELEMENTS

Interior decorative elements are exclusively decorative and, thus, play no major functional role in the design. They do, nevertheless, play a crucial role in enriching and giving expression to interior environments. We could say these are the types of elements that literally dress up a project. Included in this group are finishes, color, pattern, and ornament.

Finishes

You are likely to be fairly familiar with interior finishes by now. Even nondesigners cannot escape them, having to make choices about how to paint the walls and select the rugs and cushions for their homes. Previous design school projects have most likely required the selection of finishes. You are likely to use particular finishes because you like the way they look and they are in the family of colors you have decided to use for a project.

A major consideration of finish selection is aesthetics. Selections made have a strong impact on the nature of places. They help to determine a stylistic direction for your project, establishing a specific visual character. A project may take on a formal character, or have traditional or modernistic tendencies, because of the choice of finish. Dark woods and heavily patterned carpets will convey an entirely different character than glass, marble, and stainless steel. Materials allow you to get to a level of stylistic specificity often difficult, or impractical, to achieve by form alone. Compare the two very different looks produced by the two material palettes shown in Figure 11.21.

Beyond this broad overall distinction there are other choices possible depending on desired nuance, personal preferences, and other qualifications. In the example of the dark wood and heavily patterned carpet mentioned above, for instance, there are many possibilities. Woods and carpets are available in different varieties that would fit the descriptions of dark and heavily patterned. What is the wood type? What kind of veneer cut is being specified? Is it stained? What finish system is being used for the woodwork? How is the carpet patterned? Is there a motif? What is the size of the repeating patterns? Is it simple or complex? The answers to all these questions will produce a much more specific look for these finishes. They help to define the stylistic direction more precisely and they also force you to think about qualities you may, or may not, want for their own sake, independent of stylistic considerations, such as more or less intricacy or more or less texture.

Materials and Their Finishes

Individual materials have unique inherent qualities. They also acquire other specific qualities based on the way they are manufactured and finished. The hardness of stone, the brittleness of glass, the shine of metals, and the textures of wood are all inherent in materials. Designers need to understand these inherent qualities in order to use these materials appropriately and emphasize their best qualities. Beyond these inherent qualities, materials acquire qualities based on their manufacturing processes and the way in which they are finished. Consequently, the graining of wood will be different depending on how it is cut (Figure 11.22), the texture of carpet will be different depending on how it is constructed, and the sheen level of stone will vary depending on how it is finished.

Figure 11.21 One of the main functions of the material palette used in a project is to give it a certain characteristic flavor. The prominent use of stainless steel in (a) produces a refined and clean contemporary look, while the abundant use of wood in (b) produces a formal and dignified look.

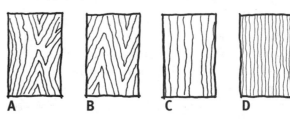

Figure 11.22 Not all woods look the same. In fact, the variety within the world of wood is enormous. One important source of variety is the way wood veneers are sliced. Different cuts will produce different graining effects. Compare the graining characteristics of rotary slicing (a), plain slicing (b), quarter slicing (c), and rift cutting (d).

Figure 11.23 Notice the three different effects produced by simple manipulations of tile and grout placement in tile floors. Drawing (a) shows an ordinary checkerboard pattern. In drawing (b), the scale is doubled by changing the size of the squares (while using the same tile size). In drawing (c), two patterns are superimposed on each other, one being the pattern created by the tiles, and the other, the pattern created by the unconventional use of grout between the tiles (shown by the darker lines).

The effect of finishes will also vary depending on its modularity. A composition with a few large pieces will look and feel very different from one with many small ones. Modular flooring produces different results, depending on the size of the pieces used. It is possible to manipulate the sense of scale by manipulating the pattern of the tiles and even the grouts (Figure 11.23).

Figure 11.24 The size of the repeating units, the density of repeat, and the contrast of the colors, values, and shapes used all make important contributions to the final effect of a patterned field. The floor in (a) features a dense pattern of small pieces in four different values, producing a rich and busy effect. The floor in (b) features larger units grouped in ways that create subpatterns. Blank spaces between them and less value variation produce a less-busy effect than the one in (a). Floor (c), despite the repetition of the stripes, does not contain identical repeating units. Every stripe is different, and the overall size of each unit is much larger than those in the other two examples.

Figure 11.25 Texture and pattern can be used to produce subtle or bold results. Compare the understated effect of the stair scene in (a) with the busier effect of the movie theater lobby shown in (b).

Certain finishes, such as textiles, usually have a pattern. The type of pattern, its size, shape, and content will all affect the final character of the finish. A large floral pattern of vivid, highly contrasting colors may delight some and offend others. A small, abstract, geometric pattern of subdued, low-contrast colors may please many and bore some. The varieties possible are enough to suit every conceivable taste. Patterns and modular arrangements may have more or less uniformity from one piece to the next. The size of the pattern, frequency of repetition, and contrast between adjacent pieces affect the overall look and many different effects are possible. Consider the different effects produced by the three floor patterns shown in Figure 11.24. Texture and pattern are two of the most important sources of articulation in interior environments. The amount and nature of the texture and pattern used will have a significant impact on the visual character and load level of the environment created (Figure 11.25).

The Feel of Materials

Other than their visual properties, materials have qualities associated with our sense of touch, such as hardness/softness, smoothness/roughness, and warmth/coldness. These are important considerations, and we have alluded to some of these before in the context of lighting and thermal qualities. The materials we walk on or otherwise touch are perhaps the most important because we are constantly in physical contact with them. A hard stone floor, a bouncy wood floor, a resilient rubber floor, and a soft, fluffy carpet not only look and sound different, they feel different! Here is one more aspect of design where criteria besides appearance and performance can be incorporated. If you really want to address the sensual aspects of your projects to enhance experience, how about playing with the degree of hardness and texture of the floor finish? The way materials feel when touched (real or imagined) is an important variable for consideration. Using the feel of materials to enrich experience should not be underestimated as one of the designer's strategies to create sense-rich qualities in projects.

The temperature of materials and finishes is an interesting consideration. On the one hand are the material's **thermal conduction** properties. Certain materials (such as metals and masonry) tend to absorb the cold or heat around them. The pleasantness of an aluminum bench, for instance, is relative. If the bench is located in a cold room during the winter but exposed to the sun's rays through a window, it can produce a very welcoming and satisfying warmth amid the cold. If the bench is located in the same room without the benefit of the warming sun or in a sunny, hot room it is likely to become too cold or hot for comfort, especially if experienced with bare skin.

Another aspect related to temperature is a material's ability to breathe, especially in the finishes we sit on or come in physical contact with. A natural textile or leather will breathe and allow air circulation through it while, say, plastic imitating leather will not. You will sweat when exposed directly to the plastic. Many of us have also experienced this phenomenon in relation to the fabric of the clothes we wear, natural ones being more comfortable than synthetic ones because of their ability to breathe.

Finally, there are the materials we come in contact with through our hands. These are the materials on doorknobs, handrails, and countertops. These also require some consideration and offer opportunities for sensual experience. Other than the relative level of pleasantness associated with the shape and proportions of the element, its temperature and texture will have some influence on the total experience, whether it is turning the doorknob or grabbing the handrail. Here again, the metals will be more thermally volatile than the woods. In terms of texture, the main distinction here is between smooth finishes and textured ones, whether regularly or randomly textured. Both

Figure 11.26 Texture, although experienced in more than just visual terms, does often contribute a strong visual statement, as shown here.

can be highly pleasurable and can be utilized at the discretion of the designer to achieve the desired effect. The smoothness of a polished metal handrail can produce a very pleasant experience when touched, but so can the reassuring effect of the good grip provided by the grainy textural effect on another handrail.

As suggested by the above example, it is clear that texture, in addition to the visual interest it produces (Figure 11.26), can be used favorably on materials that people come in contact with. It can work for us in two ways: by helping us increase users' spatial awareness, and, as we have seen, by helping us provide pleasant surfaces to come in contact with. The first strategy normally uses floor surfaces. You may have experienced the effect of encountering a highly textured part of a road while driving or of feeling a textured floor close to the platform edge when boarding a train in modern train and subway stations. In both these cases the objective is to alert us to potential nearby danger. When you feel the unusual bumpy texture under your tires or feet, you become more alert and pay more attention to the road, or to the end of the subway platform beyond. You can apply the same strategy even when there is no danger ahead. If you want to increase users' spatial awareness momentarily, you can change the floor texture, making it rough and/or bumpy.

Color

We could have included color in our discussion about finishes, because most color in interiors comes from the finishes selected for the project. However, color is an element of such power and impact that it deserves separate attention as a physical component of design. Color does a lot more than just decorate and beautify. This is an element that serves to define and articulate, thus contributing clarity and order in design. It is also an element that can have a great impact on our emotions and dictate the mood of a place. Thus, color is also an important instrument for enrichment. Additionally, color can be used in ways that make individuals and groups identify with it, making it invaluable to achieve or reinforce particular expressions.

Much of the color employed in architecture and interiors used to be inherent in the natural materials used for construction. The colors of projects were the colors of the available materials. There are many more choices now. These days, much of the color used in interiors is artificial. The colors of paints, plastic laminates, tiles, and textiles are manufactured according to what is fashionable at the time of production. A wide variety of color choices is available, giving designers ample latitude for color selection. There are still many natural materials whose color is inherently determined. Such is the case in wood and stone, for example. The color in most projects is usually a combination of materials with inherent colors and materials with artificial colors.

Figure 11.27 Color value alone can make a dramatic difference in the overall feel of an interior environment. Compare the difference between the light-colored environment shown in (a) with the much darker environment shown in (b).

Associations with Color

Color often has a strong impact on us. This is due to its power to evoke strong emotional responses and to the many associations we make in response to color. Different hues are said to have different effects on humans. Reds, for instance, tend to excite us and make us tense, while blues and greens have a calming effect. Yellows, on the other hand, excite us differently from reds because of the cheerfulness associated with them. Also important are the color's chroma and value. The greater the intensity of the color, the more it will excite, and the darker its value, the more somber a scene will get. The two scenes in Figure 11.27 show how value alone can create dramatic differences in environments. Compare the two very different moods in these two environments.

In addition to affecting our emotional states, color also influences us through some of the connotations associated with particular colors and their properties. Color brings with it associations with temperature, weight, and gender. We are all familiar with the distinction between cool and warm colors. The blues and greens are considered cool while the reds, oranges, and yellows are considered warm. Similarly, colors can feel heavy (dark colors) or light (light colors), and they can be masculine or feminine (brown and pink, respectively, at least in Western cultures).

Color carries symbolism developed through associations made over time. Therefore, we have colors that are associated with countries (red, white, and blue in the United States), school colors, colors of companies (red for Coca-Cola), and colors of organizations and clubs. Whatever the character and spirit of a person or group, whether light and lively or heavy and somber, it is possible to capture and express it through color.

Behavior of Color

The subject of color has fascinated many people throughout time, from artists to psychologists. A good deal of research has been done about color, and certain peculiarities about it have been identified. Other than the ones already mentioned, it has been determined that certain colors seem to advance toward us (warm colors), while others seem to recede and appear farther away (cool colors). This, with the relative lightness and darkness of the values used, will significantly affect our perception of the size of rooms and spaces. Perhaps one of the most significant findings about color concerns its relativity: Our perception of a particular color varies depending on what other color or colors it is seen against. The lightness or darkness of a color, as well as its warmth or coolness, will vary depending on the colors around it.

Using Color

Using color successfully requires sensitivity and appropriate response to existing conditions, knowledge about colors and their behavior, some intuition, and the ability to balance colors harmoniously. With color, what is appropriate in one case is not appropriate in another. It is one of the aspects of design requiring proper congruence between the personality of a project and the choices made. One interesting and challenging aspect of color in interior spaces is that you never see the total effect of your creation until it is all in place. As a designer, you hope that the resulting effect will be good, because once all the walls are painted or covered with applied finishes, and once all the furniture is in place with its colorful upholstery, it will be too late to recognize and change a mistake.

Context and Suitability

A great measure of the success of a color scheme in a project is dependent on the correspondence between the choices made and the physical context. Although there are many contexts with different levels of immediacy and influence, we want to focus first on what we could call **regional flavor**. We discussed the influence of the regional context in Chapter 9. Here we expand on that discussion, because color is one of the main ways designers seek good correspondence between a project and its regional context.

Some places, because of the physical characteristics of their landscape and/or regional or local cultures, develop their own native color palette. The coast, the desert, and the forest all have inherent colorings that suggest strongly what goes and doesn't go well with them. The colors of Florida are different from the colors of New Mexico or the colors of the American prairie. The colors of New Mexico, for instance, are affected by both the landscape character of the Southwest but also by the Native American cultural influences of the region. The landscape and architecture are characterized by the soft and cool earth tones of adobe, the sunbaked masonry units traditionally used for construction.

The architecture of the Southwest tends to blend with the desert background on which it sits. Doors, windows, and other architectural features are often painted with accent colors, such as white or blue, to add contrast and detail. Inside, textiles developed from the Native American traditions expand the palette, featuring white, grays, reds, and black. A local color palette has developed from these influences and projects done in the region, and while you are not obligated to follow these colors literally, you should at least understand the local palette as a point of departure.

Other than regional flavor, color responds to the context of the ebb and flow of ever-changing tastes and fashions. Every period in time has its own colors. The Victorian interiors of the nineteenth century replaced the light and airy color schemes of Georgian rooms with schemes featuring multichromatic, dark colors that made them formal and somber. The colors of the fifties by contrast were cheerful, sometimes light, often bold. Pastels were popular and colors such as pink, green, and turquoise became widely used. Also popular in interiors were the reds, oranges, and yellows of autumn, as the colors of outdoor materials were brought in to add warmth and texture.

Theory and Application

Any designer serious about the meaningful use of color in interiors must study color and become well acquainted with color theory. Theory of color, especially a good grasp of color harmony, is always a good point of reference. We do offer some words of caution about the use of color harmony systems, about the blind belief in the properties of color, and about the existing knowledge of colors' effects on humans.

Almost any color combination can be made to work if the right combinations and proportions are used. While understanding color theory is immensely helpful, it is possible to apply it unsuccessfully. Likewise, it is possible to deviate from color theory and achieve good results. While most of the basic properties of color you learned about in color theory classes have been shown to be true, it is possible to create effects that will contradict them. One example is the notion that warm colors advance and cool colors recede. Paul Zelanski and Mary Pat Fischer stress that "any color can be brought forward or pushed back in space by the visual clues to spatial organization given with it."[2]

Furthermore, while much is known about how color affects us, we must recognize, as Sinclair Gauldie has expressed, that color psychology "is a debatable land into which the psychologist himself ventures with caution, and only the painter, being guided by intuition and not accountable to science, can feel sure of his steps."[3] Whether the painter can be truly sure of his steps or not is itself debatable. The point is that, with color, there are no definite rules. The requirements of each project are so particular, and the effects of different color combinations so many, that, on the one hand, each project will have hundreds of approaches that are wrong but dozens that will work, some better than others. It is up to the designer to select which one to use.

Not only is it enough to have the right color palette for a project, the exact colors used and the way they are combined in space will also determine the success of the application. Therefore, proper consideration needs to be given to the relative sizes of color areas, their location, lighting conditions, the texture given to color, and what is placed next to what. The application of color in space is vastly different from its use on a piece of canvas or paper. In architectural space, the colors of a composition are sometimes touching, other times in proximity but not touching, and at times on opposite sides of the room! Just because two colors that are supposed to work together are in the same room does not guarantee they will achieve harmony. Their proportions and positions relative to one another have to be worked out in order for the application to be successful.

Color Strategies

Color is an important design tool. Many design strategies can be implemented successfully through the use of color. A few specific strategies follow:

- Use strong color to create focal areas. Accent colors and contrasting ones will stand out. Particularly effective are saturated vivid colors. Whether used alone or to reinforce an articulated or specially designed area, the use of strong color will ensure that it will be noticed.

- Use contrast to divide sections of the same surface. This strategy can be particularly effective in projects that feature trim. By using contrasting colors (amount of contrast to suit the job) between the wall plane and the trim (base, frames, casings, and moldings) each element can be made to stand out strongly.

- Use contrast to enhance the effect of low-relief articulations and details. By using subtle color or value changes, the three-dimensionality of the composition can be emphasized, especially for parts occurring on different planes.

- Use uniform coloring to simplify the appearance of a dense and complex space. While some color variety is possible, if there are many pieces and objects in a room and too many colors used, the result can be chaotic.

- Use varied color schemes to make plain spaces more interesting. This strategy is the opposite of the one above. Here, a varied and multichromatic approach can transform an otherwise plain and boring room into a rich and expressive one.

- Use color to unify projects and parts of projects. Color is a powerful unifying element. Whether a surface, a room, or an entire project, color can unify or fragment it. Color can be used to unify similar elements by color coding. An example would be the use of the same color for all the project's exposed mechanical ducts. Color can also emphasize rooms as units. You could paint individual rooms with different colors to distinguish them while using consistency of chroma or value to ensure some unity for the entire composition as a project. You could also just use consistent coloring throughout the project with, perhaps, different color accents in key areas.

- If variety is achieved by other elements, then unify through color. Conversely, if you unify through other design elements, then you can achieve variety through your color selections.

Dangers and Rewards

The assertive use of colors in interiors carries potential risks but also potential rewards. As mentioned earlier, it is useful to compare the application of color with the playing of a highly sensitive musical instrument. In the hands of a skilled performer, the loud sounds produced by the musical instrument will be a welcome experience, but in the hands of someone unskilled the only two possibilities are noise (not good) or the faint playing of simple patterns (not as offensive, although not quite satisfying). Perhaps due to the inherent risks involved, many interior projects lack much color. While simplicity certainly has its place in some applications of design, it is tempting to speculate that many designers shy away from using color assertively because it is hard to do well. As Allen Tate and C. Ray Smith have warned us, "If the colors of an interior are derived from a simple sequence, a designer risks little, but also tends to accomplish little."[4]

Excessive use of color can be as undesirable as too much restraint. Too much color in enclosed spaces can feel like an attack on our senses. Too much variety in color can also be disturbing, especially if used in large chunks. Edith Wharton and Ogden Codman, Jr., explain this with a useful comparison: "A multiplicity of colors produces the same effect as a number of voices talking at the same time. The voices may not be discordant, but continuous chatter is fatiguing in the long run."[5]

Color is a highly aesthetic component of design. The power of color is such that no matter how successfully all the other aspects of a project are designed and executed, if a project has unappealing colors it will be disliked despite all its other virtues. Perhaps one of the greatest pieces of advice we can give related to the selection of color schemes for interiors is the virtue in discarding unnecessary colors. An otherwise good color scheme with one or two colors too many contributes little and harms much.

CAPSULE | Color, Image, and Lifestyle

The subject of color has been studied extensively by artists and scholars alike and enjoys a fairly abundant literature. Color, as we all understand intuitively, is an extremely important qualifier of built environments. It is, in fact, an ever-present component of any visual experience. Colors carry connotations and are associated with particular attitudes and moods. When it comes to design, especially interior design, color is one of the major determinants of identity. Determining which colors are appropriate for a specific project is, largely, a search for colors appropriate for the particular identity of a client or project.

The work of Shigenobu Kobayashi and the Nippon Color & Design Research Institute (NCD) in Japan is particularly significant among the great body of literature about color. The extensive work of Kobayashi and the institute links color with its perceived connotations related to identity and personal style and presents it all in a highly usable framework. Their focus is on application, and this makes their work useful to interior designers, who are constantly faced with questions such as: What color should I use to convey an image both delicate and fashionable? Or an image that is bright and casual?

"Ours is an age of increasing sensitivity to color," says Kobayashi. "But what meanings are conveyed by the colors that surround us in everyday life? If we could grasp their real meanings, perhaps we would be able to use them more effectively. The first step toward a more effective use of color is to systematize and classify colors through key words that express their meanings and through images that express the differences between them."[1] This is not too difficult to do for single colors but becomes tricky when colors are used in combination. Kobayashi and his colleagues therefore sought to classify not only single colors but also color combinations in a systematic way and to link them to their associated meanings. They devised the Color Image Scale, a database for the systematic classification of color combinations.

The scale uses 130 basic colors, from which more than one thousand three-color combinations were assembled. Additionally, colors were matched with a collection of 180 adjectives covering the entire array of people's perceptions of their connotations and moods. From this information, profiles were prepared for each of the 130 colors and particular color combinations using each color, presenting the images connoted by each one of the single colors and each combination.

The 130 colors cover the entire color spectrum: 120 chromatic colors and 10 tones of gray. Chromatic colors are divided into 10 hues (red, yellow-red, yellow, green-yellow, green, blue-green, blue, purple-blue, purple, and red-purple), and each hue is, in turn, subdivided into 12 tones, grouped into the general categories of vivid tones, bright tones, subdued tones, and dark tones.

Colors and their combinations are positioned within a three-dimensional image scale consisting of three inter-related axes: the warm-cool axis, the hard-soft axis, and the clear-gray axis (Figure C11.1). Not only are certain hues (e.g., red) considered warm and others (e.g., blue), cool, but within each hue there is a range from warmest to coolest. The second axis, soft-hard, contains elements of shared human experience related to the relative sense of weight, brightness, and tactility of colors. It is fundamentally linked to weight. In terms of color, this is manifested by the general paleness or deepness of the color.

The third axis, clear-gray, is concerned with the amount of gray in a hue or tone.

A key word image scale was developed based on the adjectives people associated with each color and color combination. Descriptors were placed on the three-dimensional scale corresponding with the position of the colors associated with them. Figure C11.2 shows a two-dimensional representation of the key word scale. As Kobayashi explains, "Broadly speaking the key words in the warm-soft area of the scale have an intimate feeling, and convey a casual image, while those in the warm-hard section have a dynamic character. The key words in the cool-soft section have a clear feeling and suggest a good sense of color, while those in the cool-hard section convey an image of reliability and formality."[2] This is, of course, an oversimplification, as there are dozens of descriptors in each of the four quadrants. To make the scale easier to understand, similar key words were grouped under more general headings using categories from fashion, such as casual, elegant, and chic. A graphic representation of the scale with just these general image

Figure C11.2: Two-dimensional representation of the key word scale showing key words and their location according of the characteristics of colors associated with them.

Figure C11.1: The three axes of Kobayashi's model: warm-cool, soft-hard, and clear-grayish.

categories is shown in Figure C11.3. It defines the regions occupied by each of the 16 categories.

The next thing Kobayashi and his associates did to facilitate the practical use of their system was to define eight basic lifestyles associated with particular preferences of colors and adjectives. He explains, "Through the interplay of word and color images in the image scales, we can detect a general pattern in the differences between people's sensitivities. From the differences in individual patterns, we can get a feeling for different kinds of lifestyles. So, in practical terms, when you are creating a new product you can make use of the connections between words, colors, and objects."[3] The eight basic lifestyles are derived from the dominant image categories. The lifestyles are casual, modern, romantic, natural, elegant, chic, classic, and dandy. They are briefly described below.

Casual Lifestyle (key words: youthful, flamboyant, merry, enjoyable, vivid) This lifestyle is cheerful and easygoing and has an open and happy image. Preference is for vivid and clear colors, with strong and bright tones. People associated with this style are young, such as college students and people in their early twenties.

Modern Lifestyle (key words: urban, rational, sharp, progressive, metallic) The feeling of this group is cool and urbane, with a clear-cut, functional, sharp image. Neutral colors and sharp contrasts are favored. A key color is black. Vivid colors are sometimes used as an accent to create a bold effect. People associated with this lifestyle are young city dwellers who are particular about function and design.

Romantic Lifestyle (key words: soft, sweet, innocent, dreamy, charming) This style is characterized by a feeling of delicacy and sweetness. It is popular with young women. The predominant color qualities are softness, sweetness, and dreaminess. The main color combinations are light pastel tones and white. The colors used are clear.

Natural Lifestyle (key words: natural, tranquil, intimate, simple and appealing, generous) This lifestyle enjoys a natural, warm, simple appearance, with a heartwarming image. Rich, natural materials are preferred; artificial ones are disliked. The main colors are shades of beige, ivory, and yellow-green. People who aim for a cheerful, relaxed, and comfortable feeling belong in this group.

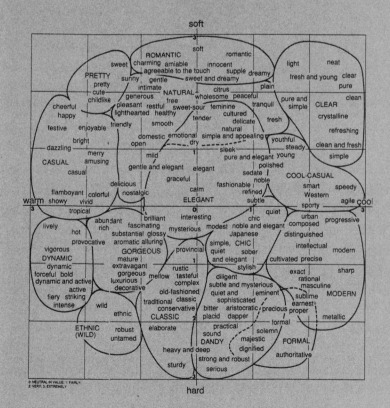

Figure C11.3: Two-dimensional representation of just the 16 general categories and their location on the chart according to the characteristics of the colors associated with them.

Source: From *Colorist* by Shigenobu Kobayashi, published by Kodansha International Ltd. Copyright © 1998 by Shigenobu Kobayashi

Elegant Lifestyle (key words: refined, graceful, delicate, fashionable, feminine) This group displays a taste for subtlety, a nonchalant style, and a sense of balance and charm. Refinement, tenderness, and calm further describe the image of this group. Grayish colors predominate and color combinations used are subtle gradations. Belonging in this group are women with a sense of gentleness, delicacy, and overall quality.

Chic Lifestyle (key words: sober, modest, simple, quiet and elegant, subtle) This group is characterized by a preference for the sober, calm, quiet, and sophisticated. They enjoy atmospheres that are quiet and polished, with an air of simple elegance. Urban, intelligent, sophisticated adults belong in this group, which has a cooler image than that of the elegant type. Sober, grayish colors predominate, with combinations displaying subtle differences of tones and grayish colors being preferred.

Classic Lifestyle (key words: traditional, classic, mature, tasteful, heavy and deep) An image of authenticity is at the heart of this type. Preferences are toward the elaborate, decorative, and formal. Preferred colors are hard and grayish, with brown, black, olive green, burgundy, and gold used widely. Belonging in this group are older, conservative people who aspire to tradition and authenticity.

Dandy Lifestyle (key words: placid, quiet, sophisticated, sound, dignified, strong, robust) This lifestyle is characterized by a self-possessed tone, stability, masculinity, and quiet sophistication. This type is simpler and cooler in feel than the classic. Preferences are toward hard colors such as brown, navy blue, or dark gray, used in combination with calm, grayish colors. Belonging in this group are adults, predominantly masculine, and with an inclination toward hard and neat atmospheres.

These insightful, research-derived lifestyle categories are the closest thing we have seen to a typology of tastes. Their potential for providing designers with useful insights about people and their taste preferences are enormous. As Kobayashi puts it when referring to his system: "I believe that this classification of colors based on images is the key to understanding the way in which color combinations are perceived, and that this system opens a path to the future, when sensitivity to color will continue to grow."[4] We couldn't agree more.

The information presented here summarizes discussion in the books *Color Image Scale* and *Colorist*, both by Kobayashi. These two books, as well as his *Book of Colors*, are highly recommended.

---

1. Shigenobu Kobayashi, *Color Image Scale* (New York: Kodansha International, 1990), 2.
2. Ibid., 12.
3. Ibid., 17.
4. Ibid., 2.

Ornament and Detail

Ornaments and special details are important decorative treatments that supply richness and expression to projects. They both share the goal of embellishing a project by supplying articulation and relief in many possible styles and expressions at a usually small and human scale. The basic difference between the two is that ornamentation usually involves the addition of some object or decorative feature to a project's space or surface, while detailing is usually an inherent part of the construction of an element, only at a smaller, more detailed level.

Ornamentation was used almost without exception in architecture and interior design until the advent of modernism, when, all of a sudden, many considered it a crime to use applied decoration. Instead, a new interest developed in accentuating the inherent expressions of materials and showing structure and its many intersections truthfully and honestly. Today, patterned materials, accessories, graphics, and artwork have become substitutes for the kind of elaborate ornamentation used in the past. Beginning around the mid-1970s there was a renewed interest in ornamentation, at least among some designers. Since then, the level of interest has fluctuated but the practice of ornamentation remains a powerful way to articulate and embellish space and surfaces. Detailing, meanwhile, continues to flourish as one of the main ways designers define the style and character of a project.

Figure 11.28 Details give character to the various elements of the environment. Example (a) shows a thoughtful detail that incorporates rich materials, lighting, and signage and adds interest to an otherwise plain column. Example (b) shows simple but crisp detailing applied to an office door and frame. Example (c) features a series of decorative pilasters of unique shape and rich material.

Detailing requires the precise shaping and articulation of smaller construction components in ways that express a particular stylistic tendency and fit in with the character of the rest of the project. All styles have their proper way of expression. The detailing of an old Victorian-style room and its components is vastly different from the detailing of a minimalist modern room and its components. The materials are different, the number of parts are different, the joints are different, and the shapes are different.

The detailing of the smaller parts of projects serves to give a project a unique style and character. Details often do this more convincingly than the main volumes and shapes of a project, which often remain fairly neutral. They all must work together, though, and require proper compatibility and consistency of approach. Whether a room or a project ends up being light-handed or heavy-handed, formal or informal, modern or traditional, it will owe much of those qualities to the type of detailing used.

Detailing takes design intent to a smaller scale and develops it more intensely. There are many types of details

in interiors. They include intersections of wall planes with ceiling and floor planes, the articulation of columns and other freestanding or protruding elements, changes in levels at the ceiling and floor, doors and frames, casework, relief, molding, reveals, custom-designed furnishings and fixtures, and so on. All these, and many others, need to be given proper expression according to the design vocabulary of the project.

Above all, detailing implies giving some element of the built environment a certain character by the treatment it is given. Figure 11.28 shows examples of three normally ordinary building elements, a sign, a door, and a pilaster, transformed into specially crafted elements through thoughtful detailing. Special detailing can also be used to make freestanding, sculptural elements stand out. Figure 11.29 shows a nicely detailed building directory and a very expressive and sculptural-looking freestanding sales kiosk. Details show concern for design. Nice detailing implies that care has been taken in the crafting of the objects and other elements of a project. Not every aspect of a project has to stand out as a highly articulated detail, but many parts present opportunities for refinement through detailing, especially if they occur in visible, prominent locations like the guardrail system/sculptural screen device and the column/ceiling/sign intersection shown in Figure 11.30.

Figure 11.29 Freestanding elements in space often require thoughtful detailing. The building directory shown in (a) is a good example of a little design project unto itself. The skillful integration of materials, shapes, and information gives it a strong design presence. Similarly, the eyewear kiosk shown in (b) integrates material, pattern, shapes, graphics, and merchandise to achieve a unique and stylish look.

Figure 11.30 Good details are everywhere in design. Intersections present special detailing opportunities, like the intersection of the column, ceiling, and sign shown in (a). Also, railing systems and other enriching sculptural fabrications, like the ones shown in (b), present opportunities to add enrichment and expression to projects.

Designers create many architectural elements and miscellaneous objects in projects; others are selected from available products. They have to ensure that there is proper compatibility between the detailing of specified products (designed and produced by others) and that of the elements custom designed by the designer for the project. The detailing will rarely be identical, but it seldom needs to be. Proper compatibility is all that is required.

The art of detailing is one that takes time to cultivate and master. Young designers need to practice it conscientiously and often. There is nothing as sad as a well-conceived space with well-chosen finishes and furnishings but lacking the richness provided by conscientious detailing, even if minimalistic and subtle.

OTHER CONSIDERATIONS

In addition to all the elements discussed in this chapter there are other important ingredients in the mix of interior places and the life that unfolds within them.

Protagonists of Place

Designers do not control the goods and the people supported by their designs; they react and respond to them. In the process of daily life, humans perform rituals involving other humans and goods. It is the role of design to support

Figure 11.31 Most interior places feature physical goods exhibited, exchanged, or consumed in them. In a store it's the merchandise (a), in a deli it's the meats and other consumables (b).

and enhance these rituals in order to make them more comfortable and meaningful than they otherwise would be.

The goods of retail stores are the merchandise sold in them. The goods in restaurants are the food items sold in them. The goods in factories are the products fabricated in them. The goods in offices are the pieces of information produced and communicated in them. These goods and the processes behind them (selling, fabricating, communicating) are at the heart of each entity designers provide services to. Understanding, facilitating, and expressing those essences are part of the design task. The goods themselves have a physical presence and often become prominent parts of the visual environment. The nature, size, and packaging of merchandise in a store, for example, can actually dominate the visual field in a store. Figure 11.31 shows the goods in a gift shop and a delicatessen sandwich shop. They have their own visual presence, and their arrangement requires careful planning and response.

The people who use the spaces we design are also a crucial part of both the drama that unfolds in these places and the look and character of the place. They are the "performers" and come equipped with general scripts according to the roles they will perform. While the nature of the scripts is generally known, its specifics are unpredictable. Nevertheless, enough is known about the basic behaviors typically associated with a place to design a responsive solution. The designer of the scene shown in Figure 11.32 had to be familiar with the basic behaviors involved in the process of checking in and boarding at an airport terminal in order to design a successful terminal gate area.

Scripts are similar to sports events where the players, the arena, and the spectators come together, knowing there is going to be a game but not knowing what the spe-

Figure 11.32: The main protagonists of place are, of course, the users. They themselves become part of the scene, adding their physical features, personalities, and behaviors.

cific outcome will be. The designer does not have much control over the people, their attire, or the scripts to be played but responds to them with the goals of facilitating, enriching, and inspiring. People and goods are really the protagonists of the play; the interior environment represents the stage and the props, themselves crucial elements for a smooth and successful play.

Truthfulness and Illusion

Designers have a great deal of power as they play the role of creator for the interior environments they design. With this comes the responsibility to use and manipulate aspects of the physical world in particular ways, depending on preferences and conditions. One interesting point of debate is the role of the designer in reinforcing reality. An important question emerges from this: Should designers portray natural physical phenomena truthfully and honestly, or is it okay to manipulate it for effect? Steen Eiler Rasmussen and others have argued for the value of presenting physical phenomena as they are, to correspond with what is natural.[6]

If a room has a northern exposure, all the natural lighting it receives is diffuse, cool lighting. That is part of the reality of northern rooms. Why alter it? Treatments for that room should, according to Rasmussen, respect and reinforce its inherent quality. Consequently, lighting and colors should be compatible with the cool natural coloring of the room. Yellowish artificial lighting and warm colors will look out of place and take away from the northern character of the room. The basic premise seems to be to let the room be what it is.

These concerns bring up an interesting point about the merits of being truthful and honest when representing reality. Is it always necessary to be truthful, though, especially in the design of interiors, where comfortable conditions often require the manipulation of natural properties, such as daylighting, color, and acoustics? Is it better to have a natural, northern room, or is the warmth of incandescent lighting reason enough to change it, against its natural tendencies? These are difficult questions, a good topic for discussion with your peers. What do you think?

Total Environmental Wholeness

Throughout this book, we have been discussing many aspects of design individually, with a special emphasis on the spatial aspects of interior design. This, obviously, is not the way things are presented to you in the real environment. We have presented them as individual topics in order to isolate them and facilitate their understanding. In reality, all these concepts and elements work together, simultaneously, complementing and affecting one another. This brings up the topic of wholeness. The many parts of a project need to both solve the design challenges they are meant to solve and provide some of the order, enrichment, and expression we have been advocating here. They also need to be perceived as a total unity, one group of many different parts that work cohesively together as a system of specific and consistent intentions. Additionally, they need to be resolved perceptually to achieve a satisfying balance and an overall sense of perceptual correctness.

Further, there is what can be called **total environmental wholeness**, the resulting wholeness of environment, occasion, and people operating smoothly and effectively as one indivisible unity. This is the kind of effect achieved when people experience environment, people, and behavior seamlessly as one. On such occasions, environment, people, and actions blend together harmoniously, blurring the perceptual edges that separate them normally, while retaining their inherent, individual characteristics.

Excellence

Your goal as a designer should be to become the best you can be and to truly make a difference in people's lives through the environments you design. There are many levels of competence. It is possible to be a good space planner with a good sense of color and produce clear, efficient, and colorful projects for the enjoyment of all. That alone would make you a fairly competent designer.

What we have been advocating throughout this book goes beyond that. When you try to transcend the limitations of efficient projects with nice finishes and attempt to provide more, then you get into a whole different level of design. It is possible to contribute more to the experiential qualities of projects through thoughtful attention to details in planning and execution. A proper and fitting response to the basic design problem starts the process. If, in addition to a good functional and efficient plan, you can also foster an appropriate sense of order, provide enriching experiences, capture the essence of the organization in the project's expression, and balance and unify the elements used with neither lack nor excess, you will be designing at a very high level.

Although so much of interior design is concerned with high style and sophistication, it is also important to know how to produce goodness and wholeness for all projects, regardless of their budget and level of sophistication. Poetic dwelling is possible at any budget, even if it takes greater effort in some cases than others. Not every project is intended to appear in a glossy design magazine. Even those not destined to be fashion statements can be special. To move and inspire its users, a project's quality must be apprehended spontaneously, without intellectual effort; a few simple, unpretentious elements, well placed and arranged, a nice and engaging flow, a detail here and there, a glimpse, a surprise, and voilà—you have touched people's hearts.

CASE STUDY
Graphics, Colors, and Materials Providing Expression: Galter Medical Pavilion
DESIGN FIRM: EVA MADDOX ASSOCIATES

The Galter Medical Pavilion project is an excellent example of expression in design. The 185,000-square-foot ambulatory health facility is part of the Swedish Covenant Hospital in Chicago. In addition to the many practical design problems associated with a project like this, there were two crucial and challenging design objectives the owners and designers wished to address. The first objective was to establish a distinct identity while embracing the multicultural philosophy of the community-based hospital. The patient population alone spoke 27 languages. The second objective was to visibly reinforce the hospital's holistic approach to healing, an approach that embodies body, mind, and spirit. In general, a special effort was made to create a facility that felt alive and to celebrate the rich cultural heritage of the surrounding community.

The design solution makes abundant use of graphic patterns, symbols, and signs. The challenge was to come up with symbols that would be understood by the diverse body of patients and staff and that would not be offensive to any one group. The designers used religion, culture, heritage, and nature as inspiration when developing the pattern identity and signage vocabulary.

Shapes, materials, colors, and patterns were selected carefully in order to communicate fitting and desirable messages. Circular patterning was used throughout the facility to symbolize the Judeo-Christian heritage of the hospital and the circle as a continuum of life. The strong circular geometry and overall patterning in the first-floor entry area is also a good example of this kind of patterning performing multiple duties. In addition to making a powerful first impression; establishing an image of openness, warmth, and professionalism; and supplying rich symbolism, the assembly also serves to center, organize, and unify an otherwise geometrically complex, and disorienting, part of the building (Figure CS11.1). At a more detailed level, iconic graphics on the floor serve to direct patients and visitors to their target destinations (Figure CS11.2).

Figure CS11.1: Among other duties, the large circular pattern in the reception area serves to add cohesiveness to a geometrically complex area of the building as seen on this partial floor plan.

Figure CS11.2: The floor pattern is rich in meaning and visually cheerful and attractive. Superimposed on the circle are layers of meaning: the circle of Christianity, multicultural symbols, and directional indicators.

The materials and colors used draw from common characteristics of the Swedish tradition. Brick, so common in Swedish construction, is used on the exterior and also inside the lobby, elevator lobbies, and restrooms. The blond finish used for the woodwork throughout is also characteristically Scandinavian. Blue and yellow, the predominant hues of the project, are taken from the Swedish

Figure CS11.3: View of public corridor area showing blue banding on the floor and blue informational signage.

Figure CS11.4: The iconic vocabulary is simple but memorable.

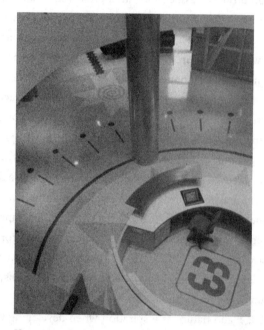

Figure CS11.5: View of reception area showing the prominent use of graphics on the floor.

flag. Yellow is used extensively in the lobby, where the patterned terrazzo flooring and the extensive blond wood paneling contribute much to the overall friendliness conveyed by the space. Blue is used as directional signage inside on the floor (as stripes), on accent vertical surfaces, and on general signage throughout (Figure CS11.3).

Color and graphics are used throughout to create easy-to-identify pathways and to highlight key points of service. They communicate at various levels, ranging from direct identification via text to iconic communication via signs associated with different floors and, at the same time, different elements such as wind, rain, and water. The iconic vocabulary consists of simple but memorable symbols, featuring simple shapes such as spirals, stars, and waves (Figure CS11.4). These appear stenciled, painted, or inlaid on both vertical and horizontal surfaces throughout the project (Figure CS11.5).

What is truly remarkable about this project is the seamless integration of architecture, interior design elements, finishes, and graphics to create a clear, cheerful, and dignified environment that expresses meanings connected to its user population and a certain attitude about their holistic and friendly way of conducting business.

REVIEW

Summary

Space and its components do not occur in a vacuum. The effects of space are modified and complemented by texture, light, pattern, and color, not to mention such nonvisual contributors as sounds, thermal qualities, and smells. All these factors together add up to the total experience of interior space.

Ambient elements contribute much to users' moods and sense of comfort in the environment. The brightness level, the size and number of light fixtures, and their distribution in space produce countless variations and effects. Light can enhance form but it can also reduce perception of three-dimensionality if used incorrectly.

Light can create or accentuate focal points or emphasize an entire segment of wall or ceiling. Furthermore, attention can be directed to a specific area in space through the use of contrast between the space and adjoining surfaces and areas. Light is also a good space modifier to use to create engaging sequences.

In addition to artificial light, daylight is an important modifier of interior spaces. Designers have to make important choices about the location of specific rooms, functions, and objects in relation to windows. Additionally, the selections made for window treatments and other light-blocking elements near the perimeter have significant effects on the qualities of a room.

Hearing is the second most prominent human sense. The acoustic properties of spaces can produce subtle effects in interior environments. The common tendency is to add sound-absorptive materials to dampen the noise level, but designers need to remember that certain spaces are meant to be acoustically lively and that acoustic variety can help produce enriching experiences.

Two other nonvisual ambient elements are important in modifying place. Although, the thermal environment is not under the full control of interior designers, with the cooperation of the project's mechanical engineer, spaces can be made purposefully colder or warmer for variety and effect. With the thermal environment, though, it is imperative to stay within the client's comfort zone. The final ambient element is smell. With smell, the object is not to produce particular smells but to respond to the desirable existing smells produced in a given environment. Accentuating and directing positive and meaningful smells in places like restaurants, perfume shops, and cookie shops is a powerful way of highlighting some of the pleasant qualities associated with those places.

Interior elements serving primarily decorative functions include finishes, colors, ornaments, and details. The finish palette chosen for a project is often one of the principal determinants of its stylistic direction. Finishes require much attention, both individually and collectively. Variables include the inherent qualities and connotations of individual materials and the subtle variations produced by the methods of fabrication, cutting, or finishing. Materials also have qualities associated with our tactile sense, such as their relative hardness, texture, and temperature.

Color is one of the most important elements in interiors. It is so prominent visually that it can contribute much to the enhancement of order, enrichment, and expression in the interior environment. Color has the power to evoke strong emotions and trigger learned associations. Different colors have specific associations with temperature, weight, gender, groups, and even countries.

Using color in interiors requires proper knowledge of its properties, as well as a sense of what is appropriate for a given client, program, and existing physical context. While color theory has good information to offer regarding the effects of color and the ways of achieving color harmony, it is crucial for designers to realize that the success of any scheme lies in its execution. The exact colors used, the relative size of colored areas, their location in relation to each other, their texture, and the lighting conditions all come into play to produce infinite effects depending on the combinations used.

Ornament and detail are to interior design what short detailed strokes are to a painting. Together they add up to give the final piece much of its flavor. Ornamentation involves the application of some nonstructural decorative embellishment to all or part of a design. Detailing is inherent in the fabrication of a piece, whether a wall, a light fixture, or a cabinet. Together with the materials and the furniture, details play a major role in establishing the visual character of a place.

Goods and people are two important ingredients of a place not controlled by the designer. They tend to have a reciprocal effect on design and affect the total experience of place. The merchandise at the store, the food at the restaurant, the clerk, the waiter, and the office receptionist all become important components of the scene and the drama that unfolds in it.

1. Simon Unwin, *Analysing Architecture* (London: Routledge, 1997), 25.
2. Paul Zelanski and Mary Pat Fischer, *Design Principles and Problems* (Fort Worth, TX: Harcourt Brace College Publishers, 1996), 238.
3. Sinclair Gauldie, *The Appreciation of the Arts: Architecture* (London: Oxford University Press, 1972), 139.
4. Allen Tate and C. Ray Smith, *Interior Design in the Twentieth Century* (New York: Harper and Row, 1986), 152.
5. Stanley Abercrombie, *A Philosophy of Interior Design* (New York: Harper and Row, 1990), 113.
6. Steen Eiler Rasmussen, *Experiencing Architecture* (Cambridge, MA: MIT Press, 1993), 218–19, 223, 235–36.

Chapter Questions

1. What factors of lighting contribute to the mood of a space?
2. What type of lighting arrangement is best for enhancing three-dimensional form? Why?
3. What types of lighting arrangements are not good enhancers of three-dimensional form? Why?
4. Name three different strategies to create focal areas with light.
5. How can light be used to create an interesting sequence? Give an example.
6. Name three things designers can do to respond to and use daylight for effect.
7. Which acoustic concept is particularly important in relation to the acoustic properties of individual spaces?
8. What manipulations in interiors help to dampen sound in a space?
9. What manipulations in interiors help to produce acoustically lively spaces?
10. Give one example of how a designer can manipulate the thermal environment for effect.
11. Give one example of how to take advantage of the pleasant smells inherent in a project type.
12. How do the pattern and modularity of finish materials affect the look produced?
13. Name three ways to use the textural qualities of finishes for effect.
14. Name five compositional considerations related to color that can be manipulated for effect.
15. How can color be used to counteract the effects of dense and complex spaces?
16. How can color be used to counteract the effects of plain spaces?
17. What are some of the dangers related to color application?
18. How does detailing relate to the rest of the interior environment?
19. What did this chapter refer to as the "goods" in a space?
20. Do you think there are instances when it is appropriate to contradict the natural, inherent properties of places by, for example, making a north-facing room warm and cozy instead of letting it reflect the natural coolness of northern light? Explain your answer.

INDEX

and contradiction, 280–81
and enrichment, 211–14
in health-care projects, 166
and hierarchy, 320
and mystery, 197–98
and order, 194–95, 196
and spatial composition, 212–13
in symmetrical compositions, 310
and system overlapping, 214
Complexity and Contradiction in Architecture (Venturi), 217
composition, 269–70, 297
asymmetrical, 310–11, 312
balance in, 307, 312
centers in, 307–8, 309, 318–19
complementary, 314
complexity in, 212–13, 310
symmetrical, 307–8, 309–10
visual harmony in, 307, 318–21
compression, tension and, 216
concentration, and enclosure, 46
concept diagram, 149f, 152f
See also diagrams, for organizational concepts
concept generation, 13
See also design concept
stages of, 153–58
concept ideas
consolidating, 157–58
evaluation of, 157
conceptual sketches, 156, 156f
configuration
circular, 227
of corridors, 190f
of interior space, 97, 98f
and massing, 152
of paths, 41
connection, 235–36
and art of joining spaces, 77
expression of, 256
segregation, 257
connectors, 44, 45
conservative tastes, 260
consistency
in detailing, 349
consistency, of approach, 187–88, 314, 315–16
constraints, 132
and freedom, 252
construction documents, 285
consumer brands, 275. *See also* branding

containment, 60, 61
See also enclosure
and grounding, 233
content, clarity of, 160, 161
context, 11–12, 32, 92, 93–99
and color suitability, 343
environmental features, 95
and expression, 261
expression of, 253–55
general, 93
contextual fit, 176–77
continuity, 314, 315
contractor, 285
contrast, 184
color used for, 344
creating focus by, 303
in sequences, 186–87
variety through, 223–24
control, 32
of mobility, 75–76
in situations, 29, 30
corporate brands, 275
corporate culture, 134–35
corporate identity, 271–72
corridors, 40, 168f
articulation of, 322, 323
breaking up linearity of, 222, 223f
changing elements in, 24
closed, in enclosed spaces, 189–90
enclosed, 222
enrichment in, 210
gradation in, 187f
in health care facility, 124f
orientation in, 189–90
visual connection to, 228
Crozier, Ray, 196
cultural capital, 263
cultural expression, 254
cultural literacy, 247–48
culture, corporate, 134–35
Curtis, Eleanor, 275

D

dandy lifestyle, and color, 348
datum, 185, 185f
daylighting, 334–36
decision making, 6
and enrichment, 208
with layouts, 250
on organizational structure, 145

decorative elements, 236
decorative tile band, 241–42
departures, 27–28
design
challenges of, 4–5
current norms, 278
intentions and strategies in, 7–8
manipulation, and enrichment, 210
synthesis in, 4, 294–97
unity in, 14, 313–14, 318, 344, 352
design, principles of, 9–15
buildings are for people, 9–10
for design completion, 14–15
for development stages, 13–14
enriching qualities in, 13–14
for establishing design, 11–13
fitting expression in, 14
general principles, 9–11
mastery of space, 10–11
order in good design, 13
organizational idea, 12–13
place as basic design unit, 10
design approach, 153
design concept, 127, 139–43
See also organizational concept
defined, 139
drivers of, 141, 142–43
stages in generation of, 153–58
statements of, 140–42
designer
becoming a, 5–8
personal expression/style of, 278–79
design guidelines, 126–30
design intentions, 7
design knowledge, sources of, 6–7
design literacy, 248
design patterns. *See* patterns
design problems, 5, 7
and design concept statement, 140–41
design solution, 141. *See also* resolution
design strategies, 7–8
design studio, 5–6
destination spaces, 37–38, 220
See also centers
domains, 37–38, 47, 180, 181f, 182
enrichment in, 210
moving to, 23–24
detailing, 118
compatibility of, 349–50
drafting of, 285
expression in, 250, 284–86

detailing (*cont.*)
>   higher levels of, 296
>   and image, 273
>   innovative, 237–38*f*
>   and ornament, 348–50
>   ornamentation, 270–71
>   and personal style, 278
>   and relief, 236
>   in restaurant, 284–86
>   and self-image, 259
>   unity in, 314

diagonal arrangements, 227

diagonal bounce scheme, 170

diagrams, for organizational concepts,
>   156, 158–62, 166, 295
>   development of, 162
>   functional, 158–59, 161
>   grammar for, 161
>   graphics for, 160
>   parti diagrams, 158, 160, 169–70, 199
>   requirements for, 160–61

difficulty, degree of, 31

disclosure, of space, 72–75, 190
>   *See also under* openings; openness
>   manipulation of, 226–30
>   and orientation, 74

discord, visual, 216

dispersion, 317, 318*f*

distinctiveness, 183

distortion, of form, 72

distraction, and relief, 74

districts, 37. *See also* domains

Doane Pet Care Company Headquarters,
>   237–38*f*

domains, 37–38, 47
>   and furnishings, 182
>   and order, 180, 181*f*

dominance, 29, 184
>   establishing, 303

doors/doorways, 44
>   size of, 300, 300*f*

double function, 281

double-loaded loop systems, 79

Drexler, Millard, 273

Duchossis Center for Advanced
>   Medicine, 166–68

Duerk, Donna, 131

dullness, avoiding, 318

dwelling, four modes of, 48

Dynamics of Architectural Form
>   (Arnheim), 176

E

economy
>   in design statement, 142
>   of means, 160
>   of order, 177

edges, 43–44, 62
>   ambiguous, 60
>   and enclosure, 73
>   ends as, 45–46
>   horizontal, 63, 67
>   and positive *vs.* negative space,
>   67–68
>   and sense of order, 182
>   vertical, 62–63

efficiency and impact, 132

El Dorado Grill (restaurant), 284–86

elegant lifestyle, and color, 348

*Elements of Architecture: From Form to
>   Place* (Meiss), 36

elevations, 319

emotional responses, 29–30, 31
>   and branding, 274–76
>   to color, 342

emphasis. *See* focus, functional

encapsulation, 60–61

enclosure/enclosed space, 46, 56, 59–61
>   common, 185, 314
>   and edges, 73
>   level of, 11
>   in offices, 104
>   of paths, 222, 223
>   in square spaces, 70
>   surface qualities in, 225–26

ends, 45–46. *See also* edges

enrichment, 13–14, 129, 206–43
>   and activity manipulation, 218
>   and ambiguity, 217
>   in building interiors, 210
>   case for, 207–8
>   color for, 342
>   and complexity, 211–14
>   and connection, 235–36
>   and disclosure manipulation, 226–30
>   general strategies for, 210–19
>   and grounding, 233–35
>   in ideation stage, 146
>   and novelty, 214–16
>   and order, 206–10
>   and pictorialness, 217–18
>   and prospect-refuge theory, 230–32
>   and relief, 236
>   and stimulation and stability, 209
>   of straightforward floor plan, 322–23
>   surface pattern as, 239–42
>   and tension, 216–17
>   and variety, 210
>   and views, 226–30, 236
>   when in transit, 219–30
>   while stationary, 233–36

enticement, 227

entrance, 21, 44, 119, 181
>   *See also* doors/doorways; lobby

environment, informal, 266

environmental factors
>   lighting, 130, 328–36, 352
>   and load level, 33, 265
>   olfactory environment, 338
>   thermal environment, 337–38

environmental features, 95

environmental imaging, 48

environmental information, 179

environmental opportunities, 132–33

environmental order, 13

environmental preference, 196–98

environmental stimulation, 29–30, 209

equilibrium, 318, 320
>   *See also* balance

eurythmy, 298

evaluation, of concept ideas, 157
>   *See also* questioning

exaggeration, 215

excellence, in design, 352

exchange, 129. *See also* interaction

exclusivity, and status, 259

exiting, 20, 27–28

exploration, 197, 220, 294

exposure, solar, 95

expression, 14, 147, 246–86, 353
>   admittance/rejection in, 253
>   ascending/descending, 252
>   and branding, 274–77
>   in ceilings, 84
>   and color, 342, 345–48
>   in columns, 85
>   constraint/freedom in, 252–53
>   of contextual factors, 253–55
>   cultural, 254
>   of current norms and conventions,
>   255
>   in design, 246–51
>   of designer, 278–79

health care facilities
Duchossis Center for Advanced
Medicine, 166–68
Galter Medical Pavilion, 353–54
interdepartmental diagram of, 123f
hedonic value, 196
Heidegger, Martin, 48
Heimsath, Clovis, 100
hierarchy, 13
attitudes about, 250
and complexity, 211
design, 131
in diagram graphics, 161
and organization, 178
in paths, 40
perceptual, 320
and placement, 148
resolution of, 296
in space-definition, 59
high culture, 263, 264
high status symbols, 259
Hildebrandt, Grant, 232
historic expression, 253–54
home, as center, 46
honesty, in expression, 278
horizontal arrangement, 319–20
horizontal edges, 63, 67
hospital. *See* health care facilities
human activities, 350–51
See also people in buildings
manipulation of, 218
users' responses, 28–32
human experience, expression of,
252–53
human scale, 299, 306
humor, 266
Husserl, Edmund, 46

I

iconic communication, 249, 354, 354f
ideation, 138–71, 294
See also concept development; design
concept
conceiving workable approaches, 155
and design concept, 139–58
externalizing approaches, 156
scenarios, 155–56
and search for proper fit, 138–39
identity, 128
and branding, 274–77

and color, 345
corporate, 271–72
expression of, 257–62
group, 259, 271–74
and image ability, 179
and kind of dwelling, 48
IKEA (Swedish furniture retailer), 140
illumination, level of, 329
See also lighting
image, 131, 261
See also self-image
and brands, 275
corporate, 272
and self-presentation, 264
image ability, 179, 182
image congruence hypothesis, 258
impressions, 24, 40
first, 22, 353
as mental maps, 177–78
and self-presentation, 264
Ind, Nicholas, 271–72
individual parts, of project, 183–84
inflection, 147, 148, 170, 199
of basic idea, 165
informal composition, 311
informal environment, 266
inherent expression, 248
See also expression
innovation, 260, 276
See also novelty
and inventiveness, 129
integration, 128
intensity, degree of, 33, 267
intention, clarity of, 160, 161
intentionality, 208–9
interaction, 128
levels of, 131
vs. autonomy, in offices, 106–7
interior context, 96
interior space
components of (*See* boundaries;
circulation systems; destination
places)
opening up of, 64–65
user's response to, 28–32
interior vistas, 200. *See also* views
internal players, clients as, 99–100
interpenetrated spaces, 77
interpretation, 247–51
and communication, 247
and meaning, 248–51

intersection, 186. *See also* nodes
intimate scale, 69, 219, 233
invitation, 133

J

Jencks, Charles, 249–50
Johnson, Philip, 65, 66f
joining spaces, art of, 77–80
Jones, Gareth, 134

K

Kahn, Louis, 163, 278
Kaplan, Rachel and Stephen, 196, 197,
198
kitchen, 121, 121f, 233
Klein, Naomi, 274
Kleinasser, William, 294–95
Kobayashi, Shigenobu, 345–48
Krier, Bob, 71

L

Lancôme (retailer), 143
landmarks, 51, 52f, 182f, 183
See also points of reference
landscape
and color, 343
and prospect-refuge theory, 230
Lazaroff, Barbara, 143
learned associations, 249
Le Corbusier, 4, 40, 206
proportional system of, 306
legibility, 183, 187, 189, 194, 197, 198
"less is more" doctrine, 65, 280
Leupen, Bernard, 176
Levi's Dockers Shop, 142
libraries, 112–13, 224–25
acoustical zones in, 125f
two master approaches, 163–64
lifestyle, and self-image, 259, 345–48
light and air, 118
light fixtures, 332–33
lighting, 130, 328–36
and color choices, 352
daylighting, 334–36, 352
foci created by, 331–33
form revealed by, 329
and mood, 329
natural, 352

of sequences and projects, 333–34
    sources of, 332
light space, 332
linear systems, 78, 115
    breaking up, 222, 223f
    for central display, 169
Linville, Ed, 284
load level, 33, 265
lobby, 19, 20f, 119, 120, 168f
local color palette, 343
locomotive activity, 24–25
longevity, of buildings, 130
loop systems, 79
loose approach, 81
Lorenz, Konrad, 231
low/lower middle culture, 264
Lynch, Kevin, 37, 39
    on edges, 43
    on environmental imaging, 48
    on image ability, 179
    on landmarks, 51
    on legibility, 197
    on nodes, 42

M

main concept, 139. *See also* design
        concept
main paths, 40
manufactured materials, 270
market research, 261
Markham, Julian E., 276
massing, 152, 237
mass-in-space studies, 190–94,
        199–200
    boundary shape in, 193–94
    irregular-shaped masses, 192
    superimposed accent in, 193
material palette, 270
materials, 118, 328
    feel of, 340–41
    and finishes, 338–40
    natural, 270, 339, 342
matrix, for analysis, 122, 122f, 124–25
meaning
    contradictory levels of, 281
    and interpretation, 248–51
    and order, 180
Mehrabian, Albert, 29–30
Meiss, Pierre von, 36, 178, 314
mental image/map, 178–79, 182, 300

mercenary organization, 134
merchandise, 351. *See also* retail stores
Mies van der Rohe, Ludwig, 66, 81, 280,
        310
    Barcelona Pavilion of, 65, 281
    "less is more" doctrine of, 65, 280
    space planning approaches of, 61
mission statements, 134–35, 274
mobility, 72
    levels of control in, 75–76
Modern Architectural Design
        (Robertson), 246
modernism, 81, 255f
    critics of, 280–83
modern lifestyle, and color, 347
modifying elements, 15, 326–56
    See also detailing
    color, 328, 341–48, 352, 354
    finishes and materials, 338–41
    interior decoration, 338–50
    lighting, 130, 328–36, 352
    ornamentation, 270–71, 348–50
    other considerations, 350–52
modular flooring, 339, 340f
modulation, 211–12
    in corridors, 223f
    of enclosing surfaces, 225
    in floors, 212, 225
modules, 120. *See also* neighborhoods
    prototypes of, 167, 167f
Modulor, the, 306
monotony, avoiding, 318
monumental scale, 68, 183
mood, and lighting, 329
mood-related concept, 139
Moore, Charles, 94, 132
Mount Angel Abbey library, 163
movement, efficiency in, 220
    See also circulation system
Moye, Gary, 126
multiple spaces, 76–81
    art of joining spaces, 78–80
    systems of spaces, 78
mystery, 197, 198

N

native color palette, 343
natural environments, 197
natural features, 94
natural lifestyle, and color, 347

natural light, 334–36, 352
natural materials, 270
    color of, 342
    wood, 339
neighborhood, 37–38, 120, 200, 259
    as context, 94
network (circulation) systems, 80
networked organization, 134
Nike (shoe retailer), 274
Nippon Color & Design Research
        Institute (Japan), 345
nodes, 42
    centrality of, 218
    and sense of order, 182
nonscreener, 30
Norberg-Schulz, Christian, 37, 38, 180
    on place and dwelling, 46–48
novelty, 31, 196, 206, 260
    and boldness, 215–16
    spatial, 214–16

O

objects, 58. *See also* accessories;
        furnishings
    role of, in place, 49–51
Observations for Young Architects (Pelli),
        92, 294
occasion, 28, 31
office design, 103
    configurations of, 97f
    disclosure in, 72
    enclosed space in, 104
    entry sequences in, 119
    functional requirements of, 56
    hierarchy in, 250
    interaction *vs.* autonomy in, 106–7
    modules, 120
    open plan, 104
    and power motive, 260
    reception area in, 310f
    secondary activities in, 26
    solids and voids in, 104
    systems furniture for, 105
    unconventional, 237–38f
    work processes and space planning
        for, 104–7
olfactory environment, 338
Olins, Wally, 272
On the Aesthetics of Architecture
        (Weber), 318–21

openings, 62–63

   See also doorways; views; windows

   and outlook, 94

openness, 130, 261

   vs. closedness, 56, 257

open plan office, 104

open space, 56, 190–92

   and destruction of the box, 64–65

   with enclosed masses, 191–92

   with one enclosed mass, 190–91

   with partial-height elements, 194,

    195*f*

opportunity *vs.* safety, 230–32

order, 13, 176–202

   case study in, 199–201

   and complexity, 194–95, 196

   designing for, 180–201

   of economy, 177

   and enrichment, 206–10

   and environmental preference,

    196–98

   establishment of, 145–46

   and factors of understanding and

    orientation, 179–80

   kinds of, 176–78

   and legibility, 183, 187, 189, 194, 197,

    198

   levels of, 13, 178

   mass-in-space studies, 190–94,

    199–200

   and mental mapping, 178–79

   and orientation, 177–78, 179, 185,

    189–90, 194

   and project understanding, 179–80,

    183–89

   and proper fit, 176–77

   role of place elements in, 180–83

   and space composition, 189–94

   and visual harmony, 177

organizational concept, 12–13, 143–53

   and circulation, 150–51

   considerations in determining,

    148–53

   diagrams for (*See* diagrams.

    organizational concept)

   and hierarchy, 178. *See also* hierarchy

   and massing, 152

   and order, 13

   and placement, 148–50

   quick approach to, 164–65

   unity in, 314

organizational structure, 295

organizational systems, 181

   and complex order, 195

organizing principle

   structure for, 179–80

orientation, 321

   and boundaries, 194

   common, 185

   in corridors, 189–90

   and landmarks, 51

   and order, 177–78, 179, 185, 189–90,

    194

   and points of reference, 188, 190

   and rotation, 214

   to space, 48, 73, 74

ornamentation, 270–71

   and detail, 348–50

overlapping, 214, 316

P

Palladio, 304, 306

parti diagrams, 158, 160, 199

   for retail stores, 169–70

passageways, 45

Passini, Romedi, 177, 180

paths, 39–41, 47

   See also circulation/circulation

    system; corridors

   articulations in, 223, 225–26

   enclosure of, 223

   height-to-width proportions of, 224

   main, 40

   and nodes, 42

   and order, 181, 181*f*

   qualities of, 221–25

   secondary, 41

   shape of, 222–25

   transitions in, 221

   and travel direction, 75–76

   zigzagging of, 221

Patio (restaurant), 143

patterns

   consistency in, 317

   dispersed, 317, 318*f*

   as enrichment, 239–42

   harmonious, 213

   repetition in, 187, 241–42, 340

   and texture, 340

   tile, 241–42, 339

patterns principle, 126

Pea in the Pod store, 273

Pelli, Cesar, 92, 280, 283, 294

people in buildings, 18–33

   See also under human

   basic events in visits, 18–28

   and context, 32

   emotional responses of, 29–30, 31

   and occasion, 28, 31

   secondary activities, 25–27

   situational factors, variables in, 31–32

perceptual hierarchy, 40

perceptual weight, 319

perimeter wall system, 191

permeability, of space, 72

personal expression, 258–59, 278

   See also expression; self-image

   and color, 345–48

personal philosophy, 209, 280–83

personal preferences, 31

phenomenology, 46–48

Philips Exeter Academy library, 163

philosophical concept, 139

A Philosophy of Interior Design

   (Abercrombie), 138

place, 36–37

   as basic design unit, 10

   character of, 46, 349

   college design, 130

   furniture groupings and, 50

   phenomenological view of, 46–47

   protagonists of, 350–51

   sense of, 206

place, elements of. *See* boundaries;

   centers; circulation systems;

   destination places; domains; paths

placement, 148–50

players, 28. *See also* people in buildings

pleasure, 29, 30, 196

points of reference, 51

   See also landmarks

   in corridors, 188–89

   mental, 300

Porphyrios, Demetri, 281–82

positional relationships, 186

   See also composition

positive *vs.* negative space, 67–68

postmodernism, 282

power motive, 260

Price, Linda, 259, 263

pride, sense of, 262

privacy, and enclosure, 223

self-esteem motive, 261–62

self-image, 258–59

   and brands, 275

   and color, 345–48

self-presentation, 264–67

sense of place, 206

sensory load, 33, 265

separation, levels of, 43, 44, 60

sequences, 186–87, 219–20, 221

   lighting of, 333

   repetition of, 187

   visibility in, 188

service brands, 275

service-oriented institutions, 101

   See also libraries; restaurants; *specific institutions*

shapes, figural character of, 268

shelter, expression of, 256

sidelighting, 329

side trips, 25

signature style, 278

Silvestrin, Claudio, 140

similarity, 314

simple form, 184

simple scheme, 145

simplicity, 318

simplification, 280

situational factors, in building use, 28, 31–32

   variables affecting users' reactions, 31–32

size, 68–69

   See also scale

   and balance, 297–301

   relation to application, 300

   relation to element type, 300–301

Smith, C. Ray, 345

sociability, 134

socioeconomic class, 263–64

solar exposure, 95

solution, and project requirements, 11–12

sophistication and taste, 262–64, 352

sound barriers, 336. See *also* acoustics

Southwest Airlines Co., 135

space, 57–61, 118

   approaches to, 80–81

   basics of, 56–85

   composing multiple spaces, 76–81

   defined, 46. *See also* spatial definition

   density of, and furnishings, 50

   disclosure of, 72–75, 190, 226–30

distribution of, in diagrams, 159

enclosed (*See* enclosure/enclosed space)

features of, 97

and function, 36

joining spaces, 77–80

mastery of, 10–11

and mobility, 75–76

modifying elements of (*See* modifying elements)

open *vs.* enclosed, 56, 257

and path relationship, 76–77

permeability of, 72

shaping of, 82–85

space planning, for offices, 104–7

spatial composition. *See* composition

spatial definition

   elements of, 57–58

   hierarchy of, 59

   levels of enclosure in, 59–61

   linear *vs.* implied space, 58–59

   loosely *vs.* moderately defined, 61

   positive *vs.* negative space, 67–68

   three-dimensional, 58

   two-dimensional, 57

spatial design, 8

   modifying elements in, 15

spatial edges. *See* edges

spatial geometry, 98, 198

   See also geometry

spatial novelty, 214–16

spatial scale. *See* scale

spatial volume, and acoustics, 337

special feature, 118

   artwork as, 51, 52f

spontaneous meaning, 248, 249

square space, 70

stability, and stimulation, 209

staircases, 183, 183f, 322f

Stanford Research Institute, 259

Starbucks (coffee chain), 274

stationary activity, 24–25

   enrichment in, 233–36

   grounding, 233–35

status, and identity, 259

Steelcase (furniture manufacturer), 105

stimulation, and stability, 209

stimuli, and approach/avoidance behaviors, 29–30

structure, 179–80

stylistic concept, 139, 297, 300, 339

subtlety and restraint, 267, 268f, 284

superimposed spaces, 77–78

support, expression of, 256

surface articulation, 322. *See* articulation

surface pattern, as enrichment, 239–42

surface refinement, 296

surface relief, 212

surprise, 196, 276

   in paths, 221

surroundings, as context, 31, 93

   See also environment

Swedish design tradition, 353–54

symbolic associations, 208–9

symbolic content, 247

symbols/symbolism

   of color, 342

   and expression, 247, 248–49, 252, 278–79

   high status, 259

   and image, 273

   spontaneous, 249

symmetry, 298, 321

   in composition, 307–8, 309–10

   vertical axis of, 319

synergy, efficiency and impact, 132

synthesis, in design, 4, 294–97

system overlapping, 214, 316

systems furniture, 105

T

target activity, engaging in, 24–25

target group, and image, 273

taste cultures, 262–64

Ten Books on Architecture (Vitruvius), 297

tension, 216–17

   and scale, 304

textile patterns, 340

texture

   and lighting, 329–30

   of materials, 341

   and pattern, 340

   spatial, 67, 226

theater, 113–14f

   lighting in, 332

   spaces and places in, 18–20, 20f, 23, 36

thematic concept, 139

thematic repetition, 316–17

thermal conduction, 341

thermal environment, 337–38

three-dimensionality, 164, 304, 346
  in compositions, 307
  and lighting, 329, 330

tile patterns, 241–42, 339

tour route, 200, 201f

Towards a New Architecture (Le
  Corbusier), 4, 206

transition point, in corridor, 190

transitions, natural, 220

transparency, degrees of, 73

travel, as source of knowledge, 6–7

triangular space, 71

truthfulness and illusion, 351–52

Tugendhat House, 65

TWA air terminal, 249, 249f

U

understanding, 92–136
  and affordance, 132–33
  and context, 92, 93–99
  and corporate culture, 134–35
  and design guidelines, 126–30
  for design solution, 11–12
  and exploration, 197
  and internal players, 99–101
  and order, 179–80, 183–89
  of project itself, 101–16, 154
  project parts and functions, 116,
    119–21
  of project type, 121–31. *See also* office
    design; retail stores; theater
  promoting levels of, 183–89
  and relationship among parts, 121–25
  of the whole, 187–89

uniqueness/novelty motive, 260

unity, in design, 14, 313–19, 352
  and avoiding dullness, 318–19
  color used for, 344
  repetition used for, 316–18

Unity Temple, 64

University of Chicago, 166–68

University of Oregon International
  College, 126–30

Unwin, Simon, 18, 328

upper middle culture, 263–64

users, 100
  See also clients; people in buildings
    response to interiors, 28–32

V

Vaid, Helen, 275, 276

VALS segmentation model, 259

value, of color, 342

variation, 130

variety, 206
  in corridors, 322
  and enrichment, 210, 223–24

ventilation, 338

Venturi, Robert, 217
  on complexity and contradiction,
    280–81
  on unity in design, 313, 318

vertical edges, 62–63

vertical elements, 319–20

views, and enrichment, 226–30, 236
  exterior views, 229
  focal points, 229, 236
  framed view, 226f, 227, 229

visibility, 186, 188

visual and physical access, 230

visual codes, 249

visual connections, 14, 228

visual disclosure, 72–73, 226–30
  See also views, and enrichment

visual discord, 216

visual elements, 215

visual harmony, 177, 318–21

visual impact
  See also first impressions
    of scale, 297

visual interest, 341

visual symbols, 273. *See also* graphics

Vitruvius, 95, 297

VOA (design firm), 237

W

waiting, 22–23, 26
  in health care facility, 124f

waiting area, 168f, 238f
  See also reception area
    enrichment in, 210

walls
  partial-height elements, 194, 195f
  as screens, 64, 65–66
  as space shapers, 82–83
  texture of, 67
  as vertical edges, 63

Weber, Raf, 318–21

weight, perceptual, 269, 319

Wharton, Edith, 345

wholeness, in design, 313–14, 352. *See
  also* unity

windows, 281
  and lighting, 335–36
  outlook in, 94. *See also* views

Wohlwill, Joachim, 197

wood, 339

work processes, in offices, 104–7
  collaboration, 107
  group communication, 106–7
  individual analysis and creation,
    107
  individual processing, 106

Wright, Frank Lloyd, 81, 278
  chair designs of, 299, 299f, 303, 303f
  and destruction of the box, 64–65
  free-flowing plans of, 310
  protective center of, 232
  space planning approaches of, 61

The Wright Space (Hildebrandt), 232

Wundt curve, 196

Z

zeitgeist (spirit of the time), 255

Zelanski, Paul, 344

Zevi, Bruno, 56

Zinkhan, George, 259, 263